# On the Edge of the Cold War

# On the Edge
# of the Cold War

*American Diplomats and Spies
in Postwar Prague*

IGOR LUKES

OXFORD
UNIVERSITY PRESS

# OXFORD
## UNIVERSITY PRESS

Oxford University Press, Inc., publishes works that further
Oxford University's objective of excellence
in research, scholarship, and education.

Oxford    New York
Auckland    Cape Town    Dar es Salaam    Hong Kong    Karachi
Kuala Lumpur    Madrid    Melbourne    Mexico City    Nairobi
New Delhi    Shanghai    Taipei    Toronto

With offices in
Argentina    Austria    Brazil    Chile    Czech Republic    France    Greece
Guatemala    Hungary    Italy    Japan    Poland    Portugal    Singapore
South Korea    Switzerland    Thailand    Turkey    Ukraine    Vietnam

Published by Oxford University Press, Inc.
198 Madison Avenue, New York, NY 10016

www.oup.com

Oxford is a registered trademark of Oxford University Press

Library of Congress Cataloging-in-Publication Data
Lukes, Igor.
On the edge of the Cold War : American diplomats and spies
in postwar Prague / Igor Lukes.
pages ; cm
Includes bibliographical references and index.
ISBN 978-0-19-516679-8 (hardcover : alkaline paper)
1. Czechoslovakia—Foreign relations—United States.
2. United States—Foreign relations—Czechoslovakia.
3. Czechoslovakia—Foreign relations—1945–1992.
4. Intelligence service—United States—History—20th century.
5. Cold War. I. Title.
DB2078.U6L85    2012
327.73043709'044—dc23        2012000393

1  3  5  7  9  8  6  4  2

Printed in the United States of America
on acid-free papers

*For Alison, Annamaria, and Marianne*

# CONTENTS

# ACKNOWLEDGMENTS

It gives me pleasure to acknowledge the generous help I have received from various foundations. The Woodrow Wilson International Center for Scholars in Washington, D.C., made it possible for me to focus on writing, and I was able to travel, do research, and write thanks to the Fellowship Research Grant from the Earhart Foundation, Fulbright-Hays Faculty Abroad Research Program, Open Society Archives Fellowship, the Philosophical Society, and IREX Individual Advanced Research Program. I also benefited from being a Senior Fellow at the Society of Fellows at Boston University.

I am most grateful to Susan Ferber of Oxford University Press, the best editor I have ever encountered, and to Ambassador Peter Bridges, Dr. Lubor Václavů, and Professor Piotr S. Wandycz. They read parts of the manuscript, noted countless errors, and helped me improve the final text. I am also grateful for the many conversations with Bill Brown of Wellesley College.

Writing this book about the Americans who had served in postwar Prague was exciting for many reasons, but the most prominent one was meeting them. Walter and Virginia Birge, George Bogardus, Robert and Dagmar Bronec, Vladimír and Otilia Kabeš, Ronald Parker, Louise Schaffner, and Spencer Taggart became admired friends. William H. Bruins, Laurene Sherlock, and Peter and Naomi Rosenblatt generously gave their time and shared previously unpublished manuscripts and important insights. I am most grateful.

Despite all the help I have received, this project could not have been accomplished without the crucial support from my wife, Alison, and our daughters, Annamaria and Marianne. Thank you.

Wellesley, Massachusetts
Choceň, the Czech Republic

# ABBREVIATIONS

| | |
|---|---|
| ABS | Archives of Special Services, Prague |
| ACC CPC | Archives of the Central Committee of the Communist Party of Czechoslovakia, Prague |
| AMFA | Archives of the Ministry of Foreign Affairs, Prague |
| AMI | Archives of the Ministry of Interior, Prague |
| AMND | Archives of the Ministry of National Defense, Prague |
| ANM-M | Archives of the National Museum, fond Vojtěch Mastný, Prague |
| APO | Archives of the Presidential Office, Prague |
| ATGM | Archives of the Thomas G. Masaryk Institute, Prague |
| AUZSI | Archives of the Foreign Intelligence Service of the Czech Republic |
| CPC | Communist Party of Czechoslovakia |
| DHCP | Libuše Otahálova and Miladá Červinková, eds., *Dokumenty z historie československé politiky, 1939–1945* |
| FMHR | Fond Minister Hubert Ripka, Institute of Contemporary History, Prague |
| JSCU | Archives of Jaromír Smutný, Columbia University |
| LOC | Library of Congress |
| MZV | Ministry of Foreign Affairs, Prague |
| NA | National Archives, Prague |
| NARA | National Archives and Records Administration, Maryland |
| OBZ | Military Counterintelligence (Czech) |
| OSA | Open Society Archives, Budapest |
| OSS | Office of Strategic Services |
| SFA | Swiss Federal Archives, Bern |

| | |
|---|---|
| StB | State Security (Czech) |
| SOE | Special Operations Executive |
| TNA | The National Archives of the United Kingdom |
| UPV-T | Office of the Prime Minister, Secret Section, Prague |
| ZOB | Security organization working exclusively for the CPC leaders |

On the Edge of the Cold War

# Postwar Czechoslovakia

## *The Master Key to Europe?*

One of the prerequisites of successful diplomacy, George Kennan observed, is recognizing one's limitations. There are occasions that call for action, and there are times to do nothing. Wilbur J. Carr, American minister in Prague from 1937 to 1939 and Kennan's boss, understood this principle. He knew that the United States was not in a position to influence the escalating European crisis, and he behaved accordingly. One evening in the fall of 1938, as the world outside the legation was frantically preparing for the coming war, Kennan found the minister asleep in an armchair:

> The sight of the old gentleman, thus peacefully at rest in the solitary splendor of his heavily curtained salons while outside in the growing darkness a Europe seething with fear and hatred and excitement danced its death dance all around us, struck me as a symbolic enactment of the helplessness of all forces of order and decency, at that moment, in the face of the demonic powers that history had now unleashed.[1]

The Allied victory over the Third Reich in 1945 thrust the United States into an entirely different position. No longer a mere observer, it now held great responsibility for the emerging political architecture of postwar Europe. This was especially true in Czechoslovakia, a country situated on the fault line between East and West. Therefore, from the spring of 1945 onward, the American embassy in Prague stood at the center of a political whirlwind as Czechoslovakia, recently liberated from Nazism, struggled to find its identity in a Europe divided into two hostile camps. Prior to the war, Kennan and other Americans in Czechoslovakia felt powerless before the coming clash with Adolf Hitler. In the postwar environment, the United States was mighty, but with strength came the burden of responsibility. Therefore, Washington instructed its embassy in Prague to be assertive and steadfast as it advanced American interests, neutralized the schemes of the Soviet rival, and protected Czechoslovakia's democratic identity.

This mission ended in failure and the American embassy in February 1948 watched helplessly while Czechoslovakia, originally a multiparty democracy, degenerated before the eyes of its astonished American friends into a Stalinist dictatorship. The crisis and its culmination, the Communist coup d'état, weakened Washington's stature, intensified the rivalry between the United States and the Soviet Union, and contributed to the militarization of the Cold War by providing the impetus for the creation of NATO a year later.

The political evolution of postwar Czechoslovakia was sui generis. The country emerged from World War II aligned with neither of the emerging blocs. Its political orientation was not a byproduct of the Stalin-Hitler pact of August 1939, its position in Europe was not discussed at Teheran and Yalta, and it did not appear on the list involving the percentages agreement between Joseph Stalin and Winston Churchill of October 1944. Like Germany and Austria, Czechoslovakia was liberated from Nazism not only by the Red Army but also by the United States. That the Red Army held most of the territory and liberated the city of Prague was a major political handicap for the democrats and a mobilizing factor for their Communist opponents. Yet it did not determine the country's future, as evidenced, in part, by the Truman-Stalin agreement to withdraw their military forces from liberated Czechoslovakia by December 1945.

Nevertheless, some Americans saw the postwar crisis and the Prague coup in 1948 as determined by the country's geographic location. George C. Marshall, for one, argued that Czechoslovakia represented a Western territorial protrusion into the Soviet bloc, a situation that was intolerable to Moscow. George Kennan, having studied the Kremlin closely, concluded that Czechoslovakia's proximity to the Soviet Union sufficed to predict the country's political future. In his view, the Soviet leaders recognized "only vassals and enemies; and the neighbors of Russia, if they do not wish to be the one, must reconcile themselves to being the other." The Poles chose to resist, and Stalin was going to crush them, Kennan predicted. The Czechs had tried to appease Stalin; nevertheless, like the Poles, they were destined to find themselves under the Russian jackboot.[2]

Others, however, did not think that the outcome of the crisis in Prague was inevitable. Instead, they thought it had been enabled by the ineptitude and lack of resolve in Washington prior to the coup. Writing at the height of the Prague Spring twenty years after the event, Eugene V. Rostow expressed the view that America's "failure to deter the Communist takeover of Czechoslovakia in 1948 was one of the most serious mistakes of our foreign policy since the war." Another voice in this category belonged to Allen Dulles, who argued that the Communists had been able to impose their dictatorship because of incompetent American diplomatic and intelligence personnel in Prague. Rostow and Dulles

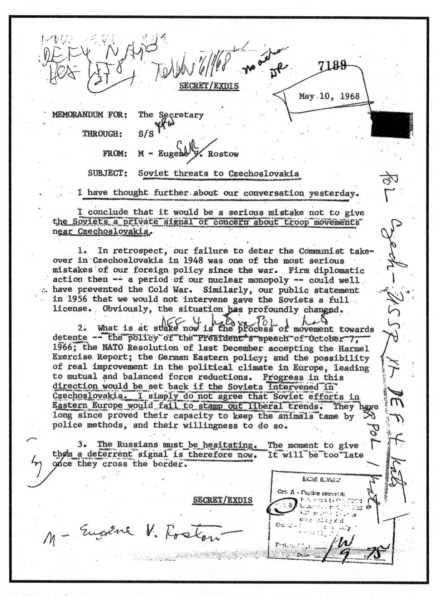

SECRET/EXDIS

7189

May 10, 1968

MEMORANDUM FOR: The Secretary

THROUGH: S/S

FROM: M - Eugene V. Rostow

SUBJECT: Soviet threats to Czechoslovakia

I have thought further about our conversation yesterday.

I conclude that it would be a serious mistake not to give the Soviets a private signal of concern about troop movements near Czechoslovakia.

1. In retrospect, our failure to deter the Communist take-over in Czechoslovakia in 1948 was one of the most serious mistakes of our foreign policy since the war. Firm diplomatic action then -- a period of our nuclear monopoly -- could well have prevented the Cold War. Similarly, our public statement in 1956 that we would not intervene gave the Soviets a full license. Obviously, the situation has profoundly changed.

2. What is at stake now is the process of movement towards detente -- the policy of the President's speech of October 7, 1966; the NATO Resolution of last December accepting the Harmel Exercise Report; the German Eastern policy; and the possibility of real improvement in the political climate in Europe, leading to mutual and balanced force reductions. Progress in this direction would be set back if the Soviets intervened in Czechoslovakia. I simply do not agree that Soviet efforts in Eastern Europe would fail to stamp out liberal trends. They have long since proved their capacity to keep the animals tame by police methods, and their willingness to do so.

3. The Russians must be hesitating. The moment to give them a deterrent signal is therefore now. It will be too late once they cross the border.

SECRET/EXDIS

M - Eugene V. Rostow

NARA. Under Secretary of State Eugene V. Rostow to Secretary of State Dean Rusk, 10 May 1968, folder 6/1/68, box 1558, POL – Czech, USSR DEF 4 NATO, Center Foreign Policy Files 1968-1969, RG 59; I am grateful to Professor Günter Bischof for a copy of this document.

shared the view that "firm diplomatic action" in postwar Czechoslovakia by the United States in defense of the democratic cause could have prevented the take-over. Rostow went even further and argued that an assertive American diplomacy in Prague could have prevented the Cold War itself.[3]

This book does not endorse either of these positions. Instead, it explores the Communist conquest of Czechoslovakia and the early years of the East-West conflict from the viewpoint of American diplomats and intelligence officers who served in Prague from 1945 to 1948.[4] Placing the activities of those who worked at the Schönborn Palace, home of the U.S. embassy, at the center of the narrative makes it possible to reveal how the Americans came to misread the postwar political situation.[5] The chapters that follow weave their personal testimonies into the fabric of the official record and provide a fresh look at the crucial early years of the Cold War.

The relations between the United States and Czechoslovakia date back to the final stages of the Great War, when President Woodrow Wilson and other allies granted *de facto* recognition to the Czechoslovak National Council headed by Thomas G. Masaryk. The first American minister in Prague and the doyen of the diplomatic corps, Richard T. Crane, had purchased the Schönborn Palace from the often impecunious Count Schönborn and sold it to the United States government in the early twenties.[6] It has been the central American diplomatic post in Prague ever since. Although Washington's relations with Czechoslovakia were cordial during the interwar period, they were of marginal importance to both parties: Czechoslovakia was small and the United States was far away. Consequently, Washington valued Prague as an oasis of tranquility in an unstable Europe, a reliable business partner with a stable currency, and an important observation post. An American minister marveled that from the ancient towers of the city he could see "the roads which lead south to the Danube, north to the Reich, and easterly across Poland to the Russian steppes." The city, he noted, was "a meeting ground of East and West."[7]

The rise of Nazism and the Czechoslovak-German crisis in the late thirties turned the Schönborn Palace, according to President Franklin D. Roosevelt, into "one of the most important posts" Washington maintained in Europe.[8] After Hitler occupied Prague and broke up Czechoslovakia in March 1939, Washington downgraded its legation to a consulate general, and closed it in October 1940. Before they left, the Americans handed the keys to the Swiss consul general and negotiated a deal whereby Switzerland would protect American interests and property in Prague. The Swiss executed their obligations to the letter.[9] They periodically inspected the Schönborn Palace and supervised the custodians who took care of its one hundred rooms and opulent gardens. As the horror of the war and the Gestapo regime unfolded outside its walls, the empty American legation suffered only stains caused by dampness and a few broken window panes.[10]

By late January 1945, the Nazis were finally retreating on all fronts. The Red Army was marching west through Poland, East Prussia, and Czechoslovakia; its soldiers held Bucharest, Belgrade, Budapest, and the ruins of Warsaw. The sweep

The Schönborn Palace, America's observation post in Central Europe (center), and the Prague Castle (top center). Courtesy of Archiv Hlavního Města Prahy.

of the Soviet offensive was impressive, especially because the Americans at the time were regrouping after *Generalfeldmarschall* Gerd von Rundstedt's offensive in the Ardennes, which had taken them unawares and complicated their position. A British historian predicted that at the end of the war Russia would be the most powerful country in Europe and might determine the course of history for decades to come.[11] As the Allies pushed Hitler off the world scene, Stalin seemed ready to establish himself at its center, although no one could claim to have much insight into Russia's postwar plans.[12]

Initially the Kremlin had tried to make the Americans and the British open the second front as soon as possible. A Russian diplomat threatened in January 1942 that if the Allies returned to Europe only after the Red Army had seized Warsaw and Prague, conquered Berlin, and marched all the way to the Champs Élysées in Paris, the future organization of Europe would be determined by Moscow.[13] Later, especially once the race for the Nazi capital was on, the advance of the Western Allies became a threat to Soviet interests. Foreign policy experts in the Soviet Union prepared and considered various theoretical scenarios for the lands between Germany and Russia after liberation.[14] Which, if any, would be realized depended on Stalin and the limits imposed by the rapidly evolving situation.

Although the strategic objectives of the Soviet Union remained opaque in early 1945, it was impossible to miss its achievements and tactics on the ground. A new political system was emerging in the countries under Soviet occupation.

As the Red Army entered each territory, local Communist organizations took control in the space that had been secured by Soviet tanks and then combed over and cleansed by the commissars who followed the combat units. It is unlikely that this policy was part of a master plan that was formulated at the highest levels in the Kremlin. It was simply the natural outcome of Soviet conquests combined with the modus operandi and ideological objectives of the Stalinist regime. The sources of Soviet behavior in Eastern Europe were unclear, as were Stalin's objectives, but there was no doubt that local Communists lost no time in taking advantage of the favorable situation created by the Red Army. By contrast, the Western Allies appeared to have no strategic plan for the postwar era; they seemed unprepared, reactive, and indecisive.[15]

Nevertheless, many influential Americans were optimistic regarding Moscow's intentions in liberated Eastern Europe, and especially in Czechoslovakia. President Franklin D. Roosevelt, for one, thought that there was ground for hope. "I believe that Russia wants to and will cooperate," he assured Czechoslovak foreign minister Jan Masaryk. "It is victorious, it has made great progress, and has every right to seek its rewards. That the Russians act tough, one must accept."[16] After his wartime visit to the White House, the exiled Czechoslovak president Edvard Beneš reported that "Roosevelt fully trusts the Soviet Union."[17] Many others, including ideological opponents of Stalinism, felt that the master of the Kremlin was sincere, and they believed his solemn promises not to interfere in the domestic affairs of sovereign states in Central Europe.[18]

Some in the Department of State were influenced by Stalin's generous declarations and by Roosevelt's optimism. In early April 1945, Paul E. Zinner, an analyst in the Office of Strategic Services (OSS), America's wartime intelligence agency, learned firsthand that various U.S. foreign service officials saw no reason for concern regarding postwar Czechoslovakia.[19] Among the cautious optimists in the State Department was Ambassador Averell Harriman. Like Roosevelt, he praised Beneš, whom he knew well, for his dealings with Stalin and said that Czech relations with the Soviet Union were "the best we can expect in Eastern Europe."[20]

Great Britain had its share of optimists. Winston Churchill's ambassador to Moscow, Sir Stafford Cripps, for one, had anticipated that the Soviet Union was likely to end the war "sitting in Berlin," which would make it possible for the Kremlin to "determine the future of Europe." This gave Sir Stafford no pause because, in his view, the Russians had no desire to impose their system abroad. They only sought borders that were "strategically sound."[21] The historian E. H. Carr shared this perspective. He argued that Stalin was not seeking to use his military successes "to promote Communism or anything like it." Carr thought that Moscow had "no aggressive or expansive designs in Europe" and only sought security. He saw no reason for Western and Soviet interests to collide, because they were "precisely the same."[22]

However, political officers of the Red Army offered an entirely different view regarding Moscow's aims in liberated Europe, and their brazen statements provided ammunition to pessimists. The chief of the Czechoslovak Military Mission in Moscow, Colonel Heliodor Píka, reported as early as August 1941 the view of Red Army officers that the war would not conclude with the defeat of Germany; at that stage it would be transformed into a "social revolution" bringing the "dictatorship of the proletariat" to Europe. When Píka retorted that the Czechoslovak electorate would have to accept such drastic changes in a free election, they laughed: "What elections? When the Red Army is in the Czech lands, everybody will vote for the dictatorship of the proletariat." They assured Píka that Czechoslovakia was destined to become part of the Soviet Union.[23]

These and other similar reports from Moscow circulated in government and political circles in the West, and some began to ask whether the Western Allies were not about to squander what could have been their moment of triumph. Lord Cranborne, former under-secretary in the Foreign Office, warned that if postwar Europe were to be governed by dictatorships, of whatever ideological orientation, "then we may have beaten Hitler, but should in fact have lost the war."[24] Public intellectuals and some politicians in Great Britain became critical of Soviet behavior in the liberated territories in the aftermath of the Warsaw Rising in 1944. An editorial in the *Tablet*, a British Catholic weekly, warned in January 1945 that Moscow probably intended to impose its system upon Central Europe, depriving millions of their freedom.[25]

U.S. ambassador William C. Bullitt was one of the pessimists. In the fall of 1944 he predicted that following the defeat of Nazism, Moscow would "dominate Finland, Estonia, Latvia, Lithuania, Poland, Rumania, Bulgaria, Hungary and Czechoslovakia." He noted that the Kremlin had learned from previous mistakes and would apply different strategies in different countries. It might come with cold steel into the Baltics and Poland, but with treaties and patience to Finland and Czechoslovakia. The outcome, however, would be the same.[26]

Many other U.S. and British diplomats refused to believe Stalin's promises not to interfere in postwar Eastern Europe. They expected the dictator to impose his will upon the region "by means of deportations and massacres," and they despaired over those who doubted the ruthlessness and inhumanity of Stalinism.[27] British intelligence sided with the pessimists. It predicted that the Soviet Union would seize large parts of Eastern, Central, and southwest Europe in flagrant disregard of any existing agreements among the Allies and then hold in perpetuity what it had grabbed.[28]

In this atmosphere of general uncertainty regarding the evolution of postwar Czechoslovakia, no country had resolved to step forward and set limits on Stalin's behavior during the great power game that had been under way at least since the summer of 1944 and was expected to intensify the moment the last German soldier surrendered. France, the country that had played a leading role in Central Europe, albeit unsuccessfully, from the early 1920s to 1939, was dishonored by appeasement before the war and its own collapse in the face of the German *Blitzkrieg*, and it had been weakened by internal ideological strife. Great Britain emerged from the fight against Nazism with prestige and moral capital. But it had paid a steep price for its victory, and the postwar era was likely to reveal its dire economic situation. Importantly, many in British political circles maintained the traditional view that Central Europe was an area in which it would be imprudent to accept obligations of any kind. Britain was thus unable or unwilling to assume a role as an advocate of democracy in postwar Prague. There was consequently only one power among the Western Allies that could resist attempts by the Soviet Union to impose Communism in Czechoslovakia, and that was the United States.

The Department of State was well aware that Washington would have to assume a central role in liberated Europe. It had even tried to develop a protocol for evaluating Moscow's behavior.[29] Some thought that the best indicator of Stalin's intentions in Europe would be Poland. The well-informed elite in the Department of State rejected this view. At a meeting of specialists on Soviet and East European affairs, Charles Bohlen noted that the fate of Poland had been irreversibly sealed. The real test, he said, was Czechoslovakia. President Beneš had done everything possible to appease the Kremlin; he had even signed an agreement with Stalin, despite opposition from his British hosts. "If the USSR really implemented that treaty and did not violate it," stated Bohlen, "then we would have an indication that it might be possible to get along with the Soviet Union. If the Soviet Union should break the treaty—the Czechs having gone as far as anybody could expect them to go—this might be an indication that cooperation with the Soviet Union would not be possible."[30]

The OSS agreed with this analysis. Its "Report on Czechoslovakia: Pivot Point of Europe" echoed the position—traditionally ascribed to nineteenth-century chancellor Otto von Bismarck—that Bohemia, Czechoslovakia's western province, was centrally important to the security of the continent. The analysts argued that the country, because of its geographical situation, was "the master key to Europe." On top of that, it now assumed the role of "a testing-ground for the two great divergent ideologies, a chessboard, where the next move in the big game between East and West is being played." The central question, the OSS claimed, was whether the country would manage to guard its sovereignty despite the fact that it had already taken various pro-Soviet steps. The answer depended on Moscow, the analysts believed, but it also depended on Washington: "If the United States is firm and strong with the Czechs and the Russians, it will help the Czechs immeasurably and add to our stature with the Russians." The study suggested that the outcome of the political crisis likely to play itself out in postwar Czechoslovakia would foretell the course and outcome of the general crisis in Europe as a whole. The report concluded: "Today Czechoslovakia has become a test case which may set the pattern for what will later happen in other countries in Central and Southern Europe, and eventually in Western Europe. Prague is the most advanced observation post in this game of powers."[31]

The central role in this book belongs to Laurence A. Steinhardt. By choosing Steinhardt to be his ambassador to the Czechoslovak "testing ground" of East-West relations, President Roosevelt signaled that American diplomacy in Prague would follow the line recommended by the OSS. It would be confident, vigilant, and assertive. Steinhardt was known as an ardent American patriot and—unusual at the time—a skeptic regarding the Stalinist regime. Even his critics among the career Foreign Service officers acknowledged that he would be a formidable and crafty opponent of the Kremlin in any schemes deployed to separate Czechoslovakia from its Western moorings. His appointment underlined Washington's desire to help defend Czechoslovakia's multiparty system and Western orientation. A high-profile lawyer and energetic diplomat, Steinhardt had excellent contacts throughout Washington, within the Democratic Party, and on Wall Street. As a political appointee he may have lacked some qualities typically found in career ambassadors, but he was a man of action, and this is what the U.S. diplomatic post in Czechoslovakia needed.

One would expect that, having agreed on the centrality of Prague as the testing ground of Soviet intentions in Europe after liberation, the Department of State and the White House would closely supervise the performance of the embassy and critically engage its reports and analyses, challenge its faulty predictions, demand more information, and request concrete action in defense of American interests. Yet Washington remained inexplicably passive even when it became apparent early on that Steinhardt had undergone a change of heart regarding his commitment to diplomacy at about the time of the Yalta Conference. Although Czechoslovakia was in a precarious position between the United States and the Soviet Union, Ambassador Steinhardt arrived at the Schönborn Palace to assume his duties only in mid-July 1945, the last of the Allied ambassadors, following by two months the return of President Beneš. He then devoted disproportionate energy to his personal comforts, while remaining an active partner at a New York City law firm with influential clients. It was occasionally unclear whether he acted in Prague in pursuit of his own or U.S. government's interests. Even as the political crisis escalated between 1947 and early 1948, Steinhardt was absent for several months at a time.

The Department of State, the White House, and the intelligence community understood that the outcome of the crisis in Prague was important, as it might shape the fortunes of Finland, Norway, and perhaps France, and the status of Berlin. Nevertheless, the official record contains no criticism from Steinhardt's superiors in Washington, not even a comment noting the ambassador's questionable involvement in the New York law firm. The chapters that follow chronologically narrate the failure of the American mission in postwar Prague and identify its causes.

Chapter 1 is focused on President Edvard Beneš from the fall of 1938 to early 1944. The chapter explores the steps he took to restore the country's legal existence and his political status. Beneš faced a difficult choice between the Western Allies, who were pleasant and cordial but noncommittal when it came to Czechoslovakia's future, and the generous offers of Soviet diplomats who were most eager to renew full diplomatic relations without delay. An analysis of the exiled president's visits to Washington and Moscow in 1943 illustrates this dilemma. After some agonizing and fuming, Beneš chose to play the Soviet card, a stratagem he had tried before, in the thirties. Although the 1935 alliance with Stalin had gained him nothing when he most needed it—during the Munich crisis— Beneš replicated it in 1943.

Chapter 2 exposes the dramatic events that marred what should have been a joyful occasion: Beneš's return from exile to liberated Czechoslovakia—via the Soviet Union. A last-minute decision made in Moscow caused the president to travel without the corpus of Allied diplomats accredited to his government and placed him—isolated from the outside—into a Soviet security bubble. This was a crucial time: while the Red Army was fully engaged in the costly battle for Berlin, the U.S. Third Army had easily broken through the collapsing positions of the Wehrmacht and had crossed into Czechoslovakia. The chapter scrutinizes the decision by Generals Marshall and Eisenhower to halt the Third Army only some fifty miles west of Prague. The drama of the last two days of the war is presented from the perspective of an OSS team that traveled in a U.S. Army jeep across many miles of occupied Czech territory in a last-minute attempt to have the city liberated by the GIs.

Chargé d'Affaires Alfred Klieforth, the leading figure presented in chapter 3, was the first postwar chief of the American embassy in Prague after it was reopened in May 1945. He is not usually ranked among the stars of the U.S. Foreign Service. Yet this unassuming American diplomat, author of many perceptive analyses of the political scene in Prague, provided ample ammunition in support of the view that the accelerating crisis would not inevitably lead to the Communist takeover. Klieforth argued that Czech society was primed to respond positively to American initiatives. Even a little effort by the United States, he argued, would have resulted in significant political gains for the West.

Chapter 4 introduces Laurence A. Steinhardt. A graduate of Columbia Law School, Steinhardt established himself as a highly competent problem solver who handled clients and cases that won headlines. His relatives and partners in the law firm introduced him to politics. By 1932, Steinhardt emerged as a prominent supporter of Franklin D. Roosevelt's bid for the White House. When FDR chose him to be the United States Minister in Stockholm, the forty-year-old Steinhardt became the youngest chief of a U.S. diplomatic post. Steinhardt fell in love with the diplomatic profession. The chapter covers his career, with focus on his service in Moscow and Ankara.

Although Steinhardt arrived in liberated Prague after an unpardonably long delay, as chapter 5 describes, he first focused on his personal needs, such as housing. Although opportunities for public diplomacy on behalf of the United States and the democratic cause were plentiful, the Schönborn Palace dealt primarily with economic matters, some of which may have involved the ambassador's private business interests. Various American claimants who received the embassy's support were also fee-paying clients of Steinhardt's law firm in New York. The chapter illustrates wasted opportunities to promote American interests and the democratic cause by reviewing General Dwight Eisenhower's visit to Prague.

While the Americans at the Schönborn Palace had barely begun to engage with the reality of postwar Czechoslovakia, a country that had made a significant political shift to the left, the Communist Party quickly scored political successes, some irreversible. Chapter 6 recounts the groundlessly optimistic reports Steinhardt issued from Prague. It also deals with the cruel expulsion of German-speaking former citizens of Czechoslovakia. The operation took place with the blessing of the wartime Allies, which was formally reaffirmed at the Potsdam Conference, and it enjoyed the unbridled support of Ambassador Steinhardt. Nevertheless, it was a crime whose consequences remain unresolved even today. Finally, the chapter explores the tendency of U.S. Army generals to conduct their own foreign relations. Its first manifestation was Eisenhower's preference for dealing directly with the Red Army chain of command in Moscow in the last stages of the war. In the postwar era, Chargé Klieforth, and later Ambassador Steinhardt, had to appeal to officials in Washington to prevent the army generals from carrying out a unilateral withdrawal of their troops from Pilsen and other cities in western Czechoslovakia. The simultaneous departure of the Americans and Russians was arranged only after President Truman's direct intervention with Stalin.

Chapter 7 introduces U.S. Foreign Service officer Walter Birge, Steinhardt's personal assistant, who later assumed responsibility for various clandestine operations in Prague. It provides an account of the U.S. Army raid on Štěchovice and Washington's decision to deny Czech requests for loans in an attempt to force

Prague to compensate U.S. citizens whose properties had been nationalized after the war. At the center of this chapter is the spectacular victory of the Communist Party of Czechoslovakia (CPC) in the elections of 1946. Despite Steinhardt's assurances that all was well on the Prague scene, the CPC gained a major and largely fair victory. Steinhardt had forcefully argued that the elections would produce a democratic coalition government. Although events proved him to be mistaken, and the Department of State had irrefutable evidence of his failure to understand the political environment in Czechoslovakia, no corrective action was taken.

When U.S. intelligence officers Charles Katek and Spencer L. Taggart arrived in Prague shortly after the war, it might have seemed that they were destined to prevail. They were far better educated and much more experienced than their provincial, occasionally barely literate, and crude Communist opponents. It was helpful that they enjoyed the unqualified support of Steinhardt, a rarity in those days, when many ambassadors did not tolerate spying. Nevertheless, as chapter 8 demonstrates, the Czechs proved to be more focused, resourceful, and crafty than Katek and Taggart. The Americans picked up gossip during lavish dinner parties, while their opponents worked at a higher professional level, developing sources among the Czech employees at the U.S. embassy and even among the American staff. The chapter analyzes the mysterious case of Kurt Taub, a U.S. intelligence officer and Katek's deputy, who frequently met under murky circumstances with representatives of the Soviet and Czech clandestine services.

Chapter 9 is focused on the Czech political scene in the crucial year of 1947. Steinhardt left the post in Prague for New York in January and returned in March. In his absence, the Communist Party grew in size but its appeal declined: those who joined were often opportunists motivated by the expectation that the CPC would soon become the sole source of authority in the country. The party no longer enjoyed its original image of a youthful and daring movement of idealists as it transformed itself into a secretive and deceitful cabal bent on gaining power. As a substitute for its waning popularity, which was confirmed by elections in workplaces, enterprises, and schools, the CPC resorted to strong-arm tactics and even acts of terrorism. The chapter studies Prague's initial acceptance and subsequent rejection of the Marshall Plan. The rudderless U.S. embassy (Steinhardt left the post again in November and would return only in February 1948) never properly challenged the CPC and its anti-American propaganda.

The penultimate chapter deals with the crucial early weeks of 1948 and the Communist coup d'état in February. It introduces several junior U.S. Foreign Service officers, including Louise Schaffner. She and her colleagues tried to maintain the appearance that the United States had a functioning embassy in Prague. When Schaffner arrived in January 1948, she was surprised to learn that the Schönborn Palace saw no signs of anything untoward in the political developments within the country. In fact, all seemed well to Steinhardt's deputy, Chargé John Bruins. At that stage, even American journalists who did not have the resources available to professional diplomats or intelligence officers came to recognize that the Communist takeover was imminent. When the coup d'état started, the ambassador was en route to Prague, and the CIA station chief was on a motoring tour of Italy. He came back four days after the Communists had seized power. The embassy could only report that all its sources of information had been cut off.

The final chapter is focused on the activities of the U.S. embassy in Prague after the Communist coup d'état. Steinhardt briefly attempted to make up for his previous spotty performance with intense activity. He fired off on a daily basis multiple analyses of the CPC dictatorship. Several were quite perceptive, particularly when one considers that he operated in a political vacuum, after his personal friends and contacts in the government had disappeared overnight. Although he could rely only on the heavily censored official press, personal observation, and his sense of history, his memoranda to Washington from that time rank among his best. But soon the Schönborn Palace operated under such pressure from the Communist police apparat that it could no longer carry out its regular duties. Steinhardt directed Walter Birge to assist Czech friends of the embassy whose arrests were imminent in escaping abroad. Steinhardt's own departure from Prague turned into a serious confrontation between the U.S. embassy and the Czech secret police. While the American team achieved several sweet but marginal successes after the coup, the large intelligence-gathering network sponsored and equipped by the United States was dismantled and its leaders were executed.

The greatest share of responsibility for the loss of Czechoslovakia's democratic identity rests with the Czechs. Blinded by an irrational fear of Germany, the nation tolerated and accepted in its midst the aggressive minority that had embraced Communism. President Edvard Beneš, Foreign Minister Jan Masaryk, and other democratic politicians bear a particularly large share of the national guilt. They had underestimated the viciousness of their totalitarian opponents, treating them as legitimate partners in a shared patriotic enterprise. Even though they privately agonized about the impact of their alliance with Moscow on their sovereignty and democratic identity, they never tried to educate the public about the dangers of Soviet Communism. They believed that their own reasonableness, good will, and polite manners would civilize their ideological opponents and bring about a distinctively Czechoslovak form of socialism. When they finally saw in February 1948 what horror awaited them under the Communist Party dictatorship, they walked away from the fight, choosing instead the brief comfort of self-pity and martyrdom, as they had during the dark time before the Nazi occupation in March 1939.

But what cause was there to defend? What star to follow? The United States embassy was expected by the president in Washington and the Department of State to promote American interests, protect the democratic cause, and engage the Soviet adversary. Ambassador Steinhardt did not exert himself to accomplish any of these goals. As a result, the Americans in Prague never provided the support and inspiration for which the democrats yearned. As the writer Egon Hostovský noted, the vanquished democratic majority in Prague had lost because it had its totalitarian enemies but no friends; it could hate but it had no one to love.[32]

# 1

# Resurrecting Czechoslovakia from Its Munich Grave

"My job," Emperor Franz Josef told an American visitor in 1910, "is to protect my people from their politicians."[1] The emperor distrusted politicians in Austria-Hungary because one of the greatest threats to the survival of his multinational realm was intolerant nationalism, and it was the politicians who used it to gain votes and power.

In the twenty years that followed the empire's dissolution at the end of World War I, the nationalistic successor states became obsessed with borders. Even minor territorial disputes among them provoked unbending and self-destructive hostility. Aggressive nationalism and fixation on territory proved to be a lethal combination, and Adolf Hitler used it in 1938 to drive the Czechoslovak-German crisis toward a second worldwide conflagration. The Munich Agreement of September, whereby the British and French handed parts of Czechoslovak territory over to the Third Reich, briefly postponed the inevitable, but the complete destruction of the country in March 1939 set into motion processes no one could arrest. The Oxford historian A. J. P. Taylor later argued that the failure of Munich and appeasement demonstrated that Czechoslovakia, despite its small size, was a "keypoint in Central Europe." The country, Taylor noted, played a surprisingly large role in maintaining the overall balance of power in Europe.[2]

World War II caused many to lose faith in the prewar European political order. They blamed liberal democracy for the rise of Hitler, while Stalingrad and the Red Army stood for the putative superiority of the Stalinist system. This led to a large-scale shift to the left of the ideological spectrum throughout Europe, and nowhere was it more apparent than in Czechoslovakia.

As the war started to wind down, thoughtful people attempted to come to grips with its horrific legacy. They also tried to imagine the future political environment.[3] It became apparent that Europe after Hitler's defeat would have to grapple not only with the seething hatreds of nationalism and the territorial disputes of old but with an additional problem, ideological conflict.

The Czechoslovak political crisis from May 1945 to February 1948 was shaped by all three of the forces driving events in postwar Europe. It involved extreme anti-German *nationalism*, fixation on recovering the *territory* that had been lost to Hitler, Poland, and Hungary, and most of all, *ideology*. As soon as the war ended, Czechoslovakia became an ideological battlefield on which the forces of liberal democracy represented by the United States clashed with their dynamic challenger, Soviet-style Communism.

The roots of the contest over postwar Czechoslovakia go back to the debacle at Munich. The agreement between the great European democracies and Hitler revealed that the system of intertwined international treaties, which President Edvard Beneš had hoped would secure his country's existence, lay in ruins. He resigned from office in early October 1938 and flew to London, where he suffered a nervous breakdown. When he recovered, he chose silence and solitude. In February 1939, he traveled to the United States to take up a teaching position at the University of Chicago.[4] His political career seemed to have run its course.

While Beneš tried to focus on his lectures in Chicago, new dramas put further stress upon the brittle political system. In his *Sportpalast* speech in September 1938, Hitler asserted that he did not desire to rule other nations and he certainly did not "want any Czechs at all."[5] Furthermore, he signed a reciprocal pledge with Prime Minister Neville Chamberlain to take only such steps in the future that would assure the peace of Europe.[6] These were lies, as in mid-March 1939 Nazi-troops were in the center of Prague. The political atmosphere in London and Paris changed considerably. Such a flagrant breach of faith as the destruction of Czechoslovakia could not be ignored. Lord Halifax stated he understood Germany's desire for "bloodless victories" but warned Hitler that "one of these days he would find himself up against something that would not be bloodless." The British ambassador in Berlin, Sir Nevile Henderson, a leading appeaser in the Foreign Office, thought that the Third Reich "definitely crossed the Rubicon," since the occupation of Czechoslovakia was a "wrong which will soon call for redress."[7] Reacting to new German threats—now directed at Warsaw—Chamberlain placed the Territorial Army on war footing and told the House of Commons on March 31, 1939, that Great Britain and France would defend Poland against any German aggression promptly and with all their might.[8] Beneš realized that he might make a political comeback after all: a large-scale war was bound to reopen the Czechoslovak question that the appeasers had thought was solved at Munich.[9]

As he sailed from the United States to Britain, Beneš had every reason to be apprehensive. His political world consisted mainly of enemies and detractors. Some charged him with having recklessly brought Europe to the verge of war in 1938 by being too obstinate with the Third Reich. Others thought it was cowardly of him to have accepted the consequences of Munich without an all-out fight, alone if necessary. Even in the circles of Czechoslovak political exiles Beneš had more critics than supporters. His situation was "cruelly difficult," one of Beneš's few British friends wrote.[10]

The French politicians, who carried a heavy burden of responsibility for Hitler's conquest of Czechoslovakia, hoped that Beneš would disappear into the mists of political irrelevance. The British were civil but at best uneasy about Beneš. Some British diplomats disliked him openly; those friendlier thought him a man of too many words and theories, not all of which could be right.[11] The United States had not been party to the Munich conference and could not be blamed for its outcome. With the disappearance of Czechoslovakia in March 1939 and the departure of Wilbur J. Carr, the last American minister, the American legation was downgraded to a consulate general. Washington accepted the "*de facto* situation prevailing in Bohemia and Moravia," but it refused to grant legal recognition to the consequences of the German occupation.[12] It assumed a wait-and-see attitude toward the nation that no longer had any home on the map.

With no country to represent and no official position in the eyes of French, British, or American diplomats, Beneš was desperate to create at least a semblance of some formal standing in London. Was there anyone whom he could realistically consider his ally?

There was the Soviet Union, of course, but a close relationship with Moscow presented significant pitfalls and challenges. Beneš knew this firsthand because he had experienced it before. In the mid-thirties, prompted by the rise of Hitler and gnawing uncertainty regarding his alliance with France, he had moved closer to Moscow and signed the Czechoslovak-Soviet Agreement. Although he cautiously subordinated it to the Franco-Czechoslovak Treaty, the pivot of Czechoslovak national security, his treaty with Stalin proved to be a bad deal. Nazi propagandists and some in East Central Europe used it to denounce Czechoslovakia as a Soviet aircraft carrier. Although groundless, the charge seemed credible to many. In addition, Beneš started to court the Kremlin just when news of a horrific famine in Ukraine was trickling out of the country, and as the Stalinist purge gathered steam. Nevertheless, he painted an absurdly idealized picture of the Soviet Union before various skeptical Western diplomats. The country, he told the British minister in Prague, was full of happy and prosperous citizens, there were no shortages anywhere, and the Communist ideology had almost completely lost its purchase.[13]

The British and others, including U.S. ambassador William Bullitt in Moscow, could not help but think that Beneš was either a naïf or a Stalinist fellow traveler, and this strengthened the French and British reluctance to defend the Czechoslovak status quo.[14] But Beneš believed that Moscow, unlike other capitals, had not written him off. The Soviet ambassador in Washington, K. A. Umanskii, took care to stay in touch with him during Beneš's tenure in Chicago; he solicited his views and generously praised his analysis of international developments.[15] This was the beginning of a game of political seduction.

Soon after Beneš arrived in London, he received a note from Ambassador Ivan Maiskii requesting a meeting. He was flattered to be invited, especially as their conversation would take place on a particularly tense day, Wednesday, August 23, 1939. Only a handful of people in the world knew what to expect when it was announced that a German delegation was in the Kremlin. Maiskii candidly explained to Beneš that a pact between Moscow and Berlin would be signed the next day. Beneš wondered whether this would mean that Hitler might attack Poland the day after next. It might take longer, Maiskii replied, "perhaps two weeks." In that case, Beneš pressed, hardly believing his ears, what was the Soviet Union going to do? The ambassador replied honestly: "Naturally, we won't stand aside." The next day, Beneš saw the published text of the Stalin-Hitler pact. The Soviets, he noted, wanted war and they had deliberately planned for it to break out. He marveled that under the circumstances "neither Poland nor Germany nor England can retreat and the war will take place." Beneš summed up his understanding of the Kremlin's viewpoint: "The time has come for a struggle between capitalism, fascism and Nazism; there will be a world revolution, triggered by the Soviet Union at an opportune moment when others are exhausted."[16]

Beneš was pleased that Moscow briefed him on its top-secret strategy, and the stratagem aimed at the insecure former president bore fruit soon enough. Stalin's invasion of Poland in September elicited not a word of protest from him. The Red Army's attack on Finland in November made the Soviet Union even more unpopular in the West. Yet Beneš again uttered not one critical word. He stayed in touch with Soviet diplomats in London, and patiently listened when they offered ideological tirades.[17] And when Hitler invaded the Soviet Union in June 1941, Beneš was triumphant and jubilant. He saw clearly that the Nazis would lose and Czechoslovakia would regain its sovereign existence. The Soviet Union, he believed firmly, would become a major force in Central Europe and beyond.[18]

Beneš's main concern in 1941 was to restore the legal status of occupied Czechoslovakia, and in this Moscow could be helpful. When it came to the great realignment that would inevitably take place after the war, the British and Americans needed to realize that Czechoslovakia no longer depended exclusively on the West, as had been the case from the early twenties to 1938. It held the Soviet card and Beneš would play it to prevent a repetition of Munich. Despite the significant contribution of Czechoslovak pilots and ground personnel in the Royal Air Force to the Allied cause, the most that the Czechs obtained in return was a statement by Lord Halifax in July 1940 that "His Majesty's Government in the United Kingdom are happy to recognise and enter into relations with the Provisional Czechoslovak Government."[19]

The term "provisional" put Beneš's government behind all the other exile governments established in London. According to diplomatic protocol, the Czech provisional government was on a par with that of General Charles de Gaulle, the London representative of the Free French. Beneš, who was quite short, was always paired up with the very tall de Gaulle at diplomatic functions. The two marched at the end of every formal procession like a mismatched and frustrated couple.

Hitler's assault on the Soviet Union and swift Soviet diplomacy combined to rescue Beneš from his political isolation. On July 16, 1941, a mere twenty-four days after the German invasion brought the Soviet Union to the Allied side, Ambassador Maiskii submitted to Beneš a draft of an agreement prepared in Moscow. It was brief, consisting of five succinctly formulated points. The first stated that the Czechoslovak and Soviet governments would exchange ministers without delay.[20] The document was signed in London two days later without great ceremony, but with gusto on both sides. Beneš was delighted that in the difficult early stages of the Soviet-German war, a time of extreme peril, the Kremlin was willing to focus on such a marginal issue as his status in London.

The act of full Soviet recognition of Czechoslovakia took the British and Americans by surprise. The Foreign Office complained to the Department of State in Washington that the Russians had "without consulting anyone extended unconditional recognition to the provisional Czechoslovak Government in London and [had] even gone so far as to pledge themselves to restoration of the pre-Munich frontiers of Czechoslovakia."[21] This did not please the British, but it would have made no sense to allow the Soviet Union, a latecomer to the Allied side, to monopolize relations with Czechoslovakia as a sovereign state under temporary Nazi occupation. Therefore, without enthusiasm, on July 18, 1941, the Foreign Office stated that "the King has decided to accredit an Envoy Extraordinary and Minister Plenipotentiary to Dr. Beneš as President of the Czechoslovak Republic." It was Anthony Eden who handed the note to Minister Jan Masaryk. The latter was only able to glance at the text—the interview lasted a mere fifteen minutes—but he quickly discerned its meaning and broke down, overcome with emotion. As soon as he left Eden's office, Masaryk threw his arms around his embarrassed English escort.[22] The sweet candy, however, had a bitter center: Eden's note stressed that the recognition did not imply a British commitment of "any particular frontiers in Central Europe."[23] This dampened the moment of victory and raised the specter of Munich in Beneš's mind.

The next obvious target of Beneš's diplomatic offensive was Washington and its cautious position regarding Czechoslovakia. In early April 1941, Beneš reminded the U.S. ambassador to London, John G. Winant, that the United States had taken the lead in recognizing Czechoslovakia during the previous war. With no attempt at subtlety, Beneš recalled that Joseph Kennedy, Sr., the former American ambassador in Britain, had encouraged Neville Chamberlain in his policy of appeasement. He argued that the United States now had an "obligation" to help the victim deal with the aftermath of the disaster. The legal status of the Czechoslovak government-in-exile was a political matter, not a legal one, and it called for a political solution. What he wanted, wrote Beneš, was "immediate recognition" by the United States.[24] Summing up the situation several days after the interview, Ambassador Winant repeated that Beneš was "extremely anxious" to be recognized by Washington. The ambassador confessed: "I personally feel very deeply about Czechoslovakia and hope that we might recognize the Czechoslovak Government in exile."[25]

The position taken by the Department of State was somewhere between London's skepticism and Moscow's eagerness. Washington refused to acknowledge "the temporary extinguishment" of the country by the Nazis in March 1939.[26] It also allowed the Czechoslovak legation in Washington to remain open, although it carefully avoided saying whether its existence had legal significance. Beneš, who had met with President Franklin D. Roosevelt in May 1939, believed that the White House would support him.[27] He wrote a letter to FDR that summed up the arguments in favor of full recognition.[28]

Ultimately, the American decision to grant recognition to Czechoslovakia was a response to the Soviet diplomatic offensive. On July 17, 1941, Ambassador Winant reported from London—"triple priority"—that the signing of a Czechoslovak-Soviet treaty involving full recognition was imminent, perhaps to take place the next day. He heard from the Foreign Office that the British Government might now "feel compelled" to provide the same, even if with reservations.[29] The speedy Soviet and reluctant British recognition created a new set of circumstances, and the creative ambiguity of the State Department's attitude toward the legal status of Czechoslovakia had to be abandoned.

On July 20, 1941, just two days after the British recognition, Roosevelt wrote to Beneš "with a very real pleasure" that an envoy extraordinary and minister plenipotentiary would be chosen to serve near the "Provisional Government of Czechoslovakia in London."[30] But there was a catch. Like the earlier British note, the U.S. recognition, signed by Ambassador Winant, stated that the "relationship between our two Governments does not constitute any commitment on the part of the American Government with respect to the territorial boundaries of Czechoslovakia or the juridical continuity of the Czechoslovak Government headed by His Excellency Dr. Beneš."[31]

Throughout his political career Beneš tended to put a positive spin on events, and he was happy to celebrate this one as well.[32] But there was little doubt that the term "provisional" made the occasion bittersweet. Luckily, at least one influential American was not certain that this limited recognition made sense. In

December 1941, Under Secretary of State Sumner Welles asked the Legal Advisor's office how it was possible for the United States to grant recognition to a government but indicate that the recognized entity had "some flaw in its title." Would this not cause endless confusion in the future?[33] It might, the advisor conceded. He then simply restated that the recognition "was not without qualification," although it was not necessary to declare it publicly.[34]

This certainly did not reassure Beneš. He knew that if the Third Reich were to be defeated, it would have to be conquered by the Americans and the British from the west and the Soviet Union from the east. And Czechoslovakia happened to lie in the path of the Red Army.

In June 1942, Ambassador Alexander Bogomolov repeated that Moscow fully supported the reemergence of Czechoslovakia with its pre-Munich borders. The Soviet diplomat inquired with a knowing smile whether the Czechs had obtained a similar pledge from their Western allies, although it was common knowledge that they had not.[35] Inspired by Moscow, Beneš and Foreign Minister Jan Masaryk renewed their pressure on the British to annul the Munich Agreement of September 1938. After all, Churchill had previously noted that it had been destroyed by Nazi Germany. But when the Beneš team tried to present this as a renunciation of the British signature, they were quickly warned against overinterpreting the prime minister.[36] Anthony Eden finally announced to the House of Commons on August 5, 1942, that Great Britain was free from any "arrangements concerning Czechoslovakia" entered into in 1938.[37] A corresponding French renunciation of the agreement, signed by General de Gaulle, arrived in late September 1942. Unlike the oblique British statement, the French National Committee generously declared that it considered the Munich deal "null and void" from its inception.[38]

Meanwhile, Beneš and Masaryk pressured Washington to drop the word "provisional" when referring to the Czechoslovak government. The U.S. minister serving near the Beneš government in London, Anthony J. Drexel Biddle, Jr., reported to Washington that Beneš kept doggedly returning to one crucial question: why was his government "provisional"? Did it differ from other governments in London? Beneš hinted he was considering a trip to the Soviet Union. Yet he was unwilling to go there before he had fully secured his relations with the United States.[39] On October 28, 1942, Czechoslovak Independence Day, Washington dropped the term "provisional." Roosevelt sent a telegram that very day addressed to Edvard Beneš, President of the Republic of Czechoslovakia.[40] A beaming Beneš announced the good news before a gathering of Czechoslovak exiles in London.[41] He was again a president, and together they represented the legal government of a country temporarily occupied by the Third Reich. They had come a long way from Munich and the dark days of mid-March 1939, when Nazi troops and the Gestapo took over Prague while the rest of Europe was enjoying its illusory peace.

Having achieved full recognition in the East and West, Beneš moved to secure Czechoslovakia in the postwar environment by means of bilateral treaties. Given the drive of Soviet diplomacy and the sluggish pace of the British and the Americans, it was hardly surprising that the first and only offer came from the Kremlin. It proved to be divisive, and Beneš showed that he had learned little from his dealings with the Kremlin in the thirties.

The British opposed the signing of a Czechoslovak-Soviet treaty that would include explicit commitments regarding Czechoslovak borders and national security matters. They did not want to take part in a competition among the great powers in winning over individual countries in Central Europe. Furthermore, they disliked the prospect of a Czechoslovak-Soviet agreement, since this would further isolate the London Poles, whose contribution to the Allied war effort was considerable.

Therefore, when the Foreign Office found out in the summer of 1943 that Beneš was planning to go to Moscow, it complained to the Department of State that a treaty between Beneš and Stalin would embarrass them and would represent a violation of their agreement with Molotov "that neither Government would enter into any treaty with the smaller European countries . . . until after the conclusion of the war."[42] The first signs of a crisis between Beneš and the British delighted Moscow, and London-based Soviet diplomats and intelligence officers with diplomatic cover, such as Ivan A. Chichayev, moved to exploit the Munich trauma whenever they dealt with any Czechoslovak officials. They sensed that Beneš might be persuaded to go against British wishes and did what they could to push him in that direction.

Counselor Chichayev was a robust fellow who stood out among his Soviet colleagues by maintaining strict sobriety.[43] His friendly demeanor, gentle smile, and boyish shock of black hair disguised his serious mission in London. From the outbreak of the war until 1943 he was in charge of the *rezidentura*, the intelligence section inside the Soviet embassy. After he was replaced by Konstantin M. Kukin, Chichayev became a liaison officer between Soviet intelligence and Allied special services.[44] He was quite open in pressing for a Czechoslovak-Soviet deal, reminding Beneš that the West had abandoned him during the Munich crisis. Chichayev asserted that the British and Americans would never help defend the Czech cause, whereas Moscow would always be reliable and supportive.[45]

Such seeds of anti-Western thinking grew quickly in the troubled mind of the president. Never having shaken off the "Munich betrayal" syndrome, Beneš could see that the British political elite still included a fair number of appeasers responsible for the traumatic events of 1938. Moreover, he detected less than full concern for the nations of Central Europe in Western postwar plans. Unlike his Polish colleagues in London, Beneš did not believe that remaining loyal to the

West during the war was enough to ensure a free and sovereign Czechoslovakia in peacetime. There was now a new force rising, the Soviet Union, and it was bound to play a role in determining the postwar order.

Conveniently, the Soviets appeared to be very supportive, but with the crucial provision that Beneš agree to pursue his plans under the auspices of the Kremlin. The president knew that getting too close to Moscow could be dangerous and was bound to upset the British and Americans. This was regrettable, but neither London nor Washington offered anything of its own regarding Czechoslovakia's postwar borders and sovereign status. The impact of British and American detachment and energetic Soviet support for Czechoslovakia was plainly visible in the daily goings-on in wartime London: the Polish government-in-exile complained that the West was not doing enough to ensure that Poland would emerge from the war as an independent country. By contrast, the London-based Czechs bristled at Western hints that they were getting too cozy with Stalin.[46]

The path toward the Czechoslovak-Soviet Treaty of 1943 was to a surprising degree a meandering one; it certainly was not as straightforward as Beneš and the official record suggested.[47] The president had initially hoped that his visit with Stalin would produce an innocuous statement on cooperation in the fight against Nazi Germany. Such an agreement would have been acceptable to his Western allies, and Eden said so.[48] But a formal treaty with a security clause was another matter altogether. British diplomat R. H. Bruce Lockhart stated that the president's trip to Moscow at this time would be "inappropriate." It would amount to breaking a "gentleman's agreement" between London and Moscow.[49] When London found out that the president had already drafted an agreement with Stalin, various officials asked him to postpone the trip indefinitely. He refused to do so. Ambassador Nichols called the affair a "wound" on Czechoslovak-British relations.[50]

Everyone could see that a relationship between Czechoslovakia, a small country with a democratic tradition, and Stalin's Soviet Union was asymmetrical, to say the least. But London was not opposed to Beneš's Soviet initiative on the grounds that a treaty with Moscow might endanger Czechoslovak sovereignty. Rather, the British criticized the plan for interfering in the arena properly reserved for great powers.[51] The problem was that no Czech politician of any ideological orientation in 1943 was prepared to allow the matter of national security to depend on an international conference. That had happened in Munich, with disastrous results. And since neither the British nor the Americans were willing to offer Beneš any guarantees of their own, the president and most of his colleagues felt that signing a treaty with Moscow was a risky but necessary endeavor.

It was only natural that Soviet diplomats watched the growing rift between Beneš and the West with delight. They wanted him to cross the bridge from West to East, and then burn it. The president felt entrapped and hurt; he fumed about it for days.[52] He thought that the Russian objective was "to turn him into an instrument" of Moscow's schemes. It was "disgusting," he said.[53]

Beneš was caught between Moscow, which was ready to offer a potentially crushing embrace, and London and Washington, whose limp handshake implied no commitment regarding postwar Czechoslovakia. He ranted against the Kremlin's "miserable tactics" in trying to alienate Czechoslovakia from the West, but he never rejected Moscow's offer. He decided to make the trip and sign the treaty, whatever its consequences. It was classic Beneš: privately seething about the cynicism of Soviet diplomacy, and then meekly submitting to it.

Eventually, Eden told Beneš that his plan to sign a treaty with Stalin "had been fully clarified."[54] In reality, the British and the Americans merely accepted the inevitable. They did not know that Beneš was scathingly critical of the Soviet Union in private—more so, perhaps, than Churchill and Roosevelt. They judged him, correctly, by his actions, not his private musings. In the end, nobody was happy, except Stalin.

Well aware of the damage his treaty with Stalin would cause to his standing with the Western Allies, Beneš hoped to minimize it by traveling first to Washington, accepting an invitation from President Roosevelt.[55] On May 6, 1943, he flew to Scotland, then Iceland and New York. Beneš liked America and he looked forward to celebrating his fifty-ninth birthday there on May 28. In preparation for his visit, the OSS and State Department analysts had created a twenty-one-page analysis of the president's personality; it described him as stiff, stubborn, simple, tough, and modest.[56] Unfortunately, the Czech delegation's arrival was poorly timed: Beneš had to compete for attention in Washington with Winston Churchill, who had swept into town with his entourage one day earlier. The British created such a sensation that Beneš, the "stubby and sad-eyed" president, almost disappeared from Washington's notice.[57]

Beneš was received by Roosevelt on May 12, 1943. He got straight to the point: for his country "friendship with Russia was essential. With Germany on one side and Russia on the other, she had no choice." Czechoslovakia could not survive another Munich. Therefore a treaty with the Soviet Union was a necessity.[58] Roosevelt agreed and was pleased to hear from his guest that Moscow stood ready to guarantee postwar Czechoslovakia's territorial integrity and sovereignty. Beneš told FDR that he had been assured by Soviet officials that the Soviet Union would respect Czechoslovak independence. It would never interfere in Czechoslovak domestic affairs. FDR apparently thought that this was good news.[59] According to a witness who saw Beneš shortly after his return from the White House, Roosevelt told Beneš that the "Czechs should look forward to cooperation with the Soviets at the conclusion of the war and in the postwar reconstruction period." Another one of Beneš's close colleagues testified that both the Czechoslovak president and Roosevelt were equally optimistic regarding the Soviet Union.[60]

American journalists asked Beneš whether he was aware of his pro-Soviet reputation.[61] He was, he replied candidly, but his views were identical with those of Secretary of State Cordell Hull and many others in Washington who desired friendly relations with Russia. Beneš asserted that Czechoslovakia's future alliance with Moscow had nothing to do with ideology; it was dictated by geography. Anyone who wished to understand him need only look at an atlas and check his country's location.[62] (Beneš used identical arguments during his trip to Moscow in 1935.) When he was invited to explain his future treaty with Stalin, Beneš answered that the rise of Nazism had made the Soviet Union indispensible to maintain the balance of power. "Just look at a map of Europe. We are at the center of it."[63]

Wherever he went in Washington, Beneš repeated that Czechoslovakia was a Western country and it would never accept a Communist government. It was a democracy that had to avoid being "crushed between opposite powers." Therefore, it needed to be "friendly and cooperative" with both sides. Asked if Russia would dominate Eastern Europe, Beneš replied that as a great power it would have an "interest in the area." But that did not mean "domination."[64]

The officials who received Beneš in Washington were respectful, but they were also brusque and always short of time with the long-winded president. Assistant Secretary of State A. A. Berle, Jr., a child prodigy who matriculated at Harvard at fourteen, saw Beneš in the Department of State and made but the barest effort to hide his annoyance with the visitor's tendency to explain points that the American considered self-evident.[65] Berle had been no supporter of the Czechoslovak cause at the Paris Peace Conference, which he attended at the age of twenty-four, and he argued in 1943 that after the war some 2,000 square kilometers of Czechoslovakia should be transferred to Germany.[66] Giving up some areas inhabited by Germans would have been a good idea for Czechoslovakia soon after World War I. But it was an obvious nonstarter to reward the defeated Third Reich with territory, however small, of a country Hitler had tried to wipe off the map. Beneš and Berle never got down to debating this matter, but their encounter was frustrating. The American record reflects it; the Czech one does not. Beneš boasted in his report that he had made it possible for Berle to understand what strategy postwar Czechoslovakia intended to pursue: it would be neither Western nor Eastern; at all times it would be independent from Russia but protected by it against another Munich.[67] Berle would have been justified to wonder why Stalin should agree to protect Czechoslovakia against all future threats without getting something substantial in return.

Beneš may have felt marginalized in Washington, but he considered the trip a success because, according to his record, Roosevelt "declared plainly" that the

United States would agree with the plan to expel the German population from liberated Czechoslovakia. The president told a colleague that Roosevelt accepted his plan to drive the Sudeten Germans into Germany without any hesitation.[68]

Throughout the war Beneš devoted much energy to making the Allies agree with the plan to expel the Sudeten German civilians from liberated Czechoslovakia as enemy aliens. The origins of the scheme dated back to September 1938, when Beneš developed a secret proposal that included territorial adjustments between Czechoslovakia and Germany and significant "transfer" of population in the Sudeten regions.[69] After the Nazi occupation, and especially during the rule of SS *Obergruppenführer* Reinhard Heydrich (1941–42), personalities involved in the home resistance (ÚVOD) took the harshest possible line regarding the fate of German speakers after Hitler's defeat.[70] They warned the Beneš government-in-exile never to speak about "good" and "bad" Germans, imagining coexisting with the former and punishing the latter after the war. Such an attitude was unacceptable, warned ÚVOD. The Czechs now recognized only one category, that of the German enemy.[71] The British Foreign Office had accepted early that some form of "transfer" of Germans from the Sudetenland would take place. Roosevelt's agreement, if it was in fact given during the visit of 1943, was important for Beneš. Stalin's consent was hardly ever in doubt.[72]

Leaving Washington, Beneš was delighted that FDR had agreed to promote the U.S. legation to his government-in-exile to embassy status.[73] He took it as a positive sign that he had stayed in Blair House, addressed the two Houses of Congress, had an official dinner at the White House, had had a friendly talk with FDR until two in the morning and met Churchill, Lord Halifax, Henry Wallace, Cordell Hull, Harry Hopkins, Sumner Welles, and even Mackenzie King during a quick side trip to Canada.[74] But when it came to Czechoslovak national security in postwar Europe, there was nothing he could take home with him.

Having done his best in the United States, Beneš focused his attention on the summit with Stalin. Did he succumb to Soviet assurances that Moscow harbored no desire to export its regime to the liberated areas?[75] Not necessarily. In private, the president had no illusions regarding Stalin's postwar intentions. Although he had been saying publicly since 1935 that exporting Communism and forcing it upon others in Europe was no longer an objective for the Soviet Union, to his colleagues he said the opposite. In his view, the Soviet Union had signed the 1939 pact with Adolf Hitler in order to "bring revolution and Communism not only to Germany, but to Central Europe as such."[76] Beneš was equally skeptical about Stalin's plans in the postwar era. He told Polish prime minister Władysław Sikorski that he did not know what the Russians intended to achieve in Central Europe after the war, but it was possible that they would come as conquerors to impose Communism, in which case no one could possibly stop them.[77] Many politicians are capable of maintaining two starkly different sets of opinions, one they express in private, the other in public. In Beneš the ability to compartmentalize the "public" and "private" spheres was extreme.

Despite the chasm between what Beneš said to other politicians and what he actually thought, there is no reason to doubt his belief that with a bit of luck Czechoslovakia might avoid succumbing to Communism after the war. The country was established on the principles of liberal democracy, pursued a progressive social agenda, and he, its president, was a lifelong socialist. Beneš hoped that this would help distinguish the Czechs from the "reactionary" and anti-Communist Poles and Hungarians in Moscow's eyes. Unlike them, he treated the Soviet Union as a power with legitimate interests. Therefore, he believed that the Kremlin might allow him to exist in the no-man's-land between the West and East. Furthermore, the alternative to his plan to establish a modus vivendi with Stalin during the war was doing nothing while hoping that the Soviet threat to Central Europe would evaporate thanks to Roosevelt and Churchill or Stalin's religious conversion. That, to Beneš, seemed naïve.

By late November 1943, the president was ready to travel. He and his party flew from London, via Gibraltar, Tripoli, Cairo, Baghdad, and Teheran, where he was granted an honorary doctoral degree, to Baku in the Soviet Union. The last leg of the trip was by train, from Baku to Moscow.[78] Beneš had been in the Soviet capital before, in May 1935, and he knew that the Kremlin bosses liked to make a grand impression on some of their visitors, just as they enjoyed openly snubbing opponents and critics. Unpredictable under the best of circumstances, Moscow in wartime was under a special regime. It was impossible to know what to expect. As the train pulled into the station, Beneš was relieved to see a red carpet, a welcoming delegation headed by Molotov and Marshal Kliment Voroshilov, and an impressive honor guard. There was also a group of Soviet foreign service officials in their splendid uniforms. Czechoslovak and Soviet flags were everywhere; a band offered a spirited version of the two national anthems, and the visitors were whisked into the Kremlin.[79]

The invisible master of ceremonies had prepared a treatment reserved for a few trusted Allies. Molotov and his aides were the first to welcome Beneš and his entourage in a heavily ornamented hall. When the introductions were complete, a voice announced the arrival of Stalin. Molotov and other apparatchiks retreated from the center as all eyes turned to the end of a long and brightly lit corridor. A small group, led by the nearly blind Kalinin, the formal head of state, could be seen slowly approaching. Behind them walked a camarilla of officials, heavily decorated generals, and finally Stalin in a simple but differently colored uniform. He greeted Beneš like an old and close friend. The banquet that followed was so formal and opulent that some of the Czechs, accustomed to British wartime austerity, found it nearly obscene.[80]

There were endless toasts. Beneš, a lifelong teetotaler, had to put up with quite a bit of teasing from the red-faced members of Stalin's entourage, for whom getting drunk under the leader's watchful eye was *de rigueur*.[81] But Beneš was happy to endure the friendly jousting, especially because Stalin and Molotov created a cozy and intimate atmosphere of mutual trust. The highlight of the evening was Stalin's declaration that "the Soviet Union will never interfere in the internal affairs of Czechoslovakia." While he was at it, Stalin warned the Communist Party of Czechoslovakia (CPC) boss Klement Gottwald that his party "had to loyally cooperate with other political parties and not rely on the Soviet Union." Gottwald solemnly accepted this charge.[82] This was vastly better than Beneš's encounters with impatient and bored American officials. At long last, the president felt appreciated. He was so relaxed that he spoke much more freely than he should have.[83]

Czechoslovakia's December 1943 treaty with the Soviet Union—a twenty-year renewable military alliance—created a foundation for, and imposed limits on, all future Czechoslovak foreign policy.[84] It reaffirmed both parties' commitment to the anti-Nazi cause and stipulated that the two would assist each other militarily against any future threat. Article Four of the agreement bound both sides to respecting each other's "independence and sovereignty."[85]

In signing the treaty, Beneš angered London and caused apprehension among some in Washington. But his actions reflected what he believed was rational under the circumstances, and they found approval among the vast majority in Czech émigré circles. The treaty reflected the sentiments that had become common in Nazi-occupied Prague, where even the wealthy saw Stalin in a positive light.[86]

While in Moscow, Beneš went to see W. Averell Harriman at the U.S. embassy. He told him he was "elated" and "thrilled" by his reception and by "the free and intimate character of his conversations with Stalin and Molotov." In a complete reversal of the harshly critical views he had often expressed to his close confidants, Beneš insisted that the Soviet Union had abandoned its revolutionary objectives. In the future, Russia would focus on its new status as a great power. "The Bolshevizing of other countries" was no longer on its agenda.[87] This was very close to what Beneš had said in Moscow in 1935, after the signing of the previous agreement with Stalin. It is remarkable that the president, a man who had spent his entire adult life in international diplomacy, had never mastered the art of saying little or nothing at all.

Beneš understood that to secure the Czechoslovak bridge between West and East in the postwar era, Washington and allies in Western Europe would have to help him maintain its Western moorings.[88] The war, the president liked to argue, had made his leaning toward the Soviet Union a necessity. He intended to be "the balance between the East and the West," safeguarding Czechoslovakia as a democratic country."[89] Referring to the Beneš government as the linchpin connecting East and West became common among the Allies.[90]

On January 8, 1944, after his return to London, the president gave a detailed report to his government-in-exile. Its conclusion was that the treaty with Stalin guaranteed Czechoslovak "existence, security, and democracy."[91] A few months later, as the Red Army approached the eastern edge of Central Europe, Beneš predicted that the region was about to undergo significant changes. But he believed throughout the year 1944 that Czechoslovakia, in contrast to Poland and others in the dangerous neighborhood between Germany and Russia, would be safe.[92]

# || 2 ||

# General Eisenhower Declines
# to Liberate Prague

In early 1945, while he was packing up his household in London before returning to liberated Czechoslovakia, President Beneš endured several affronts at the hands of his Soviet ally, as well as a medical setback. True to his character, he handled the former with resignation and the latter with exemplary courage.

Although the Kremlin had solemnly assured the president that it would help restore Czechoslovakia to its prewar borders, it wasted no time in annexing the country's easternmost district, Subcarpathian Ruthenia. By January 1945 the enormous Soviet security apparat had silenced all dissenters, and Stalin played the innocent: he had no intention to seize the region, but he could not stand in the way of the "national will" of the local population who were allegedly yearning to become citizens of the Soviet Union.[1] Beneš's official representatives in the area observed firsthand how the Stalinist agents created the kind of "national will" that the Kremlin bosses had prescribed.[2] The president accepted the loss quietly.

There was another bitter Soviet pill Beneš had to swallow. Moscow demanded that he de-recognize the Polish government-in-exile in London and grant full recognition to the Lublin Committee, which Stalin had proclaimed in January 1945 as the provisional government of Poland. Within days, Soviet diplomats bombarded Beneš with demands for recognition of this puppet organization, hinting heavily that there was a link between recognition and Moscow's willingness to respect the sovereign Czechoslovak borders, excluding the Subcarpathian province.[3] Beneš protested that the Soviet request made Czechoslovakia look like a protectorate of the Kremlin. He warned that he needed to pay attention to what the British and the Americans were planning to do in this matter.[4] Soon both parties fell back on their old patterns of conduct. Moscow resorted to threats, and Beneš surrendered. On January 31 he abandoned the Polish government-in-exile, with whom he had endured the wartime years in Great Britain, and recognized the Lublin Committee, which consisted primarily of Soviet agents.[5] The London Poles responded the only way they could—by severing their diplomatic relations with the Beneš government the next day.[6]

British ambassador Philip B. Nichols could not resist the temptation to bring up the old Czech-British dispute regarding Beneš's plan to sign the 1943 agreement with Stalin. Stressing that he was speaking only for himself, he noted with a touch of sarcasm that the president had justified the Czechoslovak-Soviet treaty with the need to secure his country's borders. But the events in Subcarpathian Ruthenia were far from encouraging. Nor did the naked pressure on Beneš to recognize the Lublin Committee fit with the British view of how to treat an ally. Nichols was obviously right but Beneš knew that he was still better off than the Poles, who had been scrupulously loyal to the West—only to be rewarded with a drastic loss of territory to the Soviet Union, an NKVD-sponsored terror regime, and a civil war in large parts of the country.[7]

On February 23, 1945, Beneš addressed the Czechoslovak government-in-exile for the last time. He ended on a hopeful note: "Goodbye, till we meet at home."[8] In two weeks he was scheduled to travel to Moscow before returning to the part of Czechoslovakia that had already been cleared of Nazi occupiers by the Red Army. No one could have predicted that getting there would be so difficult.

The president's decision to leave London and return to liberated Prague via Moscow was contentious, and it provoked strong disagreement among the exiles. Ladislav Feierabend, a financial expert, minister, and one of the few conservatives around Beneš, found it horrifying.[9] Moscow was a trap, he told the president sharply. It was the seat of international Communism and, as such, inappropriate as a way station for the government of a democratic country on its return home. He thought Beneš should stay in London until liberation, then fly directly to Prague. The president disagreed. He had to return from the east because the republic was being liberated from the east. Moreover, the president argued, the Soviet Union wished to have a "strong and independent Czechoslovakia" for a neighbor. As always, Beneš spoke with much zeal, and Feierabend knew he had no hope of winning the debate; few ever did. But like many others among Beneš's interlocutors, he was not persuaded by the president's analysis.[10] Another critic of Beneš's plan to return to Prague via Moscow was the social democrat Václav Majer. When he confronted the president with his arguments, Beneš replied that not going there would amount to giving up "everything to the communists without a struggle." Majer decided that the president was right.[11]

Distasteful as it was, the democrats would have to go to Moscow and talk directly with the leaders of the Communist Party of Czechoslovakia (CPC), empowered by the successes of the Red Army. The only alternative was to denounce the party as an agent of a foreign power, an alien and subversive force, and boycott it. That would have put the exiled democratic politicians into the same position as their Polish colleagues in London, who had been condemned by Stalin as agents of Hitler and treated by the British and the Americans as a nuisance. Beneš and his supporters had good reason to think that ignoring the CPC would be tantamount to ignoring reality.

The question about whether the president should return to Prague directly from London or via Moscow had barely been answered when another problem confronted the Beneš team. The British, who were responsible for the president's transportation to the Soviet Union, intended to take a northern route. Moscow immediately insisted that the Czechoslovak delegation arrive via Teheran. After a standoff, the southern route was decided upon.[12]

There was yet another problem that marred Beneš's return to Prague. Diplomatic protocol required that the president be accompanied on his trip home by accredited diplomats. Consequently, members of the diplomatic corps in Great Britain had taken steps to prepare for the dangerous journey with Beneš. Their plan was to sail from Glasgow to Gibraltar, across the Mediterranean, then through the Bosporus into the Black Sea, past the Romanian port of Constanţa and up the Danube. From there the diplomats would continue by train or car, as conditions dictated, into Czechoslovakia where they would meet with Beneš.

In late March 1945, the Americans responsible for joining the Beneš entourage were Counselor Alfred W. Klieforth, an experienced and knowledgeable veteran of the U.S. Foreign Service, and First Secretary John Herman Bruins, who had served at the American legation in Prague from 1935 to 1939.[13] On March 26, 1945, Bruins put fifty pieces of diplomatic luggage on board the ship in Glasgow and waited with others to commence the journey.[14] According to one source, the group of would-be travelers included fifty foreign diplomats.[15] On that day, U.S. ambassador Harriman reported from Moscow the encouraging news that the Soviet authorities would not require the diplomats to obtain Soviet visas. But there was a hint of a potential problem: Moscow warned that the accredited diplomats would need Romanian transit permits, and those could be obtained only in Bucharest. Allied diplomatic services sprang into action and used every available connection in Bucharest to secure them.[16]

While the Western diplomatic services were trying to locate a functioning visa office in Bucharest, a prominent article in *Pravda* stressed the significance of Beneš returning to Prague via Moscow.[17] Then, just after three in the afternoon on March 28, 1945, the day of the ship's planned departure, when the diplomats accredited to President Beneš stood ready to leave, came stunning news. Ivan A. Chichayev, a Soviet intelligence officer, announced that the military situation in the East was too volatile to permit the arrival of the Allied diplomats. Therefore, the Soviet authorities in Bucharest were instructed to deny transit visas to the traveling party.[18] Two hours later, Hubert Ripka, a Czech Foreign Service official, saw the British ambassador Nichols and the U.S. ambassador to London John G.

Winant and told them the trip had to be canceled. The Beneš government would be allowed by the Soviet authorities to make the journey accompanied only by Soviet ambassador Valerian Zorin.[19]

Ripka was shocked by the harshness of this Soviet decision, which was intended to cause offense. He had spoken with Chichayev about the need to arrange for the diplomats' travel in early January 1945, and the Russian agreed it was "self-evident."[20] The reversal of this position months later was humiliating. It seemed to all involved that the real reason behind the aborted plan had little to do with concern for the comforts of Western diplomats. The change was motivated by Moscow's belief that all diplomats were secret agents whose mission was to spy on Soviet machinations.[21] There was another reason the Kremlin canceled the trip: it wished to control the circumstances of Beneš's return to Prague, and Western observers would have stood in the way. As a consequence of the ban on Western diplomats, the president would be surrounded throughout the journey by Soviet officials, bemedaled generals, and the security apparat. The political message would not be lost on anyone.

Foreign Minister Masaryk told the Americans that he "greatly regretted the delay" but believed that the matter could be solved "relatively quickly," though the reason for his optimism was unclear.[22] Beneš stated that he was "most anxious" to be reunited with the Western ambassadors whom Stalin had excluded.[23] Both Beneš and Masaryk had to pretend that this was merely an episode, but in truth it hurt them deeply. When they had to tell the American, British, Belgian, French, Dutch, and possibly other diplomats that the trip was postponed, they were deeply embarrassed.[24] Although they tried to cover it up, they knew that "the affair made an extremely negative impact" on their Western friends. The boat eventually did sail out of Glasgow to the Danube, but it carried only Chichayev and other Soviet officials who had been recalled to Moscow.[25]

Washington refused to take this insult lightly. The State Department noted that the Soviet authorities had been informed as far back as February 9, 1945, that the Americans intended to accompany Beneš, as protocol required. To cancel the journey on the day of the planned departure went against the principles of diplomatic comity. In addition, the State Department stated that the Soviet decision ran contrary to the Declaration on Liberated Europe signed at Yalta and contradicted various statements made by Molotov and Stalin. The note reaffirmed Washington's determination to include Americans in the Beneš entourage. It instructed the U.S. embassy in Moscow to request individual visas for Klieforth, Bruins, a code clerk, and a stenographer. "We feel," Washington informed its embassy in Moscow, "that this representation is highly desirable during the initial stages of reconstruction of the government and civil authority on Czechoslovak soil."[26] As late as April 4, 1945, the Department demanded that the embassy secure Soviet visas so that the Americans could "proceed at once to the seat of the Czechoslovak

Government."[27] It was too late. By then Beneš was already inside a Soviet security bubble on Czechoslovak territory and out of contact with the West.

In addition to the political crises, just before his departure, the president experienced a medical emergency.[28] During the night of March 8–9, 1945, he had woken up disoriented and seemed to have become blind. His physician, Dr. Oskar Klinger, diagnosed a possible stroke, but a mild one. Nevertheless, he declared, the president would be unable to travel. A decision was made that the government would fly without him, and he would follow as soon as possible.[29]

The ministers departed after a brief ceremony, involving low-ranking British officials, headed by R. A. Butler, a prominent supporter of Neville Chamberlain's policy. The choice struck the Czechs as inconsiderate, but nobody wanted to make an issue out of it.[30] It should have been a happy occasion: Czechoslovakia, sacrificed in Munich and destroyed by Hitler in 1939, was about to reemerge as a sovereign country while the Third Reich lay in ruins. Yet no one was happy. The future hard-line Communist minister of the interior, Václav Nosek, tried to improve the atmosphere during the long flight by making fun of the bombastic style of Soviet officials.[31]

Meanwhile, Beneš, despite the medical emergency, dragged himself to his study. He summoned Feierabend, who had resigned his seat in the government and was therefore staying in London. He noticed that the president's face looked asymmetrical; one half of it drooped and an eyelid was sagging. Nevertheless, Beneš was all business. Feierabend asked him for permission to comment, yet again, on his plan to return from exile via Moscow. When this was granted, he told the president that his indisposition was a divine intervention. "I'm asking you again, please don't go to Moscow, stay in London. You have a medical reason that would explain why you had to change your mind. Nobody could read anything political into it. Mr. President, don't go to Moscow!" Feierabend spoke with emphasis on each word. Driving home, he obsessed over the president's insistence that it was too late.[32]

Beneš's recovery proceeded successfully, and on Sunday, March 11, 1945, the president was at the London airport, ready to depart. This time the farewell ceremony was attended by Prime Minister Churchill, Foreign Secretary Eden, and other personalities, such as R. H. Bruce Lockhart, R. W. Seton-Watson, and the political journalist Wickham Steed. The BBC was there to broadcast the whole affair live. Churchill spoke first. But when Beneš attempted to reply, it became obvious that something was horribly wrong. He could not utter the simplest words. His lips moved, but no sound came out. Beneš tried with all his might, but, humiliated, he abandoned the effort. He walked over to Churchill and whispered a few words of gratitude for British hospitality during the war. The BBC promptly turned off its microphones, and wartime censorship covered up any trace of the sad spectacle.[33] Even the American diplomats in London were in the dark regarding Beneš's medical condition. They reported to Washington that the president experienced a case of dizziness.[34] By then the seemingly indestructible Beneš was on his way.

Six days later Beneš and the ministers arrived in Moscow. Their reception was respectful, but measured. Stalin remained in the background for most of the visit and relied on his underlings. After the usual speeches, the president went to the Bolshoi Theater, where he was hosted by Molotov and celebrated by the diplomatic corps.[35] On March 21, 1945, Beneš and Masaryk were received by Molotov, Vyshinskii, Zorin, and others for a meeting narrowly focused on technical and financial matters.[36]

Negotiations between the Czech democrats from London and the CPC bosses from Moscow regarding the composition of the Czechoslovak government were tense. The two sides eventually reached an agreement, but just barely. They ended up endorsing a slightly altered version of the Communist Party wish list. Beneš was to remain president and Masaryk was to be the foreign minister. The other ministerial seats were divided between four parties: Communists, Social Democrats, National Socialists, and People's (Catholic) Party. Virtually all the crucial posts, such as that of minister of the interior, defense, information, education, and agriculture, went to Communists or de facto Communists. Importantly, there were two Communist deputy prime ministers, the party boss Klement Gottwald and Viliam Široký. Negotiating with the CPC at the heart of the Soviet system with its hidden microphones and informers, and at a time when the Red Army was in Czechoslovakia, clearly gave the Gottwald team the advantage.

The party negotiators knew when to show their teeth, but they also sensed when to move cautiously. For instance, they could have insisted on Gottwald becoming the prime minister and, ironically, the democratic parties would have preferred it.[37] Instead, the CPC chose to support Zdenko Fierlinger, a nominal social democrat. This was hardly a concession, because the well-informed knew that Fierlinger was a Soviet agent, as was his brother Jan.[38] Beneš had questioned Fierlinger's loyalty at least since 1941, yet he chose to do nothing.[39] The Western allies were not disturbed to see Fierlinger's name. The man was not a CPC member, and that was good enough for most of the observers who lacked a more detailed knowledge of the Czech political milieu.

Beneš had not crossed half the world to wallow in negativity and gloom. When he saw U.S. ambassador Harriman, he was as "buoyant as ever." The Russians supported virtually every one of his proposals, he claimed, and they gave him no indication of harboring any sinister designs on Czechoslovakia's sovereignty. A reorganization of the country's ruling system was inevitable, Beneš stated, but in the postwar government, only a quarter of the seats would be occupied by Communists.[40]

Others viewed the evolving situation more skeptically.[41] The negotiations gave the impression that this was a conflict between a tidal wave of Communist Party bosses and the scrupulously well-mannered democrats. Specialists in the OSS watched the situation with growing concern.[42]

Not everything was depressing from the democrats' point of view. Stalin, who had been almost invisible throughout the visit, presided over a formal reception at the Kremlin.[43] He made an excellent impression on his guests, who closely studied his every gesture. The highlight of the affair was the two toasts he delivered near the end of the evening. In the first, Stalin admitted that the Red Army, now on Czechoslovak territory, was out of control. The soldiers, he said, were "no angels." He warned that some might resort to violence in dealing with the civilians. Since these men had gone through the hell of war and because they came to Czechoslovakia to liberate it from Nazism, the Soviet leader pleaded: "Forgive them!"

In his second toast, Stalin addressed the crucial question of what kind of political systems would emerge in the countries liberated by the Soviet Union. His desire, he said, was to create in Central and Eastern Europe a "community of states, where all have the same rights and enjoy equality, a community in which no nation is oppressed" by others. At this point, Stalin paused, looked to his right where Beneš was sitting, and added: "This one here doesn't seem to believe me all that much. Or does he?" Beneš smiled, but offered no reply.[44] For once, he was truly at a loss for words. The shape of the postwar world seemed as opaque to him as it did to Churchill and other seasoned politicians.

Before leaving Moscow, Beneš called on Ambassador Harriman again. It was their second encounter in eight days; they spoke for two hours. The president was subdued but claimed to be satisfied with his visit. He reported the essence of Stalin's toasts, focusing on the assurance that the Soviet Union had no intention of interfering in the internal affairs of Czechoslovakia and imposing the Bolshevik system on Europe. Beneš also informed Harriman of Stalin's concern regarding the presence of left-wing politicians in the new Czechoslovak government since Western allies might incorrectly see it as his stratagem. In Stalin's view, asserted Beneš, Gottwald and others in the CPC were too ideological. The Kremlin boss told the president that he should "undertake to broaden their outlook."[45] It was a curious idea—Stalin, the dictator of the Communist realm, suggesting that the democrat Beneš blunt the ideological edges of Moscow's pawns Gottwald, Slánský, and Kopecký, who hardly dared to take a step without instructions from the Kremlin.

On the afternoon of March 31, 1945, members of the Beneš government were ready to leave Moscow. Those from London believed that they were all united by their wartime experience and the tasks awaiting them at home. The Communists knew better. They boarded the train "fully expecting a final showdown with the London team and reactionaries at home."[46] The delegation was seen off by Molotov, Vyshinskii, and a few other satraps; Stalin stayed in the Kremlin. Only the French, Polish, Norwegian, Dutch, Swedish, Yugoslav, and Iranian diplomats attended the farewell ceremony. Neither the Americans nor the British were invited.[47] Washington was reduced to following the train's westward journey from Ambassador Harriman's reports.

Soviet officials provided Beneš and his entourage with a luxurious train for the journey home. This was convenient from the Kremlin's point of view: it accommodated not only the Czechoslovak delegation but also a large security detachment whose sole purpose was to create a protective shield around the president. He would be unable to interact with the outside world.[48]

Aboard the train, the most splendid compartment was reserved for the president. The democrats from London were happy to accept whatever accommodations were available. But the CPC leaders, now government officials, were determined to travel in grand style. They jealously demanded their share of comfort and insisted on a rigid interpretation of diplomatic protocol, which they had previously denounced as a bourgeois farce. When the train approached Kiev, where local officials waited to greet Beneš, it was decided that Mrs. Beneš would be the only wife to alight from the train with the delegation. Marta Gottwald reacted to this plan by bursting into tears. The corpulent wife of the CPC boss had hoped to show off her new dress on this first official function of her life, and she was outraged. Her tears were persuasive, and she was included in the disembarking group.[49]

On April 3, 1945, the train reached Czechoslovakia. Shortly afterward, Beneš arrived in Košice, his temporary headquarters.[50] He was greeted by an honor guard of Czechoslovak troops commanded by Captain Richard Tesařík, a decorated Czech veteran of the eastern front, who handed Beneš a banner adorned with Thomas Masaryk's motto "Truth Conquers."[51] The president stayed in a villa that had once belonged to a Hungarian merchant. Since this was his formal residence, protocol required Benes to receive foreign diplomats who needed to present their credentials. By Soviet design, only one was at hand: Moscow's Ambassador Valerian Zorin.[52]

Washington followed these developments carefully, though from afar. Relying on articles in the official Soviet press, Harriman reported that the Czechoslovak president was on the way to Košice accompanied by Red Army generals, Zorin, and other Soviet officials. Portraits of Stalin could be seen everywhere, displayed along with those of Beneš.[53] As soon as the travelers from London and Moscow had settled in Košice, the president appointed the new government of Prime Minister Fierlinger, the composition of which had recently been agreed upon in Moscow.

The next day, the government presented its politico-economic platform, the Košice Program, consisting of sixteen chapters that dealt with political, economic, social, and cultural matters. This too had been previously hammered out in Moscow. It guaranteed basic democratic principles, including freedom of speech and religion, but it put the country firmly on the socialist path. It introduced plans to nationalize industrial plants, coal mines, banks, and the insurance industry. The program also outlined a radical approach to agrarian reform, which amounted to transferring the land confiscated from aristocrats and from the Sudeten German and Hungarian minorities to small owners. Finally, the Košice program stipulated that in towns and villages, executive power was to be vested in the so-called national committees that would replace the old *radnice* (town halls).[54] Few noticed that this resembled the Bolshevik approach to government summed up by Lenin's slogan "All power to the Soviets!" Many overlooked the radical nature of the Košice Program, as it was effectively hidden behind the façade of Czech nationalism. The program merely appeared to be "liberating" the economy from Nazi exploitation and restoring the original state of affairs that had been disturbed by Hitler.

During the last weeks of the war, few were inclined to worry about the Košice Program.[55] It was easy to calm one's fears by assuming that this document embodied policies that would be in force only during the transitional period until the first democratic elections. Even the few who were concerned about the rise of Communist influence would have agreed with Prokop Drtina, Beneš's political secretary and minister of justice (1945–48), who recorded that in April 1945 he was suspicious of the CPC but remained convinced that its leaders were going to abide by the principles of democratic competition and that they were more intelligent and humane than the uncouth Russian Bolsheviks.[56]

Not until he was in Košice did the president discover he had a serious problem: he was unable to communicate with anyone. In January 1945 Ripka had discussed with Chichayev the logistical aspects of Beneš's return to Czechoslovakia. He stressed that "right from the start the president and the government will need to have access to means of communication with the outside world."[57] Although Soviet representatives had promised that these would be made available as a matter of course, Beneš and the government were completely cut off on Soviet territory and remained so in liberated Czechoslovakia. Having forbidden all representatives of the diplomatic corps from joining the president's entourage, the Soviet authorities also imposed a total ban on all radio and telegraph equipment. Consequently, when the Americans or the British sought to contact the Beneš government in Košice, they failed.[58] The Soviet authorities claimed the ban was necessary because the front was too close for the Czech government to operate its own communications.[59] The implication of this policy—that Czechs would have acted as German spies—was offensive. The real purpose of the ban was to isolate the democratic officials in Košice from the rest of the world. It worked. During the last weeks of the war Beneš was unable to talk to anyone, including Ripka, who had remained in London for the purpose of keeping the president abreast of allied political plans and developments on the western front.

When the Košice Program was made public, a quisling newspaper published in occupied Prague suggested that, should the Red Army drive the Germans from Czechoslovakia, Gottwald was going to be the dictator while Beneš would be a mere figurehead.[60]

Not all was lost just yet. When the president was leaving London in March 1945, it seemed that only the Red Army would be in a position to liberate Prague. But on the way from Moscow to Košice, the Czechoslovak delegation found out that the Americans could reach the city first. Drtina took delight in watching how the news from the western front caused mood swings among the CPC bosses. The Third Army of General George S. Patton was approaching the Czechoslovak-German border much faster than had been anticipated. This rapid American drive through the lines of the collapsing Wehrmacht angered Gottwald and his colleagues. On April 18, 1945, they learned that the Third Army had reached the Czech border.[61] Only 316 days had passed since D-day, and the historically minded Patton was taking a look at the mountainous range along Bohemia's western border. He was "going like wild fire" and eager to press on.[62] Drtina and other democrats rejoiced. The *New York Times* took pleasure in noting that Czechoslovakia, the country that had been sacrificed in 1938 by the "weak-kneed" appeasers, was now emerging "from its fiery ordeal stronger than ever." This was good because it would have a "lasting strategic role in Europe—a role which it can fulfill only by being strong, united and independent."[63]

The CPC leaders had thought it certain that the Red Army would pave the way that would lead them to power in Prague. Suddenly the grand prize was receding into the mists before their eyes.[64] They were unprepared for the new situation. Ripka saw an opportunity and wasted no time in exploiting it. On April 20 he approached the Americans and proposed a civil affairs agreement that would provide a legal framework for the presence of U.S. troops on Czechoslovak territory. Beneš had put forward such a plan once before, in early 1944, but the Department of State did not consider the matter urgent. General Patton's advance changed all that and made it imperative for both sides to move quickly. Ripka requested the posting of two Czech officers with the Supreme Headquarters Allied Expeditionary Force (SHAEF), under General Dwight Eisenhower, and expressed gratitude for "the American advance into Czechoslovakia."[65] The State Department began to prepare the text of an agreement that would determine the status of U.S. troops on Czechoslovak soil.[66] The excitement in

Washington was palpable.[67] Journalist Anne McCormick reminded readers of the *New York Times* that Bismarck had described Bohemia as "the key to the mastery of eastern Europe."[68]

Large parts of Warsaw, Budapest, and Vienna had been reduced to heaps of rubble where Soviet security agents ruled supreme. But now there was hope that Prague might emerge from the war not only undamaged but also free. It was especially encouraging that some American and British officials began to caution that "the voice of the Soviet Government at the Peace Conference would largely depend on the actual position the Red Army held at the cessation of hostilities."[69] On April 22, Anthony Eden spoke urgently with U.S. ambassador Winant. The sole topic was Czechoslovakia. The British foreign secretary stated that, viewed politically, the liberation of Prague and other parts of Czechoslovakia by the Americans would be "most desirable." A U.S. military presence in Prague would make it possible for the United States and the British authorities "to get a footing in the country." Eden concluded that if the Western allies rather than the Russians took Prague, the "advantage to be gained" would be "considerable." He wanted to know whether the Americans shared his view.[70]

FDR's death and Harry Truman's move into the White House made the already complicated situation even murkier. The new president did not wish to begin his presidency by overruling the generals and possibly causing a conflict with the Russians. It was safer for him, he thought, not to interfere with his military leaders' plans.[71] This proved to be a bad decision. Some of the top American generals appeared to believe that U.S.-Soviet relations could be handled as a set of logistical military problems without a political context and lasting security consequences for the West. By contrast, their Soviet colleagues did not focus on the military dimension of the war alone.[72] They understood that their objective was Berlin and anything else that could be grabbed along the way. As always, the human cost was irrelevant.

This asymmetry between the Soviet and American attitudes toward the political aspects of the fighting at the end of the war was to manifest itself most clearly with regard to Prague.[73] On April 21, 1945, General Eisenhower had stated that the most important task facing his troops was to liberate the city of Lübeck and its surrounding areas. This, in his view, was more important than Berlin.[74] A week later, he was still fully focused on Lübeck and Kiel and planning a final move toward Linz, Austria. Should he find the resources, he planned to advance into Czechoslovakia, but stopping some fifty or sixty miles west of Prague. He concluded: "I shall not attempt any move I deem militarily unwise merely to gain a political prize unless I receive specific orders from the Combined Chiefs of Staff." General George C. Marshall endorsed Eisenhower's decision.[75]

Nervously pacing at the Czech border, Patton was anxious to keep going. He had hoped to be the first to drive into Paris and he would have loved to have conquered Berlin. All those dreams had been dashed.[76] Would he be able to liberate Prague, one of the last major cities still in Nazi hands?

The news that Patton's 2nd Cavalry Group, 11th Armored Division, had crossed the Czech border emboldened Churchill, Eden, and Field Marshal Bernard Montgomery to urge Eisenhower to advance as deeply as possible into Czech territory.[77] Berlin was lost—the Russians reached its outskirts on the day Patton's scouts probed the Czech border—so why not liberate parts of Czechoslovakia, or at least its capital, a mere ninety miles from the border that was now securely in U.S. hands?[78] There was no reason for Eisenhower to halt the advance and allow the Russians to take the historical city. He held the key to the country and its future. Unfortunately, no one knew what he intended to do. Ripka reported from London at the end of April 1945: "I have failed to determine how far the Americans wish to advance in Czechoslovakia and whether they have made an arrangement with the Soviets."[79]

At the height of this drama, Ripka made a bold move. Acting on behalf of the government, he requested the immediate transfer of the Czechoslovak Army and the Czechoslovak Air Force, now serving with the British forces on the western front, to the Americans in Czechoslovakia. Ripka told British ambassador Philip Nichols that there was no need to emphasize "the advantages which would ensue if these Czechoslovak forces could fight the enemy on Czechoslovak soil."[80] And there certainly was no need. A leading British expert on Central Europe, Nichols saw no reason to surrender it to Stalin.

U.S. secretary of state Edward R. Stettinius, Jr., supported the British ambassador. In a lengthy telegram, he endorsed a top-secret memorandum he had just received from Eden. It noted that the arrival of American troops at the Czechoslovak border was greeted with enthusiasm and delight, whereas the Communists were "correspondingly depressed." The British knew that Eisenhower intended to advance against the chimeric "southern redoubt." What puzzled them was "whether General Eisenhower [had] been apprized of the significance of Prague." Stettinius clearly shared these sentiments: "My reaction to the foregoing suggestion from the political standpoint is favorable." But he did not call for immediate action; he merely requested that the matter be brought before the Joint Chiefs of Staff.[81]

At the end of the month, Churchill tried to argue the case for a continued American offensive into Czechoslovakia. Addressing Truman, the prime minister declared that an allied liberation of Prague "might make the whole difference to the post-war situation in Czechoslovakia and might well influence that in nearby countries."[82] Others would have tried to accommodate Churchill's point of view, but neither Truman, nor Marshall, nor Eisenhower saw any reason to revise the original plan.

By late April 1945, the race for Prague attracted the attention of Soviet spies ensconced within the British political and intelligence establishments.

Churchill's intervention alarmed Konstantin M. Kukin, the Soviet *rezident* in London. In his report to Moscow of April 26, 1945, he stated that he found out "via agents" about Churchill's attempt to effect an Anglo-American liberation of Prague so as to orient postwar Czechoslovakia and its government toward the West.[83] Kukin's sources included such high-level Soviet spies as Kim Philby, Guy Burgess, Anthony Blunt, and Donald Maclean. If Stalin had seen the report, it would have increased his determination to get to the city before anybody else.

But then two unexpected events made Eisenhower's position difficult to defend. In early May 1945 Patton's Third Army discovered that German resistance in western Czechoslovakia was minimal or nonexistent. American journalists embedded with frontline units reported that the Wehrmacht clearly had had enough.[84] Patton's long-range patrols verified that it was in full retreat. With rare exceptions, all its dispirited soldiers hoped for was to surrender to the Americans.[85] This defused General Marshall's and Eisenhower's argument that they could not risk American lives to gain a political advantage.

The second development had to do with the outbreak of fighting between Czech insurgents and retreating German units. This news reached Eisenhower, together with signals from Patton that the fighting created a new situation that justified American advance into Czechoslovakia.[86] Eisenhower cautiously agreed. He cabled the United States Military Mission in Moscow with a message for the Soviet High Command. It stated that he intended "to advance immediately to the line Karlsbad-Pilsen-Budweis and to capture these points. Thereafter, we are ready to continue our advance in Czechoslovakia to the Elbe and Vltava for the purpose of clearing the West banks of these rivers in coordination with Soviet plans to clear the east banks."[87] Moscow's reaction was prompt. The Soviet command tersely requested that the Americans not go beyond the Karlsbad, Pilsen, and Budweis line "so that a possible confusion of forces can be avoided." It hoped that Eisenhower would "comply with [Moscow's] wishes relative to the advance of his forces in Czechoslovakia."[88] On the same day, May 5, 1945, serious fighting broke out in Prague, but Eisenhower only reaffirmed his order to Patton to halt in Pilsen and cabled the Red Army command: "The Allied Forces are under instructions to remain at the line Karlsbad-Pilsen-Budweis."[89] Patton did not hesitate to say that this was an unwise decision.[90] At this point the Russians were some two hundred miles from Prague, the Americans less than fifty.

There is reason to believe that President Truman was becoming aware of the potentially disastrous consequences of a Soviet-dominated Eastern Europe. He directed the Department of State to prepare brief surveys of the situation in the lands between Germany and the Soviet Union, and in the Balkans. The paper regarding Czechoslovakia was dated May 5, 1945. It was a brief but hard-hitting text. It recalled that the United States had played a central role in the emergence of a sovereign Czechoslovakia in 1918, which made it especially intolerable that

Washington's desire to resume its "close friendship" with President Beneš in the last weeks of the war was thwarted by the Soviet government's refusal to "grant permission to American and British diplomats" to enter the country. The report went on to stress the "political importance of Czechoslovakia, the vital strategic location of Prague," and the traditional sympathy that the Americans felt for the democratic country in the heart of Europe. It was vitally important for the United States to take part in the "liberation and rehabilitation of Czechoslovakia rather than permit the Soviet Union to continue its exclusive control over this most important area in Central Europe." Moscow had already gained "exclusive control of all the other states" in East Central Europe. This had not yet happened in Prague. Therefore, Czechoslovakia, the Department of State noted,

> is an excellent ground to test the promise of the Soviet Government of tripartite cooperation as it is the only one of the capitals of Eastern and Central Europe which has not as yet been occupied by the Soviet Army, and which could probably be occupied by us before the Soviet forces arrive there. The success or failure of cooperation in Prague will have a profound effect on our entire position in Central Europe which would be immeasurably strengthened by our occupation of Prague. The Department of State firmly believes that the interests of the United States will best be served by the immediate occupation of Prague and supports the urgent request made to this effect by Prime Minister Churchill and Foreign Secretary Eden.[91]

Thus the decision for the U.S. Army not to drive the remaining fifty miles into Prague went not only against the views of the British but also against the advice and expectations of the Department of State.

In accordance with the act of surrender, all combat operations were to cease at the end of May 8, 1945. However, on that day Prague saw the heaviest fighting since the Germans took the city some six years earlier. The SS, "crazed with vengeance," committed atrocities in parts of the city.[92] The *New York Times* recorded that the "lights went on again and the guns fell silent today all over Europe except in Western Czechoslovakia."[93] At that point the Russians were still far away. Prague and Oslo were the last great European capitals to remain in Nazi hands. The streets of Prague were blocked by nearly 1,600 barricades manned by some 30,000 volunteers. Attempts to negotiate a truce between the Czechs and their Nazi occupiers were underway, but the situation was dramatic. The overall geopolitical situation supported the insurgents, but they lacked military experience and weapons. Their German enemy was well armed and highly skilled but had run out of time, even if some of its officers seemed unable to come to terms with this fact. Moreover, the Wehrmacht was prepared to sign an honorable agreement that would allow the troops and German civilians to make a dash for the American positions west of Prague, but the SS were not ready to abandon the battlefield. This was amply demonstrated by the order issued by SS *Gruppenführer* Carl Graf von Pückler-Burghauß. The whole nest, he wrote about Prague, had to be set afire.[94] This plan enjoyed the full support of Karl H. Frank, Hitler's viceroy in Prague, who had declared Bohemia *die Zitadelle Europas* and asserted that the protectorate was the heartland of the Reich. Any attempts by the Czechs to fight for their liberty would result in great bloodshed, he warned.[95] There was no reason to treat Frank's threat lightly.

Hitler took his life on April 30 and Berlin fell to the Red Army two days later. Yet on May 8, 1945, German artillery pounded the city of Prague, and the Luftwaffe carried out several attacks on some of the positions held by the insurrectionists. Nevertheless, around seven in the evening, a U.S. Army jeep stopped on a side street near the center of the town.[96] Like many such vehicles at the time, it bore a name, Beati. Its crew, Lieutenant Eugene Fodor, Sergeant Kurt Taub, and Private Nathan Shapiro, all of the OSS, had achieved something most would have considered next to impossible: they had driven through more than one hundred miles of German-occupied territory, armed with only a rifle and a few pistols. The team's commanding officer, Major Charles Katek, ordered Fodor and Taub to go from Cheb to Karlsbad, formerly K. H. Frank's political base, and to report on the situation there.

The main road was a human river filled with retreating military units and masses of civilians of various nationalities and backgrounds. Most hoped to find safety as prisoners of war of the United States. Fodor and Taub discovered that Karlsbad was packed with refugees from Prussia and Silesia and wounded German soldiers with no fight left in them.

Shapiro, the jeep's driver, was born in the Bronx, but Taub and Fodor had both grown up in prewar Czechoslovakia; they knew its languages and its politics. They confidently strode into the city hall and discovered a prewar pro-Nazi lord mayor. They deposed him, a fate he meekly accepted, and installed a successor. The crew from the Beati was supposed to head back to the American lines to report on the situation. But when they heard over the radio about the fighting in Prague, they decided to go there and see what could be done. There was another reason for the daring trip. In Karlsbad they met Stanislav Segmüller, who informed them that hospitals in Prague had all but run out of insulin. A public health catastrophe was imminent. He had a box of the much-needed ampoules and wanted to deliver it to the city. Fodor and Taub offered to drive him and the precious insulin to Prague.

The eighty-mile trip was eventful, primarily because of trigger-happy Czech civilians who hadn't yet encountered the U.S. Army. Mistaking the jeep for a

German vehicle, they repeatedly opened fire on their own liberators. On one such occasion, Fodor and Taub took the trouble to stop and explain to a group of insurgents who had just tried to kill them that they in fact deserved their help. Apologies were offered and accepted. The Americans were delighted to find that the insurgents had access to a telephone line. Taub contacted the Czech National Committee (CNC), an underground organization established in Prague to preside over the transition from the Nazi-administered protectorate to liberated Czechoslovakia. He explained his mission, and the committee dispatched two motorcyclists, who then escorted the jeep through the remaining miles of German-occupied territory all the way to Bartolomějská Street in Prague, where the CNC was in session.

The man who came out to greet them was clad in a civilian suit. But it would have been hard to mistake Jaromír Nechanský, a twenty-nine-year-old captain in the Czechoslovak Army, for a civilian. Nechanský had always wanted to be a soldier, and his parents had supported him completely.[97] He had graduated from the Czechoslovak Military Academy in 1937 and joined the prestigious 3rd Dragoons Regiment. After the Nazis had marched into Prague, Nechanský escaped to Poland, where he met other Czechoslovak officers hoping to fight Hitler. In July 1939 they sailed to France and signed up with the Foreign Legion. Nechanský had spent only a few weeks in Algeria and Tunis when France and Great Britain realized that diplomacy had run its course and declared war on the Third Reich.

On September 23, 1939, Nechanský formally joined the Czechoslovak Army that was being mustered in France. He fought in the disastrous 1940 campaign and just barely made it to Great Britain via Dunkirk. Because of his military credentials, Nechanský came to the attention of the 2nd Bureau of the Czechoslovak Army's General Staff in Britain. Military intelligence was always looking for enterprising people willing to parachute into German-occupied Europe. In May 1942, Nechanský was ordered to undergo a special warfare and assault course, where he was taught to work with explosives. He also learned how to build and protect an underground organization. This was followed by airborne training and finally the Special Training School at Chicheley Hall.[98] Nechanský did so well throughout the course that the British Special Operations Executive (SOE) decided to make him an instructor.

It was only on February 16, 1945, that Captain Nechanský and his special forces team, code-named PLATINUM, were cleared for deployment into Czechoslovakia from an SOE base in Bari, Italy. The flight included a piquant lesson on Central European politics. The Nechanský team was greeted at the airport by an RAF lieutenant colonel who inquired whether the Czechs would be willing to fly with a Polish crew. Nechanský had served as a liaison officer with the Polish 1st Armored Division, spoke decent Polish, and knew that the Poles were among the best Allied pilots. He assured the Englishman that their nationality posed no problem at all. It was only when PLATINUM approached the plane and saluted their Polish comrades that they realized what had made the English officer so apprehensive: the Czechs walked into a barrage of invectives against their government in London. Nechanský had no idea that the Beneš government had just granted full recognition to the Lublin Committee and effectively derecognized the London Poles.[99] "Damn it all, sir," one of the pilots told Nechanský, "your president is playing footsie with the gangster Stalin without realizing that he's our, but also your enemy." The Czech commandos did not expect a political quarrel with their pilots. To their consternation, the Poles raged against Stalin and Beneš's opportunism throughout the flight. Nechanský even worried that his team might be dropped into the Adriatic Sea in retaliation for his president's politics. But the Poles not only skillfully evaded the German flak; they dropped PLATINUM exactly on target.[100] This was not at all common at the time. Pilots of all nationalities were prone to making mistakes, but Czech parachute teams dispatched from the Soviet Union and flown by Soviet pilots were especially unlucky. Although they were supposed to operate in Czechoslovakia, Russian planes dropped some in Poland, others in Hungary. In a number of cases it hardly mattered, because some agents' Soviet parachutes never opened.[101]

PLATINUM landed on February 16, 1945, and soon developed into one of the most successful of the British-trained commando teams in the country. It inflicted real harm on the enemy and gathered actionable intelligence for the allies.[102] As the front was getting closer to Prague, Nechanský received a message from Beneš that he was to be the president's military representative in the CNC On April 23, 1945, he therefore moved to Prague; he was "buoyant and full of resolve." It was Nechanský who helped to transform what had been haphazard shooting at the Nazis into an organized insurrection in May.[103]

When he heard on May 8, 1945, that a U.S. Army jeep was outside the CNC building, Nechanský, who spoke good English, went to greet the Americans. He and Taub became lifelong friends, and their encounter marks the beginning of U.S.-Czechoslovak relations in the post–World War II era.

Fodor and Taub followed Nechanský into the building where the CNC was in session.[104] The man in charge was Albert Pražák, an old-fashioned gentleman and scholar, who presided over a seven-member presidium and a plenum with twenty-six members. Although only a few were identified as Communists, there were others who were close to the party. The most aggressive Communist on the CNC was Josef Smrkovský. His job was not to help defeat the Nazis but to keep the Americans out, even if it meant (since the Red Army was nowhere in sight) keeping the city at the mercy of the likes of *Gruppenführer* Pückler-Burghauß.

After an introduction by Nechanský, Taub addressed the CNC members. The fighting in the city, he said, had created an entirely new situation, one not

envisioned when General Eisenhower had ordered Patton to remain on the
Karlsbad-Pilsen-Budweis line. The central point of the German surrender document was absolute ceasefire on midnight of May 8, 1945. Should the Nazi troops
continue fighting after that deadline, which was likely, a U.S. Army advance to
Prague would be justified. Taub told the CNC that he might be able to arrange a
meeting between the CNC and U.S. Army generals in Pilsen and that the latter
could very well be persuaded to assist the city in its hour of need. Taub sensed
that his offer took everyone by surprise, but it clearly terrified the Communists.
A period of stunned silence followed. Eventually, Pražák stated that the offer had
to be considered seriously, and he asked Taub and Fodor to step outside and
wait. After what seemed like an hour, the Americans were called in again. This
time, it was Smrkovský who spoke. The Red Army was on its way, he insisted,
and bringing in the Americans at this stage could result in confusion. The U.S.
Army was not needed.

Nechanský had just barely managed to remain silent during Smrkovský's
speech. He soon jumped up and spoke out forcefully in favor of inviting the
Americans to liberate Prague. When he realized that his intervention had failed
to persuade most of the CNC members, he motioned for Taub to meet him outside the building. There, standing on the sidewalk, he arranged for the crew of
Beati to drive him to Pilsen to see what could be done to get the GIs to liberate
Prague. Nechanský and Taub knew that whoever liberated Prague would gain a
major advantage in determining Czechoslovakia's future political orientation.
Moreover, Taub sensed that Nechanský's personality and his military bearing
would make a good impression on the Third Army's spit-and-polish generals in
Pilsen. He was convinced that this Czech officer was the kind of man who under
the right circumstances might persuade the Americans to drive to Prague.

Soon Beati was racing toward Pilsen. Although the road was jammed with
retreating German troops, the white star on the jeep's doors garnered instant
respect. Even the biggest among the retreating German vehicles made way for
the three OSS soldiers and Captain Nechanský. It was close to midnight on May
8 when the jeep reached a U.S. Army command post in Pilsen.

Fodor and Taub looked in vain for their OSS commanding officer. Major
Charles Katek was nowhere to be found, and no one among the Beati crew was
sufficiently important to contact the few flag-level officers in Pilsen. General Patton, it turned out, was most likely at his headquarters in Regensburg. Fodor and
Taub realized the madness of their project: a lieutenant and a sergeant were
hardly in a position to write the final chapter of the war. They now saw how unrealistic the whole scheme was from the beginning. Exhausted, they sat down to
contemplate their options when they heard over the radio that the forward elements of the Red Army were some twenty miles north of Prague. It was over.
They got in the jeep and drove back to Prague, arriving early in the morning.[105]

The Red Army was pouring into Prague as the Americans and Nechanský returned. The Soviets lost ten soldiers in the process of mopping up the last remnants of the once invincible German force; by the time they arrived almost all of the Germans had been able to march out toward the Americans in the west.[106] The liberation of Prague was the easiest victory the Red Army achieved during its tough fight against the Third Reich. Its consequences were enormous.

In the morning, Taub established his residence—and OSS office—in the Hotel Evropa on Wenceslas Square. He was a keen observer of the Red Army. At first glance, the troops of Marshals Ivan S. Konev and Rodion Ya. Malinovsky did not look impressive. Except for their tanks, most of their vehicles were U.S. made. Many arrived with peasant-style carts drawn by emaciated horses and even the odd camel. The soldiers came with very little of their own. Their mania for stealing every watch in sight quickly became a legend. Civilians promptly learned to understand the command *"Davai chasy"* (Give me your watch). A failure to obey meant risking one's life. The troops received almost no provisions of their own. A U.S. Army report from liberated Czechoslovakia noted that the country, having been looted by the Germans, was full of "foraging" Russians.[107] As soon as the firing had stopped the Red Army troops began searching for anything to eat and—frantically—for alcohol. Jan Stránský, a member of the Beneš entourage returning home from London, was shown a school where "Soviet soldiers had drunk to the last drop all the methylated spirit out of bottles containing frogs, snakes, lizards and even one human embryo."[108]

Violence against women and girls was among the most visible tragedies of the immediate postwar era. When Stalin had warned that his soldiers were no angels, no one imagined that they would be capable of violating eleven-year-olds or women dying in hospital beds, as Stránský learned on the spot. In large cities, such as Prague and Brno, they committed atrocities in refugee camps, schools, and hospitals. In the countryside, the Soviet troops would surround a house, burst in, and then rape every woman inside, including some great-grandmothers. On leaving, they might murmur apologies and, with their eyes fixed on the floor, offer trinkets to their hysterical victims.[109] The American troops deployed in the western part of Czechoslovakia experienced their share of conflicts with the locals.[110] But only the Red Army was capable of behavior so horrendous throughout Prussia, Poland, Austria, Hungary, and Czechoslovakia that an American journalist described it as a "terror reign."[111] In Berlin and other parts of Germany, violence against women continued until the winter of 1947–48.[112]

SMERSH, the Red Army's counterintelligence, put Sergeant Taub quickly on notice. During his first day in the liberated city, May 9, 1945, its officers tracked him down in his hotel, questioned him closely, and then placed him under house arrest. As a U.S. Army soldier Taub felt no obligation to obey a Soviet order and he kept driving around in his jeep, attracting much attention. When he awoke on

May 10, 1945, he found out that his jeep had been stolen by the Russians. This was a sign of things to come.

Watching the dramatic events from her castle at Kynžvart in western Czechoslovakia and safe under the protection of the U.S. Army, Princess Tatiana von Metternich despaired. The Americans who took over parts of her castle wore immaculate and always crisp uniforms. They seemed strong and healthy and had the best weapons in the world; they could easily have liberated Prague. The princess presumed that they had been held back by some irrational agreement. She was greatly disappointed.[113]

Eisenhower's decision to halt the American troops in Pilsen, an American diplomat conceded, had serious political consequences. It was taken to indicate that the United States was prepared to accept a strong, perhaps dominant Soviet role in Czechoslovakia.[114] This was not true as far as the Department of State was concerned. Even Ambassador Laurence Steinhardt, who watched the race for Prague from his law office in New York City, was baffled by the decision to stop the U.S. Army just fifty miles west of Prague: "The Department and I had hoped that the Third Army would be instructed to enter Prague—which it could readily enough have done, but for some reason, which we still do not quite understand, the American Chiefs of Staff could not see their way clear to giving the necessary instructions."[115]

The decision not to liberate Prague in May 1945 puzzled the State Department, but Generals Marshall, Eisenhower, and Bradley had no second thoughts. Did they really think that Prague was not worth the fuel it would have taken to move a dozen U.S. Army tanks and an infantry regiment the remaining fifty miles? It is hard to believe. As their future careers demonstrated, these men were certainly not naïfs who might be unaware of the relationship between military operations and politics. It seems more likely they were unwilling to take Prague because it would have meant displeasing their Soviet ally. And that is what they wished to avoid at all cost.

Whatever Eisenhower intended, he chose to let the Red Army liberate Prague, and this put the Americans assigned to serve at the U.S. embassy in postwar Czechoslovakia at a disadvantage. Some took it personally: "We sold the country down the river," one observed. "We could have liberated Prague. After the war we spent a lot of time trying to convince the Czechs that they weren't part of the East Bloc. But no matter what we said the Soviets came to Prague first."[116] Communist propaganda turned the Red Army's arrival in the capital city into a miraculous event and distorted the reasons behind the American decision to stay put in Pilsen.[117] There was no denying that the Russians won the title of Prague's liberator. The war ended where it had begun, noted the American press. The "first democratic capital to fall to Hitler's horde suffers the last agony of war in Europe."[118]

On May 8, 1945, still in England and unable to assume his post in Prague, U.S. consul John Bruins listened to Winston Churchill's Victory Speech with a group of Czech friends. Soon the conversation turned to their imminent return home. They wondered whether they still had a "home."[119] The exiles did not doubt the heroism with which the Red Army fought the Nazi enemy, but they had reason to worry about the consequences of its victory. Stalin had seized power in the Baltic republics, Poland, Hungary, parts of Germany, Austria, and the Balkans. What about Czechoslovakia?

While the sleep-deprived Red Army troops roamed the city, Beneš was waiting in Bratislava, still enveloped within the Soviet security bubble. Prime Minister Fierlinger and other government officials flew to Prague on May 10, 1945, in two Soviet airplanes. Several Soviet generals and Red Army infantry and armor units were waiting for them at the airport. Since there were enough Czech generals and soldiers, this was unseemly, as it cast doubt on the autonomy of the returning government.

On the way to the city, Prokop Drtina had to deal with a barrage of questions from his political comrades about why the Americans had not liberated Prague and why the Czechoslovak squadrons from the Royal Air Force had not flown missions to supply the insurgents with weapons, food, and medicine. Drtina knew nothing about the request of the Soviet high command that Eisenhower not advance toward Prague. Therefore he could not answer his friends' questions. Yet it became clear to him that the Red Army's liberation of Prague would have a crushing impact on the already precarious position of the democrats.[120]

Beneš was originally scheduled to return on Sunday, May 13. But this was postponed over alleged concerns for his safety, expressed most vigorously by Prime Minister Fierlinger. He set Wednesday as the new date for the president's arrival, and Drtina was instructed to fly from Prague to Brno and intercept the presidential entourage east of the city. He set out eastward from the Brno airport with a Soviet officer in a Red Army jeep. The driver, however, turned out to be very drunk. Soon after they left the airport, the car was zigzagging from one side of the road to the other so wildly that Drtina feared for his life. He had to wrestle the driver for control of the steering wheel. Eventually he managed to jump out of the vehicle in the middle of the countryside. He did not have to wait long before he spotted a Red Army column, with troops sitting on the fenders of the vehicles, followed by the presidential car and more Soviet guards. Drtina explained to Beneš that his entry to Prague was to be postponed. The president did not resist at all; he meekly accepted the new schedule.

Beneš's slow progress toward Prague was obviously not caused by any security concerns. Rather, Fierlinger, the CPC, and other friends of the Soviet Union needed time to secure their positions for the coming contest with the democrats.

This was the perfect time to do so: the Americans stayed in Pilsen, the Czech pilots were scattered with the rest of the Royal Air Force, the Armored Brigade was still in France, Beneš was in Brno, and Ripka and others were in London. In the nearly complete absence of any opposition or oversight, the CPC could appoint agents to crucial positions within the government. The power vacuum was also helpful for the Soviet security officers, who could arrest anyone on their lists of enemies, particularly among the prewar Russian émigré community. Some were dragged from their homes and shot on the street; those arrested were sometimes never seen again.[121]

The delay weakened Beneš's image in the eyes of the public. The president could have returned on May 9 and marched to Prague Castle surrounded by freedom fighters and the soldiers who had served the Czechoslovak cause on the fronts of World War II. The smell of gunpowder still lingered in the air, and he could have used it to his advantage. Instead, it was a full week after the end of the war before he snuck into the city. By contrast, General Charles de Gaulle marched into the not-quite-liberated Paris, a gutsy move that helped usher him in to power.

The president returned on May 16, 1945, in the midafternoon. He arrived in a convoy of thirty-four cars. It was obvious that the seating arrangement was in the hands of a CPC sympathizer. The first dignitary to appear was Minister of Defense General Svoboda, a crypto-Communist, followed by three Communists: Nosek, minister of the interior; Vacek, lord mayor of Prague; and Smrkovský, the man who had dealt with Sgt. Taub. Then came Prime Minister Fierlinger. Finally, in the eighth vehicle, were President Beneš and his wife, Hana. Keeping an eye on the couple were two gentlemen in the next car: Soviet Ambassador V. A. Zorin and General Vasily N. Gordov.[122]

It was a sunny and pleasant day. Beneš was welcomed by hundreds of thousands. Yet the crowds were restrained. The short president was barely visible amid the chain-smoking Soviet generals with bad teeth. Zorin, Gordov, and other Soviet panjandrums dominated the event.[123] Beneš's speech stressed that he was prepared to work with the Allies on both sides to reconstruct the liberated country. It was an uninspiring performance, replete with more than subtle hints of the president's alleged omniscience.[124] No wonder the Communist daily *Rudé Právo* described the occasion of Beneš's return with enthusiasm. It opined that Czechoslovakia, with the Soviet armed forces as a protective shield around it, could enjoy for the first time a truly independent existence.[125] Yet the president remained very popular. As the first Americans to arrive in Prague discovered, nobody could mistake him for a figurehead.[126]

In the national Czech collective memory, the war started in September 1938, when the British and French delivered Czechoslovakia to Adolf Hitler, and it ended with the U.S. Army sitting just west of Prague in May 1945. The CPC did not stop repeating the main lesson all were supposed to derive from the war: "The Soviet Union has never betrayed us."[127] William J. Donovan of the OSS noted that this propaganda line was successful. The commonly accepted view in the city, Donovan wrote, was: "Our cries for help were heard only in Moscow, the Western powers merely turned a deaf ear." The Communists had managed to create the impression, the OSS noted, that "the American decision not to enter Prague [was] evidence of Anglo-American indifference."[128] This was not true as far as the Department of State was concerned, but it would have been a logical conclusion for anyone who lived through the end of the war in Prague. The appearance that Eisenhower had de facto conceded Czechoslovakia to Stalin empowered the Communists and brought fear to the ranks of their democratic opponents.

The image of a Red Army tank and its cheerful accordion-playing crew became a symbol of all that was good and life-affirming.[129] Meanwhile, the Americans were invisible. Writing about the hardening "zones of interest" in Europe, C. L. Sulzberger of the *New York Times* noted the existence of a line between the Soviet and Western positions in Europe. Was Czechoslovakia already east of that line? If one consulted a map, certainly. And politically? That, Sulzberger conceded, was still unclear.[130]

# 3

# Spring 1945

## The Americans Return to the Schönborn Palace

In the glorious spring of 1945, life started returning to liberated Prague. Edvard Beneš was back in the presidential castle. He remained the most popular politician in the country, even though this was not proportionate to his power within the political system. When it came to the officials of the Communist Party, Beneš could merely argue and plead, not order. His main consolation was that his old Nazi enemies were either dead or in the hands of the justice system. *Gauleiter* Konrad Henlein, one of the leaders of the pro-Hitler elements in the Sudetenland, was arrested by the Americans. He was in their custody for only twelve hours before he slashed his wrists.[1] One of the top Nazis in occupied Czechoslovakia, Karl H. Frank, was arrested by the U.S. Army and handed over to the Prague authorities.[2] He maintained a dignified bearing but his future was bleak.

Jazz, denounced by Nazi censors as a Judeo-Negroid screech harmful to Aryan sensibilities, burst from the underground onto the popular scene.[3] American and other Western novels were being translated at a feverish pace to make up for six years of war. Movie fans who had been kept for years on a thin diet of Herr Josef Goebbels's romantic pulp-cum-propaganda stormed Prague's movie theaters, where they had no difficulty choosing between the much-loved films made in the West and a novelty in the form of Soviet movies portraying the greatness of Russian history, Soviet wartime heroism, and joyful peasants eyeing each other bashfully during the harvest.[4]

When the first team of Americans arrived to reopen the embassy in liberated Prague, the city was full of Red Army troops. This was a new experience for the vast majority of Czechs and for the small American team at the Schönborn Palace. Unlike their Polish and Hungarian neighbors, whose national identity was forged, in part, in wars with the Russians, the Czechs had had no previous contact with the eastern power. The reality of Soviet Russia, as it presented itself in

Prague during the spring and summer of 1945, collided with the idealized notions that many had formed during the war.[5]

The exact contours of Czechoslovakia's political future were beyond anyone's ken. But it was clear from the start that the Schönborn Palace would be at the center of the coming crisis and that it would have to work hard to succeed in its mission. Some in the State Department were eager to avoid turning Prague into "an area of contest" between East and West; they were hopeful that coexistence with Stalin in the heart of Europe would be possible. Others saw that the Kremlin had already created a confrontational atmosphere.[6] Those hoping that the United States would enter into the first round of competition with the Soviet Union with gusto were pleased that the man who reopened the American embassy at the Schönborn Palace was Major Charles Katek of the OSS.

Major Katek, the dashing thirty-five-year-old intelligence officer, arrived in Prague on May 10, 1945.[7] When he met Sergeant Kurt Taub, he radiated so much optimism and energy that he seemed capable of resuscitating the dazed democratic camp single-handedly. Their first stop was the Swiss legation.[8] *Generalkonsul* Albert Huber was pleased to hand over the keys to the Schönborn Palace that the Swiss authorities had protected for the duration of war.[9] He assured the two Americans that the German rulers of Prague had made no effort to violate the principle of extraterritoriality, even though the Third Reich and the United States were in a state of war. This was all the more remarkable because the departing Americans had left behind the complete archive of the prewar legation, boxes of canned food, clothes, a luxury Buick, and even a motorboat.[10]

When Major Katek found out that the Red Army had stolen Beati, Sgt. Taub's jeep, he was not surprised; he was skeptical of all things Soviet.[11] His rejection of left-wing ideologies was rooted in his upbringing in Chicago and was further developed by his study of history and wartime experience with Soviet officials in London.[12]

The first U.S. Foreign Service officer arrived in Prague almost twenty days after Major Katek. John Herman Bruins had devoted years of his career to representing American interests with the Beneš government. He was a knowledgeable and experienced diplomat.[13] It was Bruins who was prepared in late March 1945 to follow Beneš with other foreign diplomats from London to liberated Prague. He was shocked to learn that the Soviet bureaucracy would so brazenly violate such a basic principle of diplomacy and ban all but the Soviet personnel from the president's entourage. Two months later, in late May 1945, Bruins was determined to reach his post at the Schönborn Palace by one means or another. In the end he flew directly to the Prague Ruzyně Airport wearing a U.S. Army uniform with the temporary rank of brigadier general, which allowed him to negotiate various Red Army roadblocks safely. His by-the-book

Major Charles Katek. Gift from Janet Edwards.

approach to diplomacy and his cautious and prudent personality contrasted with Katek's flamboyance.

The son of a Presbyterian minister from Michigan, Bruins became a Foreign Service officer in 1924, representing American interests in prewar Latvia. He and his wife Dorothy enjoyed all their posts that followed—Singapore, Southampton, Hamburg, Danzig, and then Prague, where they served from late 1934 to 1937. On Christmas Day 1941, Consul Bruins was taken prisoner by the Japanese Army at the U.S. consulate general in Hong Kong. He was later exchanged, unharmed but desperately exhausted, for Japanese diplomats detained in Washington. In the spring of 1944, Bruins sailed with his family to London to serve near the Czechoslovak government-in-exile.[14]

As a veteran of the Schönborn Palace, Bruins was on good terms with the Czechoslovak political elite, including Beneš. Jan Masaryk was a close friend, especially since the two had shared a life-altering experience: they were driving to Headley Park, a country estate that belonged to the U.S. Embassy in London, when Bruins noticed intense activity in the sky above. Acting on a premonition, he hid the car under a bridge. "I think we should stop here," he muttered in response to Masaryk's inquiring look. Within seconds an explosion ripped up the road in front of them.[15]

When Bruins reached Prague he found the U.S. embassy was well guarded by the OSS crew under Major Katek's command. After a thorough tour of its premises, he reported to the Department of State that it was "in good condition and ready for use."[16]

The Schönborn Palace was formally opened as a working embassy by the second U.S. diplomat to arrive in Prague, Chargé d'Affaires Alfred W. Klieforth, a tall but stooped veteran of the American Foreign Service.[17] He flew to Pilsen and set out for Prague in an automobile.[18] The Russians turned him back no less than three times on the grounds that his papers were incomplete. Some would have been discouraged, but Chargé Klieforth focused on the positive: "The return of this mission to Prague," he reported to Washington, "was greeted with real joy by all classes of people. The President and Prime Minister personally expressed to me their great satisfaction and obvious relief over our arrival." At the first public function they attended, the Americans received the biggest cheer from the audience.[19]

Klieforth and Bruins conducted a survey of the magnificent Schönborn Palace and its gardens and found that neither had suffered any discernible damage, the custodial service during the war had been excellent, and nothing appeared to be missing. Therefore they officially opened the embassy on June 1, 1945 and began offering consular assistance a week later.[20] Chargé Klieforth was determined that the United States develop genuine political influence in Prague. He knew that time was of the essence. "The long delay in our arrival," he warned, "caused a certain feeling of despair in the country." He explained that some democratic politicians had started to wonder whether the Western allies had abandoned Czechoslovakia to the Russians.[21] In fact, had the Americans arrived a mere ten days earlier, he wrote in early June 1945, "it would have been a God-send to the Czechs," since the Russians would not have been able to "dig in as thoroughly as they did."[22] At this point, Ambassador Steinhardt was still in New York City.

Klieforth found Beneš to be in control in Prague and popular. By contrast, the Soviet-leaning Prime Minister Fierlinger did not, in his view, "wield much influence except as a go-between with Moscow." The American chargé showed his nuanced understanding of the political scene when he noted that the president and the democratic parties were eager to have the first postwar elections as soon as possible in order to benefit from his high standing in the eyes of the public and the declining popularity of Russia caused by the behavior of the Red Army. The Communists were anxious to postpone the elections for the same reason.[23]

After years of war, the American embassy was besieged every day by a large number of people who needed consular assistance. Hiring locals as staff would have alleviated the situation. Unfortunately, this could not be done because the embassy had no way of paying their salaries. The reason for this was simple: the ministry of finance intended to postpone fixing an exchange rate for the Czecho-slovak currency until the departure of the Soviet troops. The specter of Red Army officers and Soviet officials with Czech crowns in their pockets depleting the half-empty stores haunted all economists regardless of ideological leanings. "This is the foremost reason the action is deferred on financial exchange rates with the crown," reported Klieforth.[24] Consequently, the Americans were unable to employ any Czechs and had to handle the long lines in front of the Schönborn Palace on their own.

This was by no means easy, because on top of their consular duties, they were in demand to represent the United States at various political forums taking place throughout the country. Whenever they appeared in public, Klieforth and Bruins received the warmest possible welcome. While many Czechs and Slovaks were grateful to the Soviet "liberators," an American observed, "there was no question that America . . . was the most popular foreign country with most of the people."[25] This was a solid foundation for the Schönborn Palace to build upon.

The staff of the U.S. embassy was small but knew that that the democratic cause was not lost, especially if those seeking to halt the Communist steamroller received some encouragement. That is precisely what Chargé Klieforth had in mind. He became convinced that a robust American presence in Prague was a matter of strategic importance for the United States. Investing a little effort in support of the democratic camp in Prague, he argued, was likely to result in long-term profit. Therefore, Klieforth and Bruins made it their business to introduce themselves to every cabinet minister, ignoring the presence of the Red Army and behaving as if Czechoslovakia had been a sovereign country. Their policy was "to bend every effort towards strengthening the international position of the Beneš Government." They were determined to guide the democratic politicians toward independence, thus keeping the country "knit into Western Europe." An Ameri-can observer confirmed that the skeletal but energetic diplomatic crew at the U.S. embassy made a positive impression on Czech government officials.[26]

This attitude appeared to pay off sooner than expected. In early June 1945 the Schönborn Palace reported to Washington that Czech society was undergoing a rapid healing process. Less than a month had passed since the end of the war, and the country's ideological orientation was already shifting. The Czechs' expe-rience with the Red Army troops, observed Klieforth, was enough to cause many to abandon their "great admiration of Soviet Russia, its efficiency and its way of life." By contrast, ties with the West were from the Czechs' point of view perma-nent and not subject to change; they were anchored in the nation's history and culture. According to Klieforth, the country was anxious to resume its "relations with the Western world as soon as possible." The authorities in Prague, he wrote, "now feel that they have friends in the world other than the Russians, and they are beginning to talk back to them."[27]

Although he would spend only a short time at the Schönborn Palace, Klieforth developed a deep understanding of the issues facing Czech society. He realized that the political leaders were handicapped by fear. Its stench permeated the air everyone breathed. Until recently, people had dreaded the Gestapo. Now they worried about the Soviet secret police. This was obviously true in Poland, East Germany, Hungary, and Austria, but also in Czechoslovakia. Decades later, a British scholar endorsed Klieforth's assessment. All in Central Europe learned quickly "that the Gestapo had been replaced by the NKVD."[28] Inevitably this affected their public behavior and political choices.

As early as June 1945 some Czechs sensed that their country, its democratic tradition notwithstanding, was bound to become a Communist dictatorship. Chargé Klieforth worried that this would lead to a fatalist acceptance of such an outcome. He did not subscribe to this pessimistic vision, but he understood that in Central Europe many supposedly "impossible things [had] happened."[29]

Klieforth's analysis was corroborated by Jan Stránský, a democratic politician, who noted that the biggest challenge for those struggling against the tide of totalitarian ideology in the postwar years was "first of all to combat fear." He also confirmed Klieforth's point regarding the allegedly inevitable Communist victory. He recalled a statement by a Communist official: "You democrats are just fools. Don Quixotes—that's what you are. How can you ever hope to defeat us?" The official went on to argue that Czechoslovakia was the "springboard" for the Red Army's march to the West. Therefore, Moscow would not tolerate a democratic régime in Prague.[30] It served the interests of the CPC to advance the view that the geopolitical interests of superpowers, rather than the electorate, would determine the political orientation of the country. Why should one take any risks in opposing the inevitable? However, in the spring and summer of 1945, only a minority believed that a Communist victory was inevitable.

The jeeps, chewing gum, food and exotic liquor, jazz records, and nylon stockings, a much sought-after novelty in Central Europe, were certainly important in showing America in a better light than its arrogant but shabby, hungry, and rarely sober Soviet competitor. A U.S. Army general reported in early June 1945 that Czechoslovakia, having been looted by the Nazis, now faced massive pillaging from the Russians. This diminished the popularity they had gained at the gates of Moscow, in Stalingrad, Kursk, and when they arrived Prague in May. By contrast, the Americans' standing kept rising in the eyes of the public, in part because of the material abundance that surrounded the U.S. Army. But there was also the American openness and the universal appeal of American culture.[31]

Sympathy, even admiration, for the United States was tightly woven into the national cultural fabric. By contrast, admiration for Russia was a novelty acquired during the war, and it declined when the real Soviet troops proved to be different from the legendary Russian knights.

This trend was clearly seen on June 15, 1945, when Chargé Klieforth accompanied Beneš on a visit to the headquarters of the American Fifth Army Corps in Pilsen, where the president decorated seven generals and six officers with the Order of the White Lion, while another thirty-five officers received the Czechoslovak War Cross of 1939. Then, close to 9,500 Americans began a march across the town in what was one of the biggest U.S. Army parades in Europe. It took them ninety minutes.[32] They marched well and their equipment was shining. It was impossible, Klieforth noted, for the audience not to contrast them with the Russians who roamed the streets of Prague and other Czech cities in "filthy" uniforms. The mighty American armor also invited comparison with the Red Army, which moved about mostly "in horse-drawn old fashioned rickety carts, no different from those used in Russia over a hundred years ago." The Americans seemed strong and happy, but the Russians, wrote Klieforth, "look so miserable and dejected that when they are not feared they are pitied."

Although the U.S. Army was enthusiastically cheered at the Pilsen celebration, the real star of the event was President Edvard Beneš. Klieforth witnessed Lenin's reception in Russia, he saw Mussolini entering Rome, attended Hitler's appearances in Berlin and Churchill's in London, but none, he wrote, "approached in my opinion the unanimous and genuine welcome given to Beneš." The road from Prague to Pilsen was lined with cheering farmers and workmen. Klieforth assured himself later that no one had organized the people standing along the highway; they had come on their own. The president's reception in Pilsen was even more impressive. "I do not recall any similar experience of its kind elsewhere in Europe," wrote Klieforth. The cheering crowd did not represent one class; it "represented the people." At the height of the ovation, Beneš turned to Klieforth, who sat next to him, and said: "This frightens me, the people expect me to perform miracles." Klieforth concluded that the country saw Beneš as the only politician capable of freeing it from the clutches of its Soviet liberators-turned-oppressors.[33] It was a lot to expect from this short fellow in a double-breasted suit and a fedora, with his shy smile and polite manner.

Klieforth was not uninformed about the shifts in Czechoslovak politics between the Munich Agreement of 1938 and the end of the war. But he also knew that beneath the agitated political surface there existed a deep sense that Czechoslovakia's place was with the Western allies and that it was tied in the postwar era to the United States by shared values and aspirations. It was natural that during the war the Czechs admired Russia; the whole world did so as well. It was just as logical that the admiration increased with the arrival of Soviet tanks in Prague in May 1945. Yet Klieforth saw that by the summer of that year the Czechs were reconnected with the West.

Chargé Klieforth was not alone in noticing this trend. The Communist officials in western Bohemia witnessed the parade in Pilsen with alarm. They escalated trivialities into conflicts and made impossible demands on the U.S. Armed Forces command.[34] Less than ten days after the American triumph in Pilsen, the diplomatic team at the Schönborn Palace had to deal with a squabble that the Communists in Prague quickly blew up into a crisis. A Czechoslovak deputy prime minister, who was also a CPC official, announced that he had been "mistreated" by a U.S. Army soldier on June 24, 1945. According to his version, a GI who was directing traffic ordered his car to halt until a U.S. Army convoy had passed. The official felt inconvenienced by the delay and instructed his assistant to tell the GI, in French, who he was. "Moi," replied the soldier, stabbing a finger at his chest, "je suis un soldat américain."[35] He then indicated that the car would have to wait.

The official requested that the Foreign Ministry complain to the Schönborn Palace. Klieforth informed the highest-ranking American officer in Czechoslovakia, General Ernest N. Harmon, a tough and pugnacious soldier who personally interviewed the GI and found that his conduct was beyond reproach. But Klieforth had no desire to play into the hands of the Communists, who hoped to escalate this triviality. He and the U.S. military attaché, Lieutenant Colonel Aage Woldike, apologized for the incident.[36]

In addition to such transparently made-up affairs, there were real differences of opinion between the ordinary Czechs in the U.S. zone and the American military—especially regarding the treatment of German civilians by the GIs. The regional Czech authorities were determined to mete out the harshest treatment to any German speaker, and in this they enjoyed the support of the general public. The American soldiers approached the issue differently. The war in Europe was over; they had seen enough bloodshed and suffering. Having fought their way from Normandy to Pilsen, they felt no need to brutalize German prisoners, let alone innocent civilians. Czechs of all political backgrounds were united in their hatred of anyone who was German. They looked askance at the Americans who liked to socialize with young German women.[37] This caused problems that the U.S. military had to address on a daily basis.

The democratic politicians in Prague liked the Americans, and they reciprocated the feeling: Harmon thought Beneš "perhaps the ablest statesman of Europe . . . learned, patient, tolerant, a true patriot."[38] By contrast, the high-ranking Communists disliked the Americans intensely. They sought to dramatize any small conflict in the U.S. zone and use the negative publicity for political purposes. The population liked Harmon's troops, even though every liberation army, upon becoming an occupation force, comes to be resented over time.[39]

At this point, Ambassador Laurence Steinhardt was still engaged at his law firm in New York, far away from his embassy in Prague, and General Harmon had to deal with numerous political problems on his own. This led to tensions between his headquarters in Pilsen and U.S. diplomats at the Schönborn Palace. The Americans were surprised to discover that the soldiers had started dealing directly with the authorities in Prague behind the back of the embassy. When Klieforth complained about the general's forays into the political field, Harmon replied that it was impossible for him to avoid it. He may have been right that he had to talk with the local and regional officials. Klieforth was, however, justified in complaining when Harmon began corresponding directly with President Beneš on topics that were anything but urgent. For instance, on July 7, 1945, Harmon offered Beneš "a suitable automobile . . . a very fine limousine of German make. I am now having it painted black and will deliver it to you within a few days."[40] Ultimately, the Schönborn Palace and the U.S. Army HQ in Pilsen found a modus vivendi and patched up their relationship.

There was one potentially serious crisis that Klieforth encountered during his tenure in Prague. It provided a hint of Soviet intentions for the future and revealed a dangerous disunity on the American side, where the soldiers and diplomats no longer agreed on large issues and the White House seemed aloof. The crisis appeared out of the blue, just a week after the U.S. Army parade in Pilsen. Stalin summoned Prime Minister Fierlinger; Vladimír Clementis, the Communist who ran the Foreign Ministry in the absence of Minister Jan Masaryk; Minister of Defense General Ludvík Svoboda; Minister of Foreign Trade Hubert Ripka; and others.[41] The agenda included the territorial dispute between Czechoslovakia and Poland regarding the Těšín/Cieszyn area and the final status of Subcarpathian Ruthenia that Stalin had annexed. This produced no surprises.

However, when the delegation returned to Prague, Clementis wrote a note to the Schönborn Palace, demanding that the U.S. Army unilaterally withdraw from Czechoslovakia. In doing so, he went behind the back of President Beneš. From Klieforth's perspective, this created a tricky situation, because the American generals had wanted for logistical reasons to move the troops to their new bases in Germany for some time, but Beneš pleaded for the United States to depart only if the Red Army left as well. Others in the Prague government— with the exception of Fierlinger and the Communists around the party boss Gottwald—supported the president. Klieforth had thought that the issue was resolved and that the Americans and Russians would leave Czechoslovakia simultaneously. But now Clementis suggested that the Russians would leave behind around 40,000 soldiers, about a fourth of the overall contingent, while the Americans would withdraw completely.[42] This was the most brazen attempt so far by the CPC to disturb the balance of power.

Demanding a total withdrawal of the GIs but leaving behind a large Red Army contingent was a classic instance of the asymmetrical Soviet approach to international relations, and Klieforth was unwilling to tolerate it. In a sharply worded telegram he urged Washington to resist the pressure to pull out the troops. He warned that doing so without a simultaneous departure of Soviet military personnel would cause an irreversible loss to American prestige. As it was, the Czechs already believed that the Americans had not liberated Prague because they had meekly obeyed orders from the Kremlin. Any further signs of American weakness, warned Klieforth, would reinforce the image of the United States as a papier-mâché power.

Klieforth told Washington that the request for an American withdrawal was issued "as a result of direct Soviet pressure" and noted that most of the officials in Prague wanted the Americans to stay put. Even Beneš's wife approached the Schönborn Palace and pleaded for the U.S. Army to stay. Klieforth concluded by reporting that the Czechs' resistance to Soviet political pressure was "on the increase in all respects." It would be severely weakened should the Americans take their troops out of Czechoslovakia unilaterally.[43] Klieforth's analysis carried the day. Within hours, he had the pleasure of reading the official reply, announcing that the War Department agreed with the "recommendation that U.S. forces [should] remain in Czechoslovakia until further instructions."[44] This was Washington at its best.

Klieforth used the event to the Americans' advantage. Washington's reply to the Foreign Ministry was deft and unequivocal. The note challenged the specious argument that a complete withdrawal by the United States without a matching move by the Red Army would lead to the restoration of Czechoslovak sovereignty. The Americans, the reply stated, understood it was difficult for the Prague government to rule over a country while dealing with "problems created by the presence of two Allied Armies." Washington then praised the Czechs for the democratic course they had chosen and assured them that Washington wished nothing more for them than "the complete realization of national independence." It looked forward to the time when all the Allies would be completely withdrawn.[45] Without as much as mentioning the Russians, the Klieforth note told Moscow that the United States had no intention of abandoning Czechoslovakia. Reciprocity was the new rule.

Unfortunately, Klieforth served for less than six months in the Schönborn Palace. His service was cut short by two events. On June 20, 1945, five days after the Pilsen parade, a Czechoslovak Foreign Ministry official took Klieforth on a tour of apartments that were set aside for foreign diplomats. When the two men entered one, they discovered it had been commandeered by a group of intoxicated Red Army officers, who took immediate offense at the sight of their visitors. They hurled abuse at the United States, took Klieforth prisoner, and held him for an hour. His Czech guide was "almost speechless with fright." Eventually the American chargé managed to leave the apartment, but the Russians pursued him to the street. When they saw his diplomatic car, they claimed it. Klieforth refused to surrender it, and the Russians produced their pistols, arrested him again, placed him under armed guard, and tried to march him to a Red Army post. It was a tense scene, particularly because the aggressors were inebriated. Klieforth was ultimately released after a more sober Russian officer intervened.[46]

Acting as the doyen of the diplomatic corps in Prague, the British ambassador Philip Nichols brought the event to the attention of the Foreign Ministry, which referred the case to the Czechoslovak government.[47] The conclusion was that the Foreign Ministry would "formally apologize" to the U.S. embassy.[48] Even Beneš received Klieforth and offered his apologies. He then told him "with great joy" that all the Russian soldiers would leave Prague, although not Czechoslovakia, by early July. Beneš implied that Klieforth's "incident" was one of the factors that caused the Russians to order their forces out of the city.[49] The Soviet official reaction to the incident—delivered by Andrei Vyshinskii to Ambassador Harriman in Moscow—consisted of blatant lies. It was irrational and stood the situation on its head; it presented the gray-haired Klieforth as the aggressor and the inebriated Red Army personnel as vigilant defenders of law and order.[50] The Department of State expressed its "dissatisfaction" with the Soviet reply and rejected it. Nevertheless, it decided to drop the matter.[51] If every case of inappropriate behavior by the Red Army had been promoted to an international incident, the Department of State would have been unable to deal with much else.

In short order Klieforth developed medical problems that, he argued, made his continued stay in Prague impossible. Whether they were serious, or even existed, is unclear. He wrote to his superiors on August 23, 1945 requesting to be transferred out of Czechoslovakia for family, not medical, reasons.[52] A month later the Department of State was told by the embassy in Prague that Klieforth was dealing with a medical situation that caused him to be absent from work for periods of time. In October the Schönborn Palace notified the Prague Foreign Ministry that Klieforth was transferred to Washington.[53] His health condition notwithstanding, he soon reemerged as a U.S. consul general in Vancouver, Canada.

Klieforth was convinced that the United States had a receptive audience for its message of liberal democracy in postwar Czechoslovakia. He tried to reach this audience using the tools available to diplomats. But he spent such a short time at the Schönborn Palace that other diplomats who served there in the postwar era no longer remember his name.[54] Moreover, as a mere chargé, Klieforth was unable to leave a lasting imprint on American policy toward Czechoslovakia. His reports lacked the elegance of George Kennan's but his insights into the

Prague political scene and his willingness to seek solutions for the challenges the U.S. embassy faced set a high standard, one that his successors would not be able to attain.

The Schönborn Palace and the Department of State were relieved that they had persuaded the Pentagon to reject Moscow's demand for a unilateral American withdrawal from Czechoslovakia. But the continued disunity between the apparently apolitical U.S. Army commanders, who seemed oblivious to signs of the onrushing East-West crisis, and the Department of State was worrisome. It was one thing for Generals Marshall and Eisenhower to hold back their divisions in April and early May 1945 to allow the Red Army to take Prague as a friendly gesture toward Stalin. But it made no sense that American diplomats needed to explain to the generals the political significance of the U.S. Army presence in Czechoslovakia in June 1945.

Despite Klieforth's initial successes at the Schönborn Palace, the U.S. position in Prague was handicapped by the conspicuous absence of Ambassador Laurence Steinhardt. Klieforth wrote to him from Prague that the whole country awaited the U.S. ambassador's arrival "with interest and anxiety. I trust you may get here as soon as possible. It is a question of prestige."[55]

# ‖ 4 ‖

# Ambassador Steinhardt's Delayed Arrival

Unlike Warsaw and other capitals in Central Europe, postwar Prague offered Washington an opportunity to compete with the Soviet Union on favorable terms. America was represented by smiling GIs whistling Glenn Miller tunes, whereas Soviet soldiers were reduced to thievery and were feared for their violence. When it came to public opinion, therefore, it seemed the United States should win hands down, and many in the Department of State and the OSS believed that with the right kind of support, the democrats in Prague might keep Czechoslovakia outside the zone dominated by Stalin.

Washington naturally presumed that its embassy would energetically present the advantages of the American system and support the indigenous democratic cause.[1] Yet Ambassador Laurence A. Steinhardt, the man responsible for spearheading the effort, had gone missing and gave no indication of being ready to undertake the job. It appeared that he had experienced a professional change of heart around the time of the Yalta Conference. Until then he had viewed his ambassadorial postings as steps toward bigger jobs in Washington. Some speculated that his ultimate objective was the White House itself.[2] President Roosevelt's failure to include Steinhardt in the U.S. delegation going to Yalta constituted a sobering blow to his hopes. When the door to the inner circle of power in Washington was closed in his face, he was discouraged, even depressed.[3] From then on, he refocused on his personal finances and business deals, and his commitment to public service began to fade. This was an unexpected turn in the career of one of America's best-known diplomats.[4] From the perspective of Czechoslovak democracy, the change in Steinhardt's attitude occurred at the worst possible time.

Laurence Adolph Steinhardt spent most of his adult life abroad, but he always considered himself a New Yorker. He was born in 1892 into an upper-middle-class family.[5] Adolph Max Steinhardt, his father, was a successful manufacturer, and his mother, Addie Untermyer Steinhardt, a Virginian, was related to powerful New York attorneys, including her brother, a senior partner in an influential law firm. Young Steinhardt inherited considerable wealth, and he amassed more of his own, together with political prominence and power. But he socialized with even wealthier types, owners of stables, yachts, and residences in desirable locations, and he would never completely shake off a sense of insecurity, perhaps inadequacy, that others tended to mistake for conceitedness.

As a student at Columbia University, Steinhardt was passionate about sports and politics.[6] The 1913 Columbia yearbook predicted that he was likely to succeed in diplomacy. Yet when he graduated with a BA that summer, he hoped to become a doctor. That plan had to be abandoned when his mother died of cancer. Since his father had passed away when Steinhardt was a boy, he was now fully responsible for his sisters, Theresa and Madeline. Medical training seemed too long, so he enrolled in Columbia Law School. He received his LLB in 1915, together with a master's degree for work he had completed during previous summers.[7] As a student, Steinhardt befriended Arthur Hays Sulzberger, the future *New York Times* publisher.

After Columbia, Steinhardt joined the New York office of Deloitte Plender Griffiths & Co. but was soon called up by the U.S. Army.[8] He entered as a private and was discharged as a top sergeant, having served on the staff of the provost marshal general. Steinhardt, who could be sensitive about hierarchy, later stressed that he had been offered an officer's commission but declined it.[9]

Steinhardt married Dulcie Yates Hofmann, a wealthy New Yorker. They met when he was hired by her family to settle the estate of her father, a member of the New York Stock Exchange who had been killed in an avalanche in the Swiss Alps. The Steinhardts went to Europe every summer, mostly to Paris, but also to other, more exotic destinations, such as the fashionable spa Karlsbad (Karlovy Vary) in Czechoslovakia. The marriage was strained from early on. Their daughter, Dulcie-Ann, wrote that it "was not a dream at all, but it had power and privilege unimagined."[10] Although they often considered divorce, the Steinhardts decided against it. But there were affairs, on both sides. Most of their correspondence dealt with such practical matters as shopping, particularly for fur. The relative virtues of leopard, nutria, astrakhan, and other kinds were discussed at length.[11]

In 1920, Steinhardt joined his uncle's law firm, Guggenheimer, Untermyer & Marshall. Only family members were invited to become partners; all were relatives, either by blood or by marriage. Samuel Untermyer, Steinhardt's uncle, was a vigilant promoter of Jewish rights, and Louis B. Marshall was a cofounder of the American Jewish Committee. Steinhardt was careful not to be identified with this cause. His family treated Judaism with respect but maintained that one trip to the synagogue per year was sufficient. Moreover, it was a social, not religious, event. On the rare occasion when he was in the mood for the transcendental, Steinhardt joined his wife, an Episcopalian. His daughter Dulcie-Ann was brought up in the Episcopal Church and confirmed by the bishop of Gibraltar at

Mr. and Mrs. Laurence Steinhardt and their daughter, Dulcie-Ann, 1933. Library of Congress.

the British embassy in Anakara.[12] Yet Steinhardt was never offended when others assumed he was Jewish. When a Jew abroad sought his assistance, he reminded him: "Remember, Mr. Solomon, I'm not the Jewish Ambassador, I'm the American Ambassador."[13] After that, however, he tried to help. He felt at home at the law firm from the start and kept an office at its headquarters on 30 Pine Street in New York City for the rest of his life.

Steinhardt was an instant success as an attorney, corporate lawyer, and international negotiator. He proved to be particularly good at promoting celebrities. Among his clients were the ballet dancer Vaslav Nijinsky and his wife, the famous businesswoman Elizabeth Arden, dress designer Jean Patou, and heiress Doris Duke. Steinhardt also proved to be brilliant at solving complex legal cases that involved large sums of money and powerful competing interests. For instance, he was employed by the Habsburg archduchess Maria Theresa, whose necklace, valued at $400,000, originally a gift from Napoleon I to Marie Louise, had disappeared. The affair captured the attention of New York City as it involved, among others, Maria Theresa's nephew Leopold, the Austrian consul general, and the mysterious Colonel Charles L. Townsend, former head of the British police in Egypt.[14] Steinhardt tracked down the missing article, resolved the tricky legal issues, and returned it to its owner with minimal inconvenience to those involved, but with profit and publicity for himself.[15]

By the early 1930s, Steinhardt was well known and ready to move into the realm of political power. Conveniently, Sam Untermyer introduced him to Franklin D. Roosevelt, who was preparing to run for the White House. Steinhardt was so impressed with the Democratic candidate that in 1932 he became one of the insiders of FDR's early campaign, informally known as the "Before Chicago Club," writing speeches and raising money.[16]

The launching of Steinhardt's diplomatic career was closely linked with his legal activities. When Ivar Kreuger, a Swedish tycoon and financial wizard, took his life in 1932, the vast empire he left behind proved to be rotten to the core. Bankers and investors tried to recover at least a fraction of their claims. The situation was so complex that even specialists found it daunting. Steinhardt did not hesitate to take up the challenge and soon played a prominent role in the restructuring of Kreuger's assets and their distribution to creditors.[17] This gave him a national profile just as FDR was elected to the White House.

Steinhardt's reputation as a capable troubleshooter was enough to make him attractive to Roosevelt. But there was another reason why he captured the attention of the president. In November 1932, when the total Democratic Party war chest amounted to $1,400,000, Steinhardt contributed $5,000—the same sum as Edmund A. Guggenheim, and more than Joseph P. Kennedy.[18] Naturally, such amounts were often given by people seeking their own ends, and Steinhardt was no exception.[19]

Steinhardt's intervention in the Kreuger affair and his generosity to the party merged seamlessly when FDR summoned him to the White House and invited him to be his minister in Sweden. He accepted the offer and was confirmed without difficulty in early May 1933.[20] At forty, he was the youngest chief of an American diplomatic post. Steinhardt did well in Stockholm.[21] Upon his departure from Sweden, he received a gift from the unconventional Soviet ambassador Aleksandra Kollontay—her own picture inscribed with the words "à bientôt a Moscou."[22]

Initially, it seemed that the charming Bolshevik had been misinformed, because in March 1937 Roosevelt chose Steinhardt to be his ambassador to Peru. He accepted without protest, but hoped for better and bigger assignments. In Lima, the new ambassador worked to reduce the Axis economic offensive and helped to organize a major pan-American conference.

Soon enough Madame Kollontay's prediction was proven accurate. In March 1939 Steinhardt was appointed to serve as U.S. ambassador to the

Kremlin. It would be the first real test of his diplomatic skills.[23] Such a post was challenging under any circumstances, but Steinhardt went to Moscow at an especially dramatic time, just as the Wehrmacht marched into Prague. The Soviet Union proceeded to perform a series of diplomatic zigzags between the dispirited and confused Franco-British bloc and the purposeful Third Reich. Steinhardt despised Nazism, and when the *Völkischer Beobachter*, the Nazi Party newspaper, singled him out as one of the "rich Jews" chosen by Roosevelt because of their financial power, he was reaffirmed in his negative assessment of the Hitler regime.[24]

In Steinhardt's view, Soviet ideology was a different matter. With the rest of his family, the ambassador had held a decidedly low opinion of Tsarist Russia, and he gave the Bolsheviks the benefit of the doubt. Some of his relatives, such as Sam Untermyer, had a positive view of the new regime. Untermyer went to see the country on several occasions, once as a guest of U.S. ambassador Joseph Davies, the infamous apologist for the Stalinist system. Steinhardt supported U.S. recognition of the Soviet Union and traveled to Moscow in 1934.

As he began preparing for his own mission in Moscow, the ambassador had an open mind regarding the Soviet system. This started to change as he consulted his colleagues, especially Loy W. Henderson and William C. Bullitt. He also studied the perceptive writings on the Soviet system by journalist Malcolm Muggeridge.[25] Steinhardt devoted himself to reading the existing correspondence between Washington and its embassy in Moscow.[26] What he found gave him pause. He saw that Soviet officials serving in America used every opportunity to complain about any inconvenience, real or not, but the U.S. embassy in Moscow was expected to operate under siege conditions created by pressure from the NKVD and Soviet bureaucracy.[27] He saw that the same asymmetry existed when it came to the treatment of citizens and commercial activities.

Even before he took his post, Steinhardt suggested that reciprocity, the time-honored pillar of diplomacy, be introduced to America's relations with the Soviet Union. Some in the State Department tended to agree with him, but it is unlikely that this is why Roosevelt chose Steinhardt for the Moscow post. He did not need another Bullitt, who had slammed the door on the Kremlin, or another Davies, whose starry-eyed dispatches amounted to irrelevant fluff. The rise of the Third Reich caused FDR to consider the Soviet option seriously.[28]

While Steinhardt prepared for his new mission, the Kremlin bosses tried to learn as much as possible about him. Konstantin A. Umanskii, the top Soviet diplomat in Washington, revealed the ideas prevalent among the Stalinists when he described Steinhardt as "a wealthy bourgeois Jew who was permeated with the foul smell of Zionism."[29] The Steinhardts crossed the Soviet border in early August 1939, two weeks before the signing of the Stalin-Hitler Pact. They were "struck by the darkness of the people" they encountered. The hard faces of Soviet citizens appeared to be "completely devoid of any expression." A team of seven NKVD officers followed the ambassador around the clock. Their mission was to protect him, they asserted solemnly. "Protect? From what?" he asked provocatively.[30]

Steinhardt fully intended to move about in style: waiting for him were his Rolls Royce and a Packard. Apparently, despite his crash course on Stalinist Russia, Steinhardt still had much to learn. Shortages of everything, from spare parts to gasoline, soon caused him to give up and ship his Packard home.[31] His ill-advised entrée damaged him in the eyes of some of his staff. Charles Bohlen later described Steinhardt as "vain and highly egocentric, seemingly driven by the compulsion to make a reputation for himself." Bohlen also charged Steinhardt with being more focused on "publicizing himself" than conducting diplomacy to advance the interests of the United States.[32]

The Stalin-Hitler deal in August 1939 did not take the new American ambassador by surprise. The embassy had been tipped off on the Soviet-Nazi rapprochement by, among others, Hans "Johnny" von Herwarth, a gutsy German diplomat.[33] The combined German-Russian offensive against Poland in September, which began World War II, completed Steinhardt's education about all things Soviet.

In October 1939 the Polish government withdrew Ambassador Wacław Grzybowski after the Kremlin had declared that Poland had ceased to exist. Without hesitation, Steinhardt attended a farewell party for his departing colleague, joining others in the diplomatic corps in expressing regret that some members of the Polish embassy were unable to depart with the ambassador because they were suddenly "missing."[34] Despite their diplomatic immunity, they had been seized by the Soviet secret police and murdered.[35] Steinhardt's presence at the send-off party for Ambassador Grzybowski displeased his hosts. They preferred men like Ambassador Davies, who, upon discovering a Soviet bug above his desk, assured his staff that he was so sincere in his friendship with the Kremlin bosses that he had nothing to hide.[36]

Steinhardt did not possess his predecessor's generous attitude toward the Soviet system. Having been exposed to the Soviet reality, he quickly lost any of the hope he might have had when he was younger for the Soviet experiment. As one of the most important foreign envoys in Moscow, he watched the Soviet Union from behind the wall of his diplomatic immunity and privilege. Nevertheless, he saw clearly enough that it was a country ruled by terror, a country where anyone could be arrested anytime and executed. All of the diplomats had access to special stores and could hardly claim to be famished, but they were isolated in their ghetto. Conducting diplomacy with the host country was impossible. Steinhardt noted that in his first six months in Moscow he met with only four or five frightened Soviet officials, none of whom dared to say anything of significance. Their job was to conduct business with foreigners, yet they trembled for their lives in their presence.[37] Steinhardt occasionally thought that his life in Moscow was close to "unbearable."[38] The Kremlin bosses disliked Steinhardt and snubbed him repeatedly. Never one to overlook bad manners, he paid his hosts back in kind. "The Communist utopia," he wrote to Washington, "is probably the greatest fraud perpetrated on mankind in all recorded history."[39] He disliked not only the ideology but also its guardians. Stalin, he wrote, had so much power concentrated in his hands that he could cause the disappearance of a whole community in such a manner that it would be "neither known nor established for years." The Kremlin leaders, Steinhardt warned, were "utterly indifferent to outside opinion," and it was naïve to think that one could negotiate and reason with them in accordance with ethical standards prevalent elsewhere.[40]

Marcia Davenport, who knew Steinhardt personally, noted that he had "heart and courage."[41] This was quite true. As a diplomat in the Soviet Union he witnessed raw human suffering. His colleagues observed the same scene but suppressed their feelings and followed the rules of diplomacy. Steinhardt was incapable of indifference. He did not set out to harm his career by getting involved unnecessarily, but he helped when he could. When he received letters from parents whose children—American citizens—had disappeared in the Stalinist empire of death, he tried to assist them, and he occasionally succeeded. For instance, he secured the release of twenty-three-year-old Irene Pick from the Lubyanka prison. The Kremlin officials were resentful that Steinhardt was engaging in such activities. When articles on the topic of Soviet concentration camps and executions in Moscow reached the international press, they were angry.[42] The ambassador's admirers claimed that there were fewer ice cream parties at the Steinhardt embassy but more action.[43] There was something to this assessment. When his predecessor, Ambassador Davies, traveled, it was to go sailing on the Black Sea. Steinhardt chose a different itinerary. He went to meet American engineers working in Grozny, Chechnya, continued to the Baku oil fields, then went to Tbilisi before ending up in Crimea.[44] Some of it may have been tourism, but he was doing his job.

In late 1940 Steinhardt reported to Washington that some six hundred American citizens languished in the Soviet-occupied zone of Poland, but only a fraction were allowed to present themselves to claim their U.S. passports in Moscow. Steinhardt tried to intervene on their behalf with the Soviet authorities, but without success. He icily informed Washington that "the extent to which the Soviet Government has 'been leaning over backward' in this matter is not likely to cause it to lose its balance." Steinhardt found the overall situation in Moscow frustrating. He advised his superiors in the Department of State that they should tell his Soviet counterpart, Ambassador Umanskii, that "as a result of his years of residence in the United States, he may no longer attach as much importance to freedom of movement, housing, transportation, and a modest food supply as those of us who reside in his native city."[45] When Steinhardt came to assure Andrei Vyshinskii that the United States desired to "develop a spirit of greater cooperation" with the Soviet Union, the latter replied with platitudes. When the ambassador raised the fate of American citizens on Soviet soil, Vyshinskii was "non-committal."[46] Steinhardt retaliated by suggesting to Washington that "any concessions made to the Soviet Union" should be made only on the basis of reciprocity.[47] By 1941, the pragmatic President Roosevelt wanted to solidify his friendship with Moscow and would have liked the U.S. embassy to work in that direction. But conflicts with the Stalinist security apparat made it difficult. For instance, the embassy staff included a Roman Catholic priest, Léopold L. S. Braun, who held regular services for members of the diplomatic community.[48] In 1941 the sole remaining Catholic church in Moscow, where he celebrated mass, was vandalized by thugs from the NKVD. Instead of overlooking the episode, Steinhardt lodged a formal protest.[49]

By the spring and summer of 1941, the U.S. embassy knew that a German assault on the Soviet Union was a near certainty. Its sources included some of the anti-Nazi German diplomats in Moscow. In addition to von Herwarth, leaks regarding Hitler's intention to attack the Soviet Union could be traced to Ambassador Friedrich Werner von der Schulenburg and diplomats Gustav Hilger and Gebhardt von Walther.[50]

Just as Steinhardt had his confidential sources on German intentions with the Kremlin, so Stalin had his on the ambassador's views.[51] At least two agents kept the Kremlin leaders informed regarding the Steinhardt household. On May 4, 1941, an agent code named "Karmen" reported that Steinhardt had acquired a country house with its own electrical generator and supplies for two months, because "he believes that Germany will soon, this summer, invade the USSR and bomb Moscow." Mrs. Steinhardt revealed that the embassy personnel had started packing up and sending their luggage home. The next day, according to "Karmen," she was preparing to ship her silver and other valuables to safety. Another agent, her driver "Verny," reported that during a shopping expedition Mrs. Steinhardt pointed out a ruin of a house and said: "Soon there will be many houses like this. You heard what they have done with Warsaw and Rotterdam! Unbelievable!" While she was at it, Mrs. Steinhardt also shared her husband's opinion that Russian tanks and airplanes were all papier-mâché. On May 6, 1941, "Verny" heard another reckless conversation between Mrs. Steinhardt and an embassy wife. Her husband was convinced, she said, that the Russians would not withstand the coming conflict. The country was bound to collapse under the German *Blitz*, and there would be famine and popular revolts against the Stalinist régime, Mrs. Steinhardt declared, apparently oblivious to the presence of her driver.

In reality, the ambassador believed the opposite. Falling back on historical precedents, he thought that Russia would eventually beat back the Nazi onslaught. It may well be that his wife misinterpreted one of his casual remarks and that the eavesdropping informer "Verny" garbled it further. The result was that Steinhardt's actual opinion arrived at the Kremlin distorted. The version seen by Stalin could not have improved the ambassador's standing in his eyes. Mrs. Steinhardt's reckless talk in the presence of informers confirms the view that "she was indiscreet, self-willed, supremely self-confident and nowhere near as intelligent as her husband; an unhelpful combination for the spouse of a diplomat."[52] Her disregard for security is particularly puzzling when one considers that even her daughter understood that all their rooms and telephones in the Soviet Union were bugged and that the staff were NKVD informers.[53]

Finally, "Karmen" reported on June 19, 1941, that the American journalist Alice-Leone Moats had heard from Gebhardt von Walther that the attack would take place on June 21. Steinhardt took this information very seriously. He designed plans for the evacuation of family members, nonessential embassy personnel, and other American citizens, such as journalists.[54] Thanks to Steinhardt, Hitler's attack on the Soviet Union found the U.S. embassy prepared.

There was actually no need for Soviet agents to spy on the Americans to learn their views on likely Nazi plans for the Soviet Union. In March 1941 Sumner Wells was instructed to warn Umanskii that the Third Reich intended to invade the Soviet Union.[55] The next month Ambassador Steinhardt told Solomon Lozovsky, a high-ranking Soviet diplomat, that the German threat had better be taken seriously—even if the notion of a Nazi attack upon the Soviet Union seemed mad.[56] He received mostly scorn and sarcasm. Steinhardt saw Lozovsky one more time and reminded the official on June 5, 1941, that an improvement in U.S.–Soviet relations had been on the agenda of the Roosevelt administration since August 1940. Despite difficulties, Washington remained true to its desire to establish close ties with Moscow and showed it with economic measures. Then, however, Steinhardt turned to different topics—he demanded to know why the Soviet authorities had not returned the confiscated property of Ambassador Anthony J. Drexel Biddle, Jr., whose service at the U.S. legation in Warsaw was cut short by the German-Soviet invasion of Poland in September 1939. He also brought up the matter of American citizens imprisoned in Estonia, Latvia, Lithuania, and elsewhere and his inability to communicate on their behalf with the NKVD. Could Lozovsky help with this matter? Before he departed, Steinhardt touched yet again on the topic of German military concentrations along the Soviet border. "He is convinced," Lozovsky recorded, "that the Germans are prepared to attack the Soviet Union."[57]

A curious incident helped Steinhardt form his opinion about the forthcoming German attack. As he was tending to embassy business at the Moscow airport in the summer of 1941, Steinhardt observed Minister Counselor von Walther from the German embassy bidding a tearful good-bye to his boxer dog, who was being shipped to Berlin. Steinhardt instantly decoded the meaning of the scene: the invasion was imminent, because nothing short of an all-out war would have separated von Walther from his boxer. Steinhardt and the German diplomat met the next day for lunch. In the course of it, the ambassador learned the exact date of the imminent invasion.[58]

Stalin refused to act on the warnings he had been receiving, and Hitler's assault on his erstwhile Soviet ally took place with all its devastating consequences.[59] Steinhardt accepted the need for the United States to offer material assistance to Stalin, but he believed that this should come only after concessions were extracted from the Kremlin leaders. What about American citizens in the gulag or in the Soviet zone of Poland? Should they not be freed before the first American deliveries of trucks, planes, or food were placed in Stalin's hands? Why not demand in advance that the Soviet Union renounce title to the territories it had seized as an ally of Adolf Hitler?[60]

Roosevelt and others in Washington dismissed Steinhardt's arguments. The White House was convinced that the speed of the German offensive into Russia made any attempt to negotiate with Moscow impracticable.[61] FDR sent Harry Hopkins and W. Averell Harriman to see Stalin, bypassing his own ambassador.[62] Roosevelt's offer to extend the generous lend-lease plan of assistance to the Soviet Union came in a letter dated November 4, 1941. Even on such a momentous occasion the Kremlin boss chose not to receive Steinhardt; the ambassador had to hand FDR's letter to Vyshinskii, who then passed it to Stalin.[63]

During his visit in the Kremlin, Harriman was taken aback by the Soviet leader's attack on Steinhardt. He was, Stalin claimed angrily, "a defeatist, rumormonger, and coward."[64] None of this was true. In fact Steinhardt had dismissed the view that the Soviet system would collapse.[65] Nevertheless, Stalin thought otherwise, and it was obvious that the ambassador could do nothing useful in the Soviet Union under these circumstances. He later claimed he left because the post had been reduced to dealing with the technical aspect of delivering military supplies.[66] In reality he was pushed aside and humiliated.

Steinhardt's trip home from the Soviet Union was arduous. The ambassador traveled in a light Russian airplane, and the trip, he recalled, took seventeen days and nights of flying. He said that he had come "close to death several times."[67] The plane finally landed at Baku. After a rest, Steinhardt continued to Teheran and Cairo.[68] He arrived in Washington desperately tired and suffering from a sore tooth. When journalists asked Roosevelt what Steinhardt was going to do, the president replied vaguely that the ambassador was "reporting to him and would continue to do so."[69]

The time Steinhardt had spent in Moscow was unpleasant and frustrating. He knew that he read Stalin more accurately than Davies and Hopkins, but it was impossible to overlook the fact that he had failed to represent his president's interests. Once Hitler's assault on the Soviet Union turned Stalin into a partner in the Allied enterprise, the ambassador became an obstacle stepped around with varying degrees of tact by FDR's emissaries. It was a painful and humiliating end of his mission to Moscow.

Steinhardt was a long-term political appointee, not a career foreign service officer, and his standing in the eyes of the State Department professionals, never very high, dropped even lower. Worse, Hopkins and other enthusiastic supporters of the Soviet Union had the ear of the man in the White House. There was reason for Steinhardt to fear that the fiasco in the Soviet Union would mark the end of his diplomatic career. He was therefore relieved when he learned that FDR was sending him to run another diplomatic post.

As soon as Steinhardt discovered he would be going to Ankara, he put a positive spin on it. Turkey was "the key to the Middle East," and his job would be to reduce German influence in the region and to bring Turkey to the Allied corner.[70] The press greeted the news with enthusiasm and accolades for the ambassador. In Moscow, the *New York Times* gushed, Steinhardt performed "brilliant and valuable service" and "won the respect of the hard-boiled officials of the Soviet Government." The article concluded that Steinhardt was the best possible choice for the post in Turkey, which was "more important" than Moscow as it hanged suspended between the warring blocs. So far uncommitted, it feared the Third Reich and saw no reason to trust postwar Russia.[71]

Like many accredited diplomats in Turkey, Steinhardt preferred to conduct business out of the consulate general in Istanbul rather than the embassy in Ankara. Istanbul was an ideal listening post. During the war the State Department used it to follow events in countries inaccessible to Americans in wartime.[72] Furthermore, in Istanbul the mild breezes coming off the Black Sea produced more agreeable weather than the steppe climate on the Anatolian plateau, where days could be hot and nights freezing cold. Steinhardt also enjoyed the sophisticated atmosphere of Istanbul, with its multiple layers of history and culture.

As the war was coming to an end, western culture was seeping in. Jazz clubs were opening on both sides of the Bosporus, where late into the night "Hungarian and Bulgarian beauties would sing, and then make themselves available to dance with the patrons who might be English, American, German, Swedish, or Italian."[73] The American community was large and growing rapidly. Most worked for oil companies or other corporations; some were artists, others archeologists. Quite a few had another profession—as OSS agents. They shared the narrow streets of Istanbul with other intelligence networks. The large British, Soviet, and German services were very active throughout the area, but even the small players, such as the Czechs, used Istanbul as an important post. "There were spies in every camp," recalled the ambassador's daughter.[74]

Steinhardt was serious about his job in Turkey, and he proved to be a perceptive analyst of that complex scene.[75] When the British and American Allies put pressure on Ankara to join in the war effort against the Third Reich, its reaction followed predictable lines: Turkey's heart was with the Allies, but the country lacked the modern weapons needed to fight effectively on their side. Moreover, Ankara had reason to worry about Russia. Were Great Britain and the United States in a position to curb Soviet behavior effectively? In one of his earliest dispatches from the new post, Steinhardt noted that "the Turks fear the Germans and ardently hope for an Anglo-American victory while at the same time they mistrust the Soviets and are doubtful that the U.S. and Great Britain will be able to restrain a victorious Soviet Union from taking the Straits away from them."[76] Finally, Turkey needed a steady supply of oil and machinery, which the Allies were unable to deliver.

The Axis powers provided some of what Turkey needed, and the supplies came with conditions. Steinhardt warned that unless the Allies could substitute their own goods for those from the Axis powers, it was no use pressuring Ankara: "It is in my opinion useless for us—as well as unfair and even dangerous to our future Ally—to precipitate a breakdown in the country's economy by insisting that the Turks refuse limited shipments to the Axis in exchange for which they receive products which we either cannot or will not deliver."[77] Steinhardt recognized immediately that Ankara was in a most delicate situation. Threats were unlikely to produce the desired result. He advised patience and respect for the country's unique position on the fault line between the Third Reich, the Anglo-American Allies, and the looming Soviet realm.[78]

Finally, in July 1944, the German ambassador Franz von Papen burned his papers and left Turkey, and in February 1945 Ankara declared war on the Third Reich and Japan.[79] Steinhardt's analysis of Turkey's situation contributed to the defeat of German interests in the area.

The events that brought the Steinhardts to their next diplomatic post started to unfold in February 1945 in front of one of the ancient fortresses on the Rumeli shore. Dulcie-Ann Steinhardt, the ambassador's nineteen-year-old daughter, remembered that day clearly for the rest of her life.[80] As she recalled, she was doing her homework at the American College for Girls in Istanbul when she was summoned to the office with word that there was a phone call for her. On the line was her father. "I've sent a driver to pick you up," he announced. "We're going on a picnic." This surprised her. A picnic in February? "Are you sure?" she asked. Soon an embassy car was idling outside her dormitory. When she arrived at the U.S. consulate general in Istanbul, Steinhardt and his wife were already outside.

As the sun began to set, the Steinhardts sped south from Istanbul, on the European side of the Sea of Marmara. The ambassador knew this area well. He kept a boat, the *Hiawatha*, with a Turkish captain for long and leisurely trips along the coastline stretching from the Bosporus to the Dardanelles. From the atmosphere in the car Dulcie-Ann sensed this would not be a casual outing. The ambassador drove dangerously fast. When he finally stopped it was dark and cold.

"I'll tell you a great secret," Steinhardt started slowly. He then blurted out that he had been notified through embassy channels that the American delegation would be sailing through the Turkish Straits on their way to Yalta to meet Stalin and Churchill. It was unfair, the ambassador said bitterly, that he was not included in the team accompanying the president. He understood Stalin better than those who were with Roosevelt, especially, he stressed, "that pinko Harry Hopkins." Steinhardt railed against his enemies in Washington. It was their doing that FDR was going to Yalta without him. Dulcie-Ann had never seen her father so angry, bitter, and dejected.[81]

By now their eyes had adjusted to the darkness. Suddenly, they saw the silhouette of an impressive ship that seemed to appear out of nowhere. They all stood up and watched the majestic vessel sailing before them. The ambassador told his family that this was the ship that was carrying Roosevelt to Yalta.[82] For the rest of his life, Steinhardt was critical of the agreements reached by the Allies at the Yalta Conference, blaming all the setbacks the United States suffered in the early stages of the Cold War on this one event. As the ship slowly disappeared into the night, he retreated into silence.

During the long drive back to Istanbul, Steinhardt had another surprise for his family: President Roosevelt had decided that their next post would be— once it was liberated—Prague, Czechoslovakia. The Steinhardts had visited Karlsbad, the fashionable spa in western Czechoslovakia, before the war, but that could hardly have given them a solid understanding of the country and its history. What the ambassador understood well was that Prague might soon become a point of contention between East and West.

Steinhardt appeared to be a good choice for a post that many in Washington considered a laboratory for testing America's relations with Stalin. He had been introduced to the art of diplomacy in Stockholm. In Peru he had acquired ambassadorial rank. The Soviet Union had revealed to him the horror of totalitarianism, and it immunized him against the Communist ideology. But the most important lessons for his mission in Czechoslovakia were those he had learned in Turkey, a country in a gray zone between powerful blocs. One had to be sensitive and patient, because any attempts at economic blackmail were counterproductive, driving the country deeper into the arms of the opponent. This was the knowledge he would be taking with him to Prague.

Some hailed Steinhardt as America's ultimate diplomatic fixer.[83] Yet although he was still only in his fifties, he was no longer as single-minded, determined, or focused on his diplomatic duties as he had once been. He was hurt by his exclusion from the president's entourage at Yalta. Furthermore, he was preoccupied by an affair with an RAF officer's wife that had gone sour and threatened to erupt into a scandal.[84] Finally, he was torn between his commitment to diplomacy and his legal work in New York City.[85] Despite his postings at such demanding embassies as Moscow and Ankara, Steinhardt remained an active New York attorney. He did so out of loyalty to his partners and because he needed the income; the salary he received from the Department of State covered but a small fraction of his family budget.

There were others in the U.S. Foreign Service who could have been assigned to Prague. Kennan, for instance, was more knowledgeable than Steinhardt, but he was an analyst and intellectual, whereas Steinhardt was an activist. In choosing him FDR and the State Department concurred with the view that the United States needed to come to postwar Prague "firm and strong with the Czechs and the Russians" in order to help the Czechs and to improve America's standing in the eyes of the Kremlin.[86]

Unfortunately, it took Steinhardt more than two hundred days to take over the post in Prague. When Chargé Klieforth and Consul Bruins wrote that the politicians in Prague and the diplomatic corps accredited to President Benes were waiting for his arrival and pleaded with him to assume his post at the embassy without delay, Steinhardt was in his law office in New York City dealing with property matters. On May 21, 1945, he wrote to the Schönborn Palace that he would have to postpone his departure "for another three or four weeks."[87] Even that estimate proved to be too optimistic by one month. Steinhardt's focus on his business in New York dismayed the regular Foreign Service officers waiting for him at the Schönborn Palace, and it played into the hands of the Communists in Prague.

On June 6, 1945, President Harry Truman summoned Steinhardt to the White House and urged him to take over his post. Afterward, the ambassador faced the press. Although he could assess the situation in Czechoslovakia only from a distance of more than four thousand miles, he confidently stated that he expected the country to "return to normalcy faster than any other European country."[88] He then stayed at his law firm for another twenty days.

Making a sweeping declaration about a serious topic without evidence had never been in Steinhardt's repertoire before. In his career as a lawyer he could not afford to improvise or to be reckless. Yet here the ambassador made a bold statement regarding Czechoslovakia's political future without ever having set foot in Prague. It is likely that Steinhardt had adopted such a confident tone in order to camouflage his failure to focus on the mission entrusted to him. This proved to be a harbinger of things to come.

# || 5 ||

# A Chronicle of Wasted Opportunities

For the flight from New York to Prague, Steinhardt obtained a four-engine C-54 Skymaster plane. This was a rare privilege afforded to only a few among the powerful and mighty, including Presidents Roosevelt and Truman, General MacArthur, and Prime Minister Churchill. A military transport that was big enough to hold fifty fully equipped paratroopers, the Skymaster carried just Steinhardt and his luggage. The ambassador left New York on June 26, 1945. He landed in London, where he spent more than a week engaged in personal business. He then proceeded to make social calls in Paris and Caserta, Italy, and from there he finally flew to Turkey. There was an unanticipated problem: his family was waiting in Istanbul, but the Skymaster was too big for the Istanbul airfield and instead had to land at Ankara. The Steinhardts met on July 7, 1945.[1]

The reunited family flew to Naples for several days of visits and formal dances, and then continued on to Frankfurt.[2] This stopover had to do with another personal matter: Mrs. Steinhardt believed that she had inherited a house in the city from a relative, and the ambassador devoted much energy to proving it. Though he failed to acquire the house, Steinhardt got 50 percent of the furniture and savings. The family put everything movable, including some precious antiques, on U.S. Army trucks and sent it to Prague. Dulcie-Ann, Steinhardt's daughter, recalled that this was the very first will probated in German courts after the war.

Steinhardt announced his arrival in a cable to the embassy that read: "Ambassador Steinhardt, wife, daughter and four employees and six tons of baggage and supplies will land at Prague airfield 16 July."[3] In Frankfurt he picked up a smaller Douglas C-47 Skytrain plane that would remain at his disposal in Prague. Along with his family, Steinhardt brought a pilot, a chauffeur, a personal attendant for Mrs. Steinhardt, and another one for his daughter.

The Steinhardts touched down at Ruzyně Airport in Prague exactly two months after President Beneš had returned to the Castle. The delay at such a sensitive time was hardly excusable but, mysteriously, no one had the courage to say so. Any criticism of the boss by the staff of the Schönborn Palace would have been a career ender, but even the Department of State had not reprimanded him.

This was all the more surprising because the Department stressed the centrality of Prague for the struggle against the growing Soviet influence and the need for a vigorous American diplomatic presence in the country.

The ambassador was welcomed by Chargé Klieforth and others from the embassy, Vladimír Clementis of the Foreign Ministry, and the British Ambassador Philip Nichols. In addition to these dignitaries, scores of Czechs came to greet the first American ambassador in liberated Czechoslovakia. Decades later the ambassador's daughter still remembered the enthusiastic welcome her family had received on that sunny afternoon in July 1945. Even *Rudé Právo*, the Communist Party daily, celebrated Steinhardt's arrival with enthusiasm. This was not out of the ordinary since the paper faithfully reflected the party line, which was viciously anti-German and maudlin about everything Soviet, but positive toward the other Allies.[4]

With Steinhardt in Prague, there was another important person still missing, Foreign Minister Jan Masaryk. His down-to-earth style of political communication made him an icon among Czechs, and his wit and masterful piano style made him popular within the Western diplomatic community.[5] Many in Prague prayed for his return, but he seemed to be in no hurry; he claimed to be busy in San Francisco with the United Nations conference. In reality he stayed away because he dreaded the prospect of battling the uncouth Klement Gottwald, Rudolf Slánský, and other bosses of the Communist Party. Masaryk's aversion to confrontational politics played into the hands of the party. Steinhardt was quick to note that while Masaryk remained abroad the Communists had entrenched themselves in the Foreign Ministry and filled various posts with their followers.[6] The British diplomat R. H. Bruce Lockhart took note that during Masaryk's long absences, Clementis, the Communist who served as acting minister, "was able to staff the Foreign Ministry with Communist adherents."[7] It harmed the democratic side that the CPC developed outposts not only in the ministries it held officially (e.g., the centrally important Ministry of the Interior), but also inside those that were supposed to be in the hands of trusted friends of the United States, such as the Ministry of Foreign Affairs.

The diplomats awaiting Steinhardt's arrival at the Schönborn Palace were united by the belief that they were taking part in an important enterprise. Before they left for Prague, the Foreign Service officers were instructed in Washington that their mission was to represent American interests by strengthening the cause of democracy in Czechoslovakia. Their objective, they were told, was to "help the Czechs guard their independence." They found it agreeable, even noble work.[8]

Steinhardt brought to the embassy a sense of drama, along with drive and authority, but also camaraderie. He was scrupulously polite toward his colleagues and never tyrannical. No one ever saw him dressing down his subordinates, and junior diplomats enjoyed serving under him. He could get angry and explode, but he reserved such treatment for America's opponents, whom he would light into with the bravura of a seasoned performer.[9]

On July 16, 1945, just hours after he had landed, the ambassador went to a cocktail party in the apartment of a local socialite. He was the only Western ambassador in the crowd. The rest were junior diplomats, allied officers, and young women; the apartment was smoky and noisy. Count Leopold Sternberg and his wife, Cecilia, came only because the invitation—on formal U.S. embassy stationery—promised them an introduction to the ambassador of the United States. They stood uncertainly in the crowd full of red-faced men and their soubrettes. The hostess, wrote Countess Sternberg icily, was "a cheap little tart," who had befriended far too many German officers during the war and was now "sleeping just as readily" with Americans from the Schönborn Palace. The residence of a demimondaine was a bizarre venue for presenting the American ambassador to Prague society. Eventually a U.S. Army officer introduced the Sternbergs to Steinhardt but garbled their names. The ambassador exchanged platitudes with the couple and left.[10]

A few days later, Steinhardt was invited to the castle to present his credentials to President Beneš. The ambassador's predecessors in Prague had been ministers, a lower diplomatic rank, and Steinhardt was therefore the first U.S. ambassador to be received in Prague. He and many other American officials held the president in high esteem, and the formal ceremony had a pleasant atmosphere.[11]

Ambassador Steinhardt presides over a meeting of his staff at the U. S. embassy, Prague. Gift from Louise Schaffner.

Steinhardt made a short statement that stressed the long journey the U.S. Army had undertaken before it reached Czechoslovakia and made it possible for the two countries to normalize their relations. Beneš welcomed the ambassador as a representative of the great American democracy.[12]

Steinhardt could finally turn to a number of pressing issues that had been awaiting his attention. His first concern was the physical safety of the staff and the embassy. Although by late July 1945 only small groups of Soviet officers and virtually no enlisted men roamed the streets, Prague still suffered from occasional violence. Klieforth briefed Steinhardt on the armed attack he had endured at the hands of Red Army officers in late June. Although the Foreign Ministry apologized and claimed that steps had been taken to prevent another such occurrence in the future, there were more American victims. Soon after Steinhardt's arrival, Colonel Thomas K. Taylor, the air attaché, watched from his window as two Russians broke into his car. Hoping that his brand-new uniform would discourage the thieves, he rushed downstairs. When his insignia made no impression on them, Taylor tried to explain that this was a diplomatic vehicle and thus untouchable. One of the Russians responded by pointing his pistol at the officer. The two got in and disappeared. The car was recovered after several days, filthy and without gas. When Dulcie-Ann Steinhardt went out with a group of American pilots, they had to duck and "dash from doorway to doorway" because drunk Russian officers were expressing their momentary joy or sadness by randomly spraying bullets all around.[13]

Soviet behavior in postwar Central Europe saddened anyone who liked Russian culture. Princess Tatiana von Metternich, who was born in St. Petersburg, agonized over the reputation the Stalinist troops had given her native land. Every encounter with a Red Army soldier, she noted, was like dealing with a "wild bear," and alcohol made everything more dangerous.[14] Steinhardt instructed his staff to minimize all contact with Soviet personnel and to move about only in groups. Even this was no guarantee. As late as November 1945, a group of six Americans had a hard time protecting a secretary from the unwanted attentions of an aggressive Red Army officer attached to the Soviet embassy.[15]

The ambassador's second concern had to do with the U.S. troops in the country. The American zone in Czechoslovakia encompassed some 3,600 square miles, from Kraslice near the border with Saxony in the north to Horní Dvořiště on the Austrian border in the south.[16] On June 25, 1945, the infantry divisions of the V Corps were ordered to the Pacific theater and were replaced by the XXII Corps, commanded by Major General Ernest Harmon.[17] The large American contingent deployed fifty miles west of Prague needed a great deal of logistical and political support from the U.S. embassy. General Harmon found himself dealing with various political matters for which he had no training, and he was happy to let Steinhardt take over.

There were other pressing items on the ambassador's agenda. Chief among them was the matter of the "welfare and whereabouts" of American citizens who had been cut off from their relatives in the United States by the war. This in itself represented an enormous challenge for the embassy. Steinhardt told the Department of State that within the first ten days of his arrival he had received twenty-five telegrams from his own family requesting immediate assistance in locating missing persons. "If so many of my relatives and friends are interested I can imagine what the volume is going to be." The Nazis forced many Jews to the Theresienstadt ghetto north of Prague before sending them to the death camps. Therefore, the U.S. Embassy was the first place many Americans would turn for help in searching for missing loved ones. Steinhardt thought that a separate bureau should be created to deal with the matter.[18]

The ambassador's desk also bore a considerable pile of mail from the Department of State. Importantly, there was a long letter from the Division of Central European Affairs reminding him that Prague was "one of the key spots in Europe and perhaps the best testing ground for our future relations with the Soviet Union."[19] This was meant to be a subtle nudge that the ambassador should get on, finally, with his diplomatic business. It failed to make its intended impression.

Upon his arrival, Steinhardt became involved in three projects that distracted him from his mission. He discovered that the representation allowance assigned to the embassy for 1945 was only $3,600. In Ankara he had $6,000. Moreover, he knew that embassies in comparable cities, such as Madrid, had an allowance of $10,000 per annum. He protested this affront in a sharp note to Julius Cecil Holmes, assistant secretary of state.[20]

The ambassador was also concerned about the size of the embassy staff. This was justified, but the Schönborn Palace was not alone among the American diplomatic posts in experiencing personnel shortages. According to Czech official records, the embassy had five accredited Foreign Service officers.[21] However, Steinhardt's letter of early August 1945 mentioned that all the work was being done by the ambassador and his two colleagues, Klieforth and Bruins, who were overwhelmed by their daily agendas.[22] By September 1945, Klieforth had become incapacitated and John Bruins was the only Foreign Service officer on duty. Steinhardt and Bruins, wrote the ambassador, worked seven days a week, often late into the night. Although the Department of State mandated a forty-four-hour week, the crew at the Prague embassy regularly put in seventy-four hours, Steinhardt claimed.[23]

The ambassador was just as unhappy with the quality of his staff. Soon after he had arrived, he requested a different military attaché. Lieutenant Colonel Woldike, he wrote, was "utterly incapable." The Office of War Information at the embassy was a "complete flop." The man running it was "wholly unable to deal with the situation." Steinhardt requested more career Foreign Service officers, at least two or three, and he needed a minimum of ten or twelve stenographer clerks. He asserted that the prewar staff at the Schönborn Palace had included twenty-five administrative staff members.[24]

Finally, after a short inspection, the ambassador determined that the Schönborn Palace fell woefully below his standard. The embassy had been utterly neglected, Steinhardt claimed, and "the filth was indescribable and as to the plumbing, the less said the better." His private residence in the embassy, he wrote, was "uninhabitable."[25] On July 26, 1945, Steinhardt sent a detailed letter to the chief of the Division of Foreign Buildings Operations, claiming that the Schönborn Palace was huge and ancient, but 80 percent of it was unfit to be occupied by human beings.[26] Given the positive reports from Major Katek, Chargé Klieforth, and General Harmon, he was alone in this harsh assessment.

Steinhardt's predecessors viewed the Schönborn Palace as a jewel; they were awed by its history and significance. The ambassador saw it as a ruin. He wrote to the chief of the Central European Division: "Of all the monstrosities that I have ever seen this building is the worst." It was so huge, Steinhardt claimed, that no one seemed to know how many rooms it contained. Some thought there were 120 rooms, others counted 154. After it was fully rebuilt, Steinhardt estimated it would take at least $5,000 annually to maintain the building. He was frustrated that Washington expected him to make do with only $350 before the much-needed renovation.[27] The ambassador prepared for a long fight regarding this project. He wrote to a colleague that he was facing many uncomfortable months ahead.[28]

Steinhardt's negative assessment of the Schönborn Palace did not please the Department of State. Its Division of Foreign Buildings stated firmly that the existing ambassadorial quarters were perfectly habitable. The office produced a 1939 building inspection report in which an expert stressed the property's majesty, charm, and beauty and praised the "brass plumbing and gilt chairs." The division's response to any attempt by Steinhardt to find another house was "one hundred percent 'no.'"[29] It is quite likely that the Schönborn Palace needed to have its wiring and plumbing upgraded and that the living quarters for the Steinhardt family could have done with a face-lift. It was also probable that the representation allowance had been determined before Prague became the testing ground of America's relations with Stalin. However, such matters further diverted Steinhardt from the task of advancing American interests and protecting the cause of democracy on the frontline with Communism.

While Steinhardt set out to improve his living quarters, he suggested Mrs. Steinhardt and their daughter go to Paris. On August 17, 1945, having spent only a month in Prague, the two ladies traveled to Bagnoles de l'Orne where they took the baths.[30] Then they continued to Paris, settling down in their favorite Raphael Hotel on the Avenue Kléber. This is where Steinhardt's telegram reached them in the middle of

September 1945. The ambassador told his wife that there would be no appropriate living quarters in Prague for months to come. "Suggest therefore you take your time and acquire all the clothes you desire, irrespective of cost," he cabled.[31]

Disregarding the department's explicit directions to the contrary, Steinhardt started looking for a suitable private residence outside the embassy. A good lead emerged on July 27, 1945, a mere ten days after he had come to Prague. That day General George Patton was received at the castle by President Beneš, who decorated him with the Order of the White Lion (First Class) and the Czechoslovak War Cross of 1939. The general stayed in one of the most impressive palaces in the city.

This residence was built in the late twenties by Otto Petschek, one of the wealthiest businessmen in prewar Czechoslovakia, where his family owned coal mines and a major bank. Mr. Petschek—known in the family as "Ottolini" for his authoritative style—helped design the home with the newest modern conveniences and technology. At the center was a massive staircase; the furniture and drapes were dark and conservative, the silver heavy and ostentatious. The touch of a button set in motion a wall that opened or closed the downstairs area, to suit the size of the social event. Integrated into the living quarters was a greenhouse. The residence had a large indoor pool and a gym. The energy needs of the palace were such that it took a small train to deliver coal to a whole battery of boilers; a railroad was built in the basement for this purpose.

Otto Petschek died in 1934, and his twenty-year old son, Viktor, watched the growing Nazi threat with concern. He recognized earlier than others that he and his three sisters would never be safe so close to the Third Reich. The Petscheks therefore began selling their holdings and transferring their wealth to safer locations abroad before moving to New York City in September 1938.[32] The Nazis took possession of all Petschek real estate soon after they occupied the country; the family's bank became the headquarters of the Gestapo. The family residence was taken over by the Wehrmacht and stayed in the hands of the military throughout the war. The building then fell into the hands of the Red Army. The silver disappeared, as did some of the furniture. But, miraculously, the Ministry of Defense persuaded the Russians to leave and take over a smaller property nearby, which eventually became the Soviet embassy.

When Steinhardt attended the dinner honoring Patton in late July 1945, he fell in love with the Petschek villa. He immediately informed Washington: "I am looking around for a house of my own. I would rather pay rent out of my own pocket than have to live in [the Schönborn Palace]. The only desirable house is one of the Petschek homes taken over by the Government."[33] His friends in the Department of State saw no reason why the ambassador should pay his own rent.[34] But it was unclear how to solve the conflict between Steinhardt and the Foreign Buildings Office.

Without waiting for Washington's decision, Steinhardt moved to acquire the property. Its owner, Viktor Petschek, an American citizen since December 1943, hired Guggenheimer, Untermyer & Goodrich to represent his interests.[35] As a result, Steinhardt, a partner in the firm, entered the negotiating process with inside knowledge of Petschek's situation. By late July 1945 the ambassador wrote the Department of State that Petschek "would do well to let me occupy" the palace. To stress the point, Steinhardt suggested the Department of State inform the Petscheks: "A few days ago some Russian officers had driven up to the house with trucks and taken all of the silver, all of the linen and some of the porcelain. The furniture is still there and the house is . . . in reasonably good condition, by comparison with Mr. Petschek's other houses . . . occupied by the Russians."[36] Under such circumstances it was hardly surprising that Viktor Petschek was happy to suggest the ambassador lease his residence free of charge. Obviously, he presumed that he and his family still owned it. Therefore he was puzzled by reports that Steinhardt was negotiating with the Prague government to buy the property.[37]

Steinhardt had no second thoughts about his course of action. He went to see President Beneš and directly asked for the property. The Schönborn Palace was a ruin, he insisted, and the president did not argue. He saw the matter strictly as an opportunity to gain political favor with the Americans. In a personal letter to the prime minister, Beneš pointed out that Steinhardt had been helpful to the Czechs in the past, and the Prague authorities should indulge him. "To satisfy him," wrote Beneš, was "a matter of political wisdom."[38]

On August 14, 1945, the Foreign Ministry informed Steinhardt that it had reached an agreement with the Defense Ministry regarding the Petschek property. The next day, the Czechoslovak government decided that the palace—plus two smaller adjacent residences—would be made available to the United States ambassador by September 1, 1945. The ambassador signed an agreement, along with provisions that the government repair and clean the place and furnish it with furniture left behind by some of the wealthy Germans who escaped from the city. Signed by the ambassador and the Czechoslovak minister of finance, the document gave $1,720,000 as the total cost of the Petschek property, plus another office building and residence the United States acquired for its consulate general.[39] Then, in a stroke of genius, Steinhardt included a clause stipulating that the listed price was "credited to the Czechoslovak government against surplus property debts to the U.S. Government."[40] Put simply, the United States gained title to the exquisite Petschek palace in exchange for abandoned U.S. Army jeeps, trucks, blankets, and surplus K-rations that no one planned to ship back to America. Laughing, Steinhardt told his daughter that the residence was "paid for in 'wooden money.'"[41] In the tense fifties, Prague and Washington occasionally revisited the matter of the palace, the largest ambassadorial residence in the hands of the U.S. Foreign Service. But no one dared to challenge the validity of the deal so skillfully negotiated by Steinhardt. The contract was unbreakable.

This would not be the last of the ambassador's successes in the field of real estate. Once he started to upgrade the Schönborn Palace, Steinhardt decided to find a country place. He arranged to lease the very impressive Castle Kynžvart (Königswart) in western Bohemia, the thirteenth-century *Schloss* that belonged to Prince Paul Alfons von Metternich-Winneburg. Although the family had taken great risks in the 20 July Plot to kill Hitler, their property in postwar Czechoslovakia was confiscated.[42]

Steinhardt was a cultivated tenant at the Metternich castle. His predecessors, a group of U.S. Army officers, proved that the Red Army had no monopoly on destructive behavior. They would throw antique furniture and china out of the windows and lure girls from nearby villages by offering them suitcases of clothes and anything else that they could find.[43] The Metternichs appreciated that Steinhardt secured the castle and created a reliable inventory of all the possessions they had to leave behind.[44]

By September 1945, Steinhardt moved into his Petschek palace, spending occasional weekends at Castle Kynžvart. While he lived in the style of an early nineteenth-century European prince, the regular Foreign Service officers faced real hardship in Prague. For months they had to live in the centrally located but shabby Alcron Hotel, which carried visible traces of its previous tenants, Red Army officers.[45] Sometimes when the U.S. military attaché plugged in his hotplate, the fuses were blown. There was often no heat, and hot water was a precious

The residence that Ambassador Steinhardt obtained from the Prague government in the summer of 1945 for the United States. Photograph by Eva Heyd, Prague, 2011.

commodity.[46] An American passing through Prague in late June 1945 reported that life was anything but luxurious for the Americans. In addition to living in substandard hotels, they had to put up with a diet that occasionally consisted of U.S. Army rations.[47] Food shortages remained acute until Steinhardt organized a shuttle between Prague and U.S. bases in occupied Germany.

Having acquired appropriate lodgings, Steinhardt would have perhaps liked to turn his attention to diplomacy and politics. Unfortunately, there were further distractions. Many Americans were intrigued by reports that the Beneš government was in the process of implementing its strategy of acting as a bridge across the ideological divide between the Sovietized East and democratic West. They heard that the country was conducting an experiment that combined a partially nationalized economy with a political system that remained largely democratic. Consequently, several congressional committees descended upon the Schönborn Palace. They expected and received in-depth briefings and logistical assistance from the embassy. The ambassador had to meet all such delegations in person.[48]

Steinhardt also had to devote a lot of time and energy to accommodating various American dignitaries.[49] For instance, General Patton visited repeatedly. The ambassador's daughter recalled that on one occasion he arrived in Prague "with flags and sirens screaming" and his famous revolvers visible at all times.[50] Sometimes there was trouble. For instance, Patton's aide, Lieutenant Colonel Van Santvoord Merle-Smith, Jr., remarked during a visit in September 1945 that a war with the Soviet Union was inevitable. "We've got to finish them," he said. "Theirs is just another dictatorship and threat to democracy and peace, just like Hitler." As was to be expected, all conversations of this sort were promptly relayed by informants to various Czech security services, such as Military Counterintelligence (OBZ), which passed the information to Moscow.[51]

Even General Eisenhower came to receive his White Lion from President Beneš. Steinhardt organized the visit to the general's specifications. It must have been the fastest official tour of Prague ever accomplished. Eisenhower arrived at Ruzyně Airport at 10:30 a.m. on October 11, 1945. Having briskly reviewed the troops, he was driven from the airport so fast that he reached Steinhardt's residence before 11:00 a.m. He rushed through stops at the Defense Ministry, the Foreign Ministry, the lord mayor of Prague, and the Tomb of the Unknown Soldier. Receiving his decoration and dining with President Beneš took one hour and fifty minutes. The general was scheduled to depart at 4:00 p.m. but managed to take off fifteen minutes earlier.[52]

Eisenhower's visit was a missed opportunity to bring the United States to the center of the public arena and to reassure the Czechs that Washington had not given up Czechoslovakia to the Russians. It might have helped repair the general's reputation, which was tarnished by his decision to halt the troops in Pilsen. It may be that Eisenhower did not think there was any need to worry about Czechoslovakia's future. Perhaps he shared the view of Steinhardt that the country was in great shape and moving in the right direction. He was certainly encouraged to think so by President Beneš, who told him that he had "a definite chance" to preserve Czechoslovakia as a democracy and a strong component of the Western alliance. Steinhardt concurred but added that a U.S. military withdrawal from the country without a corresponding departure of the Red Army would seriously "endanger that possibility." Eisenhower repeated this view through his chain of command.[53] In contrast to the Department of State and the intelligence community, however, he did not seem to appreciate the centrality of the Czechoslovak enclave for the balance of power in Europe.

When he finally turned his attention to the local scene, Steinhardt realized what he as a representative of the United States meant to many Czechs. Traveling to Pilsen to inspect the U.S. troops in a convoy of official vehicles organized by General Harmon, accompanied by six motorcycles and two armored cars, the ambassador chose an open car for himself and Chargé Bruins. At the beginning of the U.S. zone outside Pilsen was a gate bedecked with U.S. flags. Steinhardt was greeted there by "hundreds of deliriously enthusiastic Czechs, cheering and crying." Mrs. Bruins pondered with a hint of sadness what the crowds would have looked like had the U.S. Army been allowed to liberate Prague in May 1945, and what influence this would have had on the future Czechoslovak government.[54]

Steinhardt was greeted in Pilsen with the ambassadorial nineteen-gun salute, scores of officers, and local officials, including the Lord Mayor. The main square was packed when he inspected the American troops. He also gave a speech. It was short, to the point, and—most important—it was in Czech, which had been transcribed for him phonetically by his staff. The crowd cheered wildly. Afterwards, Steinhardt was taken on a tour of the brewery and the Škoda Works.[55] In the evening he attended a concert performed by the Pilsen symphony orchestra, conducted by a U.S. Army officer.[56]

Steinhardt's next distraction from the political scene in Prague had to do with economic and commercial matters. The ambassador was right to be vigilant about American investments, but the commercial aspect of the embassy's work grew at the expense of its political activities, and it occasionally merged with Steinhardt's private interests.

According to official data, U.S. property in the country at the beginning of World War II amounted to $148,000,000. The largest component, $67,100,000, represented the value of U.S. shares in various enterprises; American investors owned real estate that was valued at $28,400,000; U.S. corporations had deposited $13,750,000 in Czech banks; and the rest was in bonds, personal accounts, and life insurance held by U.S. citizens.[57] Prior to the war, American corporations were invested in eleven companies operating in Czechoslovakia. The largest among them was the Vacuum Oil Company, a branch of the New York firm Socony-Vacuum Oil Company, the future Mobil Corporation. Other well-known prewar American investors were the International Telephone & Telegraph Corporation, IBM, Remington, and Paramount.[58] The Vacuum Oil Company received most of the ambassador's attention, because it was one of the main clients of his law firm and its chairman, Harold S. Sheets, was a close personal friend. The two toured the refinery in Kolín, a town thirty miles east of Prague, that the Socony-Vacuum Oil Company had owned before the war.[59] It was not clear whether in escorting Mr. Sheets Steinhardt acted as a diplomat legitimately advancing the interests of an American corporation and its shareholders or as a lawyer advising a private client—or whether the merging of the two categories was legal and ethical.

For the moment, Steinhardt and the Vacuum Oil Company could take comfort in an editorial in the Communist daily *Rudé Právo* stating that American industrialists were well known for their management skills, business acumen, and good results. The newspaper asserted that should there be a large-scale nationalization in the future, foreign owners would be compensated. There was no indication that the CPC intended to sever the country's business ties with the west. On the contrary, the article stressed that Prague hoped to secure American loans and expert assistance.[60]

The Motion Picture Producers and Distributors of America represented another challenge for the ambassador. The Czech movie industry was nationalized shortly after his arrival. The studios in Prague were among the best and largest in Europe; the new ones were equipped with the most up-to-date technology. The all-encompassing law nationalized the production and distribution of movies, as well as export and import. The signing ceremony in August 1945 included President Beneš and Václav Kopecký, the hard-line Stalinist minister of information, who thanked the president profusely for his consent to the measure. Beneš replied simply that he was glad to have signed the decree, though only a few days before, he had complained to an OSS mission that the film industry was "Sovietized."[61] The press argued that nationalized film production would make it possible to produce artistic movies, not just those designed to give the investors the greatest financial returns.[62] The state film monopoly was eager to do business with the Americans, but they ignored all offers on the grounds that the new institution was not a proper partner. The American film moguls had persuaded themselves that the political situation would not last.

Steinhardt looked into the matter and, unlike the Hollywood bosses, he understood that the monopoly was not a fly-by-night operation. Not only was it a serious partner, it was the only partner. The Russians had already signed a comprehensive contract that gave them 60 percent of all playing time in Czecho-slovak movie theaters, and the British, French, Swedes, and Italians, among others, had signed agreements for more modest shares. Steinhardt correctly sensed that the public, starved for entertainment after six years of war, "expected American films the day after liberation" and was outraged that not a single Amer-ican film could be seen. In a sharply worded letter to the motion picture industry, the ambassador warned that it was foolish for Hollywood to slumber while others were apportioning the market. There was an enormous opportunity to make a profit. Steinhardt pointed out to the film professionals that, in addition to its commercial aspect, the matter had to be seen in a political context. Czecho-slovakia was "the frontline between Communism and Democracy," and Ameri-can films were needed in the ongoing battle of ideas.[63]

The American film merchants chose a self-defeating strategy for dealing with the situation. In the summer of 1945, just after their movies had started attract-ing "huge crowds," they decided to withdraw from the market altogether. The delighted Russians responded by expanding their offerings.[64] Even the left-wing press expressed concern regarding the absence of Hollywood, noting that before the war American movies had been widespread, and the public missed them greatly.[65] An OSS analyst explained that the Czech public yearned for American movies because Russian films were "too long, too sad and too Russian."[66] Stein-hardt accurately sensed that the American film industry would soon see its error and would need to fight to regain its previous position.

Finally, Steinhardt had a significant stake in representing the property inter-ests of some truly wealthy individuals, including the Petschek and Gellert fam-ilies, two economic powerhouses in Central Europe.[67] In addition to dealing with corporations and prosperous clients, the ambassador's desk was flooded with telegrams and letters from middle-class Americans who had owned prop-erty in Czechoslovakia before the war and wanted to know what had happened to it. All of these cases—large and small—had to be investigated by the embassy staff. Steinhardt was good and efficient at this kind of work but it diverted his attention from the political dimension of his mission.

Few people could match Laurence Steinhardt's intelligence, ambition, and en-ergy. Yet some of his colleagues privately wondered whether he was still a U.S. ambassador fully committed to serving the president or a rich attorney torn between public service and private interest.

In austere Moscow Steinhardt had been focused on his ambassadorial job. He cultivated a wide array of contacts in the diplomatic community and used them to gain advance knowledge of crucial events: he accurately predicted the Stalin-Hitler pact of August 1939 and the Nazi assault on the Soviet Union in June 1941. Although he lived a privileged existence, he understood what life was like for those who lacked his status. After Stalinist Moscow, the ambassador enjoyed the permissive atmosphere of Istanbul. The war was being waged far from the Turkish nightclubs, but Steinhardt remained committed to his duties. He developed a keen understanding of the political scene, he discerned how to advance American interests, and he successfully advocated such a policy in Washington. He achieved what the White House and the Department of State expected of him. Although he was free to move without hindrance within Turkey, the war made it difficult for him to travel between his post and New York City. This curtailed his hands-on involvement in the New York firm and helped to keep him focused on his mission.

Steinhardt's posting to postwar Prague came at a time when there were no constraints on his behavior. In 1945 there was not yet any true equivalent of the NKVD in Czechoslovakia, and he had an airplane with a full-time pilot, putting European capitals within reach. Transatlantic travel enabled him to reach New York City in the course of a week. He could get involved in legal and business deals for which the war and its aftermath created ample opportunities, especially for those with his extraordinary skills and inside access. Although his superiors in Washington had every reason to demand improved performance from him, they chose to pretend that all was well.

# || 6 ||

# Steinhardt Encounters Reality

## *Nationalization, Expulsions, and U.S. Military Withdrawal*

As the country recovered from the war, the Americans serving at the Schönborn Palace began to move out of the decrepit Alcron Hotel. Some found apartments with charming views of the castle. Others rented space in upper-middle-class houses (called "villas" in Prague) in peaceful Břevnov and Dejvice near the center. Those with cars moved to Barrandov on the outskirts of the city, close to the large film studios. They learned never to speak German in public; this drew "horrible, dirty looks," one later recalled. But once they were identified as Americans, the Czechs became "dear, lovely people, most helpful in subtle and also big ways."[1] Although these events took place more than half a century ago, the retired diplomats and their spouses can even today pronounce the names of their Czech friends and neighbors with near-native accuracy. All of them subsequently served in other American diplomatic posts, but none made as deep an impression as the embassy in Prague under Laurence Steinhardt.

After the departure of Chargé Klieforth, John Bruins became the number two officer in the embassy. He was a guarded man, devoted to his duties and to his family. Such qualities made him stand out from his younger colleagues, who joyfully took advantage of the romantic opportunities available to American diplomats in the newly liberated city. The person least capable of resisting the temptations of Prague was the ambassador. "You're a very handsome man," a letter of a smitten fan read, "and all the women here are in love with you." By return mail Steinhardt invited the unknown correspondent to call on him in Prague. When she declined on the grounds that she was a medical doctor and her patients needed her, the ambassador volunteered to visit her in her hometown. Ultimately it was the instigator who ended the correspondence. "I am married," she wrote with a touch of wistfulness.[2] The two exchanged no more letters.

In August 1945 Count Leopold Sternberg and his wife, Cecilia, invited the ambassador to celebrate the American victory over Japan. He accepted and agreed to join the Sternbergs at their Častolovice castle on the occasion of the next hunt.[3] The beginning of the visit was inauspicious. Steinhardt had promised to arrive at ten in the morning but showed up at noon, a serious faux pas, noted Cecilia. The cream of Central European aristocracy, together with the head forester, the gamekeepers, a small army of bush beaters and loaders, had been standing around or sitting on their horses waiting for the guest of honor to appear. Those in charge of the highly formalized event were especially nervous, since timing was everything. The ambassador finally arrived in his new Packard, followed by a thick cloud of dust. He parked the car and sauntered toward the hunting party wearing a "broad, shiny, very new-looking cartridge belt strapped tightly round his waist, and a largish felt hat on his head." He cheerfully apologized; he had stayed up late the night before and overslept. "Diplomatic customs seem to have changed," Count Kinsky remarked sotto voce. "In my day ambassadors were always punctual."

Unperturbed by the disapproving looks of the blue-blooded crowd, Steinhardt asked where he could take a bath. "We have been waiting for two hours, Your Excellency," replied the exasperated countess. The ambassador gave up on the idea and offered Cecilia a packet. She opened it with polite interest and was amazed to discover that it contained a dozen nylons and a bottle of Chanel No. 5. "The typical G.I. gift to his girl," she thought. Nevertheless, they were immediately attracted to each other. Driving Cecilia back from the hunt at a breakneck speed on country roads, Steinhardt announced confidently: "I think you and I are going to be great friends." "Not at a hundred miles an hour," she protested. But Steinhardt continued: "Once I know my way and where I want to go, I like to get there fast. Do you understand?" he asked.[4] Of course she did.

When Steinhardt's wife, Dulcie, found out about the relationship, she confronted the countess. Was there a "little romance" between the two, she inquired. Cecilia knew how to handle such situations. "Romance?" she asked with faked innocence. "What do you mean, Dulcie? Do you mean sex?" Dulcie dropped the topic.

The affair blossomed at a time when Dulcie seemed to have entered a troubling stage in her life. Even when the weather was warm, she was cold and wrapped herself up in furs, leaving only her pale face visible. One day she could not stop crying; the next she seemed perfectly happy. Occasionally she shuffled about with a gold-headed cane, though she seemed perfectly mobile the next day. Count Leopold became her trusted confidant.[5]

The platonic friendship between Leopold and Dulcie created a convenient façade behind which the passionate love affair of the ambassador and the countess flourished. In the course of just a few months, the two abandoned all

Count Leopold von Sternberg, his wife, Cecilia, and daughter, Diana. Courtesy
of Diana Phipps Sternberg.

caution. The military counterintelligence agency, OBZ, reported that they traveled together on Steinhardt's official missions and that Cecilia Sternberg occasionally acted as "a representative of the ambassador's household." Their trips to
Brno and weekends in Karlsbad or at the Metternich castle took place under the
watchful eye of OBZ informants.[6]

Had he chosen to focus on the political aspect of his mission right from the start,
it is likely that Steinhardt would have become a perceptive analyst of the political
scene. He was smart and had direct access to some of the best sources, including
President Beneš, members of the cabinet, and important military officers. Many
Americans in Prague enjoyed access that would have been unavailable anywhere
else at that time. For instance, in early July 1945 members of an OSS team on a
fact-finding mission were received by Beneš at the presidential castle. It was

unusual for a serving president to receive officers of another country's clandestine service. The Americans asked him boldly whether he was strong enough to
defend his country's democracy. After a pause, measuring his words carefully,
Beneš replied: "Either Czechoslovakia will remain democratic or I shall not be
here." The OSS officers left believing that he had "perhaps the toughest job in
Europe." He remained popular, but for him to succeed—and for the country to
remain a stable bridge between the East and West—the two sides would have to
remain friendly and in balance.[7]

The first postwar elections were on everyone's mind. It was generally assumed
that their outcome was going to set the tone for the whole era, perhaps irreversibly.
The Communist Party apparat was mobilized to make the party's position as strong
as possible. By contrast, the democrats remained nonchalant but confident. They
believed that democracy could never be defeated in the state established by Thomas
Masaryk. They saw Beneš as a great political strategist.[8] Their faith in him had an
irrational dimension: they had seen him cornered in September 1938, yet they presumed that he would triumph in the coming crisis.[9] Unlike the great Masaryk,
Beneš was not adored, but he was respected and trusted. Even his critics in the
democratic camp thought that he was bound to find a way to democratic victory.

Steinhardt had a high opinion of Beneš, and so did many in the State Department and the OSS, including Allen Dulles, a shrewd judge of men. They may
have mistaken his gift for developing a cogent argument on almost any topic for
the ability to achieve a desired political objective. But Beneš was a leader, not a
political analyst, and should have been evaluated on his results, not his theories.
The metaphysical faith in Beneš was one of the factors that contributed to the
unpreparedness of the democrats in the struggle for power.

It was widely believed that the elections' outcome depended to an extent on
their timing. The OSS knew from the start that Beneš and the democrats wanted
to have the elections as soon as possible and the CPC wished to postpone them.
The American analysts understood that the Communists needed time to consol-
idate the power they had grabbed and to allow the memories of the Red Army's
behavior to fade.[10] Steinhardt significantly misread the situation when he argued
the opposite; he thought that the democratic parties were trying to postpone the
elections because the CPC was losing votes as time passed.[11]

As long as the timing remained unclear, even the best-informed insiders were
in the dark. The OSS thought in July 1945 that the National Socialists, the democratic party associated with Beneš, would win the elections with 30 to
35 percent. The other votes would be split between the Social Democrats (20 to
25 percent), the Catholics (20 percent), and the Communists (25 percent).
American intelligence analysts were so certain that the CPC would be seriously
disappointed by the elections' results that they worried the party or the Soviet
Union might react by resorting to force to impose the Communist system.[12]

Beneš had a somewhat higher opinion of the Communist Party's chances at the next elections. But even he thought it would carry at most 30 percent of the total. Like the Americans, he also worried that the CPC might attempt to carry out a coup d'état.[13] Within the political field of four parties, thirty percent hardly represented a failure. But in the absence of hard news from Ambassador Steinhardt, few in Washington were paying attention to the situation in Prague. They were satisfied to hear from an OSS source that Beneš was "constantly pressing the Government for the restitution of democratic institutions."[14]

Steinhardt believed that Beneš would succeed, and so the overall tone of his reports from the Schönborn Palace was upbeat. "I have found Prague in far better condition," he informed Washington in early August 1945, "the Government far better organized, and general conditions in the country much better than I expected."[15] This set the tone for a number of sanguine dispatches to the Department of State. On August 7 the ambassador wrote about "the amazing comeback that Czechoslovakia is staging." He then went on to declare: "I have no hesitancy in predicting that if the present trend continues for only a few months longer Czechoslovakia will be the first country in Europe to recover."[16] Having been fed such sunny reports from Prague, it is not surprising that the Department of State saw no reason to mobilize against the Communist threat to Czechoslovak democracy.

Admittedly, by August there were hardly any Russian troops left in large cities, and the drive among the political elite to restore national sovereignty was impossible to ignore. But Steinhardt went further and announced—just one week after his arrival in Prague—that Czechoslovakia's encounter with the Red Army and the tendency of the latter to seize whatever it desired "cured the broad masses . . . of any inclination to communism."[17] Had he glanced at the Communist press, the ambassador would have noticed that just one day after his arrival in Prague, *Rudé Právo* boasted that the CPC was the strongest political party in the country.[18] Its raw power made up for the declining enthusiasm for Russia. It was becoming common knowledge that whoever wanted a good job, apartment, or farm would do well to join the party. Therefore, the masses may have been cured, as Steinhardt noted, of their rosy-colored view of the Soviet Union, but that did not weaken the CPC.

After only a few initial calls with the Prague politicians, Steinhardt reported that there was a "conservative streak" in the CPC that would soon defeat the radical faction. The party was now in the government, and it could not afford to give in to the extremists, since this would be unpopular with the public and might even be intolerable to Moscow. "The feeling is growing," concluded Steinhardt, "that the active pro-Russian and leftist propaganda of the days immediately following the May [1945] revolution has overstepped itself and that a reaction . . . is setting in."[19] The CPC's chairman Gottwald and general secretary

Slánský determined the party's day-to-day policy and long-term strategy. They were hard-core Bolsheviks and proud of it. Nobody challenged their position. It made no sense to dismiss them as a radical faction facing defeat. How did Steinhardt form his optimistic opinion? He based it and most of his other reports on conversations with rich conservatives with whom he played bridge.[20]

In Steinhardt's view, there was another reason why the democratic cause would prevail over the CPC at the next elections. By mid-August 1945, the ambassador detected a "new trend" in the media and public political discourse in Prague. Various commentators and newspaper articles noted that the Czechs admired the United States. This may have partly reflected the appearance of material abundance that accompanied the Americans in all the countries of postwar Europe. A Czech journalist showed that the presence of American troops was a net plus for the country's economy, and even *Rudé Právo* admitted that American aid to war-torn Europe was most helpful. In conclusion Steinhardt referred to a recent interview with Beneš, who asserted that although he had signed a treaty of friendship with the Soviet Union, Czechoslovakia's links with the West were unbreakable.[21]

In mid-August Steinhardt briefly abandoned his optimistic tone. Although he had argued at the end of July that the "radicals" among the CPC bosses had been put on a short leash, two weeks later he reversed himself, stating that—thanks to the "aggressive tactics" of the CPC—the government's resistance to nationalizations had been weakened.[22] His sources still assured him that Beneš would keep state takeovers of private enterprises to a minimum, but it was possible that coal mines, lumber, armament factories, power plants, spas, and heavy industry would be nationalized. This memorandum, just like those in which Steinhardt expressed the opposite point of view, was written with considerable confidence. Phrases such as "I have little doubt" punctuated the text. At the beginning of September, Steinhardt was yet again optimistic. Beneš was skillful and the moderates in the government had lost no ground; they might even have scored some gains. "I do not believe that there is any danger . . . of revolutionary activities or of a collapse. I think this possibility is behind us. You may now look forward to steady improvement. Even the program of nationalization will probably not go as far as was first feared."[23]

Some American journalists accepted this cheerful perspective. The *New York Times* found that, although the country was still divided into two zones of occupation, Czechoslovakia was a stable and free country, and the Czechs aimed at nothing less than the restoration of full democracy. The next general elections, the paper predicted, would mark the end of the country's leftward slide. The Communists would get no more than 20 percent.[24]

Realists would have found no justification for this degree of optimism, but the ambassador formed his view and stuck to it. He reasoned that the country's swing to the left was a natural consequence of the rise of Hitler and the war, which caused the moral credit of Britain and France to decline among all social classes. At the same time, the heroism of the Red Army had improved the standing of Stalin's Soviet Union. However, Steinhardt sensed that in the postwar era the Czechs were bound to return to their middle-class values. In addition he maintained that the Communists were, deep down, patriots who would never willingly hand over the country to the backward Russians.[25] Steinhardt was not alone in this regard. The OSS also predicted in July 1945 that Czechoslovakia was going to remain a "middle of the road democracy."[26]

By contrast, British ambassador Sir Philip Nichols told Steinhardt at the end of the summer that the fate of Czechoslovakia was hanging "in the balance." The country could still be saved, he thought, but "only as the result of an all out aggressive campaign" by the United States and Great Britain. Without a political offensive by the West, it was likely to join the other Soviet colonies such as Poland, Hungary, Austria, Yugoslavia, Romania, and Bulgaria within a couple of months.[27] This warning made no discernible waves or even ripples in Washington, which evidently gave more weight to Steinhardt's cheerful assessments. Sir Philip's realistic prediction ran counter to the official belief that Czechoslovak democracy was safe as long as Beneš and Masaryk were in place.

Reality demolished wishful thinking soon enough. Ambassador Nichols's dark prediction came true in October 1945, when Beneš signed decrees that nationalized joint stock banks, coal mines, power plants, insurance agencies, iron and steel works, rolling mills, printing presses, engineering works, optical works, armament and munitions plants, chemical industries, glass works, limestone quarries, brick works, cellulose factories, paper and cardboard manufacturing plants, sawmills, veneer factories, plywood factories, cotton-spinning mills, wool-, silk-, and artificial-fiber-weaving mills, textile works, sugar and alcohol refineries, industrial distilleries, food enterprises in general, and large breweries. All mining and iron industries, more than 90 percent of power and gas plants, and over 70 percent of the remaining heavy industries were now in the hands of the state.[28]

Some could argue that Czechoslovakia had a mixed economy that combined state- and privately owned assets. But over 60 percent of all industrial workers were employed in nationalized establishments, and the state sector dominated the economic life of the country. Without its consent nothing could move forward. It controlled access to raw materials, bank credit, and even the workforce, and this was bound to stifle private enterprise. The large state factories could easily choke off all competitors by denying them supplies, transportation, and access to markets.

Some economic restructuring was inevitable in postwar Czechoslovakia. The country's heavy industry was expanded from 1939 to 1945 beyond peacetime

needs; consumer goods production had been severely restricted; and the transportation system was in ruins; just 70 percent of the prewar number of railroad
cars and 22 percent of trucks were in operable condition.[29] Moreover, the Nazis
had seized and exploited up to 75 percent of the country's industry. It was unclear
in many cases who had title to a particular property. This was especially true for
those branches that were expanded to serve the wartime needs of the Third
Reich. For instance, the aviation industry had employed only 5,000 workers in
Czechoslovakia on the eve of the war but grew to 100,000 by 1944. The Nazis
also established industries that had not existed before the war, such as plants
producing synthetic oil. This happened while textile, glass, and porcelain had
been stripped of machinery and labor.[30] The task of converting the wartime
economy to peacetime industry presented a challenge.

There were many questions without easy answers. Who should acquire title
to the properties created and left behind by the collapse of Nazi Germany? Who
should compensate the owners whose enterprises had been ruined? What about
the assets that had belonged to Jewish victims of the Holocaust and others who
died at the hands of the Nazis? Most solutions were likely to stimulate growth of
the state sector. But the decrees of October 1945 went beyond serving a practical
objective; they became not just economic but political instruments.

The nationalization decrees were a rude awakening for Steinhardt. Taken
aback, he needed time before he could admit to Washington that the measures
were "more extensive" than had been expected. Then he gave the event a positive
spin. The moderates, speculated Steinhardt, could have defeated the radicals.
They chose not to do so "in the expectation that the probable failure of so
sweeping a program will bring about a public revulsion which will afford them
the opportunity of modifying the entire program." The ambassador speculated
that Beneš, "who has for many years demonstrated his astuteness as a politician,"
signed the radical program knowing full well that it would bring about economic
decline and chaos, resulting in a political setback for the Communists.[31]

This was a creative attempt to discern a future victory in the present defeat,
and Steinhardt was completely alone in advancing this view. The State Department's Office of Research and Intelligence (ORI) pointed out that from the beginning of the postwar era there was a contradiction between the privately
owned economy and the country's left-of-center politics. The measures adopted
in October 1945 synchronized the country's economic organization with its political orientation. Czechoslovakia had thus become a socialist country. Like
Steinhardt, the ORI failed to appreciate the seriousness of the nationalization
decrees. It suggested that "formal nationalization" was not the same as an established socialist economy and that the electorate would have an opportunity to
endorse or repudiate this measure during the first postwar elections. Even the
skeptical analysts persuaded themselves that the speed with which the decrees

were written and enacted into law was a sign of weakness rather than strength in the radical camp.[32]

The State Department paid some attention to the growth of the state sector in Czechoslovak economic life, but it was focused on nationalized properties that had belonged to U.S. citizens. It estimated that the October decrees involved American assets valued at $30 to $50 million.[33] The overall situation was complicated further by another sweeping measure that had preceded the nationalization decrees by several days. On October 20, 1945, the government issued the long-expected rules pertaining to currency reform. All existing paper currency had to be deposited in banks and post offices in cash accounts that would be frozen. In return for all the money deposited, citizens were to receive no more than 500 Czechoslovak crowns (Kčs) in the new currency. Its value was pegged against the U.S. dollar at $1 = Kčs 50. Individual businessmen and private corporations were authorized to withdraw up to 10 percent from the blocked accounts in order to cover wages.[34]

The State Department initially misunderstood the extent of the currency reform. It presumed that one could simply exchange the old currency for new. Secretary of State Byrnes urged Steinhardt to request "liberal extension" of the time period for depositing the old currency held by U.S. citizens.[35] After much effort, the ambassador talked Minister of Finance Vavro Šrobár into extending the deadline for American citizens to December 31, but the sum had to be presented in denominations under 20 crowns (export of all higher denominations had been banned by a 1935 decree) and accompanied by proof that it had been taken out of the country and deposited elsewhere legally.[36] Since 20 crowns amounted to less than $1, it is doubtful that any U.S. citizens were able to avoid losing nearly all of their holdings.

Slipped under the radar of the Schönborn Palace diplomats, the October 1945 nationalization decrees and the currency reform had destroyed the market economy in Czechoslovakia and directly hurt American interests. Although there was not a socialist fiber in his body, Steinhardt came up with a sympathetic interpretation of both. In late October, he conceded that they represented a surprising setback for the democrats and a victory for the radical left. But a month later he offered the view that the measures were "practically forced on the Czech government" by the "siphoning off" of its assets during the Nazi occupation and the pressing need to reduce the currency in circulation from Kčs 120 billion to Kčs 30 billion.[37] The Department of State apparently shared Steinhardt's blasé attitude, since it saw no need at this stage to reverse its support for Prague's request for a credit of $20 million to purchase American cotton and an additional $35 million for other expenditures.

Largely misunderstood by Steinhardt and ignored by Washington, the two measures decimated the wealthy class and dissolved the upper-middle class.

Since the conservative political parties were never restored after the war, the wealthier classes' ability to influence the next elections would be minimal. Pushing the economic arrangement in Czechoslovakia so far to the left weakened the country's ability to maintain its fragile identity as an island of democracy in the Soviet sea.

The Czechoslovak government's plan to expel nearly all of the German-speaking population was another item that required Steinhardt's attention. The Germans were held collectively guilty for having contributed to the destruction of the republic by the Nazis in 1938–39. It was alleged that they committed treason by opting for German nationality and serving in the armed forces of the Third Reich. Since most of the expellees were destined for the American zone in Germany and Austria, the Schönborn Palace and U.S. authorities in Germany were directly involved. The Allies, including the United States, had formally approved the plan, but it was uncertain whether they understood the dimensions of the scheme and the danger in which it placed the German civilians.[38] When Steinhardt came to Prague, the expulsions were evolving into a monstrous enterprise. At the end of the war, there were more than three million Germans in Czechoslovakia. By the spring of 1947, just over 150,000 remained.[39]

Although many German innocents died at the hands of thugs, the expulsions enjoyed support across the political spectrum in postwar Prague. A leading advocate of the plan was Beneš, who used a great deal of his political capital to promote it in Washington and London; Stalin's backing was never open to doubt. The democrat Drtina endorsed the plan with enthusiasm. In a speech he effectively combined the themes of Nazi bestiality with a vicious and distorted version of history. "The Germans are foreigners, carpetbaggers, and colonizers," he asserted; "they were always but an open sore on our body."[40] Throughout his life Drtina embodied the courteous and well-mannered qualities of the Czech educated and prosperous upper-middle class. That he was able to utter such absurd views indicates the damage done to the national soul by the events from the Munich Agreement in 1938 to the withdrawal of the SS from Prague in May 1945.

Even more extreme anti-German cries emanated from the Communist camp, whose leaders had abandoned the principle of international solidarity, once the linchpin of Marxist ideology, and replaced it with unabashed Czech chauvinism.[41] In an example of intellectual contortionism, *Rudé Právo* linked the plan to expel ethnic Germans with the 1620 Battle of the White Mountain that marked the loss of Czech independence. The newspaper argued that the expulsions would undo the consequences of the seventeenth-century defeat as well as the Nazi occupation.[42] This CPC propaganda was heartily embraced by the public. Some Czechs found it easier to seize German farms, furnished apartments, or children's toys when it was understood to be a form of lawful retribution for Nazi crimes rather than plain looting. To underline this point, the CPC organized a political gathering under the heading "Undoing the Legacy of the White Mountain." The roster of speakers included the CPC bosses, Beneš, other democratic politicians, Soviet ambassador Zorin, and Red Army generals.[43]

By early August 1945, politicians in Prague could hide behind the edict of the Allies issued at Potsdam, where the Americans, the British, and the Soviets concluded that the Germans remaining in Poland, Czechoslovakia, and Hungary would be "transferred" to Germany. They stipulated that this "should be effected in an orderly and humane manner," but no one created a mechanism for enforcing such a standard.

Steinhardt was a surprisingly vocal supporter of the expulsions. He dismissed all arguments that they were legally and morally flawed by insisting that there were "some pretty bad actors" among the Sudetens. It was understandable, in his view, that their presence had become "intolerable." He blamed Americans for some of the bad press the expulsions received. He thought that the U.S. authorities should have been more accommodating in admitting the expellees in their zone, and he dismissed all concern for the welfare of the Sudetens as cheap and ignorant sentimentalism. The critics saw only the helplessness of the expelled civilians, Steinhardt asserted, and did not appreciate that the Sudetens had murdered many Czechs or sent them to concentration camps and confiscated their homes.[44] The truth was that many among the expellees had committed no crime.

When a congressional delegation came to Prague to look into the matter, Steinhardt spoke out firmly in support of the expulsions, suggesting a parallel with the treatment of the ethnic Japanese in the United States after Pearl Harbor. He saw no problem with the deportations. In his view, the Sudetens in the thirties chose to chant *"Heim ins Reich!"* (home to the Reich). The expulsions simply fulfilled their desire.[45]

When confronted with reports of violence against German civilians that began appearing in the U.S. press, Steinhardt claimed that they were either fabricated or exaggerated. He warned the Department of State that such articles were written by journalists who had spent little or no time in Czechoslovakia; their sole sources of information were U.S. Army officers "whose pro-German and anti-Czech feelings" were well known to Steinhardt and others at the Schönborn Palace.[46] It is remarkable that the ambassador was willing to speak out so forcefully without having been to the Sudeten areas; so far he had taken only a few short trips, and these were to Pilsen, Kolín, and the Kynžvart and Častolovice castles with Countess Sternberg. When a U.S. Army officer who had studied the situation in the Sudetenland reported an account that differed from the ambassador's, Steinhardt took serious issue with this incursion into his turf. He especially rejected the conclusion that the political situation in Czechoslovakia was dangerous.[47] The ambassador produced his own seven-page analysis of the situation, arguing that the expulsions were needed to achieve tranquility and that the Czechs should be supported, not criticized. He concluded: "I do not fear mass expulsions."[48]

Although the Moscow-inspired request for a unilateral withdrawal by the U.S. Army was successfully rejected in July, the matter was back on the agenda of the Schönborn Palace at the end of the summer. The United States Forces European Theater (USFET) requested permission to withdraw all the troops from Czechoslovakia without delay. The War Department passed the request on to the Department of State with a note stressing that the matter was urgent. Steinhardt strenuously opposed a U.S. pullout, as did the Department of State. They hoped that such a measure could be postponed until Beneš prevailed upon the Russians to leave as well. Steinhardt wrote to Washington that it was the desire of Beneš and "most members of the Government other than extreme radicals" that the Americans should stay put.[49] No one knew how many Red Army soldiers were in Czechoslovakia in the summer of 1945; some thought 165,000, while others believed the number was twice that. But Steinhardt accurately assessed the desire of the Prague government that the Americans should remain in place until the Russians withdrew.

The threat of a U.S. departure from Czechoslovakia grew when Robert D. Murphy, one of the top American officials in postwar Germany, asserted that a withdrawal was "necessary" and that there was no "overriding political necessity for the continued maintenance of U.S. troops in Czechoslovakia."[50] This was an astonishing claim. Steinhardt sprang into action and warned that this would amount to a reversal of American policy and would be perceived as an abandonment of the country to the Soviet Union.[51] Steinhardt followed up with a detailed proposal that was meant to reconcile the War Department's desire to leave Czechoslovakia with fears about the political consequences of such a move. It consisted of several sharply argued points. The central idea was to reduce the present U.S. Army strength but to fortify the border of the American zone in Czechoslovakia against any Russian attempt at advancing westward. Steinhardt warned that a total withdrawal would result in a Russian infiltration of the American zone and large-scale "requisitioning" by the Red Army. Importantly, a U.S. Army pullout would likely cause the Czechs to "feel that they had been morally as well as physically abandoned by the Americans at the very time they were beginning to show signs of courage in standing up to the Russians."[52] On the same day, Steinhardt fired off another memorandum based on his conversation with Petr Zenkl, lord mayor of Prague and a leading democratic politician, who pleaded with the Americans to stay as long as the Russians did.[53]

The State Department realized it would have to take firm action to prevent the departure planned by the military. Under Secretary of State Dean Acheson instructed Steinhardt to inquire with Beneš as to whether the Czechs would be willing to ask Stalin to withdraw from Czechoslovakia simultaneously with the Americans. Should Prague fail to do this, Acheson indicated that Washington might act directly and propose to Stalin a coordinated departure of all foreign troops. If the Kremlin turned down this offer, the United States would withdraw unilaterally and ostracize the Russians for occupying an Allied country.[54]

Steinhardt, who loved to be in the thick of fast-moving developments, requested an urgent meeting with Beneš. Within days he provided a detailed account of his audience with the president. Speaking "in strict confidence," Beneš told the ambassador that he had sent defense minister General Svoboda and State Secretary Clementis to Marshal Ivan Konev in Vienna to complain about the behavior of Soviet soldiers. The president specifically told Steinhardt that the soldiers' attacks on civilians resulted in "many murders." Svoboda and Clementis were also directed to protest the seemingly endless transits by the Red Army across Czechoslovak territory and its tendency to seize whatever it wished. Should the present situation continue, Beneš's emissaries were to warn Konev that "conflict" would be inevitable. As was to be expected, the Soviet marshal gave the two a cool reception and not even a hint of a promise that the Red Army would depart. Beneš therefore sent another team directly to Moscow with a similar agenda. Steinhardt was pleased to hear this news, but when he inquired whether the president would be willing to ask Stalin to withdraw from Czechoslovakia, he only got Beneš's counteroffer. The president thought it wiser for Washington to prepare a plan for withdrawal, including specific dates, which would be presented to the Kremlin as a basis for a general pullout of all foreign forces. Steinhardt liked Beneš's plan and endorsed it.[55]

Washington saw that there were two options. The United States could move out of Czechoslovakia unilaterally and allow an unknown but possibly very large number of Soviet soldiers to move into the vacuum, or it could suggest to Stalin that the two sides leave Czechoslovakia at the same time.[56] The first amounted to a resignation, a door slammed on Central Europe. The second offered a glimmer of hope. Therefore, on November 2, 1945, Truman brought up the issue with Stalin. The letter stressed America's close ties with Czechoslovakia and expressed appreciation for its democratic institutions. It reminded Stalin that there was no longer any need to protect the country. "I therefore desire to withdraw the American forces from Czechoslovak territory by December 1, 1945," wrote the president, and he suggested to Stalin that "the Red Army be withdrawn simultaneously with our forces." Secretary of State Byrnes authorized Steinhardt to read the text—classified top secret—verbatim to President Beneš.[57] When he did, Beneš "expressed his keen satisfaction."[58]

The problem was that nobody knew how the mysterious master of the Kremlin was going to react. George Kennan, deputy head of the U.S. embassy in Moscow, was among the pessimists. He reported that when the Czechs had asked General Aleksei I. Antonov, chief of the Red Army General Staff, to reduce the number of Soviet troops in Czechoslovakia, he replied that they had to prepare provisions for quartering 400,000 Red Army soldiers for the coming winter.[59] Even Beneš did not know what to expect. He told Steinhardt that all previous attempts by Czechs to negotiate a Soviet withdrawal had failed and "led to no reduction in the total number of Soviet troops within the country." When he was asked to estimate the actual size of the Red Army garrison in Czechoslovakia, the president could only say that he had had so many conflicting reports that he was at a loss to know which were accurate, but he confirmed a Russian demand that Prague provide food for 300,000 soldiers. The president told Steinhardt that he no longer attached much value to "Soviet statements and promises."[60] This was not the way Beneš normally spoke about the Soviet ally with foreign ambassadors; he seemed to be reaching the end of his patience.

A full week passed before the answer arrived. Teasing the reader, Stalin explained at some length why his reply was delayed before he addressed the matter itself: he welcomed the Truman proposal. It was in full accord with his own plan to withdraw the Red Army by December 1, 1945. Secretary of State Byrnes cabled the letter to Steinhardt and instructed him to inform Beneš without delay.[61] This surpassed the optimists' wildest dreams.

It turned out that Beneš was not surprised by the good news, because Moscow, always alert to the requirements of protocol, had carefully informed the Czechs just one hour before Steinhardt arrived at the castle with a copy of Stalin's reply to Truman. General Aleksei Zhadov announced that he had been ordered to depart with all the troops within three weeks.[62]

Beneš believed that Czechoslovakia would soon regain its freedom. Unlike many Polish politicians and generals who were reduced to working menial jobs in London, he was back in the highest office of his sovereign country. From March 1945, when Beneš left Great Britain, to November 1945, he had endured months of humiliating and discouraging developments. It was easy to wonder whether his conservative critics were right after all. But now that the Russians were moving out, his star was rising once again. Stalin's short note to Truman restored Beneš's reputation as a skilled diplomat.

Why did Stalin decide to withdraw from Czechoslovakia? He did not need to do so, even if the Americans had left. Was the Red Army ordered to leave because it had become too difficult to provide material support for so many troops abroad? Were Soviet ideologues worried about the consequences of the troops' exposure to Western European living standards? A reliable source told Ambassador Murphy in Berlin that the troops were taken out because their indiscipline and tendency to steal and rape "discredited not only the Soviet Union but also any pro-Soviet indigenous parties."[63] This made sense, but it applied not only in the case of Czechoslovakia and the CPC but across all the countries occupied by the Red Army. Yet Stalin did not withdraw from Germany and Austria, just as he stayed in Poland and Hungary. Czechoslovakia was the one country where he thought he could take the risk of leaving now, in the hope of reaping benefits in the future. The withdrawal would strengthen the CPC, add to its legitimacy, and make it a more effective tool for gaining absolute power in Prague. The public learned of the Allied agreement to remove all foreign troops from Czechoslovakia on November 9, 1945.[64]

This was a moment to celebrate. On November 15, 1945, the Red Army commenced its withdrawal with General Zhadov opening the parade in the center of Prague, followed by a full Soviet infantry division that was strengthened for the occasion by armor and artillery units.[65] When the Soviet troops had entered the city in May, it was perfect spring weather, and the sweet smell of lilacs was in the air. This linked the Red Army tanks in the public's eye with peace, flowers, and joyful accordion music. In November nature failed to cooperate. The weather was ghastly, even for late fall, and the citizens of Prague had become tired of endless Soviet parades.[66] The Red Army marched and its tanks rolled through a sparsely filled city center, watched by a shivering audience. The small size of the crowd was underscored by the gigantic portraits of Stalin displayed on every corner. One could interpret his enigmatic smile in various ways, not all of which were benign.

Nor were the Soviet soldiers bursting with joy at the prospect of returning home. Those better informed knew that they had become suspect in the eyes of the ruthless Soviet security apparat; some may have even heard that not a few of their comrades were shipped directly to the gulag, not home, after they had conquered Berlin. There were so many cases of attempted desertion that even the ubiquitous Soviet military police had been overwhelmed and had to request the assistance of Czech authorities.[67]

The Red Army officers did not plan to return home empty handed. For days before the final parade, the highways had been filled to capacity with convoys consisting of "hundreds of trucks." The American observers noted that the vehicles were loaded not with military equipment but "with furniture, bicycles, ice boxes and every conceivable household and farm appurtenance." The thrifty Czechs did not enjoy the sight, no matter what ideology they professed. Some bitterly complained to Steinhardt about yet another case of the "looting of their country by the Soviet Army."[68]

The American departure ceremonies started in early November 1945, when General Harmon and the sympathetic Colonel Charles N. Noble of San Antonio, Texas, were made honorary citizens of Pilsen.[69] This was followed by a parade on November 20, 1945. It was overcast and somewhat foggy, but did not rain. General Harmon, the commanding officer of the XXII Corps, welcomed on the reviewing stand Steinhardt and Masaryk, who spoke before a crowd that filled the main square beyond capacity. Masaryk lived up to the occasion. Reading from a typed text, he told the departing troops: "Soon you will pass the Statue of Liberty. Tell her from us that we, too, believe in liberty and refuse to live without her. Come back again and see what we have done with our new permanent lease on life you helped us to regain. God bless America and you, her sons, who fought to save the world."[70]

This sounded good, but it was regrettable that the minister spoke of the centrality of freedom before U.S. Army troops, who hardly needed to be reminded. On the rare occasions when he addressed a Czech audience, he related risqué anecdotes, not somber political lessons. He did not seem to have the courage to present himself as someone who would refuse to live without liberty in the presence of Gottwald, Slánský, or other CPC leaders.

Many people came to watch the parade. Conveniently situated windows and balconies were overflowing with clusters of eager spectators; some had climbed up on street lamps or balanced precariously on the wide ornamental ledges of buildings along the parade route. The GIs moved in their relaxed

General Harmon, Ambassador Steinhardt, and Minister Masaryk in Pilsen in November 1945. There was visible tension between some U.S. Army generals, who tried to conduct their own foreign policy, and the Department of State. Courtesy of the ČTK Prague.

style to the cadence, called out softly and in a jazzed-up rhythm. This was unusual in Central Europe, where armies more or less imperfectly imitated the goose-stepping Germans.

Unlike the Red Army, the Americans were eager to go home and they were taking no loot. In fact, General Harmon's XXII Corps left so suddenly that it failed to spend Kčs 555,541,000 that had been drawn from the National Bank in Prague; it was estimated that the GIs took with them an additional 10 to 20 million Czechoslovak crowns. This resulted in protracted negotiations between Czech authorities and U.S. Army finance officers that were complicated by the uncertainty over which rate of exchange should apply.[71]

The departing Americans left behind 639 of their comrades who were killed in action against Nazism on Czechoslovak soil.[72] For many Czechs, saying goodbye to the U.S. Army was a bittersweet moment, but the Americans were anxious to leave and the Czechs were looking forward to living without foreign troops in their midst. The Soviet and American troops had left the country before the beginning of December 1945.[73] No one could have imagined a more hopeful end to the year. Beneš celebrated the occasion by visiting the Schönborn Palace—freshly renovated under Steinhardt's supervision. During lunch with the ambassador, Beneš confirmed that there were no Red Army soldiers left. The two agreed that this time Stalin had lived up to his promise.[74]

# || 7 ||

# America's Warning Signs

## From the Štěchovice Raid to the May 1946 Elections

The simultaneous Soviet and American military withdrawal from Czechoslovakia in the fall of 1945 conveniently covered up the disconnect between the Pentagon and the Department of State and the passive attitude of the White House toward the political contest in Prague. It also misled Ambassador Steinhardt, President Beneš, and many Czechs into thinking that, after seven hard years, Czechoslovakia was free again. It is understandable that the public would mistake the absence of foreign occupation with sovereignty. It is less obvious why the ambassador and the president made this error.

Steinhardt and Beneš shared a number of other misperceptions. They underestimated the subservience of the Communist Party to the Soviet Union. They regarded the party boss, Klement Gottwald, as a patriot whose ideological radicalism was a libation to the Kremlin god. They thought him endowed with common sense that would prevent him from imitating the Soviet model, as this would guarantee an economic decline and secret police terror. Furthermore, the president and the ambassador were unaware of the degree to which the party dominated the postwar security services, the armed forces, education, publishing, and culture.[1] Finally, they believed the CPC when it asserted that it would never destroy private enterprise.

Steinhardt's upper-crust friends did not include any of the left-wing artists and intellectuals who had considerable influence on public opinion in the postwar era.[2] There were no young people, such as university students, many of whom found Communism initially attractive because it seemed daring and it empowered them. For instance, Milan Kundera testified that what he had found as a young student most attractive about his membership in the CPC was that it placed him within reach of the "steering wheel of history."[3] Steinhardt paid little attention to the likes of Kundera or the masses who fell for the CPC propaganda regarding the fictitious "German threat," against which the Soviet Union was hailed as the only barrier.[4] This narrowed the spectrum of legitimate political debate in postwar Czechoslovakia, since even the most determined anti-Communists among the democrats accepted the primacy of the Soviet alliance, humbly pleading that it should be complemented by a secondary alliance with the West. Thus the contest between the Communists and democrats in Prague was asymmetrical from the start.

Steinhardt also failed to note that many of the traditionally conservative farmers, who had voted for the banned Republican (Agrarian) Party before the war, changed their ideology upon discovering that they would profit from the Communist Party's policies, which included generous redistribution of land confiscated from aristocrats and the Germans driven from the country. By the end of November 1945, more than 267 million acres of confiscated land had been distributed among some 100,000 families.[5] This created a significant enclave of new land owners who, although conservative at heart, would be likely to cast their ballots for the CPC out of gratitude and to protect their property in the future.

What about Beneš? Why did the Red Army's departure cause him to think that Stalin had fulfilled his promise not to interfere in postwar Czechoslovak affairs? Beneš led an isolated existence at the presidential castle, and it is entirely possible that he did not fully comprehend how far the CPC had advanced in its march toward power during the first six months after the end of the war.[6] The one person with whom he shared confidences, Chancellor Jaromír Smutný, was a complex character whose loyalty to the president may not always have been absolute. Chargé Bruins denounced him as having played a "malevolent" role in the postwar crisis. Others noted that Smutný "liked to swim with the strongest current" and enjoyed "very good relations with the communists."[7] After years at the highest level of executive power, few manage to avoid a degree of isolation. If they have reason to question the loyalty of their staff, as Beneš did, their sense of seclusion grows exponentially.

Being isolated was not the president's only handicap. After a lifetime on the ramparts of international politics, Beneš had aged prematurely. Although he was only sixty-one, his struggles with Hitler and Stalin as well as Gottwald, Slánský, and other CPC bosses had reduced this once vigorous soccer and tennis player who neither drank nor smoked to a shell of a man, suffering from hypertension and arteriosclerosis. He often felt completely exhausted. A stroke was always a possibility.[8] The party bosses kept themselves informed regarding Beneš's medical problems. Their main source of information was the president's chief doctor, Oskar Klinger. In addition, the party could rely on at least two other secret informants who had infiltrated the presidential entourage.[9]

There was another explanation for the president's unfounded belief that postwar Czechoslovakia was moving in the right direction. Beneš was convinced that the turn toward radical socialism Czechoslovakia had just made was both inevitable and good, a stage in a natural "progress" of history. He believed that there was a global political trend sweeping postwar Europe, of which the events in Prague during the second half of 1945 were but one example.

When the law school of Charles University awarded Beneš an honorary degree in December 1945, he used the occasion to deliver a speech based on the premise that the war had rendered the prewar political system obsolete. The democracy that had existed in Europe during the interwar period, he argued, had grown out of the chaos of nineteenth century. In postwar Europe, a new style of government was emerging, Beneš claimed, one that would require a fundamental restructuring of democracy itself. The regenerated political system would have to provide social and economic justice while also guaranteeing basic political rights. There was nothing to fear about such a prospect. It was a stage of historical progress, and Beneš thought it good. He openly acknowledged the concern of some that Czechoslovakia might be sinking into a "totalitarianism of a different kind," a clear reference to Stalinism. He was not afraid of that, because the "Russian communists" knew that the transformation of prewar liberal democracy into its postwar iteration had to come about gradually and in harmony with each country's economic, social, and cultural conditions.[10] A quick glance at Poland and other countries in Eastern Europe would have shown that this sort of optimism was without any justification, but Steinhardt simply forwarded the text of Beneš's oration to Washington.[11]

Others did not share Steinhardt's and Beneš's optimism about the Prague political scene. By the end of 1945, various democratic parliamentarians and public intellectuals stopped pretending that all was well and started posing challenging questions. For instance, Ivo Ducháček, an official of the People's (Catholic) Party, wanted to know whether Czechoslovakia was drifting toward a bloc of Eastern states that was arrayed in opposition to the West. If so, then this was against the wishes of his party. He also demanded to know who had paid for the Red Army's prolonged vacation in Czechoslovakia.[12]

The CPC bosses were about to attack the insolent deputy for his lack of respect for the Great Soviet Dead, a potent weapon in their arsenal, when Speaker of the Parliament Josef (Jožka) David rose to defend the principle of free speech. All matters, he announced, including the ones deemed politically sensitive, had to be discussed in complete freedom. Encouraged by David, other deputies spoke out to defend their colleague. It is noteworthy that these ideas, commonsensical as they are, already sounded rebellious and daring at that time. Eventually Slánský, the CPC general secretary, warned that his party would not tolerate a return to the kind of democracy that had led the prewar republic to ruin.[13] This marked an important stage in the political evolution of postwar Czechoslovakia. The pro-Soviet declarations found in public statements after

May 1945 began as an expression of genuine gratitude to the Red Army. By the end of the year, they had become obligatory.

Throughout the summer and fall of 1945, there was a great deal of renovation at the Schönborn Palace. Day and night, construction crews hammered into its ancient walls to install new electric cables, pipes for central heating, and other modern conveniences. It was only in late fall that life returned to normal. At the beginning of November 1945, a thirty-two-year-old American diplomat drove through the gate of the embassy and parked his car inside the yard. He was tall and elegantly dressed, but also nervous. Having pursued various private pleasures, he had delayed his arrival in Prague by many weeks, and he expected to be chastised by the ambassador. His foreboding increased when the porter at the gate, upon determining his identity, urged him to proceed to Steinhardt's office immediately. The young man would soon become one of the central figures in a drama to be staged at the Schönborn Palace.

Walter W. Birge grew up in a wealthy family whose American roots reached back to the Puritans. His father, Walter Sr., was the founder and president of the Air Reduction Company, which had grown into a multimillion dollar enterprise. The Birge household, "Overbrook," in Greenwich, Connecticut, boasted tutors of all kinds, a butler, a young Swiss governess (followed later by a French one, Madame Espy), a German gardener, a Scottish groom, a Swedish chauffeur, and a Steinway grand piano. Walter studied at Groton School, took a cycling tour across interwar Germany, and in 1931 enrolled at Harvard. All his life he was passionate about rowing, the Harvard/Yale football rivalry, and international affairs.[14]

When the war broke out in September 1939, Birge moved to Washington to prepare for the Foreign Service exam. He joined the Department of State in January 1941; the crucial oral examination was conducted by Assistant Secretary of State Adolf Berle and four other equally formidable officials.[15] His first post was the U.S. consulate in Nuevo Laredo, Mexico.[16] In the middle of the next year, he was posted to Turkey, where he met Laurence Steinhardt. Although he was only a junior member of the embassy staff, Birge developed a close friendship with the ambassador, who entrusted him with missions requiring absolute discretion. Birge believed he impressed his boss favorably, because the ambassador "placed personal loyalty ahead of everything else." He was also on good terms with the ambassador's teenage daughter, Dulcie-Ann, whose appetite for dancing, Birge recalled, was considerable.[17]

After being transferred from Turkey to Iraq in 1944, Birge remained in touch with Steinhardt, who made use of his services for intimate correspondence that had to bypass his wife. When the ambassador found out that he would be going to Prague, he inquired whether Birge would like to join him there. Birge accepted the offer at once.[18]

The Department of State instructed Birge to transfer to Prague in mid-June 1945. He packed his small Studebaker with his possessions, added a few jerry tins with water and gasoline, and set off. The trip to Prague over the following months demonstrated that Birge knew how to enjoy life. The journey was slow and pleasant.

After taking care of official business in Saudi Arabia, Birge stopped in Beirut, where he spent "a pleasant week" with Mary, an old girlfriend, after which they "parted amicably." At a diplomatic function Birge was introduced to Clothilde, an Egyptian beauty of Circassian origin, and the two decided to share the long drive to Alexandria. When they arrived, Clothilde announced during a romantic dinner that he was a true gentleman and she would like to marry him. Birge graciously declined the offer, pointing out that they hardly knew each other and that, moreover, he would have had to resign his Foreign Service commission upon marrying a foreign national. The following morning he made inquiries about a ship that would take him and the Studebaker to Naples. Before he managed to depart, he fell into the arms of Anna, an "unusually appealing young woman of Yugoslav nationality." The blue-eyed blonde spoke perfect French, but her "eyes and smile welcomed [Birge] without words." It was mid-October 1945 by the time the young American sailed from Alexandria on a British vessel bound for Naples. He delighted in spending time traveling with Maria from Rome to Florence, Venice, and Bologna. When he reached Austria, he encountered Clara, a charming *Bürgermeister's* daughter.

The only acquaintance Birge made after he had finally crossed the border into Czechoslovakia was a clean-cut and somber young man who helped him navigate the road from Pilsen to Prague. The GIs and the Red Army were preparing to leave the country when Birge arrived, but the Soviets remained vigilant. A few miles east of Pilsen they stopped his car and checked his diplomatic credentials thoroughly.[19] It was November 2, 1945, four and a half months after leaving his previous post, when Birge climbed the ornate staircase leading to Steinhardt's office.

Ushered inside, Birge felt anxious, but the feeling dissolved when Steinhardt greeted him with a big smile: "Walter, I did not expect to see you so soon." He then motioned for Birge to sit down in front of his desk and announced: "You are going to find the Czech girls attractive." The young man was surprised by the informal reception. He was also relieved to see that Steinhardt tolerated his lifestyle. Birge believed that the ambassador saw him as a "kindred spirit."[20]

Steinhardt then turned to business. The ambassador told Birge that he would be his "administrative officer" and instructed him to work closely with Jack Guiney, a junior clerk who supervised Czech personnel. Their first task, Steinhardt decided, was to hire ten to twelve new local employees, perhaps even picked randomly off the street if necessary. The ambassador expected that the

Department of State would soon demand a 10 percent reduction of the existing staff at the Schönborn Palace. He would have to oblige, but with the recent buildup he would be able "to have just the number of employees" he wanted to have. Birge immediately thought that this was standard Steinhardt—shrewd, even brazen in pursuit of his goal. But it was hardly diplomatic for the ambassador to speak this way in front of one of the most junior members of his staff.

Guiney first took Birge around the Schönborn Palace, and then he showed him to the Alcron Hotel, where new American arrivals stayed before they found more appropriate lodgings of their own. Despite its bleakness, Guiney explained to Birge, the hotel had its advantages. One was hot water, a rarity at the time. The other was a large dance hall where a big band performed American tunes just across the street. Since jazz had been highly regulated or even banned during the war, young people were eager to make up for lost time. When Birge went that same evening, he found the place packed: "The crowd on the large dance floor was so thick that there was barely enough room to move at all. The dancers seemed just to bob up and down without moving forward in any direction."[21]

The next day Birge went to explore the city and get to know the local rowing scene. He was pleased to learn that *Český Veslařský Klub* (Czech rowing club) on the Vltava River was ready to admit him without delay. Birge went there almost daily. He learned that being a young and unmarried American diplomat entitled him to other advantages in postwar Prague. For instance, important people competed for his company. Among his first friends were Countess de Rohan and her three daughters, descended from the ancient noble French family who had until recently lived in a charming mansion in the heart of the city. The countess encouraged the developing friendship between Birge and Mabille, the oldest of the de Rohan daughters.[22]

Birge would never be promoted beyond the junior diplomatic ranks in the American Foreign Service, but soon after his arrival in Prague he became a pivotal figure at the Schönborn Palace. This was because Steinhardt directed him to get involved in missions he was reluctant to carry out himself. A man of considerable personal courage, Birge did not shy away from danger. When the Czech Communist counterintelligence services zeroed in on his activities and put him under surveillance, Birge fought back with fortitude and humor. Unlike the Foreign Service professionals, such as John H. Bruins, who took care not to get swept up by the events in the country, Birge was unable to live as a detached observer.

Initially, Steinhardt had Birge represent him at various functions that he considered unimportant. Birge traveled far and wide to give speeches and attend formal functions in smaller towns, and he assumed responsibility for the embassy's relations with the Society for Friendship with the United States (SFUSA), an organization founded in Prague in October 1945 that worked to foster

Walter Birge and his Czech friends from the ČVK rowing club in Prague.
Gift from Walter Birge.

political, economic, cultural, and scientific cooperation between Czechoslovakia and the United States. Its sponsors included Lord Mayor Zenkl, and Ministers Drtina, Šrámek, and Stránský.[23] The society expanded quickly, opening
branches in twenty-two other cities. The Fourth of July celebration represented
the highlight of the SFUSA social calendar.[24] Regularly scheduled black-tie affairs and dinner parties with a featured speaker were popular. Birge, a good
dancer and a lively conversationalist, proved to be everybody's image of a perfect
American: a Gary Cooper with a Harvard diploma.

In mid-January 1946, Steinhardt learned that after months of strategizing, the
four political parties had finally agreed that the first postwar elections would be
held on May 26, 1946. On that day, citizens of at least eighteen years of age would
be free to select the three hundred members of the Constituent Assembly.[25]
Each party was to present the voters with a separate slate of candidates in an
order chosen by the party leadership. Voters would pick one of the four slates
and drop it in the ballot box.[26] The system may have been imperfect—voters
could not alter the slates—but it was vastly better than the manner in which
governments were selected elsewhere within the Soviet sphere in Europe.

The elections of 1946 were expected to have an indelible impact on the future of the country. Their outcome would not just be a new parliament and a new constitution; it would be a referendum on the radical restructuring of Czechoslovakia's political and economic systems in the postwar era. They would reveal how the public viewed the nationalizations and what the workers in the state-owned enterprises thought about the experiment. How were other groups going to vote? The middle class? What about young people in general, and especially students? The countryside? Should the CPC come through with flying colors, it would be reaffirmed in its radicalism and would feel empowered to reach for more. On the other hand, given the high expectations, a narrow victory for the party would be tantamount to defeat.

The previously listless democratic parties finally realized how much was at stake and started to push back against the CPC bulldozer. The Communists became nervous and uncertain. Their repeated calls for "national unity" were read by their rivals as an attempt to avoid genuine public debates. Steinhardt took pleasure in reporting that editorials in non-Communist periodicals expressed the democrats' commitment to conduct a vigorous drive for electoral votes and victory in the May elections.[27]

Meanwhile, the CPC launched a no-holds-barred campaign. Its propaganda was aimed at securing the votes of artisans, shop owners, and farmers. The party assured the electorate that, notwithstanding the recent nationalizations, it fully supported private ownership of small and midsized enterprises. It also asserted that it did not intend to drive farmers into compulsory collectives. It was, the Communists stressed, the party that had given Czechoslovak farmers more than a million confiscated hectares of land.[28] The democrats had challenged this misleading argument, and the political atmosphere in the country was becoming tense. Any unexpected development was likely to have a significant impact on the outcome of the elections.

The origins of the U.S. Army raid into Czechoslovakia in 1946 were unremarkable, but its consequences far reaching.[29] The affair was set into motion on October 3, 1945 when the French Foreign Ministry wrote to its embassy in Prague that a German prisoner of war, Günther Aschenbach, revealed information that might be of interest to Czech authorities: Aschenbach had served with a team from the SS division *Das Reich* that was ordered in April 1945 to an area south of Prague. Its job was to dig an underground tunnel in which thirty large boxes were to be hidden. The French embassy informed the Ministry of Foreign Affairs that Aschenbach was willing to identify the hideout's location for the Czechs.[30]

Having done nothing for four days, the Foreign Ministry forwarded the note to the Ministry of the Interior but failed to acknowledge it to the French embassy. Subsequent inquiries determined that the Ministry of the Interior had the note translated but then put it aside. Having heard nothing from the Foreign Ministry, French military attaché general Julien Flipo followed up in January 1946 with a report addressed to the Ministry of Defense. His cover letter included a copy of Aschenbach's statement, three maps of the area, and a scheme of the tunnel. The German prisoner stated that the tunnel was some thirty or forty feet long and was located roughly twenty miles south of Prague in an area that is a quarter of a mile east of the Štěchovice hydroelectric power dam on the Vltava river. Each of the boxes in the tunnel was secured with explosives and further protected by land mines and flamethrower liquid.[31] Yet again the Czech bureaucracy failed to acknowledge this information, let alone act on it.

The French saw no alternative to passing all the known facts to the G-2 section (intelligence) of the United States Forces European Theater, USFET. Its reaction was swift. The G-2 decided to deploy a unit that was to acquire the mysterious boxes in a commando raid. The Americans may have deduced that the tunnel was so carefully protected because it contained documents regarding German nuclear research.[32] It was at about this time that media had picked up reports that uranium mines in western Czechoslovakia were being exploited for the benefit of the Soviet Union and its nuclear program.

In January 1946, USFET G-2 in Frankfurt ordered Captain Stephen M. Richards, an explosives specialist, to take part in a mission in Czechoslovakia. His team was to locate the hideout, disarm it, remove the boxes, and bring them to the U.S. zone in Germany.[33] Lieutenant Colonel Taylor, acting military attaché in Prague, received a top-secret cable on February 2, 1946, saying that a special team would enter Czechoslovakia. Taylor consulted Major Katek of the U.S. Military Mission and the SSU (Strategic Services Unit, the CIA's predecessor) at the embassy, who concluded that the mission was bound to fail. Taylor suggested it should be carried out only with the cooperation of the Czech authorities.[34] He even took the unusual step of telephoning the USFET and asking for the operation to be canceled. General Siebert, chief of the G-2, curtly replied that it was "worth the risk."[35]

On Sunday, February 10, 1946, a convoy of four U.S. Army trucks and a jeep crossed the Czech border. There were twelve GIs, each with a tourist visa; the German prisoner and his two French guards had no visas. Although no one in the echelon looked like a tourist, all the soldiers crossed the border without hindrance. Captain Richards led the convoy to Prague, where Jack Guiney of the U.S. embassy had arranged for rooms at the Alcron Hotel. They attracted attention because they were fully armed, which was unusual for a group of tourists.[36] The next day they drove south, guided by the prisoner. When they reached the wooded area next to the Štěchovice dam, Richards had it cordoned off and secured with sentries. Aschenbach quickly located the tunnel in a steep gulley, and the Americans, using a powerful air compressor, cleared all the debris and dirt. Soon the team was staring at the entrance to the tunnel.

Taking enormous risks, Richards managed to find and remove one board in the gate that was not rigged. He and two sergeants then carefully dismantled the gate. Entering the tunnel, Richards told his team that it was his birthday; he had just turned twenty-four. The three specialists disarmed all the explosives and made room for the other team members, who came in and removed thirty heavy boxes. While this was happening, Lieutenant William J. Owen, who was in charge of the intelligence component of the mission, met with Lieutenant Colonel Taylor at the U.S. embassy. Taylor restated his objections but, noting that the project was half completed, he encouraged Owen "to proceed with the operation and leave the country." Richards and his men had worked nonstop for thirty-eight hours, departing from the Štěchovice gulley on February 12, 1946, around four in the afternoon with some 12,000 pounds of documents. The cargo left Czechoslovakia in the early morning hours the next day.[37]

So far, the mission had gone surprisingly well. There had been encounters between the American sentries and locals who were surprised to see soldiers in foreign uniforms. Rumors started circulating that the men could be German saboteurs preparing to breach the dam. A Czech police patrol was dispatched to investigate. It confronted the team and was relieved to learn that they were Americans. However, the policemen were unable to find out anything regarding their mission. The Americans would say only that the operation involved classified business. The Czechs retreated but informed their superiors, who passed the information up their chain of command. Next, a Czech military squad came to inquire. When one soldier got too close, an American sentry fired a warning shot. The news that a U.S. Army detachment was removing boxes from an underground tunnel in an area outside Prague then reached the officer on duty at the OBZ (Military Counterintelligence) headquarters. During later interrogations, he could only confirm that he had sworn at the caller, who had woken him up, because he thought the group consisted of regular American GIs who had come to Prague in search of entertainment.[38] The incompetence of the OBZ had made it possible for the U.S. team to take the documents to the American zone in Germany.

While the column of trucks was moving out of Czechoslovakia on the afternoon of February 12, 1946, Captain Richards and his two sergeants decided to take their jeep in the opposite direction—back to the Alcron Hotel in Prague for rest and relaxation. It was a surprisingly bad idea. When the police returned to investigate the Štěchovice area shortly after the Americans pulled out, they found scattered papers with Nazi stamps that came from one or two boxes that had fallen apart during removal. They also came across 1,400 pounds of TNT, a thousand pounds of flamethrower liquid, twenty-nine German-made Teller antitank mines, and five boxes of various explosives. None of this dangerous material was secured in any way. It was a disaster waiting to happen. The authorities started looking for the culprits and were amazed to learn that the team leader,

Captain Richards, was asleep at the Alcron Hotel. He and his two friends were arrested in the morning.

It was hardly surprising that Lieutenant Colonel Taylor was not eager to be interviewed by the Czechs, who looked for him at his office, then at home, and finally throughout the town. But on the evening of February 13, a liaison officer from the General Staff tracked him down at an officers' club. He demanded an explanation of the Štěchovice affair and the explosives recklessly left scattered around. He also asked for the prompt return of all the purloined documents. Taylor subsequently reported that after consulting Steinhardt he "pretended complete ignorance" of the intrusion and, to gain time, offered to go to Frankfurt to find out what had happened. He was astonished to learn the next morning at the USFET headquarters that his superiors were still unable to see the negative political consequences of the raid. They stubbornly considered the operation "worth our present awkward position."

When he returned to Prague and tried to deescalate the crisis, Taylor received another unpleasant surprise. The Czechs revealed to him that Captain Richards and the two sergeants were being held in Prague under arrest, and that they had made a "complete confession." This was true, but their confession was unnecessary, because when Captain Richards was searched it turned out that he carried in his pocket the complete set of orders issued by the Intelligence Division of USFET, describing the mission and identifying all the team members by name and rank. There was nothing left to discuss. The Prague authorities made it clear that they would release the three only after all the documents had been brought from Germany back to Prague.[39]

On February 15, 1946, the Czech Government held a secret meeting. The Štěchovice incident was the only item on the agenda. Václav Nosek, the Communist minister of the interior, described the U.S. commando raid, stressing that it was an aggressive act carried out by a foreign armed unit that entered the country through subterfuge in order to steal official documents. He placed this event in the context of other questionable activities by the U.S. embassy. For once, the democratic ministers had little to add. All agreed that the government had to prepare a strong protest that would include the demand for an immediate return of all the boxes. Until then, Captain Richards and the two sergeants were to remain in detention.[40] To further complicate the situation, Richards attempted to escape. He successfully overpowered his guard and ran out of the building, only to be captured less than half a mile down the street.[41]

Ambassador Steinhardt cabled the text of the Czech protest note to Washington without any personal comments, but it was clear that the raid had seriously weakened his position in the country.[42] At one point he slammed down his fist and raved that he had had enough of Prague, he was going to ask for another appointment. Secret police informants in the room reported every word of the tirade.[43] Major Katek of the Military Mission was also convinced that the poorly designed operation would diminish his ability to access information in Prague.[44] General Egmont F. Koenig, U.S. military attaché, was conveniently not at his post in the Schönborn Palace when the Štěchovice affair unfolded. He played the innocent as he repeatedly assured the Czechs that he had had no advance warning of the mission. It seemed likely that he had been withdrawn from the country to protect him in case the mission did not go well. Acting military attaché Lieutenant Colonel Taylor was perhaps the most daring critic of the raid. He wrote to his superiors in a tone that was uncommon in military communications. "This incident," he warned, "has almost completely undermined the position of this office in Czechoslovakia." He suggested that that the documents be returned as soon as possible so that steps could be taken to clean up after the disaster.[45]

On February 27, 1946, the G-2 at Frankfurt decided it was time to deescalate the crisis by returning the boxes. Officers of U.S. Army Intelligence invited Czech representatives to observe the repackaging of the materials.[46] All the boxes had been opened, but many of the files appeared to have been undisturbed. It is possible that the G-2 searched only for specific topics, such as nuclear research, uranium production, or new weapons systems. When a cursory examination showed that a whole set of files dealt with an unrelated theme the batch remained unopened.[47] Other documents, however, had been removed and copied.[48] The loot was returned in a U.S. Army convoy to Prague Castle on March 2, 1946, along with an apology from the U.S. Army to Chancellor Smutný. Separately, Steinhardt offered his "deep regret" to Beneš.[49] The detained GIs were released soon after the boxes arrived in Prague, and General Koenig drove them back to Germany.

It was two months before Czech archival specialists examined the Štěchovice materials. They determined that the papers primarily belonged to the office of Hitler's de facto viceroy in Prague, K. H. Frank. They contained next to nothing that might be of interest to a military intelligence organization. The U.S. embassy hoped that the affair would fade from the Prague political scene as soon as possible. Unfortunately, this did not happen. The U.S. Army raid became a near sensation in the American press, because Captain Richards's unit included an embedded journalist and a photographer. Their dramatic rendering of the raid presented Richards and his team as true American supermen. The *New York Times* and other media devoted much space to the episode and proclaimed it a great success for the United States, despite the hurried return of the stolen boxes and the official apologies that the Department of State issued to Beneš.[50] Once they were returned to the U.S. zone, Captain Richards and two of his colleagues received the Soldier's Medal, America's highest award for bravery not in action against an enemy.[51]

The story was also long-lived because the CPC at last saw an opportunity to present the Americans in an unflattering light. "A Flagrant Violation of Czecho-slovak Sovereignty" was a typical headline in the Communist press.[52] It was ef-fective because it was true. When Steinhardt apologized for the Štěchovice incident, the Communist press loved it.[53] After the purloined boxes had been returned, CPC deputies started concocting various conspiracy theories. One was that the papers returned by the United States were not the ones taken from the tunnel outside Štěchovice. Steinhardt formally protested this paranoid fic-tion, but it was hardly worth the effort. The Czechs pointed out that members of parliament enjoyed immunity regarding anything they said on the floor, and the press was uncensored.[54]

The Štěchovice raid provided no actionable intelligence to the United States government, and it harmed its image in Czechoslovakia. Previously, the Ameri-cans in Prague held the high moral ground against their Russian rivals. The GIs could be as brave as the Red Army, but they were honest, paid their bills, and had manners. The Štěchovice affair caused America to lose its image of integrity. The Czech public could easily be skeptical that the ambassador, the military attaché, and his deputy had known nothing about the plan, as they claimed. It did not help that the United States came out of the episode looking incompetent. Captain Richards and his comrades were skilled engineers, but they allowed themselves to be arrested after a night of drinking, and with the orders for their top-secret mis-sion in the captain's pocket. Before the affair, the CPC and its supporters confined themselves, as Steinhardt put it, to "pin pricks, rumors, and a few sharp digs." Afterwards, the Communists resorted to an all-out barrage against the United States. The State Department feared that the new "very definite line against the United States" might become accepted by some segments of the public.[55] That is exactly what happened. Even the democratic press interpreted the Štěchovice af-fair as a sign "that the world has reached a desperate crisis in which all moral prin-ciples have been abandoned" and replaced by "gunmen and bandits."[56] It is ironic that the papers taken by the United States and then returned to Prague at a high political cost proved to be so unimportant that the whole collection was gradually dispersed among other Czech archives and forgotten.

While the U.S. raid into Czechoslovakia held the country's attention, diplo-mats and financial experts on both sides were trying to remain focused on ne-gotiating important loans the Prague government had requested at the end of January 1946. The first one involved a $50 million credit for the purchase of United States surplus war materials repayable over thirty years. Prague also requested $50 million from the Export-Import Bank and $25 million to be used to purchase American cotton, and various smaller loans, including one to purchase tobacco.[57]

In considering its options, the Department of State was torn between two objectives. On the one hand, it wished to extend economic assistance to Czechoslovakia in order to neutralize efforts by the Soviet Union and the CPC to cut the country's economic ties with the West. This was particularly urgent because Minister of Industry Bohumil Laušman, an unpredictable Social Democrat, was holding talks in Moscow in early 1946 regarding future trade relations between the Soviet Union and Czechoslovakia. Some in the Department of State believed that Czechoslovakia could in the long term maintain its reasonably free existence between the two blocs. They believed that it was necessary to weave the country into the economic fabric of the West and that the loans were one instrument for achieving this objective. Yet Washington was understandably reluctant to provide Czechoslovakia with financial injections at a time when its government would not compensate U.S. citizens whose property was nationalized under the October 1945 decrees. Furthermore, given the uncertainty regarding Czechoslovakia's political future, the Department of State had every right to worry about "granting assistance in an area which may bring neither political nor economic benefits to [the United States]." This point was effectively advanced by those who thought that Czechoslovakia was already de facto "simply a part of the Soviet Union."[58]

Steinhardt was generally supportive of almost all measures designed to strengthen Czechoslovakia's ties with the West. However, when it came to providing credit he took a different attitude: "I am disposed to advise caution . . . in extending any loan at this time for reconstruction purposes."[59] He rejected as naïve the view that loans deterred the spread of Communism, noting that the United States had already provided assistance via the United Nations Relief and Rehabilitation Administration (UNRRA). Yet it received no political advantage in Prague or even a word of gratitude. The ambassador said plainly in February 1946 that he was against the loan unless he saw evidence that the Czechs wished to free themselves from the CPC influence and were ready to provide compensation in dollars for nationalized American properties.[60]

In the spring of 1946 Steinhardt insisted that no loan be extended before the May elections took place. In June he warned against any credit on the grounds that it would feed the tendency of Czech officials to develop their "indifference toward the Western powers attributable to improved economic conditions." The next month Steinhardt stated that to extend a loan without a commitment by the Prague government to compensate for the nationalized U.S. property would amount to a "complete surrender of our bargaining position." By early fall, Steinhardt concluded his campaign against extending credit to Czechoslovakia. The United States, he wrote, should deny all loan requests "until greater appreciation is exhibited by the Czechoslovak Government and press" for the assistance the country had received from the West.[61]

Steinhardt had seen in wartime Moscow that the United States, having provided massive material assistance to the Red Army, was paid back with arrogance, lies, and spying by the NKVD. There was reason for him to be apprehensive. And yet the situation in Prague was vastly different. To begin with, the ambassador knew very well that Benes was no Stalin and the political system in Prague was not totalitarian. Moreover, the Czechs needed the loan in order to be strengthened and reaffirmed in their rejection of the Soviet system. The loan would have been a boost for the democrats. It was callous for Steinhardt to demand compensation for the original owners in dollars since the Nazis had totally depleted all currency reserves in the Czech banks. Consequently, Prague needed the American loan, in part so that it could compensate U.S. corporations, including Steinhardt's clients, and private citizens for their nationalized property in dollars.

There was also the matter of 18.4 metric tons of Czechoslovak monetary gold looted by the Nazi authorities and seized by the U.S. Army. The Paris Reparation Agreement of 1946 pooled all the gold stolen by the Third Reich in occupied Europe and established the Tripartite Commission (the United States, Great Britain, and France), which provided guidelines for the restitution of the gold to its legal owners. Less than a quarter of the Czechoslovak portion had been returned to Prague before President Truman, acknowledging the property disputes between the United States and Czechoslovakia, stopped all shipments. Washington took the position that the gold would be held until a final settlement of all claims had been reached.

The looted-gold issue could have been solved expeditiously. Steinhardt was an expert in dealing with property claims. He proved it when he had apportioned the estate of the Swedish oligarch Ivar Kreuger. If the ambassador had been focused on his job, he might have used the gold as leverage to obtain compensation for American owners. Instead the matter lingered on into the 1980s and played no positive role in solving the claims and counterclaims in postwar Prague.[62]

The debate regarding the status of the loans was further complicated by the disunity among the politicians in Prague. Steinhardt correctly reported that the loan application divided the government into supporters, such as Jan Masaryk, Jaroslav Stránský, Petr Zenkl, Hubert Ripka, Prokop Drtina, Adolf Procházka, and Monsignor František Hála; and opponents, including Klement Gottwald, Zdenko Fierlinger, Bohumil Laušman, Václav Nosek, and Zdeněk Nejedlý. This ideological division made it impossible for the Czechs to speak with one voice in Washington, and the consequences were hard to overlook. At the beginning the government formally requested the loans, but the CPC and some of its allies among the Social Democrats tended to oppose them or to support them with unrealistic conditions attached. Therefore, Czech financial specialists would be working in Washington one day to obtain the loan but would disappear the next day, having been recalled by the left-wing ministers. Another successful tactic on the part of the loan opponents was to ignore American proposals that were made in response to previous Czech initiatives. Some in the Department of State believed that Prague should receive a generous loan or loans from the United States. But their position was harmed by Prague's occasional failure to cooperate.[63]

The matter of the American loans to Czechoslovakia meandered throughout 1946. The initial application was approved, then suspended, pending guarantees from the Prague government that future U.S. claims for compensation would be handled fairly and without delay. The loans were restored again in May when the Soviet Union launched a propaganda campaign around its grain deliveries to Czechoslovakia. In late July Steinhardt argued that once the Czechs had the money in their pockets they would become even less cooperative. He warned the Department of State against extending the loan before the Prague government made a binding commitment to pay the original owners.[64] In August, Prague formally complained that the terms offered by Washington were discriminatory compared to similar loans extended to various Western European countries. Steinhardt reacted angrily: it was intolerable for Prague to "dictate" to the United States.[65]

The Department of State agreed with the ambassador. It sharply and quickly rejected the Czech protest.[66] Before Prague could react, disaster struck. Secretary of State Byrnes was outraged when Andrei Vyshinskii, Soviet deputy foreign minister, charged at the Paris gathering of foreign ministers in August 1946 that in offering various loans the United States was attempting to "bring about the economic enslavement of Europe." Byrnes also noted that this lie was "applauded and supported by the Czechoslovak delegation" headed by Foreign Minister Masaryk. Byrnes was determined "to see to it that we are not making new contracts subsidizing the Communist control of Czechoslovakia." He instructed the Department of State to deny the Czechs access to any more American credit. The time had come, he wrote, for the United States to "assist our friends in Western Europe and Italy . . . rather than to continue to extend material aid to those countries in Eastern Europe at present engaged in the campaign of vilification of the United States and distortion of our motives and policies."[67] The flow of U.S. credit was cut off on September 13, 1946. When the head of the Czech mission for the purchase of surplus war materials tried to draw more money for a transaction the next day, he discovered that the account was empty.[68]

Byrnes complained to Steinhardt from Paris that Masaryk voted without fail with the Soviet bloc and against the United States. Unless Prague presented "substantial evidence" of its independence from Moscow and friendship toward Washington, he would oppose "resuming any form of economic assistance."[69] The secretary of state was right, of course, and so was Steinhardt, who had been critical of the loans from the beginning. The Prague government—specifically its Communist elements—behaved badly. The problem was that Washington's reaction was exactly what the CPC had hoped for, and Byrnes's anger at Masaryk became an instrument for reaching their objective.

By the fall of 1946, the matter had become so politicized that those in Washington who had previously argued in favor of developing and maintaining strong economic ties with Czechoslovakia accepted their defeat. At the end of September the Department of State informed the Czechoslovak embassy that in the absence of "compensation to American nationals for their rights and properties " nationalized in 1945, the Department of State was suspending all negotiations regarding any loan applications.[70] Clementis of the Foreign Ministry downplayed the breakdown as a "passing phenomenon" caused by a misunderstanding.[71] Yet it was obvious that Prague and Washington had drifted apart. The American press, until recently surprisingly sympathetic toward all things Czech, cheered Washington's decision to withdraw from the loan negotiations. The New York Times confirmed that Jan Masaryk had in fact "applauded the Soviet Deputy Foreign Minister Andrei Vyshinskii when he charged that the United States sought the enslavement of foreign countries" with the use of loans.[72] Byrnes was unwilling to put up with Soviet arrogance, and he refused to waste resources in support of the ungrateful Prague government. In doing so, he sacrificed America's policy interest to uphold Czechoslovakia as a Western outpost in the Soviet bloc. By embargoing the hybrid government in Prague, Byrnes made it more, not less, likely that the country would become the exclusive possession of the Soviet Union.

Minister Masaryk was not free to express his real opinions openly. As Beneš explained to Steinhardt, Prague's strategy was to give Moscow full international support in exchange for a sort of democracy on the domestic front. The Czechs calculated that in voting with the Soviet Union they might benefit and the United States would not be harmed. Beneš tried to persuade Steinhardt that Washington would gain more from Czechoslovakia's democratic system than from a few votes at an international conference. Beneš refused to apologize for this kind of opportunism. He told Steinhardt that Byrnes himself would have taken the same stance as Masaryk if he had had to deal with the Kremlin as the representative of a small country.[73] Some in Washington cautiously criticized the American decision to cancel the loan negotiations. They sensed that it had weakened the friends of the West in Prague.[74] They regretted that the Czech economy would not receive the loan, as this might guarantee its fall into the Soviet camp. In that case, democracy would be the loser and the Soviet Union the beneficiary.[75]

This was exactly what Beneš feared. He complained to R. H. Bruce Lockhart that the United States had unrealistically expected him to expel the Communists from the government as a precondition of the loan. That could not be done in a democracy. With credit from the United States, Beneš argued, the Czech economy would have grown so fast that in the course of a year or two the Communists would have become harmless. Lockhart met Steinhardt, who assured him that he was in full agreement with Beneš's analysis and "had tried to convince his own government of its wisdom."[76] This was untrue since Steinhardt was one of the most committed opponents of any American credit for Czechoslovakia.

The ambassador never seemed to realize that his campaign against the loan served the interests of the CPC. It ran contrary to the principles he had advocated and practiced during his previous mission in Turkey. Unless the United States was ready to substitute for all the benefits Czechoslovakia was receiving from the Soviet Union, threats or blackmail were destined to fail, while patience and respect for the country's precarious position were more likely to produce the desired outcome.

Having contributed to the failure of the negotiations, Steinhardt made a serious analytical error. He advanced the view that the new tough approach adopted by Washington had a salutary effect on the Prague government. The hard-line policy, he argued, taught the Czechs a lesson that would improve their behavior in the future. Furthermore, he asserted that the democrats were "jubilant," whereas the Communists reacted with "gloom" to the breakup of the talks. Exactly the opposite was true. The CPC desired to integrate Czechoslovakia's economy into the Eastern bloc, and Washington's decision to walk away from any further financial deals was most welcome. Nevertheless, the ambassador asserted that Prague had "already decided . . . to take whatever steps may be necessary to remove [the Unites States'] grievances."[77] This was wishful thinking.

Steinhardt allowed even the unremarkable CPC chairman Gottwald to fool him. When the ambassador informed him that the Department of State had decided to suspend the talks, Gottwald appeared to be "impressed." According to Steinhardt, he replied that his desire was to keep the best possible relations with the United States. This was a transparent lie, but Steinhardt fell for it. He was even more pleased when Gottwald in his presence picked up the telephone and ordered the (Communist) minister of information to eliminate all articles "hostile to our American friends" from the daily press. Gottwald was, in Steinhardt's view, just as malleable when it came to nationalized American property. Yet again, as the ambassador watched, he telephoned the Foreign Ministry and demanded a complete list of owners who had to be compensated. It was all an act. Yet Steinhardt sincerely believed that Gottwald, a lifelong Bolshevik, had become so cooperative simply because of the impact of the new policy of the Department of State—that is, Steinhardt's policy.[78]

The ambassador's final analysis of the affair was breathtaking. It was obvious, he claimed, that the decision to suspend financial negotiations renewed Prague's respect for the United States that had "dissipated" because Washington had previously chosen to ignore Steinhardt's objections while advancing credits and getting nothing in return. All was now well again. He predicted that within the next two and a half months Prague was going to compensate American owners of nationalized properties.[79] He was wrong.

Behind the smoke screen of high financial politics, the Communist Party stayed focused on politics and scored successes. It worked hard to solidify its standing throughout the country, not only in the large cities. No village was too small to earn the CPC's attention, and this persistence bore results. In the middle of February 1946, local elections took place for chairmen of the National Committees that replaced the abolished *radnice* (city halls). The results shocked Steinhardt. He had expected that the CPC would win around 25 percent. It did much better than that. Although he was careful not to say exactly how much better, he admitted in his report that if "these results are an indication of the general trend, the Communist Party is making substantial progress."[80]

The data that Steinhardt omitted from his report to Washington were startling. In Bohemia, the CPC won 46.62 percent of the chair posts on the National Committees; the Czechoslovak National Socialists, who were closest to Beneš, came in second with 14.55 percent; the Social Democrats got 11.23 percent; the People's (Catholic) Party won 10.87 percent; and 16.71 percent of the elected chairmen declared no party allegiance. The results were no different in traditionally conservative Moravia—the CPC won with 46.6 percent, the People's Party came in second with 16.93 percent, then the National Socialists with 15.51 percent, followed by the Social Democrats, who got 13.61 percent, and 7.32 percent of chairmen belonged to no party.[81]

Yet Steinhardt soon regained his optimism. On February 25, 1946, he assured Washington that the regional elections were not "indicative of a national trend toward the left." He offered a number of explanations. First, the elections were held in communities where the CPC had been strong even before the war. Therefore, he argued, the recent results did not reveal a new trend. Second, he asserted that the elections were fraudulent to a degree that would have been impossible on a national scale. Finally, Steinhardt found cause for optimism in that, contrary to expectations, the young voters (the eighteen-to-twenty-six age group) had not voted exclusively for the Communist ticket. "Freedom is a very real issue to the youth of Czechoslovakia after having been deprived of it for six years," he noted. Immediately after the war, young people embraced Communism because they saw it as an "antidote to fascism." But the party lost its appeal in the eyes of the young voters when it was seen as favoring regimentation over freedom. As was the case with other claims in this memorandum, Steinhardt offered no evidence.[82] The election proved to be an indication of things to come, yet the ambassador completely missed its significance.

There was no reaction from the Department of State officials responsible for Central Europe.

On March 5, 1946, three days after the United States had returned the boxes purloined at Štěchovice, Winston Churchill spoke at Westminster College in Fulton, Missouri. Until then the Soviet Union and the West had tried to keep their disagreements regarding Eastern Europe "submerged."[83] Now the senior leader of the Western alliance spelled it out. Among the capitals that were cut off by the Iron Curtain, Churchill listed Prague along with Warsaw, Berlin, Vienna, Budapest, Belgrade, Bucharest, and Sofia. He lamented the establishment of police regimes in Eastern Europe but was careful enough to indicate that this had not happened, so far, in Czechoslovakia. No one in Churchill's audience inquired into the discrepancy between "Prague" that was behind the Iron Curtain and "Czechoslovakia" that was not.

Inspired by the speech, American journalists called on President Beneš at the castle. Would there be a war between the United States and Great Britain against the Soviet Union? they asked. Beneš answered that he did not think so. Nor did he believe that Czechoslovakia had become part of the bloc of Moscow-dominated states. The withdrawal of the Red Army was his best argument. It had left because Czechoslovakia was the one country in the region that worked sincerely toward mutual understanding between East and West.[84] A knowledgeable observer could have offered a different explanation, namely, that Stalin—better informed about the scene in Prague than anyone in Washington—planned to install his regime not by naked steel but by a combination of other means.

An indication of what was in store came in March 1946, when the Communist Party of Czechoslovakia held its eighth congress. CPC chairman Gottwald built his speech around the notion that the political and economic scene was shaped by various "basic facts." One of the facts was that the old ruling class had suffered a loss of legitimacy when Czechoslovakia fell to the Nazis in 1938–39. Another was that the country was liberated by the Soviet Union. Taken together, these two facts contributed to the dramatic rise of the CPC membership. Gottwald was pleased to announced that the party had 1,081,544 members.[85] This was a colossal achievement in a democratic country of some 7.5 million registered voters. But the CPC boss refused to gloat, stressing modesty as an aspect of political wisdom. Rudolf Slánský, the CPC general secretary, reviewed Communism's short history, conveniently omitting the Stalin-Hitler pact, the purges, the famine, concentration camps, and similar items. He focused on the Communists who had died at the hands of the Gestapo and concluded: "We have given the Republic our blood, now we help construct her with our labor."[86] The final word belonged to Gottwald, who asserted that the party stood for honesty, clear conscience, and clean hands.[87]

By early 1948 such a claim would be taken as black humor. Not so in 1946. A few days after the CPC congress, Steinhardt stated during a dinner party attended by his wife, his lady friend Countess Sternberg, her husband, and others that he was optimistic. A police informer ensconced in the group recorded the ambassador's words: "The Russians are retreating everywhere, also in Czechoslovakia, where their influence declines from week to week." Within two years, the spy quoted Steinhardt as saying, the influence of Russia would disappear altogether. The Russians were strong at home but hopeless abroad.[88]

In the spring of 1946 the whole country began preparing for the first postwar elections scheduled to take place in May. The country was divided into three districts: Bohemia, with 3,792,552 voters; Moravia and Silesia, where 2,049,789 were registered to vote; and Slovakia, with 1,741,412 voting citizens. In the first two districts, comprising Bohemia, Moravia, and Silesia, four political parties were allowed to compete for votes. They included the Communist Party, the Catholic People's Party, the Social Democrats, and the Czechoslovak National Socialists. The political parties in Slovakia were the Labor Party, the Democrats, the Communists, and the Freedom Party.[89]

Three seemingly minor events disturbed the tense Prague scene on the eve of the election. They demonstrated the absolute commitment of the CPC and its mentors in Moscow to victory, in contrast with the reactive attitude of the democratic parties. The first anniversary of the end of World War II was to be celebrated in Prague in great style at the large Strahov Stadium. The U.S. embassy learned that the Soviet delegation would consist of more than one hundred Red Army officers, including two marshals of the Soviet Union, Ivan Konev and Pavel Rybalko, and dozens of generals. Steinhardt fully understood that the Kremlin intended to use the occasion to gain political capital. He tried to campaign in Washington for the U.S. team to be comparable with the Russian one—not in size but in prominence. The Department of State rebuked him, and the U.S., British, and French delegations each consisted of some seven or eight officers. The senior American officer, General Joseph T. McNarney, was unknown in Czechoslovakia, as was the Royal Air Force officer who headed the British delegation. Given the bitter memory of Munich, the presence of the French was of questionable value.

The second event that further disturbed the choppy political waters in Prague took place just a week before the elections. Beneš discovered that Prime Minister Fierlinger had agreed that two Red Army divisions, each consisting of 80,000 to 120,000 fully equipped men, plus armor and artillery, would travel across Czechoslovakia by road and rail between May 21 and 27, that is, before, during, and after the parliamentary elections. Steinhardt learned that the news was a rude surprise to Beneš. The president demanded that the government meet without delay. When it did, all eyes were on Gottwald. He rose to the occasion and gave his "word of honor" that he had had no advance knowledge of the Soviet troop movements. Steinhardt assured the Department of State that "Gottwald's word of honor is good." The government agreed to request that the Red Army transfer be postponed until after the election. Marshal Konev decided that the troops already under way would leave Czechoslovak territory by May 23 and the bulk of the Soviet units would postpone crossing the border until May 27.[90]

The U.S. embassy was not alone in interpreting this incident as a deliberate attempt to instill fear in the electorate. Masaryk and the democratic leaders Stránský, Ripka, and Zenkl shared Steinhardt's concern. All of them thought the event had to be interpreted in light of a rumor that the CPC apparat was said to be spreading: if Moscow found the election results disappointing, it would send the Red Army back to reoccupy their former positions in Czechoslovakia.[91]

Within days, however, Steinhardt reversed his original analysis. His new interpretation of the Red Army transfer was positive. The ambassador argued that Beneš, Masaryk, and the democratic politicians came out victorious, and Fierlinger, a Moscow stooge, and Minister of Defense Svoboda were the losers. Steinhardt told Washington that the Communists were discouraged by the affair. They felt "let down by the Soviets."[92] As before, he provided no proof for such an idiosyncratic opinion.

The final event that stirred the Czech scene on the eve of the election took place in the infamous Pankrác Prison. After a five-week-long trial, Karl H. Frank, Hitler's viceroy in Prague and a vicious Nazi, was sentenced to death. If Frank's conduct during the war had revealed his cruelty, his behavior in captivity during his many interrogations and the trial was manly and dignified—all the way to the gallows. The same could not be said about the vulgar crowd that gathered to watch his execution on May 22, 1946.[93] As was to be expected, the CPC used the event to whip up anti-German hatred and advance the argument that only the Soviet Union could defend the country against any future Nazi threat.

The Communist Party approached the election with a platform that masterfully offered something important to everyone. The cogent and also detailed statement reached into every enclave of society. It made no reference to Marx, Engels, Lenin, or even Stalin, and the word "comrade" was nowhere to be found in the text. Instead the document spoke to "citizens," and, bypassing the abstractions of dialectical materialism, it focused on tangible matters in people's lives. It concluded by calling on all who meant well for the nation, the republic, and their family to vote for the CPC.[94] Some could be tempted to dismiss the platform as a public relations ploy that fooled only the simple-minded masses. This was not the case at all. Within days, the CPC manifesto was endorsed by 841 prominent writers, poets, actors, artists, scientists, and public intellectuals. *Rudé Právo* was justified when it boasted that the "best scientists, writers, artists, and engineers are with us." In one district, a priest ran on the party ticket. He insisted that whoever wished to live in accordance with the Scriptures had to join the Communist Party. A young intellectual testified he had joined the party in 1946 because it had the "most courageous and logical platform."[95]

None of this seemed to have impressed Steinhardt. In a memorandum to the Secretary of State, the ambassador predicted in mid-May 1946 that the election would produce a Constituent Assembly controlled by the moderates, who would command 171 votes out of 300. He also speculated that the CPC would lose control of the crucial Ministry of the Interior and of the Ministry of Defense. "To the extent that my prediction may be inaccurate," Steinhardt added, "I should not be surprised if the Communist vote is less than my prediction."[96]

Steinhardt's analysis of the Prague political scene prior to the May 1946 election may well be one of the most reckless documents in the annals of twentieth-century American diplomacy. Furthermore, the ambassador impressed his groundless optimism on the American journalists who gathered in Prague to observe the event. On the day of the election, the New York Times headline read "Czechs Will Vote on Regime Today: Conservative Groups Expected to Win Assembly Control despite Strength of Reds."[97] It summed up Steinhardt's view.

Steinhardt sent a version of his May 15 memorandum to his friend and business client Harold F. Sheets, chairman of the board of the Socony-Vacuum Oil Company of New York City, the first visitor the ambassador had received at the Schönborn Palace in 1945. Steinhardt assured Sheets that the Prague election was likely to establish a right-of-center government. This was important because such a government would readily agree to the standing U.S. demand that the Czechs pay compensation for nationalized properties, including those that had belonged to Vacuum Oil before World War II. Although it was marked "Personal and Confidential," the letter had reached the French newspaper L'Ordre. It published an article, "Les Etats-Unis soutiennent l'extreme droite en Tchécoslovaquie," that appeared on May 23, 1946, three days before the election; Steinhardt was quoted at length. The article questioned whether the ambassador was in the service of the White House or an employee of a business corporation.[98] Steinhardt's letter to Sheets was reprinted in the left-wing newspapers around the world and was picked up by the press in Prague.[99] The missive eventually reached the addressee on June 6, 1946. By that time it was common knowledge that the ambassador's bold predictions were disastrously wrong.[100]

Steinhardt was so confident on Election Day that he went to the Ministry of the Interior to observe as the official results were announced by Minister Nosek. Surrounded by a phalanx of journalists, he was ready to gloat. From the democratic perspective, the results were nothing short of catastrophic. The Communist Party won in Prague, won in Bohemia, and won in Moravia. In fact, it won in every single Czech electoral district but one, and it took a respectable second place in Slovakia. Altogether, the CPC received 2,205,658 votes out of a little more than seven million cast ballots.[101] It did well in cities but also in the countryside. Some villages, once strongholds of the conservative Agrarian Party, had switched from the right to the CPC.[102]

In the new parliament, 114 seats would have to be reserved for the CPC (Steinhardt had predicted 88); the National Socialists won less than half that number, 55 seats (Steinhardt: 65); the Catholic People's Party 46 (Steinhardt: 55); the Social Democrats, 37 (Steinhardt: 39); the Slovak Democrats, 43 (Steinhardt: 50); the Slovak Freedom Party, 3 (Steinhardt: 1); the Slovak Labor Party, 2 (Steinhardt: 2).[103]

When the results were final, the journalists standing around Steinhardt demanded a statement. It was a masterful performance, according to George F. Bogardus, a Foreign Service officer who accompanied his chief that night. He noted that the ambassador's first sentence was about five degrees off the topic, the next one about ten. In the end, Steinhardt spoke fluently for about ten minutes, but without addressing the matter at hand.[104] For an objective analyst, there was much to ponder. In the 1935 election, as the Nazi threat had become apparent, the CPC had won only thirty seats. It now had 114. In 1935 the party had won 9 percent in Bohemia, 13 percent in Slovakia, and around 10.3 percent of the vote overall.[105] It now held 40.2 percent in the Czech lands (Bohemia and Moravia), 30.4 percent in Slovakia, and 38 percent overall. It was obvious that Beneš would have to ask the CPC boss Gottwald to form the next government. The country was going to be governed by a former Communist International official who had been charged in the thirties with conspiracy to subvert the democratic political system.

The democratic camp was disappointed to learn that Beneš, an internationally respected champion of democracy, had decided not to participate in the elections. A failure to vote was a violation of the law, but that was hardly relevant. Before he embarked on his political career, Beneš had been a National Socialist. Had he voted, the public would have presumed that he had cast his vote with this democratic party. His decision not to exercise his democratic right was generally interpreted as a concession to the CPC.[106]

The American press had watched the elections in Prague closely. The size of the CPC victory surprised many, and everyone appreciated that the electoral campaign and outcome were free and fair—in contrast with recent elections in other countries in Eastern Europe.[107]

It took Steinhardt some time to absorb the shock. A full week passed before he wrote to Washington. He conceded that the voting was free. The democrats accepted their failure and consoled themselves with the thought that there would be another election in two years. There was no inclination among the

Communists, Steinhardt claimed, to celebrate. Instead, there were "sobered" by the many tasks ahead.[108] A detailed analysis of the election was left to the second man in the Schönborn Palace. Chargé Bruins noted that the CPC victory was so overwhelming that it surprised even the optimists in the Communist ranks.[109] It was a brave attempt to explain why the ambassador's predictions had proved to be so inaccurate.

On June 19, 1946, Beneš was unanimously reelected president. Prokop Drtina, who knew him and his limitations better than most, gushed that Beneš was a politician and a statesman but also a scholar, sociologist, philosopher, journalist, writer, soldier, and revolutionary.[110] In two weeks the reelected president named a new government with Gottwald as the prime minister. As was the case before, the crucial ministries were in the hands of CPC members or its sympathizers. Yet Steinhardt found it to be "well balanced." He maintained that it consisted of twelve "leftists," twelve "moderates," one non-Party member who was pro-Western (Foreign Minister Masaryk), and another who was pro-Moscow (Defense Minister Svoboda). The symmetry that Steinhardt projected onto the new government seemed neat, but it covered up the fact that the Communists were powerful and the democrats were not. As to the new prime minister Gottwald, a lifelong Stalinist, the ambassador held a surprising opinion: "I regard the new prime minister as a man of common sense and native shrewdness, willing to learn, a thorough Czechoslovak patriot unlikely to embark on further extremist ventures."[111] Like several other statements by Steinhardt regarding the postwar crisis, this would soon sound laughably mistaken.[112]

A more qualified analysis of Czechoslovakia's strategic position in the aftermath of the May 1946 elections came from the pen of Pavel Tigrid, a public intellectual and diplomat who had worked on the Czech desk of the wartime BBC in London. In July 1946 he attacked as unrealistically "grandiose" the notion that Czechoslovakia was a bridge across divided Europe. The relations between the two sides were in such turmoil that any bridge was bound to collapse, he claimed. The truth was that the country's position was dangerously schizophrenic: its national security was guaranteed by the alliance with the Soviet Union, but its culture was anchored in the West. Neither side could trust Czechoslovakia because it was an entity dangling above the divide. Tigrid concluded by calling for a treaty with Great Britain that would—together with a parallel agreement between Prague and Paris—effectively diminish Czechoslovakia's dependence on Moscow.[113] The article was attacked by the CPC daily Rudé Právo, while Steinhardt called it "most courageous and forthright."[114] He did not address the lack of realism that was apparent in Tigrid's proposal: neither London nor Paris would have been interested in such an alliance. Steinhardt also failed to note that Tigrid's punishment for publishing the article was immediate dismissal from the Ministry of Foreign Affairs.

In late August 1946 the Ministry of Defense in Prague unexpectedly recalled the passes of all Western military attachés, including the U.S. attaché E. F. Koenig, that had enabled them to enter the ministry and the General Staff buildings in Prague.[115] The War Department also learned two days later that the Red Army headquarters in Germany had instructed Czech military intelligence to stop operating against German targets in the Soviet zone. Henceforth, Prague would receive the information it desired from its Soviet friends.[116] Such cooperation among foreign intelligence services was most unusual and suspicious. Finally, before the month was over, the War Department discovered that Minister of Defense Svoboda, Army chief of staff General Bohumil Boček, and scores of Soviet specialists toured the Jáchymov area in uranium-rich western Bohemia. The visit concluded a three day conference that was attended by Soviet atomic scientists and nuclear energy specialists. The two sides agreed that Prague would arrange for an additional 4,500 Czech miners and engineers to accelerate the exploitation of uranium mines in western Bohemia, possibly under the supervision of Soviet specialists.[117] It was clear that Moscow's growing need for uranium was linked with Stalin's determination to construct and test a Soviet atomic bomb.

These disparate pieces of information regarding developments in Czechoslovakia arrived in Washington over the course of a few days. It was not completely clear what to make of them, but they did seem to confirm Tigrid's point that Czechoslovakia was not a bridge but at best a vanishing Western outpost in the East. Many citizens looked to the West for its culture, technology, and political openness.[118] The American standard of living was greatly admired; a Czech journalist who had spent two months in the United States reported that America "did not have 'this or that' but 'this and that.'"[119] But neither Western literature nor modern engineering and prosperity could alleviate the sense of Czech insecurity vis-à-vis Germany, and here the Red Army enjoyed far greater credibility.

That was not the way the situation appeared to Steinhardt. In his view, the elections were but a temporary setback from which the country would soon recover. He saw the current government as balanced and the prime minister as a reasonable, patriotic, and trustworthy man. He was further encouraged when in late 1946 Beneš awarded some of the highest military medals to sixteen U.S. Army officers, including General Lucius Clay.[120] He wrapped up twenty-four "corncob pipes," made popular by General Douglas MacArthur, and sent them to Gottwald with a personal card. He hoped the CPC chief and prime minister would enjoy them and that they would make his "heavy burdens" a little easier. Gottwald acknowledged the gift with a courteous note of his own.[121]

One event that had escaped Steinhardt's attention was well known to Gottwald. Shortly after Beneš rose to give an official speech in late October 1946 in Prague, he turned deathly pale and began to sweat profusely. After the first few sentences, he could not enunciate any of the words clearly printed on the page

before him. The helpless audience watched the macabre scene with consternation. Eventually, Drtina tactfully led the president back to his seat. It was a repeat
of what had happened just before the president was scheduled to depart from his
exile in London. Slánský, the CPC secretary general, was in the audience and
watched Beneš's agony with close attention. So did the rest of the country: the
incident took place in full view of the public. Somehow the U.S. embassy failed
to learn about it. Luckily the president's condition was such that its symptoms
came rapidly but disappeared just as fast.[122]

Although many Czechs were not religious, almost all of them prepared to celebrate Christmas 1946 in accordance with their elaborate customs. By mid-
December it seemed as if a magical atmosphere had descended upon Prague.
Christmas trees were available throughout the town, and the traditional carp
could be purchased live from large tubs on many street corners.

The streets of Malá Strana, where the U.S. embassy was situated, were full of
shoppers as Laurence Steinhardt's limousine with two American flags attached
to the front fenders climbed up the steep hill between the Schönborn Palace and
the presidential castle. President Beneš had asked Steinhardt to join him on
December 20, 1946, for afternoon tea. He presumed that the president wished
to exchange pleasantries to mark the end of the first year unblemished by war.
Yet Steinhardt had barely managed to sit down before Beneš launched into a
scathing critique of various officials. Fierlinger was, in the president's view,
"superficial, unreliable, tricky and ignorant." The Communist minister of information Václav Kopecký was "uncouth, garrulous, uneducated and totally devoid
of good manners." Beneš did not think highly of Zdeněk Nejedlý, a CPC propa-
gandist, either. He was a "troubled old man for whose antics and speeches the
only excuse was his senility." The president did not spare other influential figures
among the CPC officials, such as Minister of the Interior Nosek.

It was most irregular for the president to reveal his private thoughts to a foreign ambassador, but Steinhardt enjoyed this torrent of indiscretions. He agreed
with Beneš that the elections of May 1946 ushered into power a set of mediocre
figures whose main characteristics seemed to be their ability to deify the Soviet
Union. Yet it was clear that Gottwald, Slánský, and their colleagues knew how to
conduct themselves in electoral politics. Their political formula consisted of
hope (they would create a free, just, and prosperous society) combined with the
threat that their opponents were on the wrong side of history and would soon be
crushed by its weight. Should "history" miss, the Communist-dominated special
services stood ready to assist the undecided. By contrast, the democratic camp
had failed to develop comparable program of its own. Some had never realized
that such a platform was needed in modern politics. They had entered public life
some thirty years before under the wings of Masaryk and got routinely reelected

on the strength of their loyalty, patriotism, and honesty. Quite a few in the democratic camp, having endured exile or Nazi concentrations camps, had run out of energy to fight.

The second half of the visit was more apropos Steinhardt's role in Prague, since Beneš brought up the failed loan negotiations. Washington's decision to suspend the talks, he said, was regrettable, but what upset him the most was the publicity the episode received throughout the world, especially in the United States. Allowing for the disagreement between Washington and Prague to be played out in public was a bad omen, warned Beneš.[123] Even during the most desperate crises the president tended to strike unrealistically sunny poses. This was the first time he failed to insist on a rosy analysis of the situation.

Steinhardt did not share Beneš's dark premonition, but he acknowledged that the democratic camp was in a difficult position. In his memoranda for Washington he occasionally summed up the advantages the Communists enjoyed over the democrats rather well: the CPC was disciplined, organized, and had a long-term plan; it controlled the security apparat; it used the threat of the return of the Red Army to silence its enemies; it controlled all media. These factors contributed to the emergence of the CPC as the largest political party in the country. Nevertheless, the ambassador argued, the trend showed "slow but steady improvement." In Steinhardt's view this was because a psychological change was sweeping the country—people were no longer fearful and timid. They had started voicing their criticism whenever they disagreed with the Communist-dominated authorities. The Communists, announced Steinhardt, were "gradually losing the instrument of fear."[124]

The opposite was actually the case. The May 1946 elections only deepened the condition accurately diagnosed by the first postwar American chargé d'affaires, Alfred W. Klieforth—namely, fear of authorities. The problem was that this fear had thoroughly rational foundations: the wartime terror of the Gestapo changed seamlessly into the postwar fear of the Communist-dominated Czechoslovak security, the StB (Státní Bezpečnost). Empirical evidence available in any neighborhood led the public to believe that whoever attracted the attention of the men in the long leather coats (the StB recycled this uniform from the Gestapo) had little chance of escaping from their clutches unscarred.

The StB could resort to any number of tricks. It held in prison numerous Nazi officials and Gestapo agents who were made to understand that only unconditional cooperation with their jailers offered hope of survival or at least bearable treatment. With the use of false testimony obtained from such sources, almost any CPC foe could be effectively driven from public life. Take the case of Vladimír Krajina, a brilliant botanist, resistance hero, and leading figure of the democratic camp in postwar Czechoslovakia. Because he was a prominent opponent of the Communist Party, the StB tricked the imprisoned K. H. Frank into signing a statement written in Czech, a language he did not understand, that falsely accused Krajina of having betrayed his comrades to the Gestapo. When Frank was questioned by independent jurists he renounced his signature and stated that Krajina was in fact the "bravest man in Czechoslovakia." After Krajina had radioed countless intelligence reports from occupied Czechoslovakia to London, he was cornered by the Gestapo at the end of January 1943. Without hesitation he swallowed a cyanide pill, but the arresting officers came prepared for such an eventuality; they pumped his stomach and kept him alive. It gained them nothing. His refusal to divulge any information was so resolute that the Gestapo gave up and sent him to a concentration camp. He survived, although the Nazis had executed his brother in 1942 and his wife was at Ravensbrück. Obviously, Krajina was the opposite of a collaborator. Yet it took considerable effort for his friends and colleagues to prove it.[125]

In targeting him, the StB chose a very big fish—among his many admirers were Winston Churchill, who later personally thanked Krajina for the reports he had sent to Great Britain, and Lord Vansittart, who praised him before the House of Lords.[126] But there were many others who were falsely accused, and it was harder for them to prove their innocence. Even with the best possible outcome, it was an intimidating experience. The lesson was clear: standing up to the CPC/StB machine required not only fortitude but also a thick skin, since even a heroic wartime record offered no protection against accusation and scandal.

Steinhardt was familiar with cases involving the abuse of judicial authority; his reports noted that the CPC made use of the retribution decrees to intimidate its critics. But he believed that the Czechs would reemerge from these traumatic times as they gradually strengthened their democratic institutions. This proved to be unfounded. The smell of fear spread proportionally with the growth of the CPC until it fouled up the atmosphere all over the country. Prior to the 1946 elections, many had thought that staying aloof from the political contest between democrats and Communists guaranteed that one would be left in peace. The elections revealed the power of the party machinery. Not challenging it and getting out of its way no longer sufficed. One had to join it to be safe. Even conservative voters enlisted in the party, because only its members could hope to be immune from abuse by the police. Consequently the CPC membership grew until it amounted to nearly 12 percent of the total population, a surreal development in a country that prior to war had been thought of as an island of bourgeois solidity.

The rush to join the ranks of the CPC left discernible traces on society. In 1946 the Ministry of Information established the Institute for the Study of Public Opinion; its slogan was "Fascism Dictates, Democracy Inquires." Scores of young and optimistic researchers spread across the country to take the pulse of the nation. But many of the interviewers returned to headquarters with empty hands, because more than half of those selected for the experiment refused to cooperate. The short-lived monthly journal *Public Opinion* analyzed the phenomenon with remarkable honesty. It reported that the fearful public "still lived under the influence of the past." When questioned, some people refused to cooperate, since answering questions brought back memories of the Gestapo. Others spurned the interviewer because they suspected the poll was a "trick of the GPU [Soviet secret police]." Although they were promised anonymity, a significant percentage of the public was not comfortable enough to cooperate.[127] Their fears were not entirely groundless. In a different context, an StB officer had suggested conducting a fake public opinion poll, since this might shed light on cases of antistate behavior unknown to the police.[128] The failure to appreciate the centrality of fear in postwar Czech society contributed to Steinhardt's inability to read the Prague scene with accuracy.

To objective observers, the overall picture of Czechoslovakia at the end of 1946 could not be encouraging. The prime minister was a Communist, the minister of the interior was a Communist, the military was undergoing rapid sovietization, all the large enterprises had been nationalized, the country's foreign policy was coordinated with Moscow's, the security services were in the pocket of the CPC, and the public was passive and frightened. It was therefore unrealistic for Washington to demand that the Prague government stop being subservient toward Moscow as a precondition for a return to the more cordial relations that had existed prior to the first postwar elections. Secretary of State Byrnes believed that Czech officials could choose a "more discriminating course," one that would retain the good will of the United States, without provoking Moscow's interference. What this meant in practice could be summed up in two points. Byrnes insisted that Czechoslovakia should play a more independent role in international affairs, and it should compensate those American citizens whose property had been nationalized. When the Czechs fulfilled these and other related preconditions, Washington would respond positively to Beneš's plea for "close and friendly relations" between the two countries.[129] This certainly appeared to make sense—in Washington, not in postwar Prague, where the CPC had won a recent election. For Byrnes to set up impossible benchmarks came close to acknowledging that the United States had suffered a strategic political defeat in Prague.

When the secretary of state shrugged his shoulders regarding Czechoslovakia's future, U.S. intelligence joyfully stepped into the breach. Its officers, active in Prague since the last days of the war, were eager to take on and defeat the Communist adversary.

# Great Expectations and Lost Illusions

*U.S. Intelligence in Postwar Prague*

The years 1945–47 were a time of change in the organizational structure of U.S. intelligence. The wartime Office of Strategic Services was abolished in October 1945, but some of its elements became the short-lived Strategic Services Unit (SSU), which was replaced in early 1946 by the Central Intelligence Group (CIG). In 1947 President Truman signed the National Security Act establishing the Central Intelligence Agency (CIA).

Such transformations in Washington had little impact on American intelligence in postwar Czechoslovakia, where it was represented by the charismatic Charles Katek, the officer who ran the U.S. military mission. He was the man in charge of American intelligence in Prague, no matter what name happened to be on the door of the headquarters in Washington. Charlie, as his colleagues and friends called him, carried himself with an air of such importance that some U.S. embassy staff thought him to be on a par with Ambassador Steinhardt.[1]

Katek was born in Chicago in October 1910 to a family of Czech immigrants. His father, Karel, established a moving company with his two sons that specialized in delivering pianos to the houses of the rich. At home they spoke Czech and some German.[2] The young man with unusually wide shoulders and powerful arms discovered early in life that it was easy for him to make a good impression on people.[3] This was helpful, because he did not intend to lug pianos around tight corners for long. He realized that only education would free him from the confines of Katek Brothers Moving. His parents and his brother, Otto, who stood to inherit the enterprise, consented when he asked to be sent to college. With their financial support Katek enrolled at the University of Illinois. Initially, he was an average student, but he improved steadily until he had straight As in his senior year. He graduated in 1934 and married Anne Stich, from an American family of German descent.[4]

To everyone's surprise, Katek went on to pursue a Ph.D. in history at North-western University, where he defended his dissertation, "The Development of a Czech Democratic Tradition, 1840–1867," in July 1942. When the doctoral committee inquired about his future plans, Katek surprised them by answering that he hoped to become an intelligence officer in the Office of Strategic Services. In the meantime, he found a college position in nearby Cicero.[5] It was better than moving pianos, but he hoped that he would be called up by the military.[6] When he did join the Army, his doctorate and his language skills did not go unnoticed. After various basic courses, he was sent to the OSS.

Soon Katek was on his way to London to serve as a liaison officer with the Czechoslovak government-in-exile. His mission was political in nature, and he therefore received no training in the tradecraft practiced by professional intelligence officers. This would prove a handicap in postwar Prague, but it did not seem to matter in London, where all the Allies, including the intelligence services of the Soviet Union and their Communist supporters, were supposed to be on one team. Katek shone in that environment because he was smart, witty, and an engaging conversationalist. Old Europe, he found, had everything he had dreamed of during his youth in Chicago. As an American, Katek was less fettered by class conventions than others in Britain; he was as comfortable in the pubs of London's East End as he was in the mansions of the upper class, though the latter were obviously preferable. Katek was especially pleased, a colleague noted, when he found himself in aristocratic circles. Titles flattered him: "In Europe he was greatly impressed by the higher ups; bankers, very rich families, barons, *Grafen*!"[7]

The young American brought many good qualities to his job. He was a natural leader with a magnetic personality, and he understood Central Europe better than most Western politicians and diplomats. He advanced quickly, and as a U.S. Army major with connections, he could approach anyone within the Czechoslovak government circles in London. Dealing with different types of people required different strategies, and he was good at that. In January 1945 Katek and two other OSS officers received high Czechoslovak military medals. The citation identified Katek as chief of the Czechoslovak Section of the OSS and a dedicated supporter of the government-in-exile, and acknowledged that his commitment and support were centrally important for the Czech cause.[8]

Shortly after the Red Army had liberated Prague in May 1945, Katek arrived in an ostentatious green Union convertible with big white stars on the side doors, a strange choice of vehicle for an intelligence officer. He was promptly identified by the Czechs as "head of the American espionage service in Czechoslovakia."[9] He and Sergeant Kurt Taub, who had been in Prague since May 8, 1945, opened and secured the U.S. embassy at the Schönborn Palace before setting up their own shop. The original designation of Major Katek's operation in postwar Prague was the Repatriation Commission. Its ostensible duty in 1945 was to search for American soldiers missing in action; it was soon renamed the Commission for the Investigation of War Criminals. This was subsequently replaced by the generic-sounding title "The Military Mission." But it always had the same address, the same personnel, and the same objective—to gather intelligence. Other members of the Military Mission included Katek's aide-de-camp Sergeant Taub, Major Eric Vessely, Major Otto Jakes, Captain Blahoslav Hruby, Lieutenant Charles Stiassny, Lieutenant Eugene Fodor, George Homa, Donald Dunbar, and Ralph Meyer.[10] A frequent visitor to the Mission was Leo Disher, an American journalist who was in Prague as a representative of United Press International. Since his father-in-law was the legendary General František Moravec, chief of Czechoslovak military intelligence in wartime Great Britain, many assumed that Disher was in Prague in a dual capacity. This was certainly the view of OBZ, the Czech military counterintelligence, which was from its inception in the hands of Czech Communists and Soviet special services.[11] Soon all the authorities in Prague knew that the Military Mission was a branch of U.S. intelligence and that everyone associated with it was involved in gathering information.[12]

Katek initially took up rooms at the Hotel Steiner in the heart of the Old Town. Half a year later, in November 1945, he claimed possession of a most attractive piece of real estate at 2 Loretánské Square. The ceilings of the numerous rooms were majestically high, perhaps fourteen feet; each door was heavy with elaborate ornaments and had a handle at the level of a tall man's shoulders. It was close to the Foreign Ministry and within a short walk of the U.S. embassy. The Prague Castle was a few hundred meters to the east.

Shortly after Katek established himself at Loretánské Square, the American Military Mission became known as a place where high society, politicians, spies, and beautiful women met in a pleasant environment. Among the guests of the Mission were members of the most prominent noble families of Central Europe: Schwarzenberg, Liechtenstein, Schönborn, Sternberg, Pálffy, Colloredo-Mansfeld, Lobkowitz, Czernin, Kinsky, Dobržensky, Kolowrat, and Nádherný. Other visitors included government officials, such as ministers Petr Zenkl, Jaroslav Stránský, Adolf Procházka, Vavro Šrobár, Václav Majer, and František Hála. Foreign Minister Masaryk, whose American friend, the writer Marcia Davenport, was Katek's neighbor, felt so at home at the Mission that he occasionally appeared there in his dressing gown.[13] Other guests included a good dozen members of parliament, including Ivo Ducháček; Miroslav Švestka of the Knights of Malta; personalities from business circles (such as Vladimír Kabeš); influential political journalists, such as Julius Firt, Ferdinand Peroutka, and Pavel Tigrid; and military officers, e.g., General Josef Bartík, Major Jaromír Nechanský, Major Miloš Knorr, and Major Alois Šeda. Katek was also on excellent terms with members of the Baťa shoemaking family. A popular addition to the set of aristocratic,

Charles Katek with a U. S. diplomatic vehicle in front of the U.S. Military Mission on Loretanske Square, Prague. Gift from Janet Edwards.

political, business, and military guests was the brilliant athlete Karel Koželuh, Katek's personal coach and regular tennis partner.[14]

Visitors were attracted to the Military Mission by the prospect of friendly conversation and challenging political debates. But one should not underestimate the importance in postwar Prague of good food, cognac, gin, whiskey, champagne, American cigarettes, real coffee, and jazz records—all of which were made plentiful by Katek's regular truck deliveries from a U.S. Army base in Nuremberg. Dancing into the night with smart young ladies—some recruited for the occasion in a popular hair salon—represented an additional attraction. In November 1945, Tracy E. Strevey wrote to Katek on behalf of Northwestern University and invited him to come back to teach Central European history. The OBZ had read the letter before it reached the Mission. No one was surprised that Katek turned down the offer, even when Dr. Strevey repeated it in January.[15]

Soon after he had arrived in Prague in May 1945, Katek developed a relationship with Vlasta Smolíková, a cheerful divorcée, who assumed the role of hostess

Charles Katek relaxing in liberated Czechoslovakia. Gift from Janet Edwards.

at Loretánské Square. Many of the Mission's officers followed his example. They liked to debate in public whose secretary or girlfriend was closest to the ideal made popular in the hit song "So Round, So Firm, So Fully Packed."[16] By the early fall of 1946 Katek could no longer postpone the arrival of his family. He sent Miss Smolíková to the United States just as his wife, Anne, and their four-year-old daughter, Janet, arrived in Prague in September. This required the hiring of more staff. By now Katek had a stunning secretary, Eleanor Jančík, who appeared on the cover of *This Week Magazine*.[17] He also had a driver, a chef with an assistant, and two cleaning ladies.[18] Life was good.

Although the word "espionage" was never mentioned, it was common knowledge that Katek and his colleagues were collecting intelligence on behalf of the U.S. government. Whoever came and talked knew full well that their information might be passed on to Washington. Participants noted that Katek occasionally took some of his guests aside to his office for private debriefing. Overall, however, he was very open about what he was doing. His approach was to blur the line between dinner parties and espionage. Unfortunately, the goings on at the Military Mission were watched by Czech security agents. They paid close attention to the American officers and their numerous girlfriends.[19] For every one of the Mission's visitors and their relatives a file was opened.[20]

In January 1946 Katek was awarded the War Cross, with a generous citation from President Beneš.[21] It was the last time he was honored in such a manner. The Military Mission under his command had become so notorious that it could no longer be considered a covert intelligence post. The OBZ openly followed members of the Katek team and harassed the Mission's Czech employees, rudely demanding inside information. Katek studied the situation with Steinhardt, and they found a solution. On March 23, 1946, all the Americans working on Lore-tánské Square were formally transferred to the Office of the U.S. Military At-taché at the embassy. This gave them the diplomatic immunity they coveted. Katek acquired the title "attaché," although everyone knew him as "Colonel." The Mission's Czech security opponents were not pleased. When the Foreign Minis-try informed them of this change, the OBZ protested that the Mission's sole ob-jective was to "conduct intelligence operations against Czechoslovakia."[22]

Despite the formal transfer of Katek and his colleagues to the embassy, the dinner parties-cum-intelligence collection at Loretánské Square continued. This arrangement was shot through with fundamental problems. One involved the mysterious case of Kurt Taub, Katek's confidant and closest assistant, the U.S. Army sergeant who had boldly driven to Prague through a hundred miles of German-occupied territory on May 8, 1945, in his jeep Beati.

Unlike the well-built Katek, Taub was short and skinny. He was born in 1911 in Brno. His father, Siegfried, an insurance executive, became a Social Democratic politician, and a deputy president of the Czechoslovak National Assembly in the thirties; he was one of the few ethnic Germans who spoke fluent Czech. His impressive political career and the anti-Jewish laws placed the whole family in grave danger. Siegfried escaped to Stockholm with his wife and sons Kurt and Walter at the last possible moment and only thanks to assistance provided by the Swedish legation and a courageous friend, Alois Sušanka. The latter would play a significant role in the postwar careers of Kurt and his brother.[23]

Kurt's final destination was the United States. To get there from Sweden in wartime, he needed a visa to cross Soviet territory. The Soviet embassy in Stock-holm was prepared to provide one, but only as part of a quid pro quo. The Soviet diplomats extracted from Kurt and Walter their commitment to join the global Soviet intelligence network. They code-named Walter TERENTIJ and Kurt became DABL. Walter preferred to remain in Stockholm, where he was already involved in anti-Nazi activities. But Kurt was determined to continue to the United States, and the Soviet officials encouraged him. Before his departure Taub accepted two hundred Swedish kronor, and he and the Soviet operatives agreed that an officer would approach him in the United States, saying: "Greet-ings from Vojna in Stockholm." DABL's parole was: "When did I see Vojna last?" The correct answer was: "November 10th." After Taub had accepted his secret role, he received his Soviet transit visa.[24]

His journey to the United States was full of complicated turns, but Taub was lucky. He settled in Boston—not New York City, as the Russians in Stockholm had assumed—shortly after the attack on Pearl Harbor. Taub held several manual jobs that drove him to despair, but nothing had prepared him for the day in 1943 when he was drafted and ordered to Camp Croft in South Carolina for basic infantry training.[25] It was impossible for this soft and intellectual man in his thirties with a thick Czech/German accent to keep up with and be accepted by the much younger men whose bodies had been hardened by years of farm work and sports. He was therefore greatly relieved when the U.S. Army, having found out about his background, decided to send the unpromising infantryman to the OSS in London. His training for a commando mission in the Third Reich had to be abandoned, because Taub experienced panic attacks when exposed to heights and could not qualify as a parachutist. (This condition most likely saved his life, Taub later thought.) Once again uncertain what to do with this man, the army decided to make him an OSS analyst.

Although he was a mere sergeant, Taub developed a strong friendship with his commanding officer, Major Charles Katek. The two complemented each other, mainly because Taub allowed his chief to think that he, Katek, towered above him. Taub may have seemed unimposing and shy, but he was a resourceful and enterprising man with a first-rate mind. Katek liked to awe people with his physique, knowledge, and inside connections. Taub made others feel safe and comfortable. He was a sympathetic and patient listener. Although he respected his boss, he did not do so uncritically; he clearly understood Katek's professional limitations.

Taub flourished in the OSS. In May 1945 he stood again on Czechoslovak soil, this time as a U.S. Army soldier, with an advance team in front of the 540,000 men of the Third Army of General George S. Patton. No one among Patton's troops knew the country and its political scene as well as he did. Initially, all seemed well. Taub and Katek opened the U.S. embassy in May 1945 and established the Military Mission. But Taub was soon targeted by Czech intelligence. Its boss, Zdeněk Toman, repeatedly tried to recruit him as a spy inside the Mission—making use of Taub's brother Walter, who was already actively involved with Soviet and Czech special services as TERENTIJ. Taub and Toman had met several times, but they disliked each other and their conversations led nowhere. Taub later complained to a Soviet intelligence officer that he considered the Czech spy chief to be a dangerous amateur. In the end, Taub not only refused to reveal any secrets, he actually tried to extract a few from Toman on behalf of the Mission.

In 1946, Toman had had enough of this cat-and-mouse game. Taub woke up in the middle of the night in his modern apartment on Vinařská Street to find his bed surrounded by Czech security officers who told him that he was "under arrest." Although he was a U.S. citizen, he did not enjoy the privileges of an accredited diplomat. The officers ignored his protests and dragged him to the nearby Ministry of the Interior, where he encountered Toman pacing in his office. The spy chief wasted no time: "You're one of us," he barked at Taub, "and we want your help." After a pause, Toman continued. "It won't be for free," he said, pointing to his open safe with a provocatively arranged heap of cash. Taub, appalled at this crude offer from a man he disliked, merely asked to be taken to the U.S. embassy, and that was the end of the episode.[26] Or so he hoped. Toman's "you're one of us" amounted to a threat. His identity as DABL, the role he had accepted in Stockholm, had caught up with Taub in Prague.

Toman had failed to recruit Taub, but the commotion caused by his nighttime arrest alerted Soviet intelligence officers in Prague that Taub, Katek's closest assistant, was DABL, the one whom they had recruited in 1941 and then lost in America. When Soviet intelligence officers encountered Taub in Stockholm, they could not even dream that the stateless refugee would reappear as the deputy commander of the U.S. intelligence post in Prague. Naturally, they decided to renew the relationship. They approached Taub in October 1946 through an intermediary. They chose Alois Sušanka, the man who had helped the Taubs escape from Nazi-occupied Prague in 1939. Sušanka's father and his wife belonged to the elite of hard-core prewar CPC members. Unlike them, Sušanka joined the party only after the war, but he was a fully recruited operative of Soviet military counterintelligence, SMERSH; his code name was TVIST. Where Toman had failed, TVIST (according to a Soviet official review of the case) readily succeeded. DABL agreed to provide TVIST with classified information from the American political and intelligence community in Prague. TVIST later boasted that he had managed to recruit DABL by appealing to his social democratic values and their long friendship.

If one accepts the official Czech and Soviet evaluations of the case, DABL and TVIST worked together in harmony. TVIST believed he was successful because he was sincere: "There was nothing false between us. This is why DABL agreed to cooperate and willingly provided valuable materials." One of the many analyses of the case by Czech intelligence notes that the two were quite close: "DABL consulted TVIST on what he should do in certain situations because he was going through a difficult time in the office and quarreled with Katek." TVIST was also able to establish a strong relationship with DABL's wife, Beata Taub. When the Taubs desired Persian rugs, TVIST provided them; when they needed to borrow money, TVIST loaned them a considerable sum. According to Sušanka, Beata paid him back with a valuable ring, a family heirloom, and, just before she left the country in March 1948, the legal title to a house she owned.

Czech and Soviet special services were in complete agreement that the relationship between TVIST and DABL was most productive. Even in retrospect Soviet intelligence assured its Czech colleagues—as late as 1957—that it thought very highly of the services DABL rendered in Prague after the war. According to the combined Soviet and Czech review of the case, DABL was said to have revealed the structure and organization of U.S. intelligence and its sources in Prague. He had first fingered Deputy Prime Minister Petr Zenkl as the Mission's main source. Then he "revealed the names and occupations of ten American agents whom he and Katek handed over to their successor" as they prepared to leave the country. The Soviet assessment of the case concluded that DABL gave TVIST everything he could, although he told TVIST he needed to withhold—albeit temporarily—the identity of one of his sources because his arrest would inevitably reveal Taub's treason. Some of those betrayed by Taub had managed to escape from the country (Lieutenant Colonel Alois Šeda, Colonel Jaroslav Kašpar, Michal Zibrín), but the majority were apprehended and their brutal interrogations led to other arrests. For instance, DABL identified Vladimír Čepelka, an OBZ official and a source of the Military Mission, whose interrogations resulted in further arrests.[27] This is how Sergei Soloviev, a subsource for Čepelka since 1947, found himself in the hands of the OBZ. He and Čepelka were arrested in May 1948 and sentenced to death, although their sentences were later commuted to life in prison.[28]

In 1947 SMERSH withdrew from Czechoslovakia after it had handed over its human assets to the intelligence section of the Soviet embassy. Consequently, DABL's handler, TVIST, was replaced with a Soviet consul who claimed his name was Vladimir Tikhonov, even though in wartime London he had operated under a different name. Taub immediately became uncooperative—understandably so. He was put off that Tikhonov had waited for him in an official car of the Soviet embassy just around the corner from the Schönborn Palace, a sign of Tikhonov's arrogance and lack of tradecraft. When pressed, Taub conceded that in 1941 he had agreed to work with Soviet intelligence. But that was then, he noted. He was now an American citizen and a U.S. government employee. When Tikhonov threatened to reveal his work with TVIST, Taub surprised him: he had thought that the previous attempts to recruit him were American counterintelligence operations designed to test his loyalty. Therefore, he had on his own informed Washington about his wartime encounters with the Russians in Stockholm. Two weeks later the Americans, Taub told Tikhonov, sent him a list of questions regarding his past. He answered them and was fully cleared, especially because Charles Katek "took him under his protection."

Taub had yet another surprise for Tikhonov. He told the Soviet diplomat that he was ready to continue his work as a Soviet intelligence source in Prague, provided that his sole contact would be TVIST and nobody else. Taub clearly did not trust anybody else's tradecraft. Tikhonov wisely accepted the condition. He brought TVIST out of retirement, and the productive relationship between DABL and TVIST continued until Taub and Katek left for Germany in March 1948.

According to declassified documents in the Prague archives, DABL provided not only actionable information on the U.S. intelligence network in postwar Czechoslovakia but also tidbits on the American embassy. He was most critical of Ambassador Steinhardt and his assistant Birge, whom he characterized as "extreme reactionaries" and—completely falsely—sworn enemies of Czechoslovakia. He described himself as a "good Czech socialist," who was uncomfortable among his arrogant and ignorant American colleagues.[29]

After his departure from Prague, Taub changed his name to Kurt Leslie Taylor and remained an employee of the Central Intelligence Agency. He ran agent operations from Regensburg, where his unit was covered as the "Economic Research Unit." It sent spies across the Iron Curtain into Czechoslovakia. The agents were recruited from among the desperate DPs (displaced persons) in refugee camps. They went through perfunctory training before being sent on missions that were often vaguely defined ("Keep your eyes open!") but always very dangerous. Their losses were extremely high.[30] Czechoslovak intelligence tried to reestablish a professional relationship with Taub/Taylor for years to come— via Sušanka (TVIST) and Taub's brother, Walter (TERENTIJ). The Czechs treasured the Taub brothers because they were close friends of German chancellor Willy Brandt and Austrian chancellor Bruno Kreisky, whom they had befriended in wartime Sweden. Walter met with both of them repeatedly, posing various political questions drafted by Czechoslovak intelligence. Only on March 14, 1973, did Prague finally conclude that DABL was no longer of interest, and the materials pertaining to this case were sent to the archives of the StB, the civilian counterpart of the OBZ.

What is one to think about Kurt Taub? Is it plausible that he had admitted to his chain of command in the CIA that he had been recruited at the Soviet embassy in Stockholm during the war but still kept his position in U.S. intelligence after the war? Perhaps. The Americans would have understood that he had played along in order to get a Soviet transit visa so that he could travel to the United States. Everyone knew that life was desperately hard for anti-Nazi refugees in 1941. Also, it could not be forgotten that Russia had been an admired ally at that time. In 1946 Taub was an American and a pillar of the Military Mission in Prague. His loyalty was guaranteed by Colonel Katek. This part may be credible.

It is more difficult to believe that Taub had also confessed to Washington and Katek his encounters with TVIST and that their dealings were part of a sophisticated play by U.S. intelligence against its Communist adversaries. Zenkl, the first agent Taub identified to TVIST, was the one democratic politician the Americans in Prague and the Department of State respected the most. As a deputy prime minister, he was among their most knowledgeable and reliable sources. Theoretically, of course, Washington could have ordered Taub to fake working with TVIST and to throw real agents of the Military Mission to the opposition in order to build up DABL's reputation so that all future disinformation from him would be treated as reliable by Moscow and Prague. But playing espionage games involving double agents turned into triple ones—Taub pretending to be

DABL and feeding TVIST materials cooked up in Washington—was not the American style of intelligence in 1947. One is hard pressed to believe that the Military Mission, which had flagrantly failed to protect its staff and sources against OBZ and StB spies, would have become involved in a game involving a triple agent.

The DABL affair was but one of the problems that diminished the effectiveness of Colonel Katek's organization when it was needed the most. Among its weaknesses was the building the Mission occupied on Loretánské Square. Following the tradition in Central Europe, the concierge locked the main entrance promptly at ten in the evening and went to bed; no other keys were available. The only way the Americans and their guests could reach the Military Mission between 10:00 p.m. and 5:00 a.m. was by waking up the concierge (and offering a generous tip) or going through the police station that just happened to be located on the first and second floors of the building.[31] This turned the whole intelligence-gathering scheme into a slapstick comedy. Czech clandestine services were spared the need to run nighttime surveillance on the Mission because the great spy Katek, his colleagues, their agents, and party guests flawlessly signaled their comings and goings to seemingly distracted but always alert police officers who acted as informers.[32] Even an assistant chef in the Katek household thought it odd that the Military Mission had to be entered via a police station in the evening. Years later she still recalled the policemen's names and that they often asked her to give them alcohol and cigarettes from the Mission. "I presume that they kept an eye on Katek and his guests," she testified.[33] The OBZ directed a police officer to seduce one of the cleaning ladies in the Mission, then pushed her to steal Katek's discarded papers. She did.[34]

In addition to information obtained from police officers stationed on the Mission's doorstep, a good percentage of Katek's guests and friends were employed by the secret police. Judging by the voluminous archival evidence, they seem to have attended nearly every event. In addition, Czech specialists were able to break into the Mission, because it was never guarded at night. They copied pages from Katek's address book and diary for 1947, indicating which minister and parliamentary deputy attended which dinner party. From informers posing as Katek's friends, Czech special services knew how the Americans encoded the identities of their agents and what evasive measures they were supposed to take in an emergency. Although the Czechs actually knew everything about Katek, his aura of invincibility was such that they never quite believed it. And so they kept watching.

Despite Katek's zeal for intelligence and the reams of reports he sent up the chain of command, the United States had no sources in places where important decisions and plans for the future were made—among the leadership of the CPC and in the security and intelligence apparats. Washington urgently needed to know more about the Soviet exploitation of the uranium mines in western Bohemia. Moreover, the physical security of the Schönborn Palace could not be taken for granted. The StB's campaign to penetrate it, steal documents, and recruit among its numerous Czech staff members was intense. Finally, the habitués of Katek's parties were marked as opponents of Communism. In case of a major political reversal favoring the CPC, they would be the first to be fired and possibly arrested. In that case, the United States would suddenly operate in darkness, having lost its eyes and ears among the political, military, and security elites. This would be especially serious in case of war.

In early 1947, Katek was summoned to the intelligence headquarters in Frankfurt for consultations. His new mission was to leave the business of gathering political gossip to the diplomats at the Schönborn Palace and to focus instead on military intelligence. He was also ordered to create a list of individuals—military and civilian—upon whom the United States could rely in case of war.[35] He was reminded that Washington needed clandestine networks that would provide intelligence in case the U.S. embassy and the Mission were forced to evacuate.

Katek was popular among his colleagues, but some suspected that his approach to gathering information in Prague was limited. They were right. After returning from Frankfurt, Katek complained about his new tasks—to an StB informer: "Katek stated that he might have to start forming a clandestine intelligence network because of the pressure from 'above.'" The colonel explained that his superiors at Frankfurt were most interested in "long range intelligence," and he showed the informer a typed list of questions he brought for the American post in Prague.[36]

Katek complained to another informer on a different occasion that his command at Frankfurt had criticized him for not having created a network of secret agents. He disagreed with his critics. As he explained, his informants—ministers and parliamentary deputies—told him everything for free, he boasted, offering as an example an account of testimony by the defense minister before the armed services committee of the parliament that the Mission had recently obtained. The informer, a woman, was a friend of the Katek family.[37]

The OBZ, the Mission's primary opponent in Prague, had a high opinion of Katek. He was a "very intelligent, first class intelligence officer."[38] The Americans who worked with him were more critical. One was put off by his self-centered personality.[39] Another found him unprofessional. He stated that, like so many others, he was "fond of Charlie" but thought him "ill-suited to our profession." From the beginning of his career in the OSS, Katek was completely open about his line of work. Consequently, "the Soviets had had him in their records since the war and knew exactly who he was and what he was doing."[40]

Katek was pleased with his achievements in Prague: it was he who had opened the U.S. embassy and who had produced reports based on high-level sources. He never seemed to have seriously considered that his open style of work might cease being productive if the political environment were to undergo a sudden reversal. Setting aside the murky Taub affair, Katek's failure to instill discipline in his team and to protect the Military Mission against penetration by opposition services showed a lack of commitment to his job as well as disregard for the safety of the Czechs who risked their lives for the cause of democracy.

As the Military Mission was struggling to satisfy Washington's growing demands for intelligence from clandestine sources, it became obvious that a new man was needed to bring higher standards to the American effort in Prague.[41] The Central Intelligence Group thought it had the right man. His name was Spencer Laird Taggart. Like Colonel Katek, Taggart was an odd choice.

It should not have been difficult to discern that Taggart was unsuited for the world of intelligence. He was a gentle and shy man.[42] A poetic soul committed to the study of history and classical music, he would have been more comfortable doing academic research than employing questionable methods to steal secrets. As a lifelong teetotaler who found smoking nauseating, Taggart disliked cocktail parties. He was scrupulously honest and cautious, the opposite of a calculating risk taker who is willing to violate ethical principles to reach a goal. A man strictly dedicated to his family and faith, Taggart did not fit with the fast crowd of politicians, diplomats, and spies in postwar Prague.

Taggart was born in 1911 to a Mormon family in Idaho. His parents expected him to become a farmer, but it soon became apparent that his talents lay elsewhere. He enrolled at Utah State University and developed an interest in history and classical music. But the Mormon faith was central to him. Taggart was therefore delighted when, in the summer of 1931, he received a letter calling him to missionary work.

Dear Brother: You have been recommended as worthy to fill a mission, and it gives us pleasure to call you to labor in Czechoslovakia. The date of your departure is October 17, 1931. Please let us know your feelings with regard to this call, and have your reply endorsed by your bishop. Praying the Lord to guide you in this important matter, Sincerely, your brother, Heber J. Grant

Taggart immediately went to the college library to search for any information about the exotic-sounding Czechoslovakia. The map revealed only that it was an "odd-shaped country right in the center of Europe."[43]

The journey from Lewiston, Idaho, to Prague took sixteen days, and the frugal missionary managed to spend only $30 on outside expenses. He arrived on November 7, 1931. There was no one at the station, and it was chilly. As Taggart drew in his first deep breath he noticed that the air "smelled as if it belonged to a city hundreds of years old." The country's history was long, and its language extraordinarily difficult, but Taggart knew at first sight he liked the place, just as he liked Czech bread, milk, and people. "I am enjoying myself very much," he noted in his diary, "and believe that I will soon be a regular Czech. I do feel the Lord has blessed me." He found the locals treated him well, and they were "educated and cultured." What they lacked was his faith, and he set to work to remedy the situation; he spoke with dozens of people almost every day. He was soon giving speeches in Czech, and he baptized the first new Mormon in the Vltava River, immortalized by his favorite composer, Bedřich Smetana, before he turned twenty-one.

In February 1932 Taggart was at the Schönborn Palace to celebrate Washington's Birthday. "I had an excellent opportunity to observe President Thomas G. Masaryk. Next month he will be eighty-two and today he was climbing stairs like a young man of twenty. He is admired by all for his high ideals, his personality and character. His early youth resembles that of our Lincoln." Seeing the founder of Czechoslovakia in person made such an impression on Taggart that he became a serious student of Masaryk's writings.

Taggart took trips around the country to spread his faith. He traveled frequently, which proved to be useful for his later work in postwar Czechoslovakia. He even visited Jáchymov, where he noted the presence of uranium mines, which would acquire considerable importance in the early Cold War years. On weekends Taggart and other missionaries tried to teach the Czechs baseball. "The Czech people look good to me," he observed. "We are all the same except for our national dishes and language." When a beggar wearing pitiful rags once knocked on his door asking for a bite to eat, the missionary treated him to a meal and then gave him his elegant suit, a shirt, and a tie. After some two years Taggart was glad to learn that his brother, Glen, originally sent on a mission to Germany, could join him in Czechoslovakia.

At the end of January 1933, reality rudely invaded Taggart's gentle universe. As he noted in his diary, spreading the Mormon gospel on that day suddenly became nearly impossible: "No one cared to listen to my message. Everyone wanted to talk about a man named Hitler who became Chancellor of Germany. They all seem to be extremely apprehensive of how this may affect Czechoslovakia." Taggart recorded that the country was soon swept by war fever. Nearly everyone believed that Germany was certain to start another conflagration to erase its defeat in the previous war. By contrast, nobody desired war in Czechoslovakia. "They hate it and its attendant horrors, but they shrug their shoulders and say that it is inevitable."

"I have just fallen in love with them all," Taggart wrote about his new Czech friends, "and dislike thinking about leaving them." But he departed in November 1934, and the next month returned to his college studies in Utah, graduating as a history major in 1936. He married and enrolled in the Ph.D. program in history at the University of California in Berkeley, where he studied under Robert Joseph Kerner, a specialist in Slavic history. At one of Kerner's seminars, Taggart met a likeable colleague who shared his intense interest in all things Czech. It was the young Charles Katek.

Taggart watched the Munich Agreement of September 1938 and the Nazi occupation of the rest of Czechoslovakia in March 1939 from sunny California. But he recalled that the two events had hurt him as much as they hurt the Czechs. "I knew and loved the country. Munich and the sight of Nazis in Prague cut me to the core."[44] When the war broke out, Taggart quit his doctoral program at Berkeley and joined the War Division of the Department of Justice. At the end of 1942, he became an OSS officer, specializing in Czech, Hungarian, and Finnish matters. He saw Beneš when the president came to Washington in May 1943 and was alarmed when he realized that the purpose of the visit was to receive Roosevelt's blessing for his trip to Moscow. When Taggart and others in the OSS analyzed Beneš's summary of his achievements in the Kremlin, which the organization had acquired in London, they grew pessimistic about the country's future. The terms that the exiled president brought from the Soviet Union ominously pointed in the same direction as the Munich Agreement.

Taggart arrived in Czechoslovakia in February 1946. With the exception of Steinhardt, the other American diplomats typically came by train or car, but Taggart flew in from Paris, where he received a last-minute intelligence briefing. Czech security noted this and wondered why this man—a mere civilian vice-consul—was treated differently than other junior American diplomats. After some time at the Alcron Hotel, he and his wife rented an excellent house on U Nesypky Street in an exclusive section of the town. When they arrived they had almost given up hope that they might have children; their first daughter, Eileen, was born in Prague in April 1947.

Unlike the boisterous members of the Military Mission, Taggart was a serious man. He combed his hair straight back and wore round glasses. Others in the business of intelligence used scholarship as a cover for their spying. With Taggart, it was the other way around. He was a religious man, an intellectual and artist who tried to collect intelligence, a gentle idealist trying to prove himself among the tough professionals whose job was to steal secrets.[45] Unlike the Katek team, Taggart had the discipline needed to take on the StB and OBZ. But it was unclear whether he possessed the aptitude for deviousness and deceit it took to succeed.

American intelligence officers had failed to display the single-minded focus that was required to duel with the Czech special services and their Soviet advisors. Whereas Katek wasted time and energy on social activities, Taggart enrolled at Charles University as a part-time graduate student in the Department of History. One wonders what the StB and OBZ thought when Taggart informed the Foreign Ministry that he intended to study the life and times of Thomas G. Masaryk.[46]

Taggart was clear as to the nature of his mission in Czechoslovakia: "I was sent there with a long-term objective—to help the Czechs guard their independence and to promote Western democracy."[47] Seen in this light, he came to protect and promote the values shared by the democratic segment of the political spectrum. Therefore, it was not difficult for him to gain access to sources that were well informed. He identified three—Petr Zenkl, Jan Stránský and Ivo Ducháček. The problem was that all of them were among the best-known democratic politicians and close friends of Colonel Katek's Mission. They added nothing to the existing body of information already available to U.S. intelligence. Taggart kept looking for the kind of people who had the ability to run a truly clandestine network that would remain inactive in peace but would provide Washington with information in time of war. But where to find such people was a puzzle. The Prague scene had been plowed over by Katek, and Taggart did not

Spencer L. Taggart. Gift from the Taggart family.

travel much around the country, except to go fishing for trout in the Loučná, a romantic stream outside the town of Vysoké Mýto.

Colonel Katek had found the Schönborn Palace too confining. He preferred operating from his own turf at the Military Mission, and he tried to minimize the occasions when he had to pay obeisance to Ambassador Steinhardt. Taggart, by contrast, operated only from the Schönborn Palace. As an intelligence officer, he worked at the embassy under a special regime. This made the StB's job easy. A few days after Taggart had landed at the Prague airport, StB informers inside the embassy had no doubt as to the new American's real profession. They figured out exactly who he was because of the extra security around his workplace: "Taggart is the chief of U.S. Intelligence.... He has his own cipher and he personally encodes all his reports." The informers stressed that Taggart's office was in a section of the Schönborn Palace that was accessible only to a handful of Americans; it was next to the top-secret coding room. Because he had spent time around the Beneš government in London, the StB knew that Taggart was an OSS officer, that he spoke Czech, and that he had served as a Mormon missionary in prewar Czechoslovakia. It therefore quickly concluded: "Taggart is the most interesting person at the American embassy." The StB put him under a round the clock surveillance.[48]

In addition to his offensive intelligence tasks, Taggart was required to protect the Schönborn Palace against intrusions by Czech security agents. There was much for him to do in this regard. The StB owned a detailed floor plan of the embassy, and its informers helped to identify "almost completely" each diplomat's assigned office space. In addition, StB specialists were able to "remove documents from the diplomats' desks," which provided insights into their duties, interests, private lives, and weaknesses. They almost always found something of interest.[49] Consequently, the StB was able to create a catalogue of 193 Americans, with detailed—and largely accurate—professional and personal profiles.[50]

Some in the StB complained vociferously that they were operating at a disadvantage to the Americans. The embassy personnel were said to have at their disposal, in addition to dozens of private cars, eighty-nine diplomatic vehicles. This gave the intelligence unit at the Schönborn Palace speed and mobility against which the StB was, in its own words, "cumbersome and almost helpless."[51] It was certainly true that the Czechs were at a disadvantage when it came to cars. But they made up for it in other areas. After Taggart had been at his post for less than two years, in November 1947, StB specialists broke into the cordoned-off area of the embassy and into his office. They opened his desk and examined all the documents in the room. They discovered a bunch of half-burnt papers, with names and other details still clearly legible. Such information was copied, studied, analyzed, and filed for future use.[52]

Katek ran a large and boisterous team. Taggart had only one colleague, Samuel Meryn, who, like his boss, preferred to spend evenings at home.[53] Meryn was born in Prague in January 1910 as Samuel Polakov, the youngest of three brothers who shared a passion for water polo, a game they played at the national level. A graduate of the law school of Charles University in Prague, he found a good position in the foreign department of Živnostenská Banka, a leading financial institution in the country. When the Nazis occupied Prague in March 1939, Polakov and one of his brothers requested and obtained permission from the Gestapo to leave the country. Polakov spent some time in Paris, then emigrated to the United States. After Pearl Harbor, he and his brother joined the U.S. Army and became American citizens.

With the Fifth Army, Polakov took part in the Tunisian campaign, landed in Sicily, and fought his way to Rome and Austria. He specialized in interrogations of German prisoners of war. He was honorably discharged with the rank of sergeant in February 1946. At the end of the war he changed his name to Meryn, his mother's maiden name.

Samuel Meryn came to Czechoslovakia to recover his family property. The next year, he married his Austrian fiancée, Marga, and they decided to settle in Prague. In 1947, Sam Meryn was hired as a civilian employee of the Office of the Military Attaché that was commanded by Colonel (formerly Brigadier General) Joseph A. Michela. In reality, Meryn worked with Taggart and no one else, having been recruited by U.S. intelligence. It proved to be an error for Washington to employ in an intelligence capacity a naturalized American who was born in Prague and had no diplomatic cover.[54]

The main agent of Taggart's intelligence section at the embassy was Reinhold Pick. This remarkable man organized and carried out a number of missions on behalf of U.S. interests and, like Meryn, he did so without the protection that diplomatic status offered to others in the world of spying. Moreover, Pick was not even an American citizen at the time.[55]

Reinhold Pick was born in 1918 in Bakhmut, Ukraine, to a Czech father and Russian mother. He was baptized by Otto Kaiser, a Lutheran minister of the 212th Infantry Division of the German Imperial Army; it was Kaiser who insisted on the Teutonic-sounding first name. Pick's father, a successful banker, was posted in Russia by his French employer and married a Russian pianist in 1917. The next year they barely escaped with their infant boy from the Bolshevik offensive. After some years in Copenhagen, the family returned to Czechoslovakia in 1923, where they enjoyed a decade and a half of upper-class existence.

In 1935 Reinhold enrolled in a business school in Prague. His parents insisted that he spend summers in France or Great Britain to improve his language skills, and after the Munich Conference of 1938, his father ordered him to stay abroad. When the Nazis marched into Prague in March 1939, Reinhold was among the first volunteers to report for duty to the Czechoslovak military attaché in London. After the fall of France and Dunkirk, he was evacuated to Cholmondeley Park in Cheshire, England, the base of the Czechoslovak Brigade.

In May 1945 Pick was among the first soldiers of the brigade to arrive in Pilsen with the advance elements of General Patton's Third Army. Red Army roadblocks made it impossible for anyone in a Western uniform to continue on to liberated Prague. But Pick would not be deterred. He commandeered a car and, disregarding an explicit order from General Alois Liška, drove off to meet the Soviet challenge. On the way there, he satisfied the Red Army's passion for stamped documents by flashing his British Army medical card. After three days of celebrating in Prague, Pick negotiated his way back to Pilsen through a Soviet checkpoint by presenting his British military ID, which was signed—he pointed this out—by Field Marshal Bernard Montgomery. He barely bothered to return the astonished soldier's frenetically executed salute. He paid for the escapade with a three-day house arrest in Pilsen, but he showed early on that he possessed the qualities one might like to see in a secret agent.

In June 1945 Pick was honorably discharged, but he caught the eye of Colonel Thomas Crystal, a U.S. Army intelligence officer (G-2) in Pilsen who had many small jobs for this enterprising man with several languages and an uncanny way of getting around obstacles. After only a few days, the colonel was impressed by what Pick could do and recommended him to Major General Ernest N. Harmon, commander of the XXII Corps and the highest ranking American in the country. The no-nonsense Harmon named him his private secretary. He was pleased to note that Pick "has a very fine grasp of our language and can even translate our slang and curse words if required." Pick acted as an interpreter for Harmon on various occasions, but he did more than that; he helped his boss to navigate through the political minefield within and around the American zone. The general was determined not to waste this talented man. On November 17, 1945, only days before he left the country, Harmon drove with Pick to the U.S. embassy in Prague, where he introduced him to Steinhardt. He put a glowing and detailed letter on the ambassador's desk and suggested that the Americans in Prague would find Pick a welcome addition. General Harmon concluded his letter, "I shall miss him very much."[56]

Steinhardt, always on the lookout for enterprising men, hired Pick on the spot. He introduced his new employee to Walter Birge, who placed him in the administrative department. Initially, he dealt with routine duties. Soon Taggart learned that Pick—everybody at the embassy called him Noldi, short for "Reinhold"—was resourceful, and he began making use of his skills in operations. It was a sad reflection on the quality of U.S. intelligence in Prague that its best asset was a complete amateur. Since he was neither a diplomat nor a U.S. citizen, he was vulnerable to the combined forces of the StB and OBZ.

When American intelligence officers arrived in Prague in May 1945, it seemed that the cause of democracy had been dealt a lucky hand. They were highly educated and motivated; they understood the country, its language, and history; and they had time to prepare for the coming confrontation with their Communist opponent. They were also lucky in that they enjoyed the unqualified support of Ambassador Steinhardt, who, unlike some of his colleagues in the diplomatic profession at that time, appreciated intelligence.

Importantly, many among the Czech political and military elites, and some in the security apparat, were open to U.S. intelligence personnel seeking classified information. In sharing this information they felt neither dishonorable nor unpatriotic. Quite the contrary; protecting democracy and fighting off a dictatorship was their noble cause. It would be hard to imagine any other country where there existed such a harmony of interest between American intelligence collectors and their sources.

From the start, however, U.S. intelligence in postwar Czechoslovakia had failed to uncover the sort of secrets that mattered, such as strategic information from the highest levels of the CPC, Ministry of the Interior, and Ministry of Defense. The Communist clandestine services were staffed mostly with amateurs. Yet they used every imaginable technique to recruit informers inside the democratic camp, the United States embassy, and the Military Mission. By contrast, the American intelligence professionals were satisfied with relaying gossip effortlessly obtained from democratic politicians and other casual contacts.

In addition to the problematic Taub affair, it was unhelpful that Katek and Taggart failed to complement each other's efforts. Part of the problem was that their personalities were a study in contrasts. Katek was a *bon vivant* who strove to dominate every conversation, a flaw in an intelligence operator. Taggart was—in the eyes of his colleagues—stiff, passive, unimaginative, socially reserved, and too limited by the strictures of his beliefs.[57] Although he came to Prague to strengthen the clandestine component and was determined to do so, he worked with the same people whose cover had already been blown when they befriended Colonel Katek. This fatal error simplified the job of the Americans' main opponents, the StB and OBZ.

# Passing the Point of No Return

*Prague Withdraws from the Marshall Plan*

Even the best intelligence could only be an extra tool for policymakers in Washington, not a substitute for smart and assertive diplomacy. The problem was that the United States embassy in Prague excelled neither in intelligence nor in diplomacy. This was serious, because by the end of 1946 no one could rule out the possibility that the Communist Party of Czechoslovakia—acting with or without orders from Moscow—would seize absolute power. It certainly had the resources to do so. The party emerged from the war with around 40,000 members but claimed 827,000 in the second half of 1945 and more than a million before the May 1946 elections; by the end of 1947, it had 1,394,000 members.[1] This amounted to an astonishing 11.6 percent of the total population of 12,003,000.[2] Encouraged, the CPC leaders decided in January 1947 that the party's main objective was to win support of the majority of the Czechoslovak electorate.

It was impossible to discern what exactly the Kremlin wished to achieve in Prague at that stage, and it is not certain that it had a set of concrete goals. But there was no reason to doubt that it felt optimistic about its recent gains and the near future. Predicting the course the new year of 1947 would likely take, *Pravda* asserted that it was going to be filled with successes. "Time is working on our side," the paper declared; the new year would bring many "glorious victories" for the Soviet people. Since Hitler had been defeated, an American journalist wondered: Victories? Over whom?[3]

Many East Europeans would have had no difficulty understanding what sort of "successes" the *Pravda* editor had in mind. For instance, the January 1947 elections in Poland were completely fraudulent. The non-Communist candidates were harassed and terrorized, and even murdered. The U.S. embassy in Warsaw could barely function. Some Polish employees who refused to act as informers were threatened with death, and U.S. ambassador Arthur Bliss Lane was compelled to resign in protest.[4] The situation was just as bad in Hungary. The

Communists finished in a distant third place in the elections of 1945. Therefore, the next elections were rigged. Soviet authorities and Hungarian security unleashed a wave of terror upon their democratic opponents of such intensity that Lord Vansittart called Hungary "the latest police state" in Eastern Europe, and the Department of State protested that the Soviet high command in Hungary sought to substitute a dictatorship by the secret police for a government.[5]

Meanwhile, the civil war in Greece led Truman in March 1947 to ask Congress for $400 million and other resources to protect both Greece and Turkey from the Communist onslaught. Under the Truman Doctrine, Washington assumed the commitment to support and uphold democratic regimes, when doing so "was deemed to be in the interest of the United States."[6] In making this undertaking, Truman was motivated in part by the erroneous belief that the Communist insurgents in Greece enjoyed Soviet support. Not only was Stalin determined to stay away from the Greek crisis, he had even forced the Yugoslav leader, Josip Broz Tito, to follow suit. Consequently, the United States acted against Soviet "meddling" in Greece and Turkey, where there was virtually none, but maintained a resigned posture in Central Europe, where there was plenty of it.

Viewed against the backgrounds of Poland, Hungary, the Balkans, or Greece, Czechoslovakia seemed—even in 1947—to be a democracy, and the U.S. embassy in the Schönborn Palace was a regular diplomatic post. Steinhardt and the Central European Section in the Department of State maintained their optimism, as did Beneš and others among the democrats in Prague. But analysts in the Office of Intelligence Research (OIR) of the Department of State were not deceived by appearances. They conceded that the country was more independent than others in the region and its economic recovery was more rapid. Nevertheless, they warned, this once liberal democracy anchored in the West had undergone a transformation to a socialist country within the Eastern orbit.[7]

Ambassador Steinhardt disagreed with the OIR analysts. Just before the end of 1946 he stated to a Czech friend that "the Soviet Union was amidst a grand scale political retreat." His interlocutor—the man was a secret police informer—reported that the ambassador was optimistic about the future because the bosses of the CPC were, in his view, confused and uncertain.[8] The tenor of Steinhardt's formal reports to Washington was identical with his extemporaneous remarks. The ambassador reported that the Communist ministers were "giving in on almost every issue" to their democratic opponents. This was because of a combination of factors. Prominent among them was Gottwald's alcoholism, because of which the government had not conducted any serious business recently. Furthermore, Soviet foreign minister Molotov was forced to make concessions to the West, and this made the CPC more reasonable than ever before. Steinhardt concluded with an episode that illustrated why he thought the Russians and their

Czech admirers faced decline. When a Czech parliamentary delegation visited the Soviet Union, it was not a success. The deputies were unable to go anywhere individually, because NKVD agents moved them about like a herd of sheep. Furthermore, bad weather forced them to return home on a slow local train, allowing them to see parts of the Soviet Union normally hidden from foreigners. It was an eye-opening experience. They saw desperate poverty and backwardness.[9] Steinhardt, a rational and pragmatic man, assumed that members of the delegation would change their views of the Soviet Union and alter their political choices.

On January 20, 1947, shortly after he had dispatched his optimistic assessment, Steinhardt left Prague for the United States. He told the press he was going to consult with the new secretary of state, George C. Marshall, and see the president.[10] He arrived in New York City on January 31. It is unclear exactly when he returned to his post, but the first memorandum from Prague under his signature bears the date March 31, 1947. Most likely he had devoted two months to his law firm in New York City. He certainly was not at his post when the president proclaimed the Truman Doctrine. Occasionally, Steinhardt went on brief trips to Washington. For instance, in February he had dinner at the Czechoslovak embassy with Ambassador Juraj Slávik, who found him to be "extraordinarily friendly toward Czech interests."[11] It is difficult to comprehend why Steinhardt thought it appropriate to stay away from his post for so long, and why the Department of State allowed it.

In the ambassador's absence, Chargé John H. Bruins took over the Schönborn Palace. It had been difficult for this diligent Foreign Service professional to maintain a presence behind the dominant Steinhardt, and now he had an opportunity to remind the Department of State of his existence. Unfortunately, his memoranda repeated Steinhardt's mantra that the democratic parties were gaining ground and the CPC's influence was declining. When he attempted to explain the Prague scene in 1947, he meandered through a history of John Hus, the fifteenth century religious reformer; John Comenius, the 17th century Moravian polymath; and the founder of Czechoslovakia, Thomas Masaryk.[12] While erudite, such missives failed to make an impression in Washington.

In early March 1947 Bruins reported that the democratic parties had grown in strength and its leaders had become more assertive than before. He quoted Zenkl, Krajina, and Ripka, who had spoken out in defense of liberal society.[13] Bruins's tone was upbeat, yet he made no attempt to explain how mere speeches could deprive the CPC of the instruments of power it had accumulated, especially since the Communists were successful in framing public discourse, which was defined by the gratitude the nation owed the Red Army and by the fear of Germany's resurrection. Of all the weapons the CPC held, this one was the mightiest; the others were derived from it. Yet no one in the democratic camp dared to attack it.

The illusion that the overall situation in Czechoslovakia was fine and improving had to be corrected by American journalists. Albion Ross, John MacCormack, and C. L. Sulzberger of the *New York Times* painted a complex portrait of Czechoslovakia as a country that enjoyed a surprising degree of prosperity but with a fragile political system that was at the mercy of the powerful Communist Party. The latter could pounce at any moment and turn the structure of power inside out.

Ross reported that by the end of 1946 Czechoslovakia had reached prewar production levels in coal, iron, and steel. Consequently, motorcycles and other such products were coming out of factories to consumers at a fast pace.[14] This was quite an achievement, given the years of Nazi occupation and the logistical changes brought about by the shift from private to state ownership. In early 1947 there were 2,902 Czech nationalized enterprises, with 657,000 workers, and 13,439 privately owned businesses, with 416,757 employees. The state controlled some seventy percent of the overall industrial capacity.[15]

Nevertheless, private entrepreneurs were still productive and competitive, and the consequences were noticeable. Czechoslovak cities, wrote Ross, had stores offering a plentiful supply of steak, poultry, and cheese. Ross came across stores offering goose, duck, chicken, pork—and no rationing. In every town, large or small, one could find "astonishing quantities" of rich cakes, sweets of all kinds, real coffee, and beer. This was unusual in Europe after the war. A young Englishman told Ross that he had had more and better meals during a short stay in Czechoslovakia than in a whole year in postwar England.[16] Overall, the *New York Times* reported, "no formerly occupied country except Belgium had as good a year as Czechoslovakia had in 1946." It exported goods worth $287 million, thus achieving an $87 million trade surplus. Any further progress, *Times* reporter John MacCormack argued, depended on Czechoslovakia's ability to secure hard currency loans in the United States.[17] He was unaware that Secretary of State Byrnes, Ambassador Steinhardt, and the CPC leaders had forestalled that possibility.

There was more good news reported by the press. For instance, in February 1947 the whole country held its collective breath as it followed the ice hockey world championship that was taking place in Prague. To everyone's delight, the national squad won the world title, defeating the United States 6 to 1 in the last game of the tournament. The sold-out stadium was deliriously happy: little Czechoslovakia was number one—at least in hockey.

Meanwhile, one could even believe that the CPC chairman Gottwald and his rotund wife, Marta, had gone soft on class struggle and replaced it with a taste for bourgeois luxuries. They had acquired a villa in a high-class part of town and had it lavishly decorated with art borrowed from state galleries.[18] In fact, Gottwald occasionally asserted that he had no intention of replicating the harsh Bolshevik experience at home. Was his resplendent residence a sign that the CPC would try to be reasonable? In a widely quoted interview he said that his party intended to transform Czechoslovakia into a socialist country, but "the system of the Soviets and of the dictatorship of the proletariat" were not the only routes to get there. Conditions in Czechoslovakia were such that they allowed for a "specific development." These were daring words in the Stalinist realm: in just two short years they might constitute a capital crime and lead to the gallows. But in March 1947 the public had reason to hope that Gottwald had abandoned Leninism and perhaps even dogmatic Marxism, especially when he declared that the nationalization program had been completed. Both state-owned and private enterprises would be productively combined to form the economic base of Czechoslovakia. Gottwald concluded his deceptive statement by asserting that the CPC would always defend the existing democratic political system.[19] This sounded sweet, but only to those who knew little about Gottwald's career in the Communist International.

Steinhardt, who had just returned to the Schönborn Palace from New York, reported on the Gottwald interview in detail. He noted that it confirmed his previous assessments that the CPC's popularity was declining and that the party bosses feared being excluded from the next government. There was in fact partial and inconclusive evidence that Communist candidates were not as successful in workplace-level secret ballots in 1947 as they had been a year before.[20] But what may have been true in isolated samples did not necessarily reflect the situation nationwide. Moreover, Steinhardt tended to mistake popularity for power. The Party and its control over the StB, OBZ, and the armed forces did not weaken, even if the Communist cause had lost the shine it had had in the spring of 1946.

This had consequences that had escaped the attention of the U.S. embassy but were noted by American journalists who covered the Prague scene. Notwithstanding the apparent political stability and the relatively high standard of living, a troubling phenomenon manifested itself in early 1947. Albion Ross encountered more and more people who were preparing to leave the country. Nobody had persecuted them; they had had no trouble with the secret police; many were prosperous, and they had every reason to think that their future was bright. Except that they did not think so. They sensed that a crisis was imminent and they worried about its outcome. Therefore they were preparing to exchange their comforts for the uncertain existence of stateless refugees.[21] These were members of the upper-middle class, not young adventurers eager to try something new. They were prepared to face the hardships of exile because they anticipated that the political system in Prague was about to experience a catastrophic turn toward Communist totalitarianism.

Yet, according to Beneš, even in the spring of 1947 a CPC dictatorship was not the only option available in Prague. The president told the British emissary

R. H. Bruce Lockhart that the country "was out of the woods," and he had a message for the Foreign Office that Lockhart was to deliver: "Give us a fair chance in the international field, and we'll pull through."[22] C. L. Sulzberger, who—like Lockhart—enjoyed a close professional relationship with Beneš, reported in May 1947 that the Czechs would have liked to widen their repertoire of international treaties by entering into an agreement with the United States to countervail the existing treaty with Moscow. But Prague did not dare to propose it, because the Department of State would rebuff it.[23] American "coolness" toward Czechoslovakia—advocated by Steinhardt to accelerate its willingness to compensate American owners of nationalized properties—played into the hands of the radical CPC elements who wished to isolate the country from the West.

No one in the Schönborn Palace seemed to have noticed that well-to-do Czechs were preparing to leave the country in 1947, and no one reported that Beneš would have liked to negotiate an agreement with the United States. Instead, from the end of 1946 to April 1947, the embassy and the Department of State were focused on the case of Father Jozef Tiso and his trial. Tiso had served as president of the wartime Slovak state that was created in March 1939 under the auspices of Adolf Hitler. He shared responsibility for the fate of some 58,000 Slovak Jews who were deported to Auschwitz and other death camps. This murderous initiative was carried out despite pleas and interventions by the Vatican chargé in Slovakia, Monsignor Giuseppe Burzio, who denounced Tiso and his government as "servile executors" of Hitler's criminal demands.[24]

The Americans captured Tiso in Austria in the summer of 1945 and confidentially consulted the Holy See regarding the prisoner. Church officials replied that the Vatican did not oppose Prague's extradition request. The U.S. Army brought Tiso back to Czechoslovakia, where he was tried on more than one hundred charges, including war crimes.[25] At a crucial moment during the trial, his attorney urged him to show the court that he felt pity for the victims. He refused, was sentenced to death, and hanged in April 1947.[26] Executing a Slovak priest, even one as flagrantly unrepentant as Tiso, hurt Czech-Slovak relations for decades to come, perhaps irreparably. His failure to grant Tiso a presidential pardon and commute the sentence to life in prison made Beneš look like a pitiless and vengeful little man. Throughout this time, the Department of State was under great pressure from Slovak-American organizations and various congressmen to defend Tiso as an innocent victim. It was quite reluctant to do so, but the U.S. embassy had to divert its limited resources and follow the trial closely. In the end it could only report that the trial was "conducted in a fair and orderly manner." The Department of State accepted this assessment.[27]

In early May 1947, Ambassador Steinhardt and twenty other Americans from the embassy went to Pilsen to observe the second anniversary of the city's liberation and to commemorate the American soldiers who had given their lives to defeat Nazism on Czechoslovak soil. The ceremony was a success, and Steinhardt was pleased to note that his speech attracted an audience of some forty thousand, who demonstrated a "strong feeling of friendship for the United States."[28]

In mid-May 1947 the ambassador found more good news to report: the democratic parties, once timid, had shown increasing boldness and "strengthened their position with the Czech people." He specifically praised Zenkl for his attack on totalitarian ideologists. Steinhardt's analysis distinguished between the Prague government's behavior abroad and the domestic political scene. The former remained problematic, as Czechoslovakia consistently voted with the Kremlin, but on the domestic front, the democrats wrested concessions from the CPC, and even gained some ground at its expense. To be successful on the international scene, they would need American support, but, Steinhardt warned, they could hardly expect it as long as they sided with the Soviet Union. The ambassador suggested that the democratic parties had decided to focus first on strengthening the domestic scene before becoming more independent in the field of foreign policy.[29]

A five-day conference of U.S. military attachés serving in Europe and the Middle East was organized in Frankfurt in early May 1947. One of its objectives was to study the extent to which the Soviet Union had managed to take over defense and security organizations in various European countries, including Czechoslovakia. Other panels examined the work of Soviet special services operating abroad, anti-Communist resistance groups, and a variety of related themes pertaining to defense and intelligence matters. The American diplomatic post in Prague was represented by military attaché Colonel E. F. Koenig and assistant air attaché Captain Jack C. Novak. Commissioned in November 1916, Koenig was an experienced professional in the field of military intelligence. Novak, however, was a complete novice, and Prague was his first assignment; he had taken up his post at the Schönborn Palace only two months before the conference.

Captain Novak was born in 1921 in Cedar Rapids, Iowa, where he grew up in a large Czech immigrant community. He graduated from the Military Academy at West Point, went through pilot training, and flew missions as a B-17 pilot, winning the Distinguished Flying Cross with Five Clusters and other medals. After the war he served briefly as a West Point instructor, then trained for his job at the U.S. embassy in Prague.

On his way to and from Frankfurt, Novak flew in the elegant twin-engine C-45 airplane. As always on such occasions, he made ample use of his mounted K-20 aerial camera, especially as he passed over zones of interest, such as the uranium mines in the west. He later stated that, after landing back in Prague on

May 11, 1947, he left the plane to clear passport control, intending to return for the luggage he left on board, but when he came back his briefcase was missing. He implied that the Czech special services had stolen it.[30]

The Czech version of the incident at Ruzyně Airport gave a different account of how the briefcase ended up in the hands of the Military Counterintelligence (OBZ). It claimed that upon leaving the airplane Novak took his luggage but forgot to take his briefcase, which was packed with top-secret documents, and drove home. A member of the ground crew checked the plane, discovered the briefcase, and turned it over to a duty officer. The officer opened it and realized it contained classified materials. He jumped in the car and drove to the Technical Office of the General Staff, a twenty-minute trip, where two copies of each document from the briefcase were made.[31]

Captain Novak had every reason to be shocked. His briefcase included a copy of the embassy's classified report on the situation in Czechoslovakia, which contained references to the K-20 camera and also the boastful claim that the Czechs were unaware of Novak's aerial espionage. It included a detailed analysis of the Czech Air Force from the largest to the smallest units, their location, types of planes and airfields, names of higher officers, their characteristics, strengths and weaknesses. The briefcase also included the materials Captain Novak had collected at the Frankfurt Conference: the agenda of the event, a list of its attendees, and—especially damaging—the orders Novak received at Frankfurt from his superiors tailored specifically for the post in Prague. They showed what the Americans knew, what they did not, and what they wanted to discover. There can be no question that the loss of the briefcase was a serious setback.

Bedřich Reicin, chief of the OBZ, entered the scene while the papers were being copied. He swore everyone involved to secrecy and ordered that an office door at the airport be marked "Lost and Found." Captain Novak appeared at the airport the next day, May 12, 1947, sheepishly inquiring about the briefcase. He was directed to the phony lost and found office. If he hoped to recover his lost papers, he was to be gravely disappointed. In the office he encountered Reicin, who roughly demanded that Novak become his informant. Should he choose to turn down the offer, he said, the OBZ would return the briefcase to the military attaché, Colonel Koenig, who would have Novak drummed out of the U.S. Army, or the papers would be turned over to the Ministry of Foreign Affairs, which would pass them to Steinhardt. That would also bring his military career to an inauspicious end. Presuming that he owned Captain Novak, Reicin asked him to reveal the names of Czech Army officers who acted as informers for the U.S. embassy. He specifically requested that Novak provide information about General Heliodor Píka, the Czech military representative in the wartime Soviet Union.[32]

Novak refused to be blackmailed. He calmly informed the OBZ boss that he knew nothing about such sensitive matters and declined to discuss the proposition any further. Regarding the lost briefcase, he tried to put a brave face on it—the papers were without any real value, he asserted. In any case, Novak claimed that he had already informed his superior, Colonel Koenig, who imposed a small penalty upon Novak, and the matter was closed. Reicin returned the briefcase to Novak with all the papers and released him. In reality, Novak first informed Colonel Koenig the day after his encounter with Reicin.

Steinhardt protested the incident but "received no satisfaction." The Military Attaché's Office found out that "all Ministers of State had been furnished photo-static copies of the contents of the briefcase." Colonel Koenig filed a short report regarding the briefcase, minimizing the seriousness of the loss, on July 23, 1947, some seventy-two days after the event.[33] Soon after the incident he was replaced in Prague by Colonel Joseph Anthony Michela, another West Point graduate and a close friend of Steinhardt; the two had served together in Moscow during the war.[34] The second consequence of the briefcase affair was that the C-45 was flown to Germany and never returned.[35] Yet Captain Novak remained at his post. This turned out to be a quixotic decision on the part of the Pentagon. The absent-minded captain was lured into a trap in November 1949, caught red-handed ser-vicing a dead drop under a cobblestone, and expelled from the country amid a highly publicized campaign.[36] "It was ridiculous for us to think that we could get away with what we were doing," Novak later admitted. "If we did anything, we did it with the Communists' acquiescence."[37]

Despite events of this kind, the stream of optimistic reports from the U.S. em-bassy continued. At the end of May 1947 Steinhardt analyzed various scenarios for the coming 1948 elections. He concluded that the democrats would likely make "substantial gains," in which case the CPC would lose control over the important ministries, and "Communist prestige and Communist influence would be weakened" throughout the country.[38] Steinhardt saw another sign of a trend favoring the forces of democracy. One of the last remaining Czech conser-vative politicians, Ladislav Feierabend, ran for a seat on the presidium of Koop-erativa, the purchasing agency of agricultural cooperatives. The Communists despised him, and they mounted a frenzied campaign to defeat him. To every-one's surprise, he won decisively: 108 to 25. Steinhardt thought this event signif-icant, not least because of the hysterical reaction by the CPC and its print media. They attacked Feierabend as a former "agrarian magnate" and made the prepos-terous claim that he had received a large estate from Hitler's viceroy, K. H. Frank.[39] Feierabend had escaped from Nazi-occupied Prague to London in Janu-ary 1940 and spent the war in London close to Beneš. He sued the Communist periodicals for spreading lies about him and won.[40] This affirmed the view of the Schönborn Palace that the overall trend was positive, especially when the mod-erate wing in the Social Democratic Party gained ground at the expense of

Fierlinger and other pro-Moscow agents. Steinhardt joyfully quoted the leader of the moderate faction, Minister Laušman, as saying that Czechoslovakia should not "copy any foreign socialism." He also denounced censorship and attempts by the CPC to treat the courts, the police, and the armed forces as if they belonged to the Communists.[41]

On May 25, 1947, Steinhardt detected signs of more good news. He attended a parade of some 120,000 cheerful and confidence-exuding young Catholics who marched through the streets of Prague, supported by delegations of like-minded youth from France, Belgium, the Netherlands, Italy, Austria, and Spain. Steinhardt was delighted by this event. He was particularly pleased with some of the slogans: "The People's Party Defends Private Enterprise," "Down With Fascism—Left and Right," "Workers Are Found in All Classes," and "Down with Dictatorship, Whatever Its Color."[42] A similar parade was organized by the National Socialists on the occasion of their fiftieth anniversary. The slogans were witty, and some were explicitly anti-Communist. The ambassador thought the National Socialists had displayed "great strength."[43]

In early June 1947, Steinhardt watched with pleasure a speech given by Minister Laušman, the rising star in the Social Democratic Party. The Czechs, he said, did not want to become a satellite; they wanted to remain free. He even promised that Prague would soon secure an alliance with England—although he took care to describe the country as the "new Socialist England" and did not indicate how he intended to lure the British into such an arrangement, given their age-old reluctance to enter into alliances of any kind in Central Europe.[44]

Steinhardt was right to focus on the Laušman speech. It was important because it showed that the Social Democrats, much like the Catholics in the People's Party and the National Socialists, at last understood what the stakes were. The alternative to the imperfect postwar Czechoslovak democracy was not only a CPC dictatorship, which was bad enough, but a loss of sovereignty to Moscow. The democratic parties seemed ready to fight against this threat.

But were the people ready to follow? *Public Opinion*, a monthly publication of the Ministry of Information, provided some insight into Czech society in mid-1947. Only 13 percent of those polled felt they lived behind the Iron Curtain; 53 percent did not, and 34 percent chose the "don't know" option. When the researchers asked, "Will the Germans become a peace-loving and democratic nation?" only 2 percent of Czechs answered "yes," in contrast to the British (23), the Americans (22), and the Canadians (20), as well as the Dutch (14) and the French (10), who had experienced Nazi occupation. The final question was: "Will Germany attempt to start a new war in the future?" The results were comparable for the Americans, the British, the Canadians, the Dutch, and the French—the range was from 43 to 63 percent answering positively. But an astonishing 81 percent of Czechs expressed the view that Germany would launch yet another world war.[45] The irrational fear of postwar Germany, a country in ruins and under foreign military occupation by the mightiest armies in the world, drove Czechoslovakia toward the camouflaged trap set up by the CPC and the Soviet Union.

In June 1947 Secretary of State George C. Marshall, in a speech at Harvard University, presented a plan for the economic rehabilitation of Europe: the European Recovery Program (ERP).[46] "Europe's requirements for the next three or four years . . . are so much greater than her present ability to pay," Marshall stated, "that she must have substantial additional help or face economic, social, and political deterioration of a very grave character."[47]

The news that the United States offered tangible assistance in the form of the ERP was received with much enthusiasm among the democratic parties in Prague. They saw in it an instrument that could accelerate global economic renewal. There was every reason to believe it would alleviate poverty and blunt the edge of political radicalism. It might also help reduce the chasm between East and West, thus making the Czechoslovak position of standing astride the two blocs more comfortable. Naturally, Gottwald and the CPC were apprehensive about it. It was obvious to them that the scheme—coming on the heels of UNRRA and the Truman Doctrine—was going to further increase America's image as a superpower. But Gottwald was occasionally able to set his ideology aside and focus on practical concerns; he did not lack an understanding of economic matters. He knew that his country needed American credit so that it could purchase materials, such as cotton, that would put its idle textile factories back to work. It seemed that Prague's participation was assured.

The ensuing events demonstrated that the cancer attacking the Czechoslovak political system had spread farther than the reports from the U.S. embassy in Prague had so far allowed. On July 1, 1947, Masaryk told the American press that Prague was ready to "take action in line with the proposal of U.S. Secretary of State Marshall."[48] The next day Molotov made clear that Moscow would not participate in the Marshall Plan. Nevertheless, on July 4, 1947, the Prague government confirmed Masaryk's previous declaration that Czechoslovak representatives would be coming to Paris soon. Trouble came the next day. Gottwald received an encoded message from Moscow via a secret radio channel.[49] It ordered Prague to send its delegation to the Paris Conference so that it could "demonstrate on the spot that the Anglo-French plan [regarding the implementation of the Marshall Plan] is unacceptable and to prevent its unanimous acceptance. Whereupon, the delegation will walk out, taking along as many other delegates from other countries as possible."[50]

Then Stalin changed his mind and summoned the Czechs to Moscow. On July 9, 1947, Gottwald, Drtina, Masaryk, and others listened in the Kremlin to his tirades against the West and the Marshall plan. For the Czechs to go to Paris, Stalin declared, would be intolerable. "We consider this to be a matter of fundamental importance. Our friendship with Czechoslovakia depends on it. By going to Paris you will only prove that you wish to assist in the attempt to isolate the Soviet Union."[51] To underline his point, he directed the Czechs toward a map of Europe. Using sweeping gestures, he demonstrated the precarious geographic position of Czechoslovakia. Sooner or later, Germany was bound to rise again and start another war. Neither Drtina nor Masaryk had the courage to disagree, and Gottwald, who knew what happened to those who crossed Stalin, was visibly frightened and remained silent.

After a dramatic meeting of the Prague government on July 10, 1947, Czechoslovakia renounced its planned participation in the Marshall Plan. It stated that no one from Eastern and Central Europe would be attending the Paris Conference and that Czechoslovakia's "participation would be understood as a measure directed against its friendship with the Soviet Union."[52] When the Czech delegation returned from the Kremlin to Prague, Gottwald had to audacity to state: "We have returned from our short visit with great results." Friendship with the Soviet Union and Stalin's support for Czechoslovakia, Gottwald said, were "inestimable."[53]

In the end, some of the leading beneficiaries of the Marshall Plan were the very countries that had contributed to the outbreak of the war, and the first victims of Nazism, Czechoslovakia and Poland, were prevented from taking part in it. To make matters worse, Beneš, who had very much wanted for Czechoslovakia to take part in the Marshall Plan, suffered another stroke on July 2, 1947. Neither the public nor foreign diplomats found out about this new medical emergency. The president was released from the hospital but went to a resort for physical therapy. He returned to Prague only at the beginning of October.[54]

While the Marshall Plan crisis was unfolding, the American embassy was rudderless. Steinhardt and Bruins were attending a boar hunt organized by the Ministry of Foreign Affairs. Colonel Katek's deputy, Kurt Taub, who did not find shooting appealing, got the story first, directly from Deputy Prime Minister Zenkl. The Military Mission felt very proud of this scoop. George Bogardus, second secretary at the U.S. embassy, also got the news—from Drtina's office. Now the question was what to do with the information, since the only Americans on duty at the Schönborn Palace were Charles W. Yost, a Foreign Service Officer, and Bogardus, and neither of them held a senior rank. Eventually, a report on the debacle in the Kremlin went under Yost's signature.[55]

Just as the Americans found out about the meeting in the Kremlin, so the Czech clandestine services were quick to learn what the Americans knew and who had told them. An informer at the embassy reported: "The Intelligence Section of the American embassy has a copy of the telegram sent by Masaryk and Gottwald from Moscow to Prague, explaining how the Soviet Union views our acceptance of the Marshall Plan. The telegram also indicates how the Government is to proceed and that the original acceptance of the Plan is to be reversed."[56]

The story leaked to the *New York Times*. An article accurately described the Marshall Plan fiasco and the tense situation in Prague. But then it quoted "observers here," possibly a reference to U.S. diplomats, as being skeptical that the Russians would try to impose upon Czechoslovakia "the kind of communist state that prevails in Rumania, Bulgaria and Poland." The hopeful view, the paper reported, was that in following its tradition the Kremlin might in fact decide to withdraw altogether back to Russia, lest its people become contaminated with the West.[57] This groundless optimism reflected the views held by the ambassador and his loyal deputy John Bruins.[58]

Steinhardt later stated that the Marshall Plan episode was the one case where he had "definite proof" that Czechoslovakia had received "orders from Moscow."[59] But as had happened before—such as after the 1946 elections—he soon allowed his proclivity toward positive predictions to replace his original, skeptical assessment. On July 19, 1947, he conceded that the first reaction to Stalin's diktat regarding the Marshall Plan was one of shock among the democrats. He noted that some of the democratic leaders had prepared ways of escaping from Czechoslovakia, transferring hard currency abroad, and possibly even setting up a government-in-exile. That mood of panic had passed, Steinhardt reported. He thought it unlikely for the Kremlin to interfere in Czech domestic affairs.[60] The political scene in Prague was "tranquil" and he thought it would remain so.[61]

Having made this bold prediction at the end of July, the ambassador left on vacation. "During the summer months," wrote his daughter, Dulcie-Ann, "we took the opportunity to reacquaint ourselves with Europe. Austria, which was our great love, saw us at the musical festival in Salzburg." They stayed at a romantic castle. When they returned home late on August 13, 1947, they discovered that all their belongings and suitcases had been taken. It "looked as though a vacuum cleaner had gone through" the rooms. The family lost their diplomatic passports, Steinhardt his pearl-handled pistol, and his wife her mink coat. The passports were found early; the rest, including the pistol and mink coat, after several months. The robbers, desperate Ukrainian refugees, received draconian sentences.[62]

The first document under Steinhardt's signature is dated September 18, 1947. This added a month and a half to the two months Steinhardt had spent in the United States in the winter. His absences went against the directions of the Department of State. It repeated on July 9, 1947, the day Stalin saw the Czech delegation in the Kremlin, that Czechoslovakia was a

> testing-ground in the conflict of ideologies between the East and West.... Every development in the state and the Government's foreign

affairs has much significance as evidence of Soviet and Communist policy.... The Mission is accordingly charged with an arduous task, and is expected to put in as effective an appearance on official and unofficial occasions as other diplomatic missions.... It is of much importance for the American Embassy to be able to play an equally influential role.[63]

This implied criticism of the embassy's performance is the only one on record.

The summer of 1947 was unusually hot and dry and, contrary to Steinhardt's prediction, anything but tranquil. It was ugly, filled with anger, malice, and fear. For the first time, threats of violence became political arguments. Slánský fired the first shot by stating that anyone who criticized the Soviet Union or other countries in the Soviet bloc was a "saboteur and had to be treated as one."[64] In August 1947 the Communist daily *Rudé Právo* weighed in with a series of articles attacking the "reactionary" democrats.[65] Those who had the courage to criticize the Soviet Union had to brace themselves for an apoplectic response. For instance, the CPC caught in its crosshairs Jan Slavík, a respected scholar. It charged him with being an "anti-Soviet agitator and slanderer" and an ally of "Nazi anti-Soviet pogromists." Hidden behind such wild rhetoric, a new argument started to emerge—that the United States was in the process of reviving "German imperialism." Czech paranoia regarding Nazi revanchism, fed by the Communists, made such allegations insidious. The CPC hinted that the central purpose of the Marshall Plan was to rebuild German industry and armed forces, and then to deploy both in the service of an anti-Soviet crusade led by the United States.[66] On August 24 Prime Minister Gottwald warned that "reactionary agents" had managed to sneak into the democratic parties. He pledged that his party would enlarge its base from the current 1.2 million to 1.5 million members.[67]

Even the weather seemed to have played into the hands of the CPC. Heat and drought conditions in the summer of 1947 led to a crop failure. This was an opportunity for the propaganda machine. It played up an offer of emergency grain from the Soviet Union and invented a scheme whereby farmers who sustained losses would be compensated by a capital levy imposed on the wealthy, dismissively called "millionaires." The CPC claimed that there were 35,000 such creatures in the country, whose total wealth allegedly amounted to Kčs 50 billion.[68] In early September 1947 the party launched a campaign to raise Kčs 4 billion from the accounts of the rich in support of farmers and to pay for grain purchased abroad. Even the Social Democrats opposed this assault on private property, and it was duly defeated by a vote. The U.S. embassy (without its elusive ambassador) followed the CPC campaign, which made use of the press and billboards posted around the city. The Party named the ministers who had opposed the extra tax and called them "defenders of reactionaries and enemies of the people."[69] In addition, orchestrated delegations of coal miners and farmers flooded the corridors of government offices, demanding to know why their elected representatives expected them to face extreme hardship while the rich bathed in gold. The campaign cleverly exploited the egalitarian instincts of many Czechs. In just two weeks, the Communists reached an agreement with the Social Democrats to cooperate regarding the extra tax initiative, and at the end of October 1947, a compromise version of the original plan was passed by the parliament. The CPC had scored another victory and gained more power.

On Wednesday, September 10, 1947, the already unstable scene in Prague received another jolt. When an assistant of Minister Drtina's went through the morning mail, she noticed an unusual parcel that was apparently mailed to the minister from a nearby shop that specialized in perfumes. This was unusual. She unwrapped it and discovered a wooden box covered with a sliding lid. When she tried to push it open, she realized that it was held in place by a string that disappeared inside the box. She called for help. A colleague cut the string, opened the box, and saw two explosive charges connected to a detonator. Bomb disposal specialists found that had the box been opened as it was designed, its explosive power would have most likely killed all staff members present and destroyed the large room. It turned out that Zenkl and Masaryk had each received a similar deadly present. Zenkl's staff found the box suspicious and called the police; Masaryk's "perfume bomb" was intercepted en route.[70]

Thus far, terrorist violence was unheard of in Czech political culture. Since Steinhardt was not in Prague, Chargé Yost reported the event to Washington, predicting it was bound to increase the bitterness among the competing political parties, since two of the three targets (Zenkl and Drtina) were among the democratic notables denounced by the Communists as "reactionaries and enemies of the people."[71]

Communist propaganda had never been subtle, but what it churned out in the aftermath of these assassination attempts was astonishing. Slánský attacked those who asked whether there was a connection between the bombs and Communists as "agents of international reaction." He escalated the campaign further by asserting that the perfume bombs and Reichstag fire in Germany in 1933 were similar anti-Communist provocations. Those suggesting that the CPC was behind the boxes, Slánský implied, were just like Hitler.[72]

The party propaganda machine could hardly have been more explicit in denying any responsibility for the three acts of terrorism. But the Communist-dominated police force seemed lost as it proceeded to investigate the affair. It claimed to have deployed no less than four hundred investigators. They analyzed the wrapping paper and traced it to a manufacturer who, unfortunately, supplied its wares to half the country. The string was studied under a microscope, but whatever discoveries were made led nowhere. Then the authorities asserted that they had identified the man who had made the boxes, and that he had confessed. The announcement had to be quickly withdrawn as groundless. In fact, no one was identified, no one confessed. Finally, a box of explosives was found and linked with those used in the three boxes. Like the alleged manufacturer of the three boxes, this also proved to be a diversion.[73]

The CPC bosses seemed surprisingly reticent in their private dealings with the democratic ministers. When the government met, Zenkl, Drtina, and Masaryk expected that the prime minister and minister of the interior would denounce this act of terrorism. With their eyes glued to the floor, the Communist ministers acted as if the event had never taken place. Only after Beneš had written personal letters to the three ministers did the government follow suit. Yet it did so with a text so evasive and illogical that Drtina began to entertain the idea that the boxes were sent by a Communist outfit. Finally, a gutsy journalist asked who stood to profit from the outrage. The CPC claimed that the culprit must have been a "reactionary," i.e., a democrat. If so, why did he target three democrats and not Gottwald, Nosek, and Kopecký?[74]

The police seemed ready to give up in early October 1947, when Minister of Justice Drtina learned that a credible source had recognized the boxes shown in the newspapers. He contacted the intrepid wartime resistance leader Vladimír Krajina and a trusted subordinate, Zdeněk Marjanko, who followed the link and determined that the boxes were made by a CPC member who acted on orders from high-ranking regional party bosses, including Alexej Čepička, a CPC deputy and future son-in-law of Klement Gottwald.[75] Other individuals involved in the perfume affair included a CPC deputy, a Communist mayor, and other party activists. On November 18, 1947, with ironclad evidence in hand, Krajina formally charged the suspects at the district court in Olomouc. The authorities could not ignore this legal submission. Several suspects were arrested, and the majority confessed that they had acted on instructions from their party bosses. The investigators also found out that the regional CPC bureau had several illegal weapons caches.

The democratic press celebrated this breakthrough in the investigation and eagerly waited for the culprits to be identified by name. Gottwald was desperate and ready for extreme measures. He invited Drtina and Stránský to his quarters and, without preliminaries, asked Minister of Justice Drtina to suppress all further investigation into the affair. Drtina icily declined. Gottwald sank into prolonged silence, then exploded: "Drtina, I'm telling you, you'll end up just like van der Lubbe." For the prime minister to bring up the fate of the man the Nazis charged with the Reichstag fire in 1933 was shocking. Drtina was speechless. He was grateful that his colleague Stránský quickly jumped in: "Prime Minister, what are you saying? Who would then play the role of Göring? That would be Nosek?! Yes?!"[76]

Just as the Marshall Plan reversal represented a point of no return in Czechoslovak foreign policy, so the bombs marked the breakup of the domestic alliance. The democrats gave up their illusions about coexisting with the Communist Party, and the Communists, who were caught red-handed, faced monumental embarrassment. Gottwald realized that he would have to overturn the entire political system to suppress the affair altogether.

The U.S. embassy had initially paid little attention to the perfume drama. Chargé Yost had predicted in September 1947 that the lethal boxes had been sent by "some crank."[77] But at the end of November Steinhardt conceded that "Communist Party members were probably directly implicated."[78] In January 1948, Minister Drtina analyzed the affair before the parliament. His evidence proved that the perpetrators were all members of the CPC who acted on orders from their superiors. Drtina demonstrated that the reason why it had taken so long for the investigators to solve the puzzle had nothing to do with the criminals' sophistication. It was caused instead by the security officials—all CPC members—who had deliberately mismanaged the investigation.[79] The U.S. embassy eventually reported there was proof that the acts of terror had been carried out by important CPC members and that the party had done its best to suppress this fact.[80]

In the fall of 1947 the CPC was included as a founding member in the Cominform (Communist Information Bureau) that the Kremlin created for the Yugoslav, Bulgarian, Romanian, Hungarian, Polish, Czechoslovak, and also Italian and French parties. Posing as a forum for "coordinating" the Communist movement, it was an instrument for consolidating Moscow's gains in Europe and imposing discipline within the Soviet realm. Some saw the Cominform as Moscow's reaction to the Marshall Plan, until new archival evidence proved that the intention to establish it predated Secretary Marshall's speech at Harvard.[81]

George Kennan analyzed the new organization for Under Secretary Robert A. Lovett and noted that Western pressure forced Moscow to choose between two alternatives. It could either retain its popularity among Western liberals and watch discipline in the Communist bloc erode, or it could tighten discipline and lose popular support. Moscow chose the latter. The creation of the Cominform, Kennan argued, meant that the Kremlin bosses planned to "seize" Czechoslovakia "by strong-arm tactics" in the course of a few months.[82] There is no trace in the archives of any attempt in the Department of State to question the gap between the position taken by the sharp Kennan and the optimistic predictions coming out of the embassy in Prague. The two camps simply continued their parallel lives.

While the CPC was being woven into the fabric of the Cominform, the Communist-controlled Ministry of the Interior demonstrated some of the strong-arm methods Kennan had in mind. It announced that the security organs had found evidence of a conspiracy in Slovakia that could be traced to the highest levels of the Democratic Party (DS). Minister Nosek alleged that the plotters had formed armed units bent on sabotage, political assassinations, and pro-Nazi propaganda. He asserted that the DS shielded fascist and other disreputable elements. That was highly convenient, because this party had won the May 1946 elections in Slovakia, defeating the Slovak Communists. The DS leaders were arrested, even though Nosek was unable to present any evidence against them. Claiming that the ship of state had been saved at the last moment, the Ministry of the Interior detained some eighty people, then suddenly 237. The number grew to 380 and eventually up to about seven hundred.[83] The CPC had eliminated a major rival.

The Schönborn Palace followed the "conspiracy" in Slovakia closely. Steinhardt and Chargé Yost initially reported that the CPC bosses had "decided to make use of the secret police to intimidate their political opponents, beginning with the Slovak Democrats." The ambassador still thought Gottwald to be a "moderate" who had intended to win the next elections by "relatively democratic means." But after the Marshall Plan fiasco, Steinhardt surmised, Moscow decided to bring Prague "into complete subservience to the Kremlin as rapidly as possible."[84]

Steinhardt got it right—finally—but the change in tone of his and Yost's most recent reports occurred too late to make much of a difference in Washington. When military attaché Colonel Michela requested more staff for his office, the Intelligence Division in the Pentagon agreed, on the grounds that Czechoslovakia was "very friendly to the United States, and [presented] a broad base along the periphery of the 'iron curtain' from which an observation post could operate most successfully."[85] One wonders how it was possible for the Intelligence Division of the Pentagon to be so uninformed.

At the beginning of October 1947 Steinhardt warned that Moscow probably intended to impose its will upon Prague once and for all. After a week, he changed his mind. No evidence of the alleged conspiracy in Slovakia was made public, but he was inclined to think that the CPC must have had "some proof." Even if it turned out to be less than conclusive, Steinhardt said, it might justify the measures taken against the DS. Yet again he thought that a compromise between the CPC and the democratic parties could be achieved.[86] Gottwald's current public speeches provided sufficient grounds to abandon such hopes. For instance, the CPC boss warned that "reactionaries," i.e., democrats, dreamt about the "good old days when they were the masters and exploiters." But all traces of that era would be "mercilessly suppressed and stamped out."[87] Obviously, these were not the words of someone who wished to maintain a spirit of cooperation with the democrats.

From his time in Moscow the ambassador understood that "evidence" of criminal wrongdoing by political opponents could be manufactured. Yet he adopted the view that the blows aimed at the Slovak democrats were necessary, because the Democratic Party was in great "need of a housecleaning."[88] Consequently, it seemed to Steinhardt that by early November 1947 everything had again returned to normal. He believed that the CPC was focused on the next elections and that the resistance of the democratic parties to Communist machinations was vigilant and firm. All was calm in Czechoslovakia, the Steinhardt embassy was pleased to report. The Communists were probably going to achieve "some political gains" as a consequence of the crisis in Slovakia but it was unlikely that they would "succeed in what must have been their original intention—to take over the government."[89] The truth was that the CPC had no intention of using the crisis in Slovakia as a pretext to carry out a coup d'état. It was a preparatory step in that direction.

On November 12, 1947, the ambassador asserted that the situation in Slovakia would be solved by a compromise that was "far more acceptable to the Democrats than to the Communists."[90] He persisted in this optimistic mode to the end: "The total solution of the Slovak crisis . . . is in fact a severe setback for the Communists."[91] Was it? The president of the governing body in Slovakia was the arch-Communist Gustáv Husák, later immortalized by Milan Kundera as the "president of forgetting."

There was in fact some good news. The Social Democrats held their congress in the middle of November 1947, and the pro-Moscow Zdenko Fierlinger, whose main ambition was to hitch the Social Democratic Party wagon to the CPC engine, was removed from the top position in the party. He was replaced by Bohumil Laušman, a man of socialist convictions but no Russian stooge; the final vote was 280 to 182.[92] Steinhardt had been saying for some time that if the rule of secret ballot could be obtained, the defeat of the Soviet agent Fierlinger was a "foregone conclusion."[93] The democratic press welcomed Laušman's victory as a gain for the parties committed to democracy. As was to be expected, *Rudé Právo* was disappointed.[94]

The Communists had another reason to be concerned. A series of student government elections that took place in November 1947 at Charles University in Prague and universities in Hradec Králové, Pilsen, and Brno, as well as various technical colleges, resulted in a stinging setback for the Communists. The National Socialists won with 37 percent; the People's Party came in an unexpected second with 28 percent; and the Communists were third with 20 percent, followed by Social Democrats (9 percent) and nonaffiliated candidates (6 percent). The performance of democratic candidates was especially impressive because they had to withstand harassment from CPC demagogues.[95] The elections—a harbinger of young peoples' attitudes—surprised the party chiefs, who thought of students as a source of strength for the CPC; it was a bad omen for Gottwald, who had gone on record with his desire for the Party to win the 1948 elections with 51 percent of the vote.[96]

Encouraged, Beneš invited Steinhardt to see him at the castle on November 20, 1947. The ambassador was pleased to note that, although there were some traces of the stroke he had suffered in July, the president seemed fit. Beneš told his visitor that he was more than pleased with Fierlinger's defeat. He went on to say that the Communist attack on the political system had been defeated and the balance of power restored. Beneš also brought up the topic he knew to be close to Steinhardt's heart: the lingering case of restitutions for nationalized American property. He assured the ambassador that he had reminded the government of this outstanding obligation. Gottwald had apparently replied that "the matter would be given immediate attention and that all the ministries would be instructed to seek prompt settlement." Throughout the audience, Beneš demonstrated a hostile attitude toward the CPC and concluded by expressing the hope that the U.S. government "would succeed in its efforts to restore tranquility to the troubled world."[97]

Looking at the international scene in the fall of 1947, the *New York Times* found the Western strategy for dealing with the Soviet Union in Eastern Europe to be unimaginative, barren, and a failure. Cyrus L. Sulzberger warned that all the allied hopes and pledges, including those made at Yalta, had been thwarted by Stalin. The Americans and the British based their dealings with Moscow on the fact that, disagreeable though it was, the Russian Communists resided on the same planet, and everyone simply had to coexist. This led the Western allies to "concessions." Yet this policy had borne nothing but "withered fruit." The last remaining democrat in the Polish government, Stanisław Mikołajczyk, had barely managed to escape from the country. Czechoslovakia was the one outstanding sliver of land not "fully tamed to the Soviet pattern."[98] By now even the perpetually optimistic Beneš allowed the possibility of defeat. He stressed that Prague merely sought to find a balance between "economic coordination," that is, socialism, and "individual freedom." If this were to fail, then the Czechoslovak experiment was lost and both the United States and the Soviet Union would have to pursue a destructive arms race and face prolonged conflict.[99]

Once again many eyes turned toward the American team at the Schönborn Palace only to find that no one was at home. On November 23, 1947, Steinhardt announced that he was going to the United States.[100] He left the next day and arrived in New York City on December 4. He spoke briefly with the press on arrival, said nothing about his post in Prague and immersed himself in the business of the law firm on Pine Street. Admittedly, he took a brief trip to Washington; he saw Ambassador Slávik on December 19, 1947, and complained, according to Slávik, that the U.S. government and media failed to understand Czechoslovakia and Gottwald, for whom he had respect.[101]

By leaving his post at this time, Steinhardt again demonstrated that his private interests trumped his commitment to public service. It was his third prolonged absence from the embassy, and it would last almost three months. From January 1947 to February 1948 he was away from the embassy for some two hundred days.

While Steinhardt sailed across the Atlantic, events accelerated in Prague. Stalin doubled the originally promised 200,000 tons of wheat that the Soviet Union had agreed to deliver to Czechoslovakia.[102] Just before Christmas, the U.S. embassy in Prague announced that it had broken off all negotiations with the Czechs regarding American movies and none would be shown in the future.[103] With commitment and focus on the matter, Steinhardt could have protected the interests of Hollywood as well as the Czech public, which was hungry for glimpses of America. Instead, he had left it in the hands of junior staff and walked away. Finally, an opinion poll in Germany found that at the end of 1947 Germans preferred Nazism to Communism by a very wide margin.[104] This headline alone brought countless new members to the ranks of the CPC.

At the beginning of 1947 many in Washington had still believed that a conciliatory path with Stalin could be found. By the end of the year the optimistic camp had shrunk significantly, and knowledgeable observers expected that Soviet pressure on the existing balance of power in Europe's center would increase further.[105]

Prominent among the pessimists was Secretary of State Marshall. In his memorandum for Truman he predicted that Moscow "will probably have to clamp down on Czechoslovakia, for a relatively free Czechoslovakia could become a threatening salient in Moscow's political position."[106] Marshall's analysis, based on common sense and military experience, offered more insight into the crisis in Prague than American diplomats and intelligence personnel based in the city provided. It is an indictment of Steinhardt that the secretary of state, a man who had spent no time in Prague, should have come up with a more accurate assessment of the crisis than Schönborn Palace personnel with doctorates, language skills, and confidential sources at the highest ranks of the government. In its daily summary of December 23, 1947, the newly created Central Intelligence Agency embraced Marshall's perspective. It warned that as early as January 1948 the Communists might "make every effort to achieve their objectives in Czechoslovakia by constitutional rather than extralegal means."[107] Yet at this crucial moment Steinhardt was absent from his post.

# || 10 ||

# The Communists Exchange Popularity for Absolute Power

Following tradition, Edvard Beneš addressed the country on Christmas Eve 1947 with a speech that was carried live on the radio in every corner of the country. Many households tuned in, wishing for a soothing assurance that 1948 would bring peace and continued economic recovery. They were disappointed. In the past, Beneš had always accentuated the positive, but this time his tone was mournful. He was clearly worried and depressed.[1]

Steinhardt's continued absence became painfully obvious on the first day of 1948. As the dean of the diplomatic corps in Prague, the American ambassador was required to lead the accredited envoys in a formal ceremony at the castle. Since he was in New York, his deputy—the Soviet ambassador—was pleased to fulfill his duty. And then another problem arose: no sooner did the New Year arrive than fresh rumors circulated about Beneš's health. Cyrus Sulzberger reported the insiders' view that although the president seemed to be well, he was actually seriously ill. This caused much concern, he wrote, because the president's condition was "of prime importance to the balance of power in Europe."[2]

Washington had been hearing from other posts that the president's health was declining rapidly, and its embassy in Prague had reported an unconfirmed rumor that he had chosen his successor ad interim.[3] Soon the Schönborn Palace revised its view. In late January 1948 the embassy stated that Beneš was unwell but warned that reports regarding his imminent collapse were exaggerated.[4] This did not stop the speculation, and Beneš decided to do something about it. He sent his wife, Hana, to call on Mrs. Steinhardt at the Petschek residence. After pleasantries, Mrs. Beneš, a charming blonde with a gentle smile, dismissed her husband's most recent medical emergency in the summer as a simple case of sunstroke that had been complicated by a case of vertigo. The latter could cause occasional embarrassment, but overall her husband was in "reasonably normal health." The two diplomatic wives then moved from the medical field to politics. Mrs. Beneš brought good news. She thought the 1948 election campaign would be tough and bitterly contested. But her husband believed, she told Mrs. Stein-hardt, that the CPC would decline by 5 or 10 percent in comparison with 1946, and he was hopeful that the next prime minister would not be a Communist. The embassy found such expectations to be largely accurate.[5]

While he was in New York, Steinhardt was kept informed by Chargé Bruins, whose reports dealt with various property claims and offered anecdotes from the political scene and tidbits from the American community. Occasionally, Bruins also addressed serious matters. He noted, for instance, that the CPC had launched an effective campaign claiming that while the Red Army was racing to save Prague from the SS in May 1945, the Americans were playing baseball in Pilsen. This was a distorted version of what had happened, and Bruins thought it would be a good idea to declassify the documents showing that Generals Mar-shall, Eisenhower, Bradley, and Patton had stopped the troops as a result of ex-plicit Soviet demands. But it was unlikely that such sensitive documents would be cleared for publication any time soon.[6]

On a different occasion in January, Bruins conceded that there were "the usual number of rumors and alarms." Some of the pessimists, such as Georges Bidault in Paris, thought that a Communist coup d'état would take place in Prague within weeks. But Bruins, doggedly following Steinhardt's line of argu-ment, was completely blasé. He had no feeling of "any dire impending events hanging over our heads."[7] Such news only encouraged the ambassador in his erroneous view that events in Czechoslovakia were under control and he was not needed.

At the end of January, there was correspondence between the Schönborn Pal-ace in Prague and Pine Street in New York regarding "rifle cartridges suitable for a Winchester rifle of 30-06 caliber with soft nosed bullets for deer shooting." Two weeks later, when the Prague political scene was on the verge of a civil war, Bruins informed Steinhardt in New York that the embassy and the residence were in need of new linoleum.[8]

American journalists stationed in Prague did not have the same means for gathering information as U.S. Foreign Service and intelligence officers. But what they knew from open sources gave them pause. In late January 1948, the *New York Times* reported that the electoral campaign in Prague had started with full force, and the parliamentary debates were more violent than ever.[9] One of the points of contention involved the perfume box bombs.[10] The CPC denounced Drtina, Krajina, and their allies as reactionaries and conspirators. *Čas*, the peri-odical published by the Democratic Party in Slovakia, was suppressed alto-gether.[11] The small island of democratic media shrank to a handful of dailies—all handicapped by paper shortages. The picture was bleak. Even Beneš thought so. When he received Drtina on the afternoon of Friday, January 23, 1948, he expressed the view that a clash between the CPC and democrats was imminent and its outcome would determine the future of the country. He then told his guest that if the two democratic parties decided to resign from the government, he would seize the opportunity to enter the political scene on their side. He warned Drtina that the coming clash was going to be "bad, very bad." The minister agreed and told the president that he would rather put his life on the line than watch freedom being lost without a fight.[12]

At this point Bruins and the Schönborn Palace had no inkling of how serious the crisis had become. The chargé reported that the electoral campaign had not even started, and he chose this time to unveil his plan for strengthening the "very friendly pro-Western sentiment" in Czechoslovakia. Offering a loan at this late stage might seem cheap, Bruins conceded. Instead he proposed a "quick Commercial Treaty or a Cultural Treaty or both." Such measures would show, he wrote Steinhardt in New York, "that we do not intend to 'desert' this country." But it would not commit the United States to anything. It would amount to no more than a "lot of nice words."[13]

On January 28, 1948, Bruins submitted a polished-up version of this "plan" to the Department of State. He argued that 80 percent of Czechs favored Western democracy over Soviet Communism but were too timid to express their views. To make it easier for them, Bruins suggested that Washington quickly negotiate a commercial agreement and a cultural convention. He thought that this would involve a minimal risk to the United States while contributing to the task of "containing" Communism in Czechoslovakia.[14] Secretary Marshall responded with his own ideas, which included offering stipends for Czech students.[15] It was obvious that competing with Stalin over Czechoslovakia would take a little more than this.

And so it happened that the only good news in January 1948 came from the figure skating championships held in Prague. Dick Button, the eighteen-year-old sensation from New Jersey, won by a wide margin. His popularity may have had to do with the double Axel that he introduced for the first time earlier that year. But in Prague he was cheered and admired because he was an American, and his performance exuded that freedom and creativity that many Czechs believed came naturally to those who were lucky enough to have been born in the United States.[16]

When Steinhardt took over the embassy in 1945, he requested more staff. Paradoxically, newly minted Foreign Service officers descended on Prague at a time when Steinhardt's own interest in diplomacy had declined. But arrive they did, and the embassy that had had only two active Foreign Service officers in the summer of 1945 (Klieforth and Bruins) would boast a staff of more than two hundred men and women two years later.

For some of the young diplomats, such as Nathaniel Davis, the Steinhardt embassy was the beginning of their careers in the U.S. Foreign Service. They were disappointed by the ambassador's long absences, but they remained with the Department of State for many years.[17] Others, however, found their experience at the Schönborn Palace so discouraging that they decided to go into entirely different professions.[18]

Ralph S. Saul was one new arrival. He had been a student at the University of Chicago when he was drafted into the Navy after Pearl Harbor. He served in the Southwest Pacific, taking part in some of the deadliest battles in the theater under General Douglas MacArthur; he was lucky to survive when his ship was badly damaged by a kamikaze attack. Saul left the Navy in 1946 and passed the Foreign Service examination; the whole process took only three weeks. When he discovered he was going to Prague, he thought that it could have been worse.

In short order Saul reached Le Havre, then on to Paris and Prague, where he arrived in December 1947. There had been no training whatsoever before his departure. No one had mentioned Beneš to him, let alone Gottwald and Slánský. What Saul knew about the Soviet system had been derived from Arthur Koestler's *Darkness at Noon*, which he had read while in the Pacific. Looking back he could only say that "all in Washington were naïve about Communism."

When the new third secretary of the U.S. embassy disembarked in Prague, the air was heavy, damp, and smelled of coal. Only a few lights guided him on the way to the nearby Alcron Hotel. There was no one to receive him at the Schönborn Palace the next day. Steinhardt was in New York, and the embassy seemed deserted. Saul eventually found a desk for himself, sat down, and wondered how he was expected to write reports on the political situation that he knew nothing about. Therefore he asked to be assigned to the visa section, where he served under a fellow war veteran, Thomas A. Donovan. Following his advice, Saul quickly found an apartment to rent. After only a few days, he came home from work and found himself facing two burly Czech plain-clothes officers who were in the process of examining his possessions. They blushed, murmured something, and left in a hurry.

Soon people he had never met would press into his hands papers filled with words and numbers he did not understand. Some would do so on the street; others came to his door. It was impossible to tell who was doing this in an effort to assist America and who wanted to plant secrets in his pocket in order to entrap him. No one at the Schönborn Palace had given him any guidance. Compared with the combat he had survived in the Pacific, the spying game seemed to be a joke. But he took seriously the warning of his friend Donovan that what seemed like a thrilling diversion to the Americans was deadly serious to the Czechs. Nevertheless, Saul became a go-between for papers purloined from a high-ranking Czech Army general. He thought the people involved "incredibly naïve; they were endangering their lives." But he passed what he had received to Spencer Taggart, feeling uneasy about his role in the scheme.

Saul tried to use his time in Prague constructively, but living under the pressure of secret police agents bothered him, and he was appalled to discover that "our CIA was even more amateurish" than the StB. He was unhappy about the embassy's political section. Its lack of commitment, focus, and professionalism were obvious to him, a complete beginner. He applied to Yale Law School and was delighted to be admitted. Leaving Prague in the fall of 1948, he thought, "I hope I'm never coming back."[19]

In contrast to Saul, other young Americans who came to the Steinhardt embassy between 1947 and early 1948 were deeply affected by the experience. Louise Schaffner spent only twenty months at the Schönborn Palace, but for years to come she was unable to listen to Bedřich Smetana's symphonies: the music brought back painful memories and was too "poignant."[20]

Schaffner graduated from Wellesley College and started working for *Life*, where she was disappointed to learn that there was no chance for her to get an overseas assignment. Her next option was the Department of State, and in the spring of 1944 she knocked on its door in the Old Executive Building. "Would

Louise Schaffner, a U.S. Foreign Service Officer in Prague, 1948. Gift from Louise Schaffner.

there be an opportunity for a woman to become a Foreign Service officer?" she inquired. The bureaucrats in the personnel office were aghast. Female typists, secretaries, and assistants of all kinds were common in the Foreign Service. But a female Foreign Service officer? After much consulting, Schaffner received a somewhat encouraging answer: "Conceivably." But there was a catch. Because of the war, the Foreign Service examination was not being offered. Therefore, Schaffner arrived at her first post, Madras, India, as a temporary vice-consul in December 1944.

As soon as the war ended, Schaffner took the exam and advanced to the second round. There she faced Joseph Green, director of the Foreign Service Board of Examiners and a man many aspiring diplomats feared. He was friendly but paternalistic: "Is this a job for a woman?" he inquired. "Won't you be led to a frivolous life-style?" The young woman managed to soothe his fears, and in September 1947 she was sworn as a Foreign Service Officer.

When she learned that she would serve in Prague and no training would be offered, she made every effort to educate herself about the country. Having read all relevant books and newspaper articles she could find, she went in December 1947 to speak with the staff of the Czechoslovak desk at the Department. In light of what she had read, she was astonished to discover that the desk officers were "very optimistic." They had heard so often from Steinhardt that the country was a "solid bridge" between the two blocs that they had failed to register the cracks that had appeared in its pillars. Schaffner thought that the specialists were on "autopilot" and that "the country was riding high on its prewar reputation." The experts told her that Czechoslovakia was "democratic and prosperous." She did not know what to expect.

Accompanied by her mother and wearing the latest Chanel dress, Schaffner arrived in Prague on January 10, 1948. The ladies were directed to the bleak Alcron Hotel, which reminded them of a college dormitory. When the new third secretary went to work at the Schönborn Palace the next day, January 11, 1948, she was surprised by its tranquil atmosphere. Without Steinhardt to stir things up it was quiet and sleepy. The young woman found nothing "to shake you in your boots."[21] After she had introduced herself to her colleagues, she inquired about the current situation. "There is no evidence of anything untoward," Chargé Bruins assured her. Schaffner did not believe him, but she found only one person who shared her premonition, Labor Attaché Milton Fried. He was well read and educated, and while other Americans socialized with the titled and the wealthy, his main contacts were among trade unionists. He believed that the CPC was about to seize absolute power.

In short order, Schaffner met Colonel Katek, Walter Birge, Reinhold Pick, and other lively personalities in the embassy, and this improved the gloomy first impression. Her colleagues were surprised how much she had learned about

Prague before she arrived. Using his vast network of well-to-do friends, Katek arranged for the Schaffner ladies to rent a beautiful apartment with a view of the Vltava river, the Charles Bridge, and the Prague Castle.

From the beginning, the Czech secret police surrounded the Schaffners with informers. Some of the staff the American women hired for their household were agents when they applied for the job. Some were not, and they were befriended by young StB agents who then blackmailed them into cooperation. They regularly searched their employers' private possessions and kept a record of all visitors and their opinions—mostly guessing, because their knowledge of English was minimal. Archival documents show that, unlike many of her colleagues, Louisa Schaffner was well aware of the hostile environment in which she worked. When she was accompanied home by LIST, an StB agent posing as a love-stricken adorer, she alerted him to the presence of several undercover agents following them and asked him, as if *en passant*, whether he too worked for the police. The agents' reports reveal how absurd and twisted life in Prague had become: the operation against Schaffner was run by an StB unit called 701-A; its chief was a comrade named 10/SA; and the agent who controlled LIST was called AK.[22] It is worth remembering that when the Communists surrounded Schaffner with this elaborate network of informers inside and outside her household, she was merely a third secretary in the U.S. Foreign Service, one of the lower ranks of the American diplomatic hierarchy.

In early January 1948 the enterprising Vladimír Krajina discovered that the Communists had learned from a secret opinion poll that they were likely to get only 28 percent in the elections scheduled for the spring. This would be highly embarrassing for them, since Gottwald and Slánský had publicly promised to win at least 51 percent.[23] Krajina believed that the CPC escalated the crisis because it feared it might decline to 28 percent.[24] Even if it were to win the election, which was not certain, such a victory would amount to a defeat. Krajina was not alone in thinking along such lines. Beneš thought the CPC would get 5 or 10 percent less than in 1946, which would be 28 to 33 percent, and Chancellor Smutný confirmed that a secret opinion poll in January 1948 indicated that the combined democratic voters might win the coming elections.[25] Some Americans shared this view. Walter Birge wrote that the CPC "was fearful of losing votes in the election," and Nathaniel Davis stated that it was "clear that the Communist Party would lose the elections in 1948."[26] Secretary of State Marshall believed that the CPC stood to lose "at least eight percent" in the next elections, in comparison to May 1946.[27]

For the party to regain popularity by political means was certainly not simple, and it might have already become impossible. Under such circumstances, the CPC strategists realized that they would have to resort to power, in which case the security apparat would play a central role. Luckily for them, the Ministry of the Interior was under the command of Václav Nosek, a party member since 1921. In addition to the top post in the Ministry, the CPC gradually filled many other positions with Communists. Any attempt by the democrats to criticize and reverse this policy was met with loud denials and counterattacks. In most cases, democratic politicians retreated.

But reality could not be ignored forever. On Friday, February 13, 1948, Minister Drtina informed the government that StB agents Müller and Kroupa, posing as "Edy" and "Tony," operatives of an American intelligence service, had tried to entrap regional democratic politicians in a conspiracy.[28] They approached several officials and asked for help hiding weapons and explosives that were supposedly smuggled into the country from the West in preparation for a coup d'état. In addition to being illegal, the method of using agents provocateurs was all the more repugnant because it was copied from the playbook of the Gestapo. Gottwald refused to allow any discussion of this report on the grounds that Minister Nosek was absent. While the meeting was still in progress, Drtina learned an additional fact: Nosek had dismissed eight police officials whose only flaw was that they did not belong to the CPC. The majority of the government passed a resolution instructing the minister to stop treating the police as an instrument of his party and to reverse the illegal dismissals. Only the Communists opposed it; even the fence-sitting Social Democrats supported it.[29] To lose a vote, especially one involving national security, was novel to the CPC.

Some surmised that the democrats forced the vote in order to bring about early elections so that they would profit from the favorable trend revealed by the public opinion poll. The Communist press protested against this "complot" of democratic parties.[30] There is no evidence to support this speculation. The memoirs of all the leading democratic politicians reveal that they stumbled into the confrontation completely unprepared. Drtina and his friends acted on the spur of the moment and out of ethical principle, not tactical calculation.[31]

According to another theory, the democrats decided to take a stand on the personnel issue at the Ministry of the Interior on the recommendation of Western diplomats.[32] That was impossible. Ambassador Steinhardt was not at his post, and Bruins did not believe that a crisis existed. British ambassador Sir Pierce J. Dixon did. He told Drtina on January 20, 1948, that London expected the CPC to establish a dictatorship—soon. Drtina inquired whether his guest had any evidence. Dixon nodded but did not present it and offered no further opinion.[33] French prime minister Robert Schuman and Ambassador Maurice Dejean in Prague had information that a CPC coup d'état was to be expected on or around February 15, 1948. However, they never led anyone in Prague to believe that France would become involved in the imminent crisis.[34]

Czechoslovak intelligence worked exclusively for the CPC during the crisis. It kept the party bosses accurately informed that neither Washington nor anyone else would take action if the Communists escalated the crisis and established a monopoly on power.[35] Gottwald therefore decided to ignore the resolution passed by the majority of his ministers and waited for the democrats' next move. He knew that their options were few. Nosek was instructed by the CPC to come down with a case of diplomatic influenza, and he stopped appearing in public. Gottwald used his absence as a pretext for not putting the resolution regarding the fired police officials back on the government's agenda. The last meeting of the government, on February 17, 1948, degenerated into a row. The democrats demanded a restoration of the dismissed police chiefs, but Gottwald and the other Communists refused to discuss the matter. The tension escalated when one of the Communist ministers physically attacked Zenkl. In the midst of the commotion, Gottwald accused the democrats of preparing a coup d'état. He then gathered his papers and left the room. The meeting was over. That government would never meet again.

The U.S. embassy's record during the decisive first half of February 1948 is not impressive. In Steinhardt's absence, Chargé Bruins reported on February 5, 1948, that the election campaign was getting "into full swing."[36] There was no evidence, Bruins assured the Department of State, that the Communists intended to skip the elections altogether.[37] The word "crisis" appeared in Bruin's reports only on February 18, 1948, and then as "impending." The chargé described the events accurately, but he failed to realize that the political parties could no longer work together.[38]

Ambassador Steinhardt set off for Prague in the middle of February 1948. On the boat from New York to Europe, fellow passengers heard him say that "the Communists would never be able to take power by force because the roots of democracy were too deep in Czechoslovakia." This reached the journalist Marquis W. Childs, who used the quotation as evidence that the ambassador had but a superficial understanding of the crisis. The ambassador insisted he was misquoted.[39]

In Paris Steinhardt stopped to visit his colleague Ambassador Jefferson Caffery. According to a report by Czechoslovak intelligence, Steinhardt assured him that people in Czechoslovakia were fed up with Communism, that Beneš was going to maneuver the CPC out of the government, and that Czechoslovakia would join the Marshall plan. No one at the U.S. embassy in Paris agreed with this analysis. The document gives no hint as to how this information was obtained, but the views expressed therein correspond closely with the written text of Steinhardt's talk on the Czechoslovak situation that he gave at the National War College in Washington in November 1947.[40]

On Thursday, February 19, 1948, Steinhardt flew from Paris to Prague. Chargé Bruins, Colonel Katek, Consul Bogardus, and other Americans who came to Ruzyně to welcome him sensed that the airport personnel were nervous. Katek went to see one of his informers, a Pan Am manager, who told him that Steinhardt's flight from Paris was still in the air, but that the one from Moscow had landed.[41] On board was Valerian Zorin, the first Soviet ambassador in postwar Prague (1945–47) and Stalin's diplomatic fixer du jour. Uninvited and unexpected, he simply appeared, and the news of his arrival spread like wildfire throughout the city. The emissary came ostensibly to supervise the delivery of Soviet grain and to attend a Czechoslovak-Soviet friendship ceremony. But his arrival had the same impact as the landing of a Soviet airborne division on the outskirts of Prague.

The timing could not have been more political. The visit reminded the democratic parties that they would have to take on the Kremlin, the Red Army, and the Soviet intelligence services if they wished to defeat the CPC. From Gottwald's perspective, the Zorin visit presented a complex dilemma. On the one hand, the CPC could not be certain it had prepared for all the possible scenarios; a coup d'état is always a messy affair. This is why the party longed for a credible sign of Stalin's support. Even a hint would have signaled to Czechoslovakia's Western supporters to stay out of the coming fight. On the other hand, the Communists hoped to create the appearance that they had won on their own. Few in Eastern Europe admired Russian political culture, and no one thought of the Soviet Union as a model of openness and the rule of law. Gottwald and other CPC bosses hoped to grab power, but not while holding Stalin's hand. They feared it would deprive them of legitimacy. This is why Gottwald is rumored to have made a disparaging remark when he heard that Zorin was in town. He met with him but amid minimal publicity.

What exactly transpired at the meeting is not clear. The traditional view holds that Gottwald felt he was in full control of the situation and wanted the Kremlin to stay away. Evidence from Russian archives disproves this speculation. According to Zorin, the CPC leaders were "fantastically scared" and very concerned about the legal connotations of their actions—a cardinal sin in Bolshevik circles. In Zorin's view, Gottwald was indecisive and uncertain. He even requested that Red Army units in Germany and Austria should conduct maneuvers along the Czechoslovak borders to bring pressure to bear on Beneš and "all those on the right." In the end, the Red Army did not need to leave the barracks. An editorial in *Pravda* on February 22, 1948, described the democratic ministers in Prague as conservative extremists whom the forces of "international reaction" used as tools to bring about chaos in the ranks of the bloc of "people's democracies." There could be no compromise with such "reactionary agents," *Pravda* warned.[42] The article told the West to stay away from the coming dénouement, and the West had no inclination to disobey.

Steinhardt knew little about any of this when he landed in Prague on February 19, 1948. Nevertheless, he stated at the airport that the political situation would likely lead to a victory for democracy and freedom, and possibly even bring Czechoslovakia back into the zone covered by the Marshall Plan.[43] His first report from Prague, dated the next day, touched on the unexpected appearance of Zorin and asserted that it was a sign that the Soviet Union was "suddenly taking a more active interest in the local situation."[44] There was nothing sudden about Moscow's concern regarding the crisis in Prague, of course. The Kremlin followed it in detail and supervised it.

On February 20, 1948, the democrats resigned from the government, claiming that the Communists were preparing a dictatorship. They had run out of options. Zenkl, Drtina, and others hoped that the government would fall and new elections would reveal the decline of CPC popularity, but that did not happen. The Social Democrats and Minister Masaryk did not join the democrats. At the decisive moment, out of twenty-six ministers, fourteen stayed and only twelve resigned. The government did not collapse, and the prime minister could start looking for different personalities to fill in the empty seats.

Many have criticized the democrats' tactics during the crisis, but Drtina was right to point out that when the Communists established their dictatorship, the choice was clear: "Either collaboration or resignation. . . . Tertium non datur [no third option exists]."[45] The democratic ministers who resigned their seats believed that they had acted with Beneš's approval. The president had received Zenkl and Ripka two days before their resignation. They described the crisis in the government and told Beneš that they might have to resign within forty-eight hours. They testified that the president indicated his full support: "The sooner you do it, gentlemen, the better."[46] He also warned them against having any illusions that the contest would be civilized. The Communists, he noted, had no scruples and were capable of great brutality. Chancellor Smutný cast doubt on some parts of the democratic ministers' testimony, but he was not present and had to rely only on the president's word.[47] Beneš told Steinhardt—via Arnošt Heidrich of the Ministry of Foreign Affairs—that he had had absolutely no advance knowledge of the ministers' plan to leave the government.[48] But if one were to pit Drtina against Beneš in a credibility contest, the former would win hands down. Steinhardt felt the same way because in his memorandum to Washington he wrote that Beneš "promised the moderate ministers that he would stand by them."[49]

In its confrontation with the democrats the CPC could rely on its own might and on Moscow's political support. The democrats were prepared to take a stand on a procedural matter, but once the contest evolved into a question of raw power, they meekly retreated into a passive stance. One episode illustrates this point. On February 20, the day the democrats resigned, Vladimír Kabeš and his wife, Otilia, were giving a dinner party for a few friends.[50] The host was a lawyer—he worked for Lockheed—a close friend of Colonel Katek and other Americans, and a landlord of the Schaffners. One of the invited guests was Foreign Minister Jan Masaryk, an old family friend. At about two in the afternoon a messenger came with a handwritten note from him—the foreign minister regretted to say he had a case of "little laryngitis," which put him "in the cradle." He hoped to be invited on a different occasion.[51] It was characteristic that Masaryk should react to the first hint of a crisis by climbing into bed; he lacked courage. The man whose great name alone would have brought masses to the streets and inspired them to defend democracy had decided to hide at home.

Masaryk was not the only one to be immobilized by a defeatist mood. Among those present at the dinner party was General Heliodor Píka, a remarkable officer with a distinguished war record. Many looked up to him as a guardian of the democratic system. After the dinner Mrs. Kabeš invited the general to look with her at the majestic panorama of the city spread out before their windows. "Isn't it beautiful?" she asked him. Then she suddenly sharpened her tone: "I'm mad that men like you are so passive," she said. "Can't you do something, finally? Are you all scared?" "My dearest," Píka replied with a benevolent smile. "I'm afraid, you're right. And I'm also sick and old. It's all over." He was only fifty-one years old. Steinhardt told Washington that Gottwald's basic strategy was to isolate the democrats.[52] He was right, and it worked. Píka, who had never abandoned a fight during the war, now considered himself defeated and helpless, although not a single shot had been fired.

On the next day, Saturday, at ten in the morning the CPC held a mass rally with Gottwald as the main speaker in the Old Town Square. The event was broadcast live throughout the country. The Communists who had organized the meeting did not suffer from the malaise displayed by Masaryk, Píka, and other democrats. Angrily spitting out his words, Gottwald urged the Communists to set up "action committees" throughout the country to guard against the so-called reactionaries. Regarding the democratic ministers who had resigned, Gottwald demanded that they be replaced with progressives. Other fiery speakers warned that the reactionaries wished to "take nationalized industries from the workers" and place them "at the feet of foreign capital."[53] The message was clear. The CPC was holding out for a legal path to absolute power, but it was ready to use force should constitutional means prove inadequate. If Masaryk had had some reason not to resign his post in the government before the rally, now there was no excuse for staying, yet he did nothing.

That Saturday evening Vladimír Kabeš went to the annual black-tie ball of the National Socialist Party in the center of Prague. Although the CPC rally in Prague and similar meetings held in other cities had involved hundreds of thousands, some of the elegant people who came to celebrate the National Socialist

Party knew nothing about it. In the ornate Smetana Hall, Kabeš met Milada Horáková, a leading democratic politician. Did he know that the democratic ministers had resigned? Horáková asked him. He did not, and he found it worrisome. "No need," she assured him, "things are under control." But then she noted in passing that some of the highest party chiefs were attending a skiing championship ten hours away from Prague.[54] Krajina, like Kabeš an impeccable source, testified that he had asked a leader of Sokol, the Czech athletic and patriotic organization, to put his men on alert. The Sokol organizer replied he could not do that because he was leaving to attend a skiing championship.[55]

The National Socialists, who had waltzed into the night or admired daring skiers, were probably still asleep early on Sunday, February 22. By contrast, the CPC bosses presided over a gathering of some eight thousand trade union leaders. They explained to the delegates that the reactionaries (i.e., democrats) intended to harm the interests of the working class. Many in the audience found this assertion plausible. The CPC had prepared for the confrontation, while the democrats walked into it casually, with their hands in their pockets. This was reflected on the streets and in the media, where the party was visibly in charge, although islands of supporters of democracy could also be found debating in the town's center.

The Communists had detailed contingency plans to keep their opponents from making use of any institution (such as the army or the parliament) against their interests. One of their great advantages was timely intelligence. This was provided by the StB, OBZ, and by the shadowy Zemský Odbor Bezpečnosti (ZOB), an intelligence apparatus under the exclusive control of the Communist Party.[56] It was primarily oriented against the democratic parties, but it also covered foreigners in Prague, especially the Americans. It produced a steady stream of reports on the U.S. Military Mission, the U.S. embassy, and Steinhardt. ZOB had an informer close to the American deputy military attaché, Lt. Col. Thomas Foote, and it had a detailed and accurate understanding of the leading personalities in the U.S. embassy.[57]

The StB, OBZ, and ZOB provided Gottwald and Slánský with insights regarding their political enemies. The democrats in contrast knew nothing about the Communists' deliberations and intentions. They could not effectively communicate even with Beneš, whom they considered the leader of their team and who—they believed—had encouraged them to challenge the Communists.

French foreign minister Georges Bidault told U.S. ambassador Caffery on February 22, 1948, that Czechoslovakia's fate was sealed. The Iron Curtain fell "with a loud thud" along the country's western border.[58] The next day Steinhardt reported snippets from the crisis: units of armed men marched in the streets of Prague; all passports were declared invalid; Zdeněk Marjanko, the Ministry of Justice official who had tracked down those responsible for the perfume bombs, was arrested and disappeared, together with many others; CPC-dominated "action committees" took over ministries, enterprises, and the media.[59]

On Monday, February 23, 1948, Beneš received Zenkl, Ripka, Drtina and Jaroslav Stránský at the castle. He told them that if Gottwald tried to force him to accept a government in which the democrats were replaced by Communists or their puppets, he would decline.[60] The scene was later described by Steinhardt: "Beneš knew that the majority of the Czechoslovak people were looking to him for guidance and for leadership, that they expected him to stand firm against the ever rising flood of Communist intimidation and terror. As yet the President showed no signs of weakening—but the sands were running out." The embassy now read the situation with accuracy: the CPC determined to seek nothing short of "complete control," regardless of what Beneš might or might not do.[61] The country became a prison.

On Tuesday, February 24, Secretary of State Marshall commented that the imminent seizure of power by the Communists in Prague would change nothing, because Czechoslovakia had been faithful to the Soviet line from the start.[62] However, he was worried that, left unchallenged, a Communist coup d'état in Prague might send the wrong signal to countries in Western Europe. He wanted to explore what options the United States, Great Britain, and France had.[63] When two French diplomats went to the Department of State to discuss Czechoslovakia, the American specialists on Central Europe told them that the events in Prague came "as a surprise to many in the Department." The discussion was long, detailed, and erudite. But the protocol could only reflect that the French "had no suggestions to make as to what might best be done." It was obvious that their American counterparts were just as helpless.[64]

At three in the morning on February 25, 1948, the CPC strategists sent a letter to Beneš stressing that the "reactionary ministers" had violated the principles of "people's democracy." Therefore the Communists would never negotiate with them. Twice that day Gottwald, Nosek, and other CPC bosses confronted Beneš at the castle. They combined threats of civil war with promises of a speedy return to the kind of politics that had been prevalent so far in the postwar era—only without the "reactionaries." Such assurances were obviously hollow, and the president knew it. He understood that the CPC had asked him to legitimize Czechoslovakia's descent into totalitarianism. The broken and defeated man accepted the list of new ministers dictated by the victorious CPC, and at five in the afternoon Gottwald addressed a large crowd on Wenceslas Square. Shouting out isolated words rather than reading full sentences of his speech, he informed the world that the president had accepted the new government without any reservations.

The Communists had won an absolute victory. For their boss, Gottwald, it was the culmination of an astonishing career. One wonders whether he cared to recall the beginning of his political life, when as a novice parliamentary deputy of the CPC in the late twenties he hurled abuses at his astonished bourgeois colleagues. They reacted with condescension and bemused laughter, and Gottwald angrily shouted: "We'll wipe those smiles off your faces soon enough! We'll fight with no regard to losses, with persistence and purpose, until we have overturned your rule."[65] Nobody believed him at the time. How could such an uncouth man seize power in a democratic country that adored its elegant president-philosopher, Thomas Masaryk? But Gottwald believed it, and he was now in a position to destroy those who had laughed at him two decades earlier.

Although the masses had cheered and applauded during the speeches by CPC bosses, they seemed confused once the show had ended.[66] Steinhardt noticed that the streets were filled with isolated and silent observers and paramilitary crowds. The people he encountered mostly struck him as being apathetic, sullen, and disoriented. He suggested that they behaved "much as they did when the Germans entered Prague" in March 1939.[67] The ambassador knew what the Czechs could only intuit: the populace would soon experience dictatorship by one party, loss of national sovereignty, murderous show trials, rule by terror, concentration camps, the end of all civic freedoms, decades of shameful mismanagement, and shortages of everything. He had seen it in Moscow.

To avoid any trouble, the party sent its armed activists to march through Prague's center to secure all public spaces. The headquarters of the democratic parties were taken over by police and militia units. Detectives, a few openly embarrassed by the task, entered the premises to seize "evidence" that the democrats had planned a coup d'état.[68] This was a standard Stalinist trick—a thief crying "Thief!" Radio Moscow announced on February 26, 1948, that "reactionary plotters had tried to establish a right-wing dictatorship in Prague." They failed thanks to the vigilance of the Communist Party.[69]

On February 27 Beneš endured one more humiliation. He received the new government chosen by Gottwald. It was especially painful to see Foreign Minister Jan Masaryk standing sheepishly in the ranks of this outfit. It was all over. Stalin could add another pearl to the necklace of countries he had seized in the aftermath of the war. "Czechoslovakia has today become a totalitarian police state under a Communist dictatorship," wrote the *New York Times*, "and the last flickering lights of freedom that shimmered through the Iron Curtain are going out." This marked the end of the system designed at Teheran and Yalta, the article continued, "in the same manner that Hitler's seizure of Czechoslovakia meant the collapse of the world of Versailles."[70] The Communist power grab in February 1948 was achieved swiftly and with minimal violence, even though in the U.S. embassy's estimation only 25 percent of the population supported it.[71]

The Americans, the British, and the French discussed what steps, if any, to take in response. They quickly admitted that protests unaccompanied by action would only underscore their weakness. Nevertheless, a joint statement was released by the three powers. As was to be anticipated, it had no impact on either the CPC or its Kremlin masters. The note merely condemned the events in Prague and predicted that the Communist takeover would be "disastrous for the Czechoslovak people." When journalists asked Secretary Marshall why the U.S. Army had stopped so close to Prague in May 1945, he said he no longer remembered the reason.[72] Gottwald was quick to dismiss expressions of Western concern for free Czechoslovakia as pathetic when coming "from those with Munich on their conscience."[73] Undeterred, Minister Bidault spoke forcefully about the Prague coup before the French assembly, repeatedly making references to the Munich Agreement, for which his country did in fact bear considerable responsibility.[74]

Even if the Communist coup d'état in Prague did not surprise Secretary Marshall, he considered it a watershed in East-West relations. He told the press that Czechoslovakia was under a "reign of terror." The situation, he warned, was "very, very serious," and he called for "urgent and resolute action" if the United States were to defend the West.[75] President Truman wrote to his daughter that he was dealing with "exactly the same situation with which Britain and France were faced in 1938–9 with Hitler. Things look black."[76]

The coup jolted Steinhardt out of his slumber. Firing multiple reports to Washington every day, he blasted the CPC with passion. In his view, "February" was the same as Munich. He saw similarities between the methods Hitler had employed in the thirties and the way the CPC had tired Beneš out and then shocked him into capitulation.[77] The ambassador portrayed the president's role generously. The Communists, he wrote, gave Beneš "no alternative than to capitulate."[78] The *New York Times* cited Gottwald's speech before the parliament in 1929 in which he declared that he learned in Moscow how to break the necks of the rich. This appeared to be one of the few promises the CPC meant seriously.[79]

On February 27, two days after the CPC's triumph, Minister Masaryk's "little laryngitis" had subsided enough that he could see Steinhardt. With tears in his eyes he explained his decision to remain "temporarily" in the new Gottwald government. He believed he could "soften the impact of Communist ruthlessness" by helping those who needed it; he asserted he had already "'saved' about 250 people," an absurd claim. He also told the ambassador that Beneš was a broken man with little time left.[80]

This at least was true. Beneš retreated to his country estate in Sezimovo Ústí, where he collapsed. The crisis had sucked out all his energy and hope, leaving the empty shell of a defeated man. Václav Černý, a scholar and member of the wartime resistance, visited him there just three weeks after the coup. "It was much worse than I expected," he recalled. Černý thought Beneš had aged twenty years. He seemed like a tiny man wearing someone else's large clothes. His face was ashen, his eyes frightened and watery. Yet he somehow found the energy to heap invectives on the Czech and Russian Stalinists, whom he had previously defended in countless debates with Western politicians and diplomats: "Liars, cheats, bastards."[81] He refused to sign the new constitution in May 1948, resigned from the presidency in June, and died in September. Just before he died, Beneš told his secretary that his greatest failure was not having recognized that Stalin had systematically lied to him from their first encounter in 1935 to the very end. All his assurances, the dying man fumed, were lies and deceptions.[82]

Masaryk's time was shorter still. He was found dead on March 10, 1948, beneath the bathroom window of his apartment in the Foreign Ministry, wearing only soiled pajamas. Excrement and pillows in the bathtub, scratches on his body and more excrement on the windowsill were possible indications of struggle. The police formally declared he had died by his own hand, but many aspects of the tragedy quickly made his death one of the persistent mysteries of the Cold War.[83]

Masaryk's death caused Secretary of State Marshall to declare only a few hours after the event that the international situation was "very, very grave." Czechoslovakia, he added, lived under a "regime of terror." But he also stressed that the American strategy would be based on cool calculation, not emotions. On March 11, 1948, President Truman admitted that he had become less optimistic that it would be possible to secure a lasting peace.[84] Washington's original position regarding the Masaryk death was that it was a mystery, but in August 1951 Truman told the new Czechoslovak ambassador in Washington Vladimír Procházka that Masaryk had been "murdered."[85] Western Europe saw Masaryk's death as a major escalation of the tension between East and West. In France, only the Communist press accepted Prague's statement that the minister had suffered from a "nervous malady." Moderates and conservatives presented the event as an outrage of totalitarianism. *Le Figaro*'s André François-Poncet denounced it as violence committed by agents who acted on behalf of a foreign power.[86]

Steinhardt initially accepted the view that the foreign minister had taken his own life.[87] He thought it "authentic," but he acknowledged that many did not.[88] He later changed his mind—somewhat. On April 7, 1948, a month after the tragedy, Steinhardt wrote that he was "less convinced" than before that Masaryk took his life. If the minister was murdered, however, it was not a "'local operation' but was undertaken by imported [i.e., Soviet] gunmen."[89] Two days later, the ambassador listed all existing theories circulating in Prague and concluded: "The rumors that Masaryk's death was involuntary should not be wholly discarded."[90] Taggart recalled that Masaryk's death shocked the public and made the mood in Prague darker still.[91] The ambassador reported the view of his fast vanishing friends that the atmosphere of fear and sense of gloom was "even greater than during the German occupation."[92]

How others died is all too clear. General Píka was hanged by the Communists in June 1949. According to the tribunal, one of his "crimes" was that he had cooperated with British intelligence during the war, without acknowledging that Great Britain was the host and principal ally of the Beneš government-in-exile. Most likely Píka, an intelligence officer, was murdered on the instigation of Soviet security because the general's reports from the wartime Soviet Union made clear he saw through the Stalinist façade. Milada Horáková, who had survived a Nazi death sentence, was executed a year after the general. They were among the first of close to 250 victims executed by the CPC for political reasons.

Drtina had told Beneš that he would rather give up his life than lose his freedom. He lived up to his promise. On February 28, 1948, he watched police and StB agents swarming around his house.[93] Having previously determined not to be taken alive, he threw himself out of the window. He survived and came to, in chains, inside a prison. He was freed only in 1960 and viciously persecuted for the rest of his life. Drtina's colleague Zdeněk Marjanko, the Ministry of Justice investigator who solved the case involving the perfume terror bombs, was never released. He died after torture and severe beatings in 1949. Such criminal behavior was made possible by the installation of Alexej Čepička, the central figure in the terrorist plot, as minister of justice. "They already had a Communist Minister of the Interior to arrest people," said a Western diplomat; "now they have a Communist Minister of Justice to execute them."[94]

Throughout the crisis in February 1948, U.S. intelligence did next to nothing. The Military Mission lost access to its sources as soon as the democratic ministers resigned. Czech special services followed Katek's every step. But when the crisis was over, none had anything to report for the simple reason that the colonel did not try to do anything worth reporting. The CPC victory marked the end of the Katek era in postwar Prague.[95] On March 18 Katek, Taub, their colleagues, and families flew out of the country, utterly defeated.[96]

Spencer Taggart's CIA section in the Schönborn Palace did nothing during the coup. When Steinhardt was in New York City, Taggart decided in early 1948 to take his wife, Ila, on a two-week motoring tour of Italy.[97] On February 25, when the Communists seized power, the Taggarts were in Rome. Incredibly, they took an additional four days before they finally approached the Czech-German border. Ila Taggart was the first to notice a long line of trucks parked on the Western side with their engines off. She cried: "Oh, no, the border is closed." And so it was, but not to those with diplomatic passports.

As soon as the Taggarts started the two-hour drive from the border to Prague, they realized the impact the putsch had made everywhere: "It was as if a gigantic funereal gloom had enclosed the entire country. There was very little traffic. It seemed we were virtually alone. The Czechs are great walkers, but this Sunday we saw only a few, their bearing was solemn and dirgeful." In the embassy Taggart could only confirm that "the whole power structure had been turned upside down and shaken out." He learned about Drtina's failed suicide and that many friends of the Americans had been arrested. Zenkl, Taggart's close comrade, was under house arrest, guarded around the clock by teams of detectives. The embassy had lost all its sources: "All contact of any significance between the Americans and the Czechs was cut off."

In early March 1948, Taggart sent his pregnant wife and daughter to the United States. Things were likely to become dangerous, and he had already had one close call. In the summer of 1947 Taggart took two women from his office—both U.S. Army reservists—for a lunch in Barrandov. They ate the same dishes but Taggart alone got deathly ill. His whole body swelled up. All his friends and colleagues suspected he had been poisoned. President Beneš's niece found a trusted doctor. He asked for a list of medications unavailable in Prague, and Steinhardt immediately had the drugs flown in from Paris. Taggart recovered, but only after being in a stupor for five or six weeks.[98]

The Katek team had departed, Taggart's intelligence section was paralyzed, and Steinhardt admitted that he was no longer able to gather information: "The embassy's reporting difficulties increased immensely as formerly well-informed contacts disappeared or ceased to be well-informed." In the course of one week, Steinhardt marveled, Czechoslovakia became "almost as isolated as Soviet Russia."[99] How could this have happened, many were asking, if some 70 percent of the population or more opposed the Communist coup d'état?[100] The experts in the Department of State and the intelligence community were left shaking their heads in disbelief. In February 1948, Czechoslovakia, the "pivot point" and "master key" of Europe, as American analysts had seen it, disappeared for a few days behind the Stalinist curtain for a change of clothes. When it came out again, it fit neatly into the political pattern Moscow had created between West Germany and Russia. The country now wore a Soviet-style uniform.

CPC boss Gottwald had successfully cut Czechoslovakia loose from its Western moorings and delivered it to the Kremlin. It is remarkable that he was able to do so with the support of a minority at home while escaping the scrutiny and wrath of the United States and the West. Of course, this was made possible by historical factors he had neither created nor controlled. Had it not been for Hitler, Munich, Stalingrad, and Stalin's victorious march through Central Europe, Gottwald would have remained an obscure alcoholic peddling extremism. But here he was—preparing to move to the Prague castle and rule the country.

Shortly after the coup Gottwald read a report by Zpravodajská služba (ZS), the CPC-controlled foreign intelligence service. It analyzed Western responses to the February takeover and predicted that, "unless seriously provoked,

[Secretary] Marshall and the State Department will not resort to any precipitous measures."[101] Since they had won a complete victory, Stalin and the CPC had no reason to do anything provocative.

The final word on the February crisis came from Steinhardt. His analysis confirmed that when he applied himself to the job, he possessed a first-rate analytical mind. He noted that the Czechs had felt "written off" by the West since 1943, when Beneš had had a noncommittal reception in Washington, in contrast to the false promises he had been getting from Moscow. Then came Yalta and the sense that Europe was divided into spheres of influence, and that the Czechs were placed on the Soviet side. This may not have been accurate, but it was confirmed—from the Czech perspective—when the U.S. Army stopped in Pilsen. "Hindsight now indicates that further attention by us to the political aspects of the war might have given us control of Central Europe at a nominal cost," wrote Steinhardt. This bold statement was addressed to Secretary Marshall who (as General Marshall) had supported Eisenhower's tendency to prosecute the final stages of the war as if it had existed outside the realm of politics.

The future of Czechoslovakia, Steinhardt knew, was hopeless. He dismissed as fanciful all plans to create a resistance organization against the Communist regime. It had no chance of success, he warned, for the simple reason that Czechoslovakia was a "police state."[102]

# 11

# The Schönborn Palace under Siege

## Americans as "Spies and Saboteurs"

The West accepted the loss of Czechoslovakia to the totalitarian behemoth calmly; it was a fait accompli. But it was a laud wakeup call, and from now on, Washington was quick to say, there would be no easy victories for the Kremlin. "The westward march of Communist totalitarianism" had to be arrested, declared an aide to General Lucius Clay, the military governor of the U.S. zone in Germany.[1] Western policymakers agreed that the United States and the Europeans had to remain united in the task of lifting Europe up from the rubble as well as in defending it against any further advances by Stalin.[2]

A problem facing Washington was that the Communist victory in Prague was not accomplished through the use of Soviet arms and could not easily be attributed to Moscow. The world could see only that the Communist Party of Czechoslovakia had made use of the democratic political system in order to destroy it. However, the form and extent of the Soviet role were debatable.

The United States had proven it could successfully respond to a massive provocation such as Pearl Harbor. It was less clear that it would know how to arrest the kind of Soviet penetration of Western Europe that had been successfully tested in Prague. Former Secretary of State James Byrnes used strong language to stress that no other country would be lassoed and pulled into the Soviet camp through subversion by local proxies. "It is our duty to let the Soviet Government know that they must not be misled by our forbearance in the case of Hungary and Czechoslovakia." Byrnes mentioned Greece and Turkey, already covered by the Truman Doctrine, and added Italy and France as countries watched over by the United States. Should the Kremlin threaten the independence of any one of these four countries, the United States would not merely "write a letter of protest." It would take action.[3]

The combined power of American diplomacy, treasure, and intelligence was mobilized in defense of those four countries, but Washington made

defensive moves also in the direction of Norway and Sweden and even projected its power into the gray zone, toward Finland. Threatening signals from
Moscow only added a sense of urgency to such defensive measures. Soviet
military periodicals charged that Stockholm intended to make its armed forces
into an "appendage" of the U.S. war machine. *Izvestia* accused Norway of planning to open itself to "foreign imperialists." Regarding Finland, there was talk
about the Red Army moving in to "protect" it against foreign enemies.[4] The
wife of the Finnish (Communist) minister of the interior asserted that the
model of the February coup in Prague was the example Finland intended to
follow: "The road Czechoslovakia has taken is the road for us."[5] Finland had
already signed a treaty of friendship with the Soviet Union, and there was pressure on Norway and Sweden to do the same. In response, a U.S. naval task
force was ordered to sail into the area. The purpose of the visit was to assure
the three countries that they were not up for grabs.[6] Such assertive behavior
produced desirable results.

It was different at Europe's center. By April 1948, Soviet authorities were restrict-
ing traffic between the Western zones of Germany and Berlin. The crisis seemed
to be spiraling out of control. It diverted international attention away from the
Prague coup d'état, and the rising East-West tensions made the position of the
Americans in the Schönborn Palace more precarious. Ambassador Steinhardt
refused to take part in a ceremony observing the sixth hundredth anniversary of
the founding of Charles University, as most Western academic institutions
withdrew from the event to protest the Communist assault on freedom.[7]

After the Communist putsch all Western diplomatic posts in Prague felt
increased pressure from the StB. The intrusions were so brazen that many embassies lodged protests. On April 23, 1948, Jindřich Veselý, a high-ranking StB
officer, sent out a circular demanding improved performance since too many
agents had been caught in flagrante delicto. The apartments of American diplomats, Veselý noted ironically, had "been searched without proper authorization
and in the absence of the owners." Attempts to recruit informers were crude, and
telephone bugging and mail interception were incompetent. He warned his
team that such tasks had to be performed in a professional manner.[8]

Veselý's note confirmed that the U.S. embassy was the primary target for the
StB. It became an outpost of America under siege. All mail, telephone calls, and
movements in and out were openly monitored by the Czech security apparat.
Steinhardt formally protested to the Ministry of Foreign Affairs against "the
wholly improper practice of opening mail addressed to the Ambassador of the
United States." He noted that the envelopes often arrived damaged. The embassy
submitted some to an FBI laboratory to determine whether they had been
opened and received "conclusive proof" of StB tampering.[9]

The embassy protested that American citizens had been detained without any notification given to the U.S. consul and warned that this could result in bearers of Czechoslovak passports being barred from travel to the United States.[10] The Americans also complained that the StB pressured Czech employees of the Schönborn Palace to become informants. Such demands were always followed by threats concerning the personal safety of the employee in question.[11] The Americans in Prague, wrote Steinhardt to Washington in April, were "regarded as spies and saboteurs."[12] A few months later the official Czechoslovak Press Agency (CTK) charged that the U.S. embassy had organized a plot in which assassins from the American zone in Germany were to kill the minister of defense, General Ludvík Svoboda.[13] Charges of sabotage or acts of terror were completely unfounded. Even the accusation involving spying was questionable. The Katek team had left. The CIA section run by Spencer Taggart and the Office of the Military Attaché were still functional, but barely, as their sources of information had dried out so completely and so suddenly that they had little to do. The only people still willing to socialize with Taggart and others from the embassy were—almost exclusively—secret police informers whose job was to mislead the Americans.

Even in this extreme environment, Ambassador Steinhardt got his Schönborn Palace crew, especially his courageous assistant Walter Birge, involved in activities that were not approved by Washington and would be regarded as most irregular at any diplomatic post. When Birge came to Prague, he thought he would be a regular Foreign Service officer. After the coup, however, Steinhardt directed Birge to help his friends who were in trouble. Later, he became a volunteer for Taggart's CIA section. Czechoslovak special services believed Birge to be a "great American spy" with up-to-date tradecraft, an endless supply of money and latest technology. Some even thought that he was the "chief of the intelligence section" at the embassy.[14] In reality, Birge never received any intelligence training. His only previous experience with clandestine work involved carrying letters between Steinhardt in Istanbul and his mistress in Bagdad; his method of avoiding surveillance by the StB was to drive faster than his minders.

Steinhardt asked for Birge's help the day after the CPC had seized power. Walter drove to the Schönborn Palace through mostly empty streets.[15] There were no cars, and even pedestrians were few. The city seemed to belong to armed detachments of the Communist militia and the police. Karla, the Czech receptionist in the Schönborn Palace, could not stop crying and looked frightened; her boyfriend had been arrested the previous night. Steinhardt received Birge almost immediately. He looked grim. "Walter," he asked, "are you ready to drive to the German border?" Without a pause he explained that his friend Josef Max Hartmann, the "sugar king," and his wife had to be taken into the safety of the U.S. zone. The StB had already tried to arrest them as known anti-Communists

Ambassador Steinhardt and Birge at work. Gift from Louise Schaffner.

and financial supporters of the defeated democratic cause. At the moment they were hiding at the British embassy under the protection of one of the legends of British intelligence, Harold (Gibby) Gibson. Steinhardt told his assistant to guide the couple across the border and dismissed him.

It was characteristic of the ambassador to think of the safety of his personal friends before anyone else's.[16] There were democratic politicians, diplomats, army and intelligence officers, and others whose lives were in grave danger because of their close association with Colonel Katek and the U.S. embassy. Some, such as General František Moravec, won high U.S. military medals for their contribution to the allied cause during the war. They were on their own.[17] Yet Steinhardt rushed to protect the Hartmanns, to whom he was connected merely by their shared love of bridge.

The ambassador told Birge that he would only need to get the couple to the border area, where a professional guide would take over. Even that was no small feat. To cover over a hundred miles on icy roads with police roadblocks would be a challenge for anyone. Furthermore, Birge drove a new luxury Cadillac that would attract attention anywhere in war-torn Europe. In addition, the 6'1," 175-pound athletic American was a snappy dresser. That day he wore a "long suede Hungarian overcoat with frog button fasteners, plus a white sheepskin hat." It was a near certainty that such a car, with such a driver, would be scrutinized by the police. When it happened, west of Karlsbad on the road to Cheb,

Birge was ready. He stopped as directed, lowered the window, waved his gray diplomatic card, carefully putting his two fingers over the letters "USA," and announced authoritatively in passable Russian he had picked up in Istanbul that he was from the Soviet embassy: "*Sovietskoye posol'stvo!*" The officer came to attention, saluted, and indicated that the car could proceed. Birge and the Hartmanns, now pale with fear, were greatly relieved when they finally reached a hamlet in the border area.

The first guide failed to show up. A smuggler was found who was willing to take the couple's luggage, which he promised to bring to the U.S. zone but stole instead. Birge decided to act. Without any knowledge of the terrain, and armed only with a small compass and three white sheets he got from the smuggler, he led the Hartmanns into the woods. After a considerable hike, they detected and avoided two border guards engaged in a loud conversation. Luckily, the group's next encounter was with two German officers. They made it. Birge introduced himself and the Hartmanns, and the officers readily agreed to take the refugees to the nearest U.S. Army post.

Birge still had to retrace his steps through the forbidding forest, recover his car, and get back on the road to Prague. He dealt with the first flat tire—a very common occurrence in those days—swiftly. But after the second one he pulled over and called Walter Burke, the embassy's security officer on duty. It took several more hours before he made it to Steinhardt's residence and was able to report that the mission was accomplished.

Within a short time, Steinhardt called Birge again. Miloš Hanák, a Czech diplomat, and his wife, Karla, were old friends of the ambassador from the days when they served in Turkey, where they played countless games of bridge. There was reason to believe, the ambassador told Birge, that the Hanáks were about to be arrested. Steinhardt assured him that they had made their own arrangements from Kdyně, a small town about one hundred miles southwest of Prague. As was to be expected, the plans quickly fell apart. After the Hanáks exchanged passwords with their contact, he took them to the woods and instructed them to wait there for his partner, who would guide them across the border. But the couple did not trust the man. Acting on intuition, they waited for him to disappear and then ran back to where Birge had dropped them off. To their relief, he was still there. He had also sensed that the plan was likely a trap and had decided to wait before returning.

In a few hours the would-be refugees were back in Prague in Birge's apartment at Barrandov. This was a reasonably safe hideout, because the StB thought it had recruited Birge's chef, François Ryšavý, as an informer.[18] In reality, Ryšavý had immediately warned Birge about his recruitment, and they had agreed to compose his reports for the StB together. The Hanáks would be in safe hands in Barrandov. Steinhardt was angered the next day to learn what had happened to his friends. By now he truly detested the Communist regime, and he decided to take the Hanáks out of the country in his official car. When the majestic vehicle with two U.S. flags approached the border area, the Hanáks lay at the feet of their American protectors, who placed blankets on their laps. The border guards did not dare to inspect the official vehicle of the ambassador, and so the refugees reached the West safely. Some would have criticized this misuse of diplomatic privilege, but Steinhardt obviously believed it was justified.

Next came Jan Stránský, who had worked with Colonel Katek's Military Mission and Taggart. In addition, his father had been a leading democratic politician, a deputy prime minister, and minister of education prior to the coup d'état. Stránský was consequently one of the prime targets of the StB. He hid for several days in Birge's apartment—attended to by Ryšavý—before being taken out of the country hidden in a huge 1939 Hudson with white stars on its side doors that had belonged to Colonel Katek.

By now the Gottwald government abandoned all of its electoral promises and ruled openly by terror. This increased the number of people who needed to escape from the country. Many who had hesitated in the winter saw no alternative to leaving in the spring and summer. At this point Birge received a phone call from a man who spoke educated British English and suggested they meet at a pocket garden down the street from the U.S. embassy. The mysterious stranger came late, but explained that he needed to be sure that Birge was not followed. Such caution was encouraging. The Czech refused to introduce himself, but told Birge that he had created a small organization specializing in taking people wanted by the StB across the border. The network included safe houses in the border area and border guards who had been turned on ideological grounds or bribed into cooperating. Acting on an impulse, Birge accepted the proposition. Before they parted, they agreed to call their organization BLACKWOOD.

The StB eventually learned of the organization's existence and came to believe that BLACKWOOD was a vast, sophisticated, and lavishly funded intelligence network run by the CIA. In reality it consisted of one Czech and one American volunteer. The two met only six times but arranged a number of escapes; the last one involved a friend of U.S. chargé d'affaires James Penfield. Unfortunately, one of the refugees praised Birge as his savior during his debriefing in the U.S. zone, and this triggered an invitation for Birge to face a State Department security officer at the U.S. embassy in London. He subjected Birge to a tough interrogation and made it perfectly clear that the Department was not pleased with BLACKWOOD. Birge was ordered to discontinue his private role as the Czechoslovak Scarlet Pimpernel immediately.[19]

Overall, the number of people who escaped from the Communist regime with the assistance of the U.S. embassy was small in comparison with the masses of refugees who crossed the border on their own. From 1948 to the early fifties, many Czechs and Slovaks escaped to the West.[20] In mid-April 1948 Ambassador Murphy reported from Berlin that on average about two hundred Czech displaced persons arrived every day. Many were destitute and survived with the support of various charitable refugee commissions. Their condition, wrote the ambassador, was "deplorable." He urged the Department of State to get them out of Germany soon.[21]

This was not easy to achieve, because at that time Washington was fully focused on the fast-evolving crisis in Berlin. In early April 1948 the United States responded to the tightening blockade of the city by bringing some supplies by air, and less than a week later, a Soviet fighter plane collided with a British airliner, killing everyone aboard. The two blocs were on the verge of an armed conflict.

The Czechoslovak exile community grew rapidly in the West. Within months it included ministers, members of parliament, ambassadors and diplomats, Army and air force generals, and hundreds of officers. But there was no Thomas G. Masaryk, Beneš, or even Jan Masaryk in their midst, and without a well-known figure the value of the group declined in the eyes of its Western sponsors. It became obvious to the Department of State and U.S. intelligence that they would need to help the exiles achieve unity and organize themselves. The first priority was to install a leader the Americans could trust. From the start, Steinhardt thought that the best personality for such a task was Petr Zenkl.[22] His life reflected the eventful history of Central Europe in the twentieth century. As a democratic politician, he was arrested by the Gestapo and sent to Dachau and then to Buchenwald, where he faced death repeatedly. In postwar Prague Zenkl was one of the most determined champions of the democratic system. He provided valuable information to Taggart at the embassy and to Katek at the Military Mission on a regular basis.

Steinhardt and other Americans respected Zenkl, and they decided to bring him to the West. In the early summer military attaché Colonel Michela summoned Walter Birge to his office. They had a long talk about the escalating crisis in Berlin and "about the robust possibility that before long World War III might break out." They needed to make sure that at least one significant Czech democrat was in the United States ready to create a government-in-exile just as Beneš had done in Great Britain.[23]

Taking Zenkl and his wife, Pavla, across the border would be a challenge, because they were under house arrest in their apartment, which was located a short distance from the Ministry of the Interior and guarded around the clock by three rotating pairs of secret police officers. Katek, who was at the U.S. Army headquarters in Frankfurt, assumed overall control of the Zenkl operation, but its execution fell to Reinhold Pick, a Czech employee at the Schönborn Palace since November 1945, whom the Americans called "Noldi." Since he had an exit permit stamped into his Czechoslovak passport, Michela could fly him to Frankfurt under a pretext. At the meeting, chaired by Katek and attended by Assistant Military Attaché Taylor and Eleanor Jančík of the Military Attaché's office, the Americans gave Pick the name of Jaroslav Švejdar, a police detective in Prague who had done favors for the Military Mission. Pick obtained a password that would prove his bona fides to the policeman.

Švejdar was obviously a man of courage. Involvement in such a scheme was dangerous for everyone, but a police official could expect nothing but the death penalty were he to fall into the hands of the StB. Yet the detective accepted Pick's proposition without hesitation. He suggested that the obvious obstacle—the agents who guarded the Zenkls—could be removed by one method only: the United States would have to offer them and their families political asylum. Therefore, the Zenkl operation would require arranging for the escape of Mr. and Mrs. Zenkl, the two agents, and their families. Švejdar suggested to Pick that he would simply go and ask whether they might be interested in such a deal. It seemed to be an insanely risky proposition. Pick briefly pondered Švejdar's plan and then agreed to it. The two agents accepted the offer on the spot.

Meanwhile, Pick discovered that Zenkl was allowed regular visits to Ferkel and Mandl, a barbershop on Panská Street in Prague's center. He also learned that the two agents typically waited for their man outside. Having ascertained the date of Zenkl's next appointment, Pick, who knew the owner, positioned himself in the back room of the establishment. "I was sent by Katek," he started. "What about the guards?" asked Zenkl. "They will come along." No further discussion was necessary. Years in Nazi concentration camps taught Zenkl how to behave in a crisis. All was clear. Or so it seemed. When everything was ready, the whole scheme collapsed, because the original StB watchers were suddenly replaced by three brand new teams. This time Švejdar insisted that Pick should make the proposal to the new duo. And, like Švejdar before him, he was also successful. The new guards, Luděk Kopecký and Karel Tománek, agreed to let go of Zenkl on the condition that Washington expedite their immigration applications. Of the original team, one agent insisted on coming along, although he was no longer involved with the Zenkls. This further increased the number of Pick's customers. And then there was Švejdar, the detective, who decided to leave as well—with his wife, two children, and elderly parents.

On August 7, 1948, the Zenkls, followed by the two security officers, went for a walk in their favorite park, Chotkovy Sady. Standing by were Pick, Michela, Birge, Jack Guiney (Birge's assistant at the embassy), and Frank Volek, a Czech employee. Michela drove Zenkl; Birge took his wife. The others escorted the officers and their families. Before Michela and Birge approached the border zone, they asked their guests to hide in the trunk. The only problem was that after he had arranged the Hartmanns' escape, Birge replaced his Cadillac with an even more ostentatious Alfa Romeo roadster, which had little luggage space. Consequently, Mrs. Zenkl had a hard time fitting in the trunk, and holes had to be drilled in the seats so that she could breathe. The border crossing was uneventful, and several hours later Military Attaché Michela delivered the couple to Alaska House, a.k.a. "the Golden Cage," in Oberursel, northwest of Frankfurt, where Katek concentrated prominent Czech exiles. The policemen's group had grown to thirteen. Crawling through a wooded area full of border guards with attack dogs in the middle of the night with a child and an infant was nerve-wracking, but they all made it safely to the other side. Zenkl never forgot "Noldi." As late as September 1965, he sent a card to "my dear friend who helped save my life."[24]

About two weeks after the Zenkls had crossed the border, around August 20, 1948, Spencer Taggart summoned Pick to his office and explained that staying in Czechoslovakia was too risky for him.[25] There were indications, Taggart said, that the StB had learned about his role in the Zenkl escape. The Americans could not afford for him, who had neither diplomatic immunity nor U.S. citizenship, to be interrogated. Taggart was characteristically gentle but allowed no discussion. He understood that Pick had already experienced one exile, from 1938 to 1945, and it was regrettable that he would have to leave his family again. His father had been murdered by the Nazis in 1942, but there was his mother, siblings, and fiancée, Milada. Regarding Milada—the Americans called her "Mila"—Taggart hinted that he would see what could be done for her. But he promised nothing and insisted that Pick should get ready to depart within days. Pick told his mother he would have to leave for some time but he hoped to come back soon; like many others at that time, he thought that the CPC dictatorship would crumble in a matter of months. It would be decades before he could return for a visit.

On August 30, 1948, Taggart drove Pick out of the country and left him in Nuremberg. The next day Pick met Katek in Griesheim, a suburb of Frankfurt. The colonel was pleased to inform the new arrival that a position had been arranged for him with the U.S. embassy in London. Regarding his fiancée, he was evasive, but eventually he admitted that he was not in a position to help. Pick refused to proceed to London, moved to Alaska House, and sulked. He hinted that unless the Americans brought his Mila to him, he would go back and take her out by himself. He said so forcefully to Walter Birge, who was returning from Paris to Prague via Frankfurt. It was obvious that Pick's plan could easily end in disaster—for Pick, his fiancée, and the United States. It would have been a catastrophe if the Czech propaganda were to reveal that Americans had smuggled the Zenkls and others across the border in their diplomatic vehicles.

When Birge returned to the Schönborn Palace, he learned that President Truman had asked Steinhardt to become his ambassador to Canada, and that his departure was set for September 19, 1948. Birge told Colonel Michela and Taggart that Pick was on the verge of making a fatal decision. They agreed that his threat was credible and could be diffused only by taking Mila across the border. In the middle of the meeting, Birge realized that Steinhardt was going to fly out of the country, and because he was the doyen of the diplomatic corps in Prague, protocol required all the accredited chiefs of mission to appear at Ruzyně for a grand reception. The airport would be packed, and that would create an opportunity not to be wasted.

Birge warned Steinhardt that Pick was desperate and might do something reckless unless he were reunited with Mila in the West. "I asked the boss whether he would be willing to take her out of Czechoslovakia in his plane when he left Prague en route to his new post if a feasible way could be devised to bring this about. Steinhardt was unpredictable, but this was the kind of adventure that appealed to him." Birge believed that the ambassador would play along because he wanted to look like an "intrepid hero." He was right. "If you can get Pick's girl on my plane safely and undetected," replied Steinhardt, "I'll go along."[26]

The scheme to smuggle Mila to Pick aboard the ambassador's airplane directly involved the Steinhardt family, Birge, Michela, Taggart, Guiney, a group of five or six young secretaries, and Steinhardt's pilots, Mark Bellenger and André Duchaene. They dubbed it Operation Flying Fiancée. On September 19, 1948, Birge, wearing a French-style black beret, picked up Mila in front of the Wilson train station in his conspicuous Alfa Romeo. As instructed, she wore a light, summery dress and carried a bouquet of flowers but no suitcase. Birge drove fast, but when he and Mila arrived at the airport, the VIP lounge was already filled to capacity. In the center was Mrs. Steinhardt and a group of flower-bearing young ladies in nearly identical summer dresses. The rest of the space was taken up by the diplomatic corps; champagne was flowing freely. Birge left Mila under the protection of Mrs. Steinhardt, who placed her at the center of her group, and he made his way through the boisterous crowd to study the situation.

Birge was dismayed to discover that the door connecting the VIP lounge to the runway was locked. He then looked outside through a glass panel and saw two sturdy secret police officers in leather jackets. Steinhardt's airplane, and another one that carried a "mountain" of luggage for the ambassador's family, were plainly visible and ready for takeoff. It occurred to him that the Czechs might allow only those cleared for departure—Steinhardt, his wife and daughter, and their small staff—to leave the lounge. At this point, Jack Guiney motioned for Birge to step outside the room: "Walt, I'm afraid they suspect something." He then drew Birge's attention to the flight board, which listed Steinhardt's plane as "US Embassy Aircraft. Destination Frankfurt. Awaiting Clearance."

Birge went to the office of the flight director. "I see that my ambassador's flight has not yet been cleared for take-off. Could you please explain this unusual situation?"[27] The director was Birge's acquaintance, and he was obviously uncomfortable as he lied that there was a logistical matter that needed to be fixed. Birge could read between the lines. He went back to the reception area, found Steinhardt, and whispered the news regarding his flight's status. The ambassador loved challenges of this kind. Moving "like a panther approaching its prey," he burst into the flight director's office. He skipped all formalities and demanded "in his most menacing tone" an explanation for the delay. When the Czech began stammering the same transparent excuses, Steinhardt interrupted him: "Get me General Boček [chief of staff of the Czechoslovak Army] on your phone." When the director made the connection, the ambassador tore the receiver from his shaking hands. Steinhardt became even angrier when Boček tried to hide behind excuses: "This is no explanation, General, and it is an insult, not only to me, but to the United States. Now, let me tell you something, General. If my flight is not given immediate clearance, do you know what I'm going to do? I'm going to call the US Air Force base at Rhein-Main and I'm going to ask the officer in command of that base to send a flight of fighter-bombers over here to bomb the hell out of your Ruzyne Airport." It is not known how General Boček replied, but when Steinhardt handed the phone back to the flight director, the latter listened intently. "Mr. Ambassador," he said, smiling, "your flight to Frankfurt is now cleared."

Birge acknowledged that this scene, and especially Steinhardt's unbelievable threats, might sound "utterly fantastic." But he was there and could confirm "that those were Mr. Steinhardt's words." The problem was that this victory neither unlocked the exit door nor eliminated the two StB guards. Birge discovered that there was a service door in an adjacent room and quickly agreed with the ambassador that he would physically push aside the soldier guarding it and force it open just when the crowd would follow the Steinhardts from the VIP reception. The timing was perfect. As soon as he heard the noise of the largest collection of accredited diplomats Prague had seen in a long time, Birge shouted some incomprehensible phrases at the big and fully armed soldier, pushed him aside, and opened the door. At that point, Mrs. Steinhardt and her flock of nearly identical girls in summer dresses stepped onto the runway, followed by the pack of excited diplomats. Some remained outside, but others went to admire the ambassador's plane. After a while, the visitors departed—all, that is, but Mila, whom Mrs. Steinhardt locked in a small cabinet. The ambassador was the last to board his plane. He climbed the steps, turned to face the diplomats, waved, and disappeared. It seemed that Operation Flying Fiancée was a success.

It turned out that the StB had greater stamina than General Boček. Its agents surrounded the two planes and indicated to the pilots that they were not to start their engines. A leather-jacketed colonel appeared and demanded to be allowed on board. Steinhardt came to the door and, playing to the sympathetic crowd of his colleagues, announced: "He seems to think I have a stowaway on board." Birge noticed that only a very few of the envoys in the crowd laughed. It was obvious that the situation had become tense and dangerous. The powerful Steinhardt poured scorn on the StB colonel from above, while the foreign diplomats on the ground lectured his colleagues that the ambassador's airplane, like his residence, was inviolable. Nevertheless, the colonel made his way on board and checked everyone's passport. Luckily, he was so nervous that his search of the plane was at best perfunctory. He did not dare ask Mrs. Steinhardt to step aside and let him open the small door she was guarding with her arms crossed. As the agent began descending the steps, Steinhardt took one more risk: "Are you quite satisfied?" It was obvious to Birge that the colonel was not but that he had run out of the courage needed to prove his point. The door was shut and the two pilots, Mark Bellenger and André Duchaene, started their engines. When the plane reached cruising altitude, Steinhardt invited Mila to join them. In Frankfurt they were welcomed by Katek and grateful Pick, who married Mila a week later.

As Birge and Taggart watched the airplane take off, they felt an enormous burden lifted from their shoulders. They knew, however, that the Czechs were not fooled. Most likely, they were already planning their revenge. The airport incident was bound to leave a deep imprint on Czechoslovak-American relations. Unfortunately, the U.S. embassy was yet again without a leader, and Steinhardt's successor would not be named until October. Ambassador Joseph E. Jacobs, a career Foreign Service officer, arrived in December and presented his credentials to Klement Gottwald on January 5, 1949.[28] Much would happen during the interceding four months.

The Czechs formally protested the actions of "three Americans"—presumably Birge, Guiney, and Michela—who had manhandled a guard, forced a side door open, and allowed a crowd onto the runway. They also said that Steinhardt's threats were unacceptable. The embassy replied that the ambassadorial party's passports had been checked twice. This "not only delayed the Ambassador's departure but caused him and his family intense embarrassment. The Embassy is at a loss to understand this discourtesy to the departing Ambassador of a friendly nation and would appreciate an explanation."[29] However, on December 10, 1948, the Schönborn Palace changed its tone. "I wish to express my regret," wrote Chargé James K. Penfield, "for any improper action on the part of members of this Embassy."[30]

By then the ambassador was already far away, back in New York taking care of his private affairs on Pine Street. There is no indication in the official records that the Department of State considered his performance in Czechoslovakia objectionable or that his irregular departure from Ruzyně Airport raised any eyebrows. In the aftermath of the routing of the democratic cause, it would have been natural for all eyes to turn to Steinhardt for an explanation. The gap between his rosy predictions and the harsh reality of Communist terror in Prague cried out to be studied by the Department of State. This did not happen. In fact, Steinhardt was rewarded with the United States embassy in Ottawa. True to form, he would arrive there only in November 1949, after a break of thirteen and a half months. Sumner Welles had only praise for Steinhardt: "I can't tell you how much pleasure and satisfaction I have had from the news. . . . Ottawa is unquestionably one of the most important posts we have, and I'm delighted that you're going there."[31]

Back in Prague, as Birge and Taggart pondered the events of September 19, 1948, it occurred to them that Operation Flying Fiancée revealed a security problem at the Schönborn Palace. They had attended several ceremonies in the VIP lounge at Ruzyně and knew that the door to the runway had always been open. Moreover, they had never seen StB guards posted in that area or a soldier with a submachine gun guarding the side door. They realized the StB must have received an advance warning that someone would try to escape on Steinhardt's airplane. Taggart believed that the culprit was a Communist sympathizer at the French embassy with an American girlfriend.[32] Birge focused directly on the Schönborn Palace team. He formed a theory "that one of our girls might have unintentionally leaked to a Czech boyfriend that something was in the wind."[33]

Birge was right. Irene Foster had arrived at the U.S. embassy in Prague in April 1947 as Steinhardt's secretary. Within weeks she befriended Václav Václavík, a thirty-six-year-old charmer. A survivor of the Mauthausen concentration camp, Václavík returned to Prague and contacted one of the CPC-controlled intelligence services, offering "information from the American Embassy, where he had as a mistress Steinhardt's personal secretary." Ms. Foster trusted Václavík, and she spoke freely about her daily tasks at the Schönborn Palace, which included taking Steinhardt's dictation. She was recruited to be one of the young American women in summer dresses whose task was to help smuggle Mila aboard the Steinhardt airplane. This is how Václavík could reveal to the Czech special services the details about the U.S. embassy's daily operations, Steinhardt, and Operation Flying Fiancée.[34]

In the aftermath of the drama at Ruzyně, the Americans in Prague got to know the state secretary at the Ministry of Foreign Affairs, Arnošt Heidrich. It was he who delivered the official protests, albeit mechanically and without conviction. "We gradually gained the impression," recalled Birge, "that this very knowledgeable individual would eventually seek asylum, probably in the United States."[35] Heidrich made his move at a British function. He motioned for Colonel Michela and Birge to follow him to somewhere they could speak in private and asked the two to help his family escape to the West. "You can count on us," Michela replied. The military attaché quickly outlined a simple clandestine code for their communication and promised to contact Heidrich soon. Could his two-year-old son's nurse come as well? he inquired. "Of course," replied Michela. But the practical Birge wanted to know her size. He was already concerned, as Heidrich was a big man, around 300 lbs., and his wife "was almost equally large." The small boy presented another problem, since few two-year-olds react well to being locked in the dark and noisy trunk of a car. He was relieved to hear that the nurse was small.

For the Heidrich operation Birge recruited Consul Frank G. Siscoe, who came to Prague with a grand American car. On November 22, 1948, Heidrich climbed into the trunk of Michela's car, and Siscoe took Mrs. Heidrich, who was obviously frightened but said not a word. The nurse and the boy (with a sleeping pill in his system) traveled in Birge's black Alfa Romeo. The convoy was headed by an impressive U.S. Army vehicle driven by Michela, and the experienced Birge was last. As was to be expected, the Americans were stopped by the StB roadblocks, once just outside Pilsen and another southwest of Domažlice. The cars bore diplomatic plates and were inviolable, but it was unclear what the guards might do should the child start crying in the trunk. The nurse was instructed by a family physician to administer a second sleeping pill at about the time when the convoy cleared the last roadblock and was moving toward the crucial border-crossing post. The guards at the border moved with deliberate slowness to humiliate the representatives of American imperialism. But they had to let them go, and they did, eventually. As Birge's Alfa Romeo was cleared and moved across "the last yard of Communist-held territory," the child in the back started shrieking. By the time the convoy reached Fürth-im-Wald the boy again turned silent. The next day, as Birge was cleaning the trunk of his car, a small white pill fell to the ground. He realized that the nurse faithfully administered the second pill, but the boy must have spit it out. Heidrich reached Washington safely and became a respected consultant with the Department of State.[36]

The StB knew full well that some of the American diplomats were involved in activities that had nothing to do with diplomacy. The man they disliked the most was Walter Birge, in part because he took such joy in his triumphs over the Communist agents, and also because he stood for everything the StB hated and envied. He was an elegant and rich young American who drove spectacular cars and liked the company of beautiful women. So the StB decided to hurt him where his diplomatic immunity offered no protection.

Birge met Božena in 1946 at the annual ball given by the Friends of the USA Society in Pilsen.[37] She was a "beguiling, vivacious, lovely blond girl of twenty." They danced into the night as the orchestra—lacking sheet music for other

American numbers—played endlessly "It's a Long Way to Tipperary," a song everyone knew by heart from the BBC. Their relationship blossomed. They spent time in Birge's house in Barrandov, went on long walks along the river, or talked in one of Prague's many cafés. When they met one afternoon in the summer of 1948, she burst into a tirade against the Communist regime, which was, she complained, in the process of destroying her life. She eventually calmed down, and as Birge put her on the Pilsen train in the evening, she hugged him and smiled: "Maybe the next time we meet, it will be in the West."[38]

Then unexpectedly, Božena dropped out of existence. No matter how hard he tried, Birge was unable to track her down. Two months later, he found Štěpán, an acquaintance from the Friends of the USA. When he asked about Božena, the man gripped his hand and made him sit on a bench: "Prepare yourself for a shock, Mr. Birge."[39] Štěpán explained that his cousin had told him some time ago that he had discovered a safe plan for escaping from Czechoslovakia. Božena learned about it and enthusiastically embraced it. She even brought additional friends into the enterprise. The group grew to eight. The guide charged Kčs 5,000 up front and an equal sum when the escapees reached to border. He claimed that the money was for the border guards. Several days later, Štěpán learned that a group of eight young people were found deep in the woods, close to the border. All had been mowed down by bullets fired from an automatic weapon. Birge was never able to determine whether the refugees had been murdered by the StB or the border guards, or whether the guide lured his victims into a trap and killed them for private gain. Since there is no evidence that the crime was ever investigated or the culprits tried, it would appear that the murderer or murderers acted in an official capacity.[40]

Soon after the February 1948 coup d'état in Prague, the StB proved to be good at adapting the techniques of the Gestapo and Soviet special services to suit its needs in the struggle against the Americans and their Czech associates. One scheme involved the United States directly, and it triggered two official protests from Washington. Operation KÁMEN (meaning "stone" or border marker) was a copy of a stratagem that Stalin's special services had invented and practiced before World War II and again in postwar East Berlin.[41] Typically, an StB provocateur contacted a government official, a military officer, a Czech employee of the U.S. embassy, or a businessman. Claiming to have been sent by U.S. intelligence, the agent told the victims that their arrest was imminent, and then offered to guide them to safety across the Iron Curtain.

Individuals or families with little children, carrying only cash and jewelry, were escorted to the border area by a group pretending to be members of a resistance organization who were in fact StB agents. They introduced the refugees to another StB agent, posing as a bribed border-guard official, who took them into the woods. Under his supervision, the group crossed the "border" and reached a "U.S. Army" post that was visible from afar at night. In reality, the building was still inside Czechoslovakia. The fake U.S. Army post was guarded by StB agents in the uniforms of the German border police and manned by StB agents in U.S. Army uniforms. The role of the "American" intelligence officer was often played by StB agent Amon Tomašoff.[42]

The final stages of Operation KÁMEN followed various possible scripts. Some victims were instructed to take a copy of the protocol of their interrogation to the next American post. On the way there, they were arrested by Czech guards. They could not deny their guilt, as they still carried a signed statement in which they had boasted of their anti-Communism. This took place at night and in the woods, and the victims tended to blame themselves for having lost their way between the two U.S. posts, never realizing that they had fallen for an StB ruse. Some believed that they had already been on German soil but were kidnapped by the border guards and brought back into Czechoslovakia. The fake U.S. Army officer occasionally chose a different ending. He told the applicants that their petitions for political asylum were denied and handed them over to the Czechs. The news that the Americans had apparently forced some refugees back into the arms of the StB trickled out of prisons and labor camps and had its intended effect on the rest of the population.

Among the first victims of KÁMEN were Jan and Jiřina Prošvic.[43] Jan was an engineer, designer of household products, and the founder of a highly successful company. As parents of four young children, the Prošvics were unwilling to risk exile, although the authorities had started to harass them. Six weeks after the February coup d'état, an StB agent approached the couple, introduced himself as a U.S. intelligence operative, and offered to arrange their escape. Mrs. Prošvic energetically turned it down and refused to discuss it, and even her husband was far from eager to risk crossing the border and starting anew abroad.[44] It took two more visits by the fictitious American agent to change the minds of these desperate people.[45]

On April 23, 1948, the couple and their two older daughters, Věra and Jana, met the agent; the two younger children, Eva and Jan, had been left with relatives, because the supposed American had refused to take them. The would-be refugees and their "American savior" drove to Kdyně and rested in Hotel Modrá Hvězda, located on the scenic town square lined with trees. At ten that night the agent introduced them to a police officer, Stanislav Liška. After Prošvic had paid a hefty fee, Liška left to make sure that the scene was ready. At midnight the policeman came back to report that all was well. He drove the family to Všeruby, a gloomy hamlet on the border. They were stopped several times at roadblocks manned by security personnel, but Liška, wearing his uniform, "always knew what to say." The Prošvics were impressed. From the outskirts of Všeruby, the family and their guide continued on foot through another hamlet, Mysliva, and around a lake. Standing by a border marker, Liška pointed out a well-lit building in the distance: that was, he asserted, the U.S. Army office, their destination, their safety.

The couple reached the post without difficulty, and two "German border guards" invited them inside. There, "U.S. Army Officer" Tomašoff offered the Prošvics a delightful choice—between Lucky Strike and Camel cigarettes; he gave their daughters Swiss chocolate and allowed them to go to sleep in the waiting area. The office was decorated with a large American flag and portraits of Roosevelt and Truman. A bottle of whiskey stood on the table. All seemed well.

Tomašoff began by interrogating Prošvic on his connections with the anti-Communist underground, of which the engineer knew nothing. All other questions, such as "What do you think of Communism?" sounded politically illiterate to Prošvic. The interrogation continued: who knew about his escape, who helped him, what reliable friends could he recommend for the Americans to contact in Prague? Prošvic resented the interrogator's tone, and the atmosphere became tense. Nevertheless, he signed the protocol, as the "American" requested, and was shattered to hear that his application for political asylum was denied. "We have no interest in Czech Communists," said Tomašoff. He drew his revolver and forced Prošvic into a car where his frightened wife and daughters were already waiting.[46] The family was speechless as the "Germans" drove them back to Všeruby and into the arms of the StB. Within hours, the parents and their sixteen-year-old, Vera, were back in Prague, torn apart in Pankrác Prison; the youngest in the group, Jana, was only eleven, and so the StB placed her in a convent. At that point, the two younger children, Eva and Jan, were barely alive, kept hidden by their frightened relatives in a hellish, small, always dark room that they were never allowed to leave.[47]

The protocol, dated April 24, 1948, noted with satisfaction that "Prošvic carried with him lots of valuables, especially jewels." But that was trivial compared with the property the family had left in Prague, including a beautifully furnished ten-room apartment in Prague's center and a spectacular villa in Vonoklasy, outside the capital, filled with works of art. All the Prošvic possessions were confiscated.[48] The crass nature of the CPC bosses was revealed when the villa in Vonoklasy was purchased on September 17, 1949, by Antonín Zápotocký, one of the top party leaders and later president of Czechoslovakia from 1953 to 1957. A subsequent review of the Prošvic case by the Ministry of the Interior concluded that the "seizure of the Prošvic villa took place outside the legal framework, the confiscation of the apartment by the state was illegal, and the sale of the villa in Vonoklasy to comrade Zápotocký was inappropriate."[49] The report made no reference to members of the Prošvic family who were crushed by Operation KÁMEN.

Only five days after the Prošvic family had been sent back to Prague in hand-cuffs, the next victims of KÁMEN, Oldřich and Ludmila Maláč, were on their way.[50] As an official of the Ministry of the Interior and a lawyer with contacts in the United States, Maláč was a difficult target. He immediately noticed that the two StB agents pretending to be Germans were not native German speakers, while Tomašoff's English was heavily accented. Moreover, Maláč saw that Tomašoff's used a Czech-made typewriter with a keyboard that an English-speaking user would have found confusing. He realized he was surrounded by actors from the StB. He refused to cooperate and was arrested and sentenced to fifteen years.[51]

Operation KÁMEN was frequently used against military officers. Pilot Officer Josef Hnátek, RAF, a decorated veteran of the Battle of Britain, was dis-missed from service shortly after the Communist coup. An StB agent approached him and offered to help him escape across the Iron Curtain in May 1948. The police protocol puts it simply: "From the very beginning the escape was arranged and directed by the security organs (Operation KÁMEN)." Hnátek was interro-gated by a phony American, who told him that he was "unreliable for the West" and handed him over to Czech authorities. The military court sentenced Major Hnátek to death; this was changed on appeal to sixteen, then fifteen years in prison.[52] Operation KÁMEN claimed many other victims in the officer corps. Air Marshal Karel Janoušek, RAF, the highest-ranking Czech Air Force officer in Great Britain during the war, was lured into KÁMEN shortly after the Communist takeover, and sentenced first to nineteen years, then life in prison.

The StB was understandably pleased by the productivity of Operation KÁMEN. But there was a problem. The Americans found out about the scheme and protested it with a note of June 15, 1948. It described the whole setup in surprising detail:[53]

For approximately four weeks, representatives of the Czechoslovak State Security Police (S.N.B.), dressed in full uniform with insignia of officers of the United States Army, have been conducting an office in a house on Czechoslovak territory in the Western outskirts of the village of Vseruby. In the conduct of their business, these representatives are seated behind a desk on which there is conspicuously displayed a bottle of American whiskey, packages of American cigarettes and a small American flag. On the wall behind their desk is a large American flag and pictures of Presidents Truman and Roosevelt. These S.N.B. repre-sentatives, dressed in uniforms of the United States Army, are assisted by other S.N.B. representatives who are dressed in uniforms of the German border police. According to factual evidence in the possession of the Government of the United States, the purpose of this office, as

well as of the fraudulent misuse of the uniform of the Army of the
United States and of the German border police, as well as the display of
the American flag and pictures of the former and present presidents of
the United States, is to supplement other measures taken by the Czechoslovak Government to prevent illegal departures from Czechoslovakia.

Some two weeks later, on July 2, 1948, there was another U.S. protest. It
stated that Czech personnel had been seen moving around the border area in
"American cars and wearing United States Army uniforms." The embassy
made it clear it disapproved of the misuse of U.S. insignia and symbols of any
kind.[54] Prague authorities rejected the protests with a note of their own,
denying everything.[55] Yet they were worried: how did the Americans find out
about KÁMEN? And so quickly?

The answer was all too obvious. Stanislav Liška, the chief of the police station
in Všeruby and a central player in Operation KÁMEN, was part of a network that
gathered information for U.S. Army Intelligence from the winter of 1945 to the
summer of 1948.[56] Liška relayed information about KÁMEN to the Americans
without delay. The speed with which the U.S. protest arrived at the Foreign Ministry in Prague provoked suspicion, as did the details contained in them. It was
clear to the StB that the description of the fake U.S. Army post could have come
only from someone who had been there. An internal investigation concluded
that the traitor was the station chief Liška, and he was arrested on December 10,
1948. But the experienced policeman knew how to conduct himself in such circumstances. Despite long interrogations, he was released in May 1949. He wisely
decided not to test his luck any further and crossed the border to the U.S. zone.[57]

In June or July 1948, during the first weeks of the Berlin blockade, General
Lucius Clay summoned Spencer Taggart to his headquarters in Germany and
told him to expect war to break out with the Soviet Union within four months.[58]
The general asked him to build a network of agents equipped with radio stations.
It was to remain inactive during peacetime but spring into action in case of war.
Its mission would be to gather military intelligence.[59]

Taggart was eager to carry out his orders, but he was scheduled to leave the
Prague post by October 1948 at the latest. Moreover, he and his assistant, Samuel Meryn, a U.S. citizen with no diplomatic cover, could rely on only two people
at the embassy, Walter Birge and Louise Schaffner. Each had the rank of third
secretary and neither had undergone any intelligence training. There was an additional problem: the new U.S. ambassador, Joseph Jacobs. A traditional diplomat, Jacobs had made it clear that he disapproved of mixing diplomacy with
espionage. He warned at every staff meeting that "strict disciplinary action"
would be taken against anyone in the embassy acting in disregard of his edict.[60]

When Birge and Schaffner became involved, they jeopardized their careers. Their Czech contacts put their lives on the line.

Like almost everything else U.S. intelligence attempted to achieve in Czechoslovakia after the war, this network came into existence as a result of coincidences and improvisation. It originated in the winter of 1947 when Steinhardt delegated Birge to represent the U.S. embassy at a black-tie event at the Grand Hotel in Pardubice. Because Birge arrived alone, Jarmila Dudešková, a twenty-three-year-old English speaker, was assigned to be his escort for the evening.[61] They danced often, and before he left, Birge slipped her his telephone number. In March 1947 Jarmila came to Prague to see Birge, and their assignations soon became routine. In June she persuaded Birge to visit her friend Táňa Wahl at her hunting lodge about thirty miles northeast of Prague.

On the way, Jarmila talked about her friend's family history.[62] Táňa's father, Josef Růžička, a successful attorney, had built for his family one of the most beautiful houses in Prague with a grand view of the city. The Nazis murdered him in Mauthausen in 1943 and expelled his wife, Anna, and children, Táňa and Primus, from the house. In March 1947 Táňa had married Veleslav Wahl, who also came from a family that had experienced more than its share of tragedies: Wahl's father, Veleslav Sr., and his uncle Karel were executed by the Nazis in 1942. Both men had joined the struggle against Nazism stoically accepting of the risks involved.[63]

Young Wahl grew up as a pampered only son. Initially he seemed to be passionate only about ornithology.[64] But at the age of twenty, after his father and uncle had been executed, he stepped into the gap left behind by the two men he adored. He helped organize the Intelligence Brigade (IB), a clandestine organization that provided the allies with accurate and actionable intelligence on the Wehrmacht.[65] In recognition of his wartime record, Wahl and others from the IB were honored by Beneš at the castle in February 1946.[66]

Jarmila sensed that Birge, who was not enthusiastic about the outing, barely listened to her story.[67] But he warmed up as soon as they arrived. After lunch, Birge and Wahl left for a walk. By the time they returned, they had become close friends, and on the way back, Birge had complained that Jarmila had not introduced him to the Wahls earlier. Veleslav and Walter became inseparable. They celebrated Christmas 1947 together, on which occasion Birge received from his friend two lovely presents that he kept proudly for the rest of his life. They grew even closer when it transpired that Wahl was on excellent terms with Major Jaromír Nechanský, the British-trained commando officer who had fought against the Nazis, and befriended Sergeant Kurt Taub of the OSS in May 1945.[68]

Major Nechanský was a professional Army officer with a great war record, and he had every reason to expect an easy career in the liberated country. But he soon discovered that "all the parachutists from England were considered to be agents of British Intelligence." His telephone was tapped and he was followed. Rumor had it that Nechanský's career was over because "he was too close with the English and the Americans."[69] This charge was true. The military counter intelligence noted in 1946: "Recently Katek has been visiting Captain Nechanský often in his apartment. They used to know each other superficially in the past, but now Katek is there more often than he is at home." Elsewhere the OBZ noted that "Nechanský is in frequent contact with Katek; he most likely works for him."[70] Furthermore, it was well known that Nechanský was a close friend of Kurt Taub ever since the two had tried to persuade the Third Army to advance further into Czechoslovakia. For this reason alone Nechanský was high on the black list of the communists.

The plan to establish a U.S. intelligence network that would be controlled from the Schönborn Palace was hatched in the elegant house that the Wahl family had reclaimed after the defeat of the Third Reich. Birge appealed to Wahl's and Nechanský's sense of patriotism and argued that all good Czechs were now obligated to work against the dictatorship, much as the two had done during the war. "He assured us," Nechanský later confessed to the StB, "that in our struggle we would enjoy unlimited support from the United States Embassy." The two accepted the challenge and acted quickly. In mid-summer 1948 they reported to Birge that they had put in place two networks, PISEK in southern Bohemia, and MOST in the north; preparations for a third network, code-name JIHLAVA, were under way. Birge was delighted. He told Nechanský that future contacts would be with intelligence professionals.[71]

There followed a series of clandestine encounters between Nechanský and Samuel Meryn and, later in August 1948, also Taggart. They met outside the Bubenec train station that is on the Western edge of Stromovka, Prague's largest park. On that occasion, Nechanský testified, "Taggart said that it was necessary to expect in the near future, maybe in the fall or perhaps winter, a dramatic reversal on the international scene. . . . He therefore demanded that I finish building my network. The time for its use, Taggart said, was near." Everyone involved understood that the situation was deadly serious. Taggart was talking about war.

The rest of the story involves a series of errors, culminating in tragedy. Meryn delivered to the Czechs four American radio transmitters. The transaction was bungled because he had waited at the wrong place. Then it turned out that the manuals and coding directions that came with the stations were for an entirely different model. Weeks passed because Meryn had to consult Taggart, who had left for the United States. Then the Americans decided to withdraw the worthless manuals and they demanded that Nechansky and Wahl give them the complete list of all their subagents. Nechansky was concerned about the lack of tradecraft on the part of the Americans, and he refused to release the names of his agents.

In early November 1948, Meryn requested another meeting, but only to announce that he was leaving the country. Furthermore, he told Nechanský that Washington no longer expected an imminent armed conflict with Moscow. Nevertheless, he urged the major to keep building the networks but insisted they had to remain inactive for the time being. He failed to deliver the correct manuals and coding instructions, without which the radio transmitters were not usable but, if discovered, represented a sure ticket to the gallows. The two Czechs found the whole situation puzzling.

Birge reappeared and met the major several times in Wahls' house. He passed on to Nechanský and Wahl Taggart's letters that had arrived via the diplomatic pouch and consisted of lists of questions. The two agents would take "twenty or thirty minutes" to reply in writing, while "Mrs. Wahl served tea, or drinks, depending on the time of day." During one of these dangerous and unprofessional encounters Birge invited Nechanský and Wahl to his wedding. (Birge's leather-bound address book included entries for "Nechanský" and "Wahl" with full addresses and telephone numbers.) Incredibly, the two Czechs attended the resplendent affair. At the reception Birge introduced them to Isaac Patch, an assistant political attaché at the U.S. embassy. Then he announced that he too was leaving Prague very soon. Their next contact with the embassy, Birge stated, would be his colleague, Louise Schaffner. On May 9, 1949, Birge and his bride drove out of Communist Czechoslovakia in his Alfa Romeo. Their destination was Park Avenue, New York City.[72]

Schaffner met both Nechanský and Wahl several times to hear their reports, get the latest on the condition of their networks, and pass on requests from Taggart. She told them that U.S. intelligence planned to have several members of the networks attend a radio training course in the U.S. zone in Germany. Nechanský and Wahl were to help them across the border, then put them to work once they returned. This would eliminate the need for manuals. Schaffner, just like Birge before her, met the agents in the Wahls' house. Unlike her colleagues, she never believed that the operation was secure, and she was gravely worried. But by the summer of 1949, the appearance of normalcy had returned to the Schönborn Palace. The Americans, who had withdrawn Meryn from Prague in late 1948, felt that it was safe to send him back in August 1949.

This is what the StB had been waiting for. The first to be arrested was Nechanský. There was nothing Wahl could do but wait for his own turn and the interrogations and torture that were bound to follow. He tried to find serenity in his ornithological studies, mostly at his hunting lodge, having rejected Schaffner's suggestions that he should escape from the country on the grounds that it would worsen Nechanský's situation.[73] It was his wife, Táňa, who opened the door to the StB. The network's subagents were arrested in September 1949. Samuel Meryn's turn came several weeks later. It defies comprehension why this "employee of the Office of the Military Attaché without diplomatic status" had not been taken out of Czechoslovakia right after Nechanský's arrest; the whole affair smacked of shocking amateurism. Meryn's house was searched on October 21, 1949, and he was arrested the next day. In deference to his U.S. citizenship he was released after twenty-one days and no violence was used against him. He showed stoicism during his interrogations, doggedly denying everything, despite all the evidence. At one point he was asked to identify Wahl, whose bloodied face showed signs of severe beating. "I'm sorry," announced the poker-faced Meryn, "but I've never met this gentleman before."[74] The network's subagents never had a chance. All—men and women—were tortured; even the police photographer who took their pictures for the court did not bother to hide this.[75]

In the aftermath of the fiasco, the Czechoslovak government declared John Heyn persona non grata. He came to the Schönborn Palace as a diplomat in June 1949, and the StB immediately ransacked his apartment. Yet he left quietly, without U.S. protest or retaliation, which led Schaffner and others to believe that Heyn was an intelligence officer who came to help with the

Photographs of Major Jaromír Nechanský and Veleslav Wahl from their StB file. Nechanský's picture is taken from a wartime British document; Wahl was photographed by the StB. Courtesy of Archiv Bezpečnostních Služeb, Prague.

Nechanský-Wahl crisis.[76] Prague formally charged five U.S. embassy diplomats with involvement in the intelligence network. First was Walter Birge, who was identified as the chief of the conspiracy. Then came Taggart and Schaffner, and finally Meryn and Isaac Patch. Of these, Birge and Taggart had already left. Schaffner was declared a persona non grata and left just as Meryn went to prison. Isaac Patch, a political attaché, who had met Nechanský and Wahl only once, was given twenty-four hours to leave.[77] After his departure, another alleged spy ring tied to the U.S. embassy was rolled up. The *New York Times* published a photograph of Schaffner, whom the StB charged with having been in close contact with the second network's members, mostly officials of the Ministry of Foreign Affairs.[78] And indeed she was on friendly terms with some of the diplomats, but there was no clandestine activity. After a brief pause, Captain Jack Novak from the Military Attaché's Office was lured in early November 1949 into an ambush prepared by Czech security. He was detained, released, and ordered to leave immediately.[79] The intelligence component of the embassy ceased to exist.

The Nechanský and Wahl trial in April 1950 became an orgy of anti-American propaganda.[80] The names Birge, Taggart, Meryn, Schaffner, and Patch appeared repeatedly in the state-controlled press, accompanied by photographs of the four radio transmitters that had been delivered by Meryn and weapons the StB claimed to have uncovered in the houses of the agents.

The verdicts had been determined in advance. Nechanský and Wahl were sentenced to death. Their friends received life, twenty-five years, twenty years, eighteen years ... Wahl's wife was also arrested and brutalized, then sent to serve eleven years in prison. Nechanský and Wahl were executed on June 16, 1950. Before he was hanged, Wahl bequeathed a large sum of money to the Ornithological Society and made provisions for future editions of his book. (The Ministry of Justice ignored the will and all its provisions; it seized the Wahls' estate for the benefit of the CPC elite.) In his final letter, Wahl quoted a poem that contrasted the sorrow of humans, who were haunted by their fear of death, with the joyful existence of birds. The condemned man wrote that, like his father, uncle, and father-in-law had done before him, he would face his last moments "calmly and at peace." Death would come gently for him, he predicted, as it would for Nechanský, "who has been very brave." Under the gallows, both Nechanský and Wahl protested that they were not allowed to see their wives. Vladimír Trunda, the executioner, submitted a report asserting that the procedure was orderly, but there was a persistent rumor that the StB mocked Nechanský and beat him when he looked away from his younger friend's long agony. The prisoners' last words were recorded verbatim. Wahl reached out to his wife: "Good-bye, darling," and Nechanský, having smoked a cigarette, said: "I die for justice, democracy and country, the land for which I fought in the last war." A soldier to the

Police file photographs of the Americans who worked with Major Nechanský and Wahl.
Courtesy of Archiv Bezpečnostnich Služeb, Prague.

Evidence presented at the Nechanský and Wahl trial. The weapons were added by the StB but the radio stations are likely to be authentic. Courtesy of the ČTK, Prague.

end, he added: "There will be retribution."[81] Wahl's grandmother had lost two sons and a grandson to Nazi and Communist executioners. When Wahl's mother asked the authorities to release the letters her son wrote on death row and his wedding ring, the prosecutor recorded his decision "to leave Anna Wahl's request without reply."[82]

Birge heard the news regarding the trial in Prague on his car radio while driving to give a lecture in Atlanta. The announcer stumbled over the names of Veleslav Wahl and Major Nechanský but had no problem to report that Walter Birge, a U.S. diplomat formerly posted in Prague, was identified as the mastermind of a network of terrorists and spies. When he reached Atlanta, Birge received a telegram from Washington tersely instructing him to make no comment regarding the Prague affair, and he learned that his next post was Dakar, Senegal, the last of his brief diplomatic career.[83]

The state media in Prague made no mention of Nechanský and Wahl's executions. Washington found out about it from Louise Schaffner. Before she reported to her next post, at the U.S. consulate general in Palermo, Italy, she was granted a short home leave. When she checked her mail in Lancaster, Pennsylvania, she discovered an envelope mailed anonymously from Prague. It contained a formal notice of Major Nechanský's death. It came without any accompanying letter, and she sensed that it was meant to be a sarcastic present from the victorious StB.[84]

As the affair unfolded, Washington had hinted repeatedly that the charges were another manifestation of Communist paranoia. Officials described them as being "entirely without foundation."[85] But when Taggart, Taub, Birge, and Schaffner had an opportunity to examine the official Czech protocols of the case, they found them to be largely accurate.[86]

Prague escalated the crisis by demanding that the Americans close down their Consulate General in Bratislava and reduce their diplomatic staff in Prague to eighteen. Washington complied and then retaliated by shutting down the Czechoslovak Consulate General in New York and consulates in Cleveland, Pittsburgh, and San Francisco. It also requested a two-thirds reduction in personnel at the Czechoslovak embassy. Prague responded by demanding a further decrease, and soon the staff of the Schönborn Palace consisted of five diplomats, seven administrators, and one janitor.[87]

Such was the inauspicious end to Washington's plan to treat Czechoslovakia as the "master key to Europe" and a testing ground for the contest with Stalin. Before he left Prague, Spencer Taggart paid one final visit to his favorite restaurant. Having learned of his imminent departure, the chef came out of the kitchen, looked around to make sure that nobody was watching, then threw himself into the American's arms and sobbed like a child. The next day, when the airplane lifted off from the runway at Ruzyně Airport, Taggart felt tears come to his eyes. He knew that the cause he and his colleagues had come to defend had been crushed.[88]

A bitter verdict on the Steinhardt embassy in Prague came from a man who made it his business to be better informed than most, Allen Dulles. Reflecting on signs of unrest in Eastern Europe in the fifties, he stressed how important it was for the United States never to repeat the mistakes that had been made in postwar Czechoslovakia. That country, Dulles said, "would never have been lost if someone had been there doing something about it."[89]

With the Communist putsch of February 1948, Czechoslovakia had been irretrievably lost to the Kremlin, and its future was bleak. The CPC had promised that it would introduce its radical program slowly, showing respect for established customs and traditions. It also postured as a committed defender of Czechoslovak sovereignty. Gottwald spoke along such lines as late as 1947. He broke all his promises immediately, and the "age of the Barbarian," as R. H. Bruce Lockhart called it, was about to commence.[90] Soviet security advisors who had spread out throughout Eastern Europe made quite clear to the recently installed Communist leaders that for them to accommodate their non-communist majorities or to adjust the inhumane and failing Russian model of socialism in any way was tantamount to betrayal and punishable accordingly. Therefore, Gottwald and the CPC no longer believed—or pretended to believe—that they were creating their own kind of socialism and following their own timetable. Instead, they joined other Communist countries as they trudged along the sorrowful Stalinist path.

The human cost of Stalinism in Eastern Europe was enormous throughout the region, especially in Poland, and Czechoslovakia did not get off lightly. At least 248 political prisoners were executed, and 4,500 died as a result of cruel treatment in detention, prisons, and labor camps. In addition, more than 300 died while trying to escape from the country; most were shot by border guards and others were killed while contending with electrified fences. Some drowned while swimming or were shot down as they flew toward the border. A few were killed by land mines or military dogs. State prisons were always kept full: from 1948 to the Velvet Revolution of 1989, the courts sentenced 205,486 persons for political "crimes."[91]

The February 1948 coup helped to reveal the aggressive and uncompromising essence of Stalinism and alert the United States and the democracies of Western Europe to the seriousness of the challenge they faced. Charles Bohlen had suggested during the war that liberated Czechoslovakia would have to be watched carefully as it was the most accurate test of whether the West could peacefully coexist with the Stalintis realm. The imposition of the CPC dictatorship provided a clear answer to the Bohlen test. Only nine days after the CPC had seized power in Czechoslovakia, General Clay sent a startling telegram from Berlin warning

The Iron Curtain as it appeared from the U.S. zone in Germany in 1948. Photograph by Major Miloš Knorr. Gift from Major Knorr.

darkly of a possible Soviet aggressive move that could come with "dramatic sud-denness." Secretary Marshall, Kennan, and the CIA refused to countenance this interpretation of Soviet intentions. However Moscow's conquests to date and new threats directed at several Scandinavian countries, and the possibility that the events in Prague would embolden the Communists in France, Greece, and Italy could not be ignored.

President Truman addressed the situation in two speeches he gave on March 17, 1948 to Congress and in New York City. Solemnly reading the long list of countries the Soviet Union had already claimed in Eastern Europe, the presi-dent warned that it might soon become longer unless measures were taken that would erase any doubt as to American military strength and determination. He called on Congress to approve funding for the Marshall Plan and to help rebuild the U.S. Armed Forces. On the same day, representatives of Western European democracies met in Brussels and formed a defense pact, the Western Union, from which NATO emerged a year later, with the crucial participation of the United States. Having retreated from Prague, the West would retreat no further.

# NOTES

## Introduction

1. George F. Kennan, *Memoirs 1925–1950* (Boston: Little, Brown, 1967), 89–90.
2. The Harry S. Truman Library, Papers of Harry S. Truman, Files of the White House Naval Aide, G. C. M., Secretary of State, Memorandum for the President, November 7, 1948. Kennan's views are in National Archives and Records Administration (NARA), George Kennan, Department of State, to Robert Lovett, Department of State, October 6, 1947, 861.00/10-647. See also Kennan, *Memoirs*, 254–55.
3. NARA, Secret Memorandum of Under Secretary of State Eugene V. Rostow to Secretary of State Dean Rusk, May 10, 1968, folder 6/1/68, box 1558, POL—Czech, USSR DEF 4 NATO, Center Foreign Policy Files 1968–1969, RG 59; I am grateful to Günter Bischof for giving me a copy of this document. The view of Allen Dulles regarding the Prague coup can be found in "Memorandum from the Assistant Secretary of State for European Affairs to the Under Secretary of State," January 4, 1955, *Foreign Relations of the United States, 1955–1957*, vol. 35 (Washington, DC: GPO, 1990), 7.
4. The first to address this topic was Walter Ullmann, *The United States in Prague, 1945–1948* (Boulder, CO: East European Quarterly, 1978). A more recent work is Justine Faure, *L'ami américain: La Tchécoslovaquie, enjeu de la diplomatie américaine, 1943–1968* (Paris: Tallandier, 2004).
5. Brigitte Hauger, "The Schönborn Palace: A History of the American Chancery Building in Prague," unpublished manuscript, no date. See also Archives of the Czechoslovak Ministry of Foreign Affairs (AMFA), "History of the Site and Building of the American Embassy, Prague III, Trziste 15," 1945–54, 6th Section, USA, box 16. A good description of the palace can be found in Franz Kafka, *Letters to Felice*, ed. Erich Heller and Jürgen Born; trans. James Stern and Elisabeth Duckworth (New York: Schocken Books, 1973), 540–43.
6. The Richard T. Crane Papers are deposited at Georgetown University.
7. Lewis Einstein, *A Diplomat Looks Back* (New Haven, CT: Yale University Press, 1968), 192.
8. Peter Bridges, "Mr. Carr Goes to Prague," *Diplomacy and Statecraft* 8, no. 3 (November 1997): 187–98.
9. Consul General Huber served in Prague from June 1939 to September 1945. References to this period can be found in Daniel C. Schmid, *Dreiecksgeschichten: Die Schweizer Diplomatie, das 'Dritte Reich' und die bömischen Länder, 1938–1945* (Zurich: Chronos, 2004).
10. Swiss Federal Archives, Bundesarchiv Bern, 1000/113 Bd 7 DO 13, "Report," Frank Beranek, Custodian of the United States government–owned property in Prague, July 1, 1942. Similar reports can be found in E 2200. 190 (-),-/3, Bd 1, 1928–1945, "Jahresbericht 1941 des Sweizerischen Generalkonsulates in Prag," "Jahresbericht 1942," and "Jahresbericht 1943."

11. Anonymous [E. H. Carr] "Russia, Britain, and Europe," *Times* (London), November 6, 1944. Anthony Eden expressed a similar view in a milder form to Polish politicians in December 1943. General Sikorski Historical Institute, *Documents on Polish-Soviet Relations*, vol. 2, *1939–1945* (London: Heinemann, 1967), doc. no. 67, 117. See also Anne O'Hare McCormick, "The Shadow of Things to Come," *New York Times*, February 12, 1944.

12. Evidence on Soviet thinking regarding postwar Eastern Europe is sparse. Among the most helpful publications are T. V. Volotkina et al., eds., *Vostochnaya Evropa v dokumentakh rossiskikh arkhivov, 1944–1953*, 2 vols. (Novosibirsk, Russia: Sibir'skii Khronograf, 1997–99), and T. V. Volotkina et al., eds., *Sovietskii faktor v Vostochnoi Evrope, 1944–1953*, 2 vols. (Moscow: ROSSPEN, 1999–2002).

13. Fond Minister Hubert Ripka (FMHR), Ústav Soudobých Dějin, Prague, inventory unit 1559, box 46; record of Ripka's conversation with Minister Aleksandr Bogomolov and other Soviet representatives on January 30, 1942. Similar views were expressed in the highly controlled Soviet press. An article suggested that the war might end with Soviet soldiers in Berlin and other great European capitals, and entrenched along the English Channel. At that point, the author predicted, distinguished politicians, the Pope, and several kings would try to restore the old order. But all they would see around them would be the encampments of the Red Army that had fought its way to the westernmost edge of France. See Boston University, Private papers of General František Moravec, "Esteemed Guests," *Krokodyl*, no date. The article was brought to the attention of General František Moravec in London by General Helidor Píka.

14. See Vladimir O. Pechatnov, *The Big Three After World War II: New Documents on Soviet Thinking about Post-War Relations with the United States and Great Britain*, CWIHP Working Paper 13 (Washington, DC: Woodrow Wilson International Center for Scholars, 1995).

15. James B. Reston, "Russia Acts While We and the British Ponder," *New York Times*, March 5, 1944; and Hanson W. Baldwin, "Dual Policy of Russia Traced," *New York Times*, March 8, 1944.

16. Masaryk's Memorandum of Conversation with F. D Roosevelt, February 4, 1944, in Jan Němeček et al., *Československo-sovětské vztahy v diplomatických jednáních, 1939–1945* (Prague: Státní Ústřední Archiv, 1999), 229–30.

17. Ladislav Karel Feierabend, *Beneš mezi Washingtonem a Moskvou: Vzpomínky z londýnské vlády od jara 1943 do jara 1944* (Washington, DC: published by author, 1966), 34.

18. In March 1945 Stalin told a Czech delegation he intended to create in Central Europe "a communion in which all have the same rights, all are equal, and no nation is oppressed" by another. Prokop Drtina, *Československo můj osud: Kniha života českého demokrata 20. století*, vol. 1, part 2, *Emigrací k vítězství* (Toronto: Sixty-Eight Publishers, 1982), 27–28.

19. Interview with Paul Zinner, April 5, 2005, Washington.

20. Eduard Mark, "Charles E. Bohlen and the Acceptable Limits of Soviet Hegemony in Eastern Europe: A Memorandum of 18 October 1945," *Diplomatic History* 3, no. 2 (April 1979), 205–6.

21. "Russia and Post-War Europe: Sir S. Cripps's View," *Manchester Guardian*, February 10, 1942.

22. "Russia, Britain, and Europe," *Times* (London), November 6, 1944.

23. Report by Heliodor Píka, Moscow, to Edvard Beneš, London, Regarding the Conditions of the Czechoslovak Military Mission in the USSR, August 10, 1941, in Němeček et al., *Československo-sovětské vztahy*, doc. no. 98, 220–26. The Russian special services obviously read Píka's reports and did not mind advertising the fact, because they complained about his reports in London. See FMHR, Hubert Ripka, London, to Edvard Beneš, London, June 4, 1942.

24. Lord Cranborne, "Britain and the Central Europeans," *Tablet*, January 13, 1945, 15. See also Francis A. Gerth, "Who Saved Whom?" *Chicago Daily Tribune*, May 19, 1945.

25. Cranborne, "Britain and the Central Europeans," 15–16.

26. William C. Bullitt, "The World from Rome," *Life Magazine*, September 4, 1944.

27. NARA, Cecil B. Lyon, First Secretary, U.S. Legation, Cairo, Egypt, August 25, 1945, 861.00/8-2545. See the attached memorandum by T. H Preston, the British resident representative in the Middle East.

28. Such was the view of British intelligence in 1943, see Gordon Brook-Shepherd, *The Storm Birds: Soviet Postwar Defectors* (New York: Weidenfeld & Nicolson, 1989), 63.
29. The Harry S. Truman Library, Independence Missouri, Harry N. Howard, "Oral History Interview," October 7–8, 1976, interview by Richard D. McKinzie.
30. Howard, "Oral History Interview." The meeting was attended by Charles Bohlen, Elbridge Durbrow, Llewellyn Thompson, and others.
31. NARA, Office of Strategic Services, Research and Analysis Branch, "Report on Czechoslovakia: Pivot Point of Europe," July 4, 1945.
32. Egon Hostovský, *Missing: A Novel*, trans. Ewald Osers (New York: Viking, 1952), 245.

## Chapter 1

1. Franz Josef is believed to have made this statement in 1910 during a conversation with Theodore Roosevelt. See *Beruf: Kaiser*, exhibition catalogue, Vienna, June 2006.
2. A. J. P. Taylor, *Czechoslovakia's Place in a Free Europe* (London: Czechoslovak Institute, 1943), 5.
3. See for instance Helmuth James von Moltke, *Letzte Briefe aus dem Gefängnis Tegel* (Berlin: Henssel, 1951).
4. NARA, "Eduard Benes," Department of State, Washington, DC, May 10, 1943, 860F.001/135. His biographers assert that Beneš was a success as a professor. One wonders. An observer placed in the audience by the State Department noted that the first lecture had lasted for eighty minutes without a break and that the "audience was slightly groggy when he was done."
5. R. G. D. Laffan, *Survey of International Affairs, 1938* (London: Oxford University Press, 1951), 2:403.
6. Laffan, *Survey of International Affairs, 1938*, 2:447–50.
7. *Documents on British Foreign Policy, 1919–1939* (London: Her Majesty's Stationery Office, 1951), doc. nos. 279 and 308.
8. House of Commons, *Parliamentary Debates, Official Reports* (London: His Majesty's Stationery Office, 1939), vol. 345, col. 2315.
9. Frank Munk, "My Century and My Many Lives," unpublished manuscript, 44.
10. Robert Bruce Lockhart, *Jan Masaryk: A Personal Memoir* (London: Philosophical Library, 1951), 27–28.
11. Anthony Eden, *Facing the Dictators: The Memoirs of Anthony Eden, Earl of Avon* (Boston: Houghton Mifflin, 1962), 192. Attlee noted that the Czechoslovak president "put far too much confidence in his own cleverness." See *As It Happened: The Autobiography of Clement R. Attlee* (New York: The Viking Press, 1952), 131–132.
12. Secretary of State Cordell Hull, Washington, to Charge d'Affaires, Alexander Kirk, U.S. Embassy, Berlin, July 8, 1939, *Foreign Relations of the United States Diplomatic Papers, 1939: General, the British Commonwealth and Europe* (Washington, DC: Government Printing Office, 1939) 2:458–59.
13. The National Archives of the United Kingdom, TNA, Foreign Office, 371/19461 N 3240, Minister Sir Joseph Addison, British Legation, Prague, to London, June 27, 1935.
14. NARA, William C. Bullitt, U.S. Embassy, Moscow, to the Secretary of State, Washington, June 14, 1935, 760F.6111/10.
15. Toman Brod, *Osudný omyl Edvarda Beneše, 1939–1948: Československá cesta do sovětského područí* (Prague: Academia, 2002), 16.
16. Ústav Tomáše G. Masaryka (UTGM), Beneš Papers, USSR 1939, box 169.
17. Jaroslav Kraus's record of his conversation with the Soviet diplomat Mikhail V. Korzh, London, May 21, 1941 in Jan Němeček et al., *Československo-sovětské vztahy v diplomatických jednáních, 1939–1945* (Prague: Státní Ústřední Archiv, 1999), doc. no. 81, 188–89.
18. Jaromír Smutný's Record of his conversation with Beneš, London, June 23, 1941 in Němeček et al., *Československo-sovětské vztahy*, doc. no. 84, 192–96.
19. Edvard Beneš, *Memoirs: From Munich to New War and New Victory*, trans. Godfrey Lias (London: Allen & Unwin, 1954), 110.
20. Beneš, *Memoirs*, 157, 166.

21. NARA, Ambassador John G. Winant, U.S. Embassy, London, to the Secretary of State, Washington, July 17, 1941, 860F.01/398.
22. Lockhart, *Jan Masaryk*, 36–37.
23. NARA, Ambassador John G. Winant, U.S. Embassy, London, for the President and the Secretary of State, Washington, July 18, 1941, telegram in three parts, 860F.01/398.
24. NARA, Ambassador John G. Winant, U.S. Embassy, London, for the President and the Secretary of State, Washington, April 2, 1941, 860F.01/370. Beneš wrote that Ambassador Kennedy "stood expressly and consistently behind Chamberlain's policy of appeasement," that the U.S. ambassador in Berlin, Hugh Wilson, came to Prague in August 1938 where he lectured Beneš on Hitler's "peaceful intentions," and that, finally, the U.S. ambassador in Paris, William Bullitt, worked "incessantly" on behalf of appeasement. Beneš, *Memoirs*, 172–73.
25. NARA, Ambassador John G. Winant, U.S. Embassy, London, to the Secretary of State, Washington, April 10, 1941, 860F.01/377.
26. NARA, Ambassador John G. Winant, U.S. Embassy, London, to Jan Masaryk, Minister of Foreign Affairs, London, July31, attached to a note from U.S. Embassy, London, to the Secretary of State, Washington, August 5, 1941, 860F.01/410.
27. NARA, Ambassador John G. Winant, U.S. Embassy, London, to the Secretary of State, Washington, May 7, 1941, 860.01/381.
28. Beneš, *Memoirs*, 188–90.
29. NARA, Ambassador John G. Winant, U.S. Embassy, London, to the Secretary of State, Washington, July 17, 1941, 860F.01/397. Regarding the agreement, see Němeček et al., *Československo-sovětské vztahy*, doc. nos. 91, 92, 93, pp. 210–14.
30. Beneš, *Memoirs*, 177.
31. NARA. Ambassador John G. Winant, U.S. Embassy, London, to the Secretary of State, Washington, August 5, 1941, 860F.01/410.
32. Beneš, *Memoirs*, 177–78.
33. NARA, Under Secretary of State Sumner Wells to Green H. Hackworth, Legal Advisor, Department of State, Washington, December 10, 1941, no call number.
34. NARA, Legal Advisor Green H. Hackworth to Under Secretary of State Sumner Wells, Department of State, Washington, December 10, 1941, no call number.
35. Fond Minister Hubert Ripka (FMHR), inventory unit 1559, box 46, Hubert Ripka, London, to Edvard Beneš, London, June 4, 1942.
36. Beneš, *Memoirs*, 302.
37. Beneš, *Memoirs*, 207–8.
38. Beneš, *Memoirs*, 231–32.
39. NARA, Minister Anthony J. Drexel Biddle, Jr., serving near the Provisional Government of Czechoslovakia, London, to the Secretary of State, Washington, September 21, 1942, 860F.01/456.
40. NARA, Franklin D. Roosevelt, the White House, to Edvard Beneš, London, October 28, 1942, 860F.458/21A.
41. NARA, Anthony J. Drexel Biddle, Jr., London, to the Secretary of State, Washington, November 16, 1942, 860F.01/471.
42. NARA, Sumner Welles, Memorandum of Conversation with Viscount Halifax, June 28, 1943, 760f.61/99.
43. Christopher Andrew and Oleg Gordievsky, *KGB: The Inside Story of Its Foreign Operations from Lenin to Gorbachev* (New York: HarperCollins, 1990), 322.
44. E. M. Primakov, eds., *Ocherki istorii rossiiskoi vneshnei razvedki*, vol. 2, *1917–1933* (Moscow: Mezhdunarodnye otnoshenia, 1997), photo section, and V. I. Trubnikov et al., eds., *Ocherki istorii rossiiskoi vneshnei razvedki*, vol. 4, *1941–1945* (Moscow: Mezhdunarodnye otnoshenia, 1999), photo section.
45. FMHR, inventory unit 1559, box 46, Hubert Ripka Memorandum of Conversation with I. A Chichayev and P. D Orlov, October 20, 1943.
46. Interview with Paul Zinner, April 5, 2005, Washington.
47. Beneš, *Memoirs*, 254–75.

48. Smutný's Memorandum, October 16, 1943, in *Dokumenty z historie československé politiky, 1939–1943*, ed. Libuše Otáhalová and Milada Červinková (Prague: Academia, 1966; henceforth DHCP), vol. 1, doc. no. 324, 393–97.

49. Record of President Beneš's conversation with Robert Bruce Lockhart, London, September 13, 1943, in Němeček et al., *Československo-sovětské vztahy*, doc. no. 24, 57–58.

50. Hubert Ripka, Memorandum of Conversation with Ambassador P. B Nichols, December 3, 1943, in Němeček et al., *Československo-sovětské vztahy*, doc. no. 56, 117.

51. Ripka, Memorandum of Conversation with Ambassador P. B Nichols, December 3, 1943, in Němeček et al., *Československo-sovětské vztahy*, doc. no. 56, 117.

52. Directives of Edvard Beneš, London, to Zdeněk Fierlinger, Moscow, regarding the Czechoslovak-Soviet agreement, October 13, 1943, in Němeček et al., *Československo-sovětské vztahy*, doc. no. 36, 77–79.

53. DHCP, vol. 1, doc. no. 324, 393–97.

54. Beneš, *Memoirs*, 254.

55. Jan Němeček, Helena Nováčková, and Ivan Šťovíček, "Edvard Beneš v USA v roce 1943: Dokumenty," *Sborník Archivních Prací* 49, no. 2 (1999): 475–76; Beneš, *Memoirs*, 180–96; and Ladislav Feierabend, *Beneš mezi Washingtonem a Moskvou: Vzpomínky z londýnské vlády od jara 1943 do jara 1944* (Washington, DC: published by author, 1966), 30–35.

56. NARA, Department of State, "Eduard Benes," Washington, DC, May 10, 1943, 860F.001/135.

57. "Visitor Bound for Illinois," *Time*, May 24, 1943.

58. Beneš, *Memoirs*, 184–86.

59. Record of the 92nd extraordinary meeting of the Czechoslovak Government, London, Report by President Edvard Beneš Regarding His Trip to the United States, June 17, 1943, in Němeček et al., *Československo-sovětské vztahy*, doc. no. 253, 501–4. It is not possible to check Beneš's record of his conversation with FDR against the relevant American documents, since they have never been found. See Department of State, *Foreign Relations of the United States, 1943*, vol. 3 (Washington, DC: Government Printing Office, 1963), 529. The editors noted that the U.S. records of the meetings between the Czechoslovak and American presidents "are not in the files of the Department of State nor in the Franklin D. Roosevelt Library at Hyde Park, New York."

60. NARA, Record Group 84, Confidential file, 1949, box 7, Chargé d'Affaires John H. Bruins, U.S. Embassy, London, to the Secretary of State, Washington, November 8, 1949. The first witness was Ladislav Feierabend, a former minister in Beneš's government-in-exile, who traveled with the president to Washington in 1943. The other was Jaromír Smutný, Beneš's closest confidant and chancellor.

61. In his memoirs Beneš blamed his pro-Soviet reputation on "German and Hungarian propaganda." *Memoirs*, 183.

62. NARA, CIA [*sic*] declassified report, May 19, 1943, 860f.001/144. Source and addressee redacted.

63. Archives of the Ministry of Foreign Affairs, AMFA, Chargé d'Affaires Josef Šust, Czechoslovak Legation, Moscow, to the Ministry of Foreign Affairs, secret, June 22, 1935.

64. NARA, A. A Berle, Jr., Department of State, May 31, 1943, Memorandum of Conversation, 860f.00/1009.

65. NARA, A. A Berle, Jr., Department of State, May 31, 1943, Memorandum of Conversation, 860f.00/1009.

66. Marie-Luise Goldbach, ed., *1. Januar bis 31. Dezember 1943, Amerikanische Deutschlandpolitik*, Dokumente zur Deutschlandpolitik, 1st ser., 4 (Munich: Oldenbourg, 1991), 88–101; and Roland J. Hoffmann, Kurt Heißig, Manfred Kittle, eds., *Odsun: Die Vertreibung der Sudetendeutschen*, vol. 2, *Dokumentation zu Ursachen, Planung und Realisierung einer "ethnischen Säuberung" in der Mitte Europas* (Munich: Sudetendeutsches Institut, 2010), 374–75.

67. Němeček et al., "Edvard Beneš v USA," 526.

68. Notes by Smutný on Beneš's conversation with Roosevelt, May 13, 1943, in Němeček et al., "Edvard Beneš v USA," 491.

69. See "Dossier Necas," *Revue des Études Slaves* 52 (1979): 135–40, Jonathan Zorach, "The Nečas Mission during the Munich Crisis: Nečas' Own Account from the Hoover Institution Archives," *East Central Europe* 16, nos. 1–2 (1989): 53–70, and Igor Lukes, *Czechoslovakia between Stalin and Hitler: The Diplomacy of Edvard Beneš in the 1930s* (New York: Oxford University Press, 1996), 221–22.

70. Vojtech Mastny, *The Czechs Under Nazi Rule: The Failure of National Resistance, 1939–1942* (New York: Columbia University Press, 1971).

71. Vladimír Krajina for Ústřední Vedení Odboje Domácího (ÚVOD) to Beneš in London, in Hoffmann et al., *Odsun*, doc. no. 78, 166–67.

72. The literature dealing with the postwar expulsions and other forms of retribution is vast. See Detlef Brandes, *Der Weg zur Vertreibung, 1938–1945: Pläne und Entscheidungen zum "Transfer" der Deutschen aus der Tschechoslowakei und aus Polen* (Munich: Oldenbourg, 2001), Benjamin Frommer, *National Cleansing: Retribution against Nazi Collaborators in Postwar Czechoslovakia* (New York: Cambridge University Press, 2005), and Norman M. Naimark, *Fires of Hatred: Ethnic Cleansing in Twentieth-Century Europe* (Cambridge, MA: Harvard University Press, 2001), 108–38. See also the German publication, quoted above, Hoffmann et al., *Odsun*.

73. Beneš, *Memoirs*, 195.

74. Record of the 92nd extraordinary meeting of the Czechoslovak Government, London, Report by President Edvard Beneš Regarding His Trip to the United States, June 17, 1943, in Němeček et al., *Československo-sovětské vztahy*, doc. no. 253, 504. See also Beneš, *Memoirs*, 183–87.

75. FMHR, inventory unit 1559, box 46, Hubert Ripka's Memorandum for the President, London, October 21, 1942.

76. Jaromír Smutný, London, to Colonel Hubert Píka, Istanbul, January 30, 1940, in Němeček et al., *Československo-sovětské vztahy*, doc. no. 45, 116–17.

77. NA, ACC CPC, f. 100, inventory no. 24, file 175, archival unit 1566. Polish Prime Minister Władysław Sikorski warned Beneš that Stalin would impose Communism upon Central Europe in May 1942. Beneš shrugged his shoulders: in that case there was nothing either of them could do about it.

78. Beneš, *Memoirs*, 259–60.

79. "New Partnership," *Time*, December 20, 1943.

80. Archives of Jaromír Smutný, Columbia University, New York (JSCU), BBC Broadcasts, 1950–56, "Stalin, moje vzpomínky z Moskvy."

81. Teresa Toranska, *"Them": Stalin's Polish Puppets*, trans. Agnieszka Kolakowska (New York: Harper & Row, 1987).

82. JSCU, Jaromír Smutný, "Stalin, moje vzpomínky z Moskvy."

83. Vojtech Mastny, "The Beneš-Stalin-Molotov Conversations in December 1943: New Documents," *Jahrbücher für Geschichte Osteuropas* 20, no. 3 (September 1972): 367–402.

84. NARA, Rudolf E. Schoenfeld, Charge d'Affaires, London, to the Secretary of State, Washington, January 6, 1945, 860f.01/1-645. Schoenfeld quotes Jan Masaryk's speech of December 31, 1944, in London that presented the treaty as a "solid, unalterable and mighty foundation" of Czechoslovak foreign policy.

85. Beneš, *Memoirs*, 255–58.

86. Jan Stransky, *East Wind over Prague* (New York: Random House, 1951), 22.

87. NARA, Ambassador W. Averell Harriman, Moscow, to the Secretary of State, Washington, December 18, 1943, 860f.001/163.

88. LOC, Steinhardt Papers, William Walton Cable no. 22, Sans Origine (Austria) to David Hulburd, sent June 30, 1945. "Russo-Czech Accord Covers Rule in War and Free Zones," *Christian Science Monitor*, May 1, 1944.

89. NARA, Office of Strategic Services, Research and Analysis Branch, "Report on Czechoslovakia: Pivot Point of Europe," July 4, 1945.

90. NARA, Rudolf E. Schoenfeld, Charge d'Affaires, London, to the Secretary of State, Washington, January 6, 1945, 860f.01/1-645.

91. Feierabend, *Beneš mezi Washigtonem a Moskvou*, 103.

92. General Sikorski Historical Institute, *Documents on Polish-Soviet Relations*, vol. 2 (London: Heinemann, 1967), doc. no. 73, 733.

## Chapter 2

1. "I. V. Stalin's letter to E. Beneš, President of the Czechoslovak Republic, on the events in the Trans-Carpathian Ukraine, January 23, 1945," quoted in Galina P. Murashko and Albina F. Noskova, "Stalin and the National-Territorial Controversies in Eastern Europe, 1945–1947 (Part 1)", *Cold War History* 1, no. 3 (April 2000): 161–72.

2. See F. Němec and V. Moudrý, *The Soviet Seizure of Subcarpathian Ruthenia* (Toronto: Anderson, 1955), Paul Robert Magocsi, *The Shaping of a National Identity: Subcarpathian Rus'*, *1848–1948* (Cambridge, MA: Harvard University Press, 1978), and Ladislav K. Feierabend, *Politické vzpomínky*, vol. 3 (Brno, Czech Republic: Atlantis, 1996), 193–201.

3. Zdeněk Fierlinger, Moscow, to Edvard Beneš, London, regarding Fierlinger's interview with V. Z. Lebedev, January 17, 1945, in Jan Němeček et al., *Československo-sovětské vztahy v diplomatických jednáních, 1939–1945* (Prague: Státní Ústřední Archiv, 1999), doc. no. 223, 462.

4. Edvard Beneš, London, to Zdeněk Fierlinger, Moscow, regarding the recognition of the Polish Government, January 18, 1945, in Němeček et al., *Československo-sovětské vztahy*, doc. no. 224, 463.

5. Record of Hubert Ripka's conversation with Ivan A. Chichayev, London, January 27, 1945, in Němeček et al., *Československo-sovětské vztahy*, doc. no. 234, 478.

6. "Czechs Recognize 2 Polish Regimes," *New York Times*, February 1, 1945; "London Poles Break with Benes Regime," *New York Times*, February 2, 1945.

7. Hubert Ripka's record regarding Jan Masaryk's and Hubert Ripka's conversation with P. B. Nichols, O. Sargent, A. Schoenfeld, and Jacques Emil Paris, London, January 29, 1945, in Němeček et al., *Československo-sovětské vztahy*, doc. no. 235, 480.

8. NARA, Rudolf E. Schoenfeld, Charge d'Affaires ad interim, London, to the Secretary of State, Washington, March 19, 1945, 860F.01/3-1945.

9. Feierabend (1891–1969) was trained as a lawyer in Prague, Switzerland, and Great Britain. He was a leading official of the Republican (Agrarian) Party.

10. Ladislav K. Feierabend, *Soumrak československé demokracie* (Washington, DC: published by author, 1967), 132–34.

11. Josef Korbel, *The Communist Subversion of Czechoslovakia, 1938–1948: The Failure of Coexistence* (Princeton, NJ: Princeton University Press, 1959), 111.

12. NARA, John G. Winant, London, to the Secretary of State, Washington, March 13, 1945, 860F.01/3-1345.

13. Interview with William Henry Bruins, the son of John Herman Bruins, April 29, 2004, Wellesley, MA.

14. Bruins, "Life of a Family," 218; unpublished manuscript.

15. Zdeněk Fierlinger's record of his conversation with V. A. Zorin, Moscow, March 25, 1945, in Němeček et al., *Československo-sovětské vztahy*, doc. no. 256, 524–25. It is unlikely that the group included as many as fifty diplomats.

16. NARA, Averell Harriman, U.S. Embassy, Moscow, to the Secretary of State, Washington, March 26, 1945, 860F.01/3-2645.

17. NARA, Averell Harriman, U.S. Embassy, Moscow, to the Secretary of State, Washington, March 27, 1945, 860F.01/3-2745.

18. NARA, John G. Winant, London, to the Secretary of State, Washington, March 28, 1945, 860F.01/3-2845.

19. NARA, John G. Winant, London, to the Secretary of State, Washington, March 28, 1945, 860F.01/3-2845; Hubert Ripka, *Únorová tragédie: Svědectví přímého účastníka* (Brno, Czech Republic: Atlantis, 1995), 48.

20. FMHR, Institute of Contemporary History, Prague, inventory unit 1559, box 46, "Conversation with Chichayev," London, January 8, 1945, Secret.

21. Feierabend, *Soumrak československé demokracie*, 147.

22. NARA, John G. Winant, London, to the Secretary of State, Washington, April 7, 1945, 860f.01/4-745.
23. NARA, Averell Harriman, U.S. Embassy, Moscow, to the Secretary of State, Washington, March 31, 1945, 760F.61/3-3145.
24. NARA, Department of State, Washington, to the U.S. Embassy, Moscow, summary of a telegram from the embassy near the Czechoslovak Government in London, April 4, 1945, 860F.01/3-2945.
25. Hubert Ripka's telegram, London, to Edvard Beneš, Moscow, regarding the postponed trip of the diplomatic corps to the liberated areas of Czechoslovakia, in Němeček et al., *Československo-sovětské vztahy*, doc. no. 263, 534–35.
26. NARA, Department of State, Washington, to the U.S. Embassy, Moscow, summary of a telegram from the Embassy near the Czechoslovak Government in London, April 4, 1945, 860F.01/3-2945.
27. NARA, Department of State, Washington, to the United States Embassy, London, for Rudolph E. Schoenfeld, Chargé d'Affaires ad interim, serving near the Government of Czechoslovakia, April 4, 1945, 860f.01/3-2845, CS/EG.
28. Prokop Drtina, *Československo můj osud: Kniha života českého demokrata 20. století*, vol. 2, part 1, *Emigrací k vítězství* (Toronto: 68 Publishers, 1982), 7–14; Feierabend, *Soumrak československé demokracie*, 133–47.
29. NARA, John G. Winant, London, to the Secretary of State, Washington, March 13, 1945, 860F.01/3-1345.
30. "Czechs Leave London," *New York Times*, March 10, 1945; Drtina, *Československo můj osud*, 9.
31. Drtina, *Československo můj osud*, 10–11.
32. Feierabend, *Soumrak československé demokracie*, 146.
33. "Czech Leader Returns Home, Ends 6 Yr. Exile," *Chicago Tribune*, March 12, 1945; "Exile of Benes Ends," *New York Times*, March 12, 1945.
34. NARA, John G. Winant, London, to the Secretary of State, Washington, March 13, 1945, 860F.01/3-1345.
35. NARA, Averell Harriman, U.S. Embassy, Moscow, to the Secretary of State, Washington, March 19, 1945, 860F.001/3-1945.
36. AMFA, March 31, 1945, Moscow, PO 1945–1954, box 93.
37. Ripka, *Únorová tragédie*, 45–46.
38. George F. Kennan, *Memoirs 1925–1950* (Boston: Little, Brown, 1967), 254; John Earl Haynes and Harvey Klehr, *Venona: Decoding Soviet Espionage in America* (New Haven, CT: Yale University Press, 1999), 385.
39. Ripka, *Únorová tragédie*, 46.
40. NARA, Averell Harriman, U.S. Embassy, Moscow, to the Secretary of State, Washington, March 22, 1945, 860F.01/3-2245.
41. Korbel, *Communist Subversion of Czechoslovakia*, 114.
42. Interview with Paul Zinner, April 5, 2005, Washington, DC.
43. "Soviet-Czech Talks End," *New York Times*, March 31, 1945.
44. Drtina, *Československo můj osud*, 27–28; Jan Stransky, *East Wind over Prague* (New York: Random House, 1951), 30–40.
45. NARA, Averell Harriman, U.S. Embassy, Moscow, to the Secretary of State, Washington, March 31, 1945, 760F.61/3-3145.
46. Václav Kopecký, *ČSR a KSČ: Pamětní výpisy k historii Československé republiky a k bojům KSČ za socialistické Československo* (Prague: Státní Nakl. Politické Literatury, 1960), 383.
47. NARA, Ambassador Averell Harriman, Moscow, to the Secretary of State, Washington, April 3, 1945, 860.01/4-345.
48. Drtina, *Československo můj osud*, 29–43. The bubble is also noted in Dorothy Bruins, "Life of a Family," 225. Beneš's isolation is stressed by Ripka, *Únorová tragédie*, 48–49.
49. Drtina, *Československo můj osud*, 29.
50. Most sources have Beneš arriving at Košice on April 3, 1945. Some, however, put Beneš's arrival to Košice a day earlier, April 2, 1945. The State Department was informed that Beneš

arrived in Košice on April 3, 1945. NARA. Ambassador Harriman, Moscow, to the Secretary of State, Washington, April 7, 1945, 860F.01/4-745.

51. František Hanzlík and Václav Vondrášek, *Armáda v zápase o politickou moc v letech 1945–1948* (Prague: Ministerstvo Obrany ČR, 2006), 98–99.

52. Drtina, *Československo můj osud*, 35.

53. NARA, Ambassador Averell Harriman, Moscow, to the Secretary of State, Washington, April 7, 1945, 860F.01/4-745.

54. For instance, NARA, Ambassador Harriman, Moscow, to the Secretary of State, Washington, April 11, 1945, 860F.01/4-1145.

55. The most vocal critics of the Košice Program were those who, like Feierabend, stayed behind in London; they would have no or minimal political influence in postwar Prague. Feierabend, *Politické vzpomínky*, 233–35.

56. Drtina, *Československo můj osud*, 38.

57. FMHR, inventory unit 1559, box 46, Ripka's "Conversation with Chichayev," London, January 8, 1945, Secret.

58. NARA, Secret Telegram, Department of State, May 11, 1945, 860F.01/5-245.

59. Drtina, *Československo můj osud*, 38.

60. " Beneš má 'vládnout'—Gottwald diktovat," *Večerní České Slovo*, April 5, 1945.

61. "Patton Bisects Reich and Enters Czechoslovakia," *Christian Science Monitor*, April 18, 1945; "Patton Crashes Deeper Inside Czechoslovakia," *Los Angeles Times*, April 19, 1945; "Into Czechoslovakia," *New York Times*, April 19, 1945.

62. Bruins, *Life of a Family*, 231.

63. "Into Czechoslovakia," *New York Times*, April 19, 1945.

64. Drtina, *Československo můj osud*, 40–41.

65. NARA, Rudolf E. Schoenfeld, Chargé d'Affaires ad interim, London, to the Secretary of State, Washington, April 21, 1945, 860F.01/4-2145 and NARA; John G. Winant, London, to the Secretary of State, Washington, April 21, 1945, 860F.01/4-2145.

66. NARA, United States Embassy, London, for Rudolf E. Schoenfeld, Chargé d'Affaires ad interim, London, April 25, 1945, 860F.01/4-2145.

67. "Czech Policy under Survey at Washington," *Christian Science Monitor*, April 21, 1945.

68. Anne McCormick, "First Exiled Government in Eastern Europe Goes Home," *New York Times*, April 21, 1945.

69. NARA, Cecil B. Lyon, First Secretary of U.S. Legation, Cairo, Egypt, to the Secretary of State, August 25, 1945, 861.00/8-2545. Lyon attached the January 1943 memorandum prepared by T. H. Preston, a British diplomat.

70. NARA, John G. Winant, London, to the Secretary of State, Washington, April 22, 1945, 860F.01/3-2245.

71. Harry S. Truman, *Memoirs*, vol. 2, *Years of Trial and Hope* (New York: Doubleday, 1956), 216–17.

72. John Wheeler-Bennett and Anthony Nicholls, *The Semblance of Peace: The Political Settlement after the Second World War* (New York: St. Martin's, 1972), 289; Milovan Djilas, *Conversations with Stalin*, trans. Michael B. Petrovich (New York: Hartcourt, Brace & World, 1962), 114.

73. Forrest C. Pogue, "Why Eisenhower's Forces Stopped at the Elbe," *World Politics* 4, 3 (April 1952): 356–68.

74. NARA, General Eisenhower, SHAEF, to the United States Military Mission, Moscow, April 21, 1945, FW 860f.01/12-1748. See also Joseph Patrick Hobbs, ed., *Dear General: Eisenhower's Wartime Letters to Marshall* (Baltimore: Johns Hopkins Press, 1971), 222.

75. Alfred D. Chandler, Jr., ed., *The Papers of Dwight David Eisenhower*, vol. 4, (Baltimore: Johns Hopkins Press, 1970), doc. no. 2462, 2662. See also Ed Cray, *General of the Army: George C. Marshall, Soldier and Statesman* (New York: Norton, 1990), 529–30.

76. "3rd Army Diverted from Third Goal," *New York Times*, April 24, 1945.

77. Charles M. Province, *Patton's Third Army: A Daily Combat Diary* (New York: Hippocrene Books, 1992), 258; Jindřich Marek, *Šeříkový sólokapr: Příběhy spojeneckých novinářů a vojáků z května 1945* (Cheb, Czech Republic: Svět Křídel, 2002), 179.

78. Stephen E. Ambrose, *Eisenhower*, vol. 1, *Soldier, General of the Army, President-Elect, 1890–1952* (New York: Simon & Schuster, 1983), 395.
79. NA, F1/1-114, Hubert Ripka, London, to the Czechoslovak Embassy, Moscow, and the Czechoslovak Government, Košice, April 30, 1945.
80. NARA, Rudolf E. Schoenfeld, Chargé d'Affaires ad interim, London, to the Secretary of State, Washington, April 28, 1945, 860F.20/4-2845.
81. NARA, Secretary of State, E. R. Stettinius, San Francisco, to Acting Secretary of State, Joseph Grew, Washington, April 28, 1945, 740.0011 E W/4-2845.
82. Martin Gilbert, *Winston S. Churchill*, vol. VII, *Road to Victory, 1941–1945* (Boston: Houghton Mifflin, 1986), 1322.
83. V. I. Trubnikov et al., eds., *Ocherki istorii rossiiskoi vneshnei razvedki v shesti tomakh*, vol. 4, *1941–1945* (Moscow: Mezhdunarodnye Otnoshenia, 2003), doc. no. 75, 649.
84. "Patton Drives to Smash Czechoslovakia Pocket," *Los Angeles Times*, May 6, 1945.
85. Tomáš Jakl, *Květen 1945 v českých zemích: Pozemní operace vojsk Osy a Spojenců* (Prague: Miroslav Bílý, 2004).
86. George S. Patton, *War As I Knew It* (Boston: Houghton Mifflin, 1947), 326–27.
87. NARA, General Eisenhower to the United States Military Mission, Moscow, May 4, 1945, FW 860f.01/12-1748. A slightly different version of the message is in Chandler, *Papers of Dwight David Eisenhower*, doc. no. 2482, 2679–80.
88. NARA, United States Military Mission, Moscow, to SHAEF, May 5, 1945, FW 860f.01/12-1748. See also Chandler, *Papers of Dwight David Eisenhower*, doc. no. 2482, 2679–80.
89. NARA, General Eisenhower to United States Military Mission, Moscow, May 6, 1945, FW 860f.01/12-1748. See also Chandler, *Papers of Dwight David Eisenhower*, doc. no. 2496, 2693–94.
90. David Eisenhower, *Eisenhower at War, 1943–1945* (New York: Random House, 1986), 801–2.
91. Harry J. Truman Presidential Library, Joseph C. Grew, Acting Secretary, Department of State, to the President, Washington, May 4, 1945, President's Secretary's Files, box 153.
92. Callum MacDonald and Jan Kaplan, *Prague in the Shadow of the Swastika: A History of the German Occupation, 1939–1945* (London: Quartet Books, 1995), 192.
93. John MacCormack, "Fight After Surrender," *New York Times*, May 8, 1945.
94. "Slavná Rudá armáda," *Rudé Právo*, September 23, 1945.
95. K. H. Frank, "Ein Wort zur Stunde," *Der Neue Tag*, September 9, 1944; "Eine Mahnung zur rechten Zeit," *Tageszeitung für Böhmen und Mähren*, September 10, 1944.
96. The description of the jeep's journey to Prague is based on my interviews with Kurt Taub, March 5–6, 2000, Salzburg, Austria.
97. AMI, Prague, Jaromír Nechanský et al., V 5443, podsvazek no. 1.
98. AMI, V 5443, Attachment.
99. "London Poles Break With Beneš Regime," *New York Times*, February 2, 1945.
100. AMI, V 5443, Nechanský's interrogation, October 10, 1949.
101. Antonín Benčík and Karel Richter, *Vražda jménem republiky: Tragický osud generála Heliodora Píky* (Prague: Ostrov, 2006), 191–96.
102. Radomir Luza, *The Hitler Kiss: A Memoir of the Czech Resistance* (Baton Rouge: Louisiana State University Press, 2002), 195–99.
103. Luza, *Hitler Kiss*, 228.
104. The scene was described to me by Taub in Salzburg, Austria, March 5–6, 2000.
105. John MacCormack, "Swift Soviet Dash Liberates Prague," *New York Times*, May 10, 1945.
106. Zdeněk Roučka, *Skončeno a podepsáno: Drama Pražského povstání* (Pilsen: ZR & T, 2003), English summary. In addition to the ten casualties, the Red Army lost about twenty additional soldiers to accidents.
107. NARA, HQ, Communications, European Theater of Operations, U.S. Army, Paris, France, to the War Department, June 1, 1945, 860f.01/6-245.
108. Stransky, *East Wind over Prague*, 30–40.
109. Luza, *Hitler Kiss*, 231–33.
110. NARA, A. W. Klieforth, Charge d'Affaires, Prague, July 7, 1945, to the Secretary of State, Washington, 860f.01/7-745, and same, July 11, 1945, 860f.01/7-1145; ACC CPC, 1945–51,

100/1, vol. 64, unit 524, "Report on the Territory Under U.S. Occupation," July 20, 1945, and Stanley B. Winters, "Conflicted Partners—Czech Opposition to the U.S. Occupation of Western Bohemia in 1945," paper presented at the 38th National Convention of the AAASS, Washington, DC, April 18, 2006.

111. John MacCormack, "Red Army Accused of 'Terror Reign,'" *New York Times*, August 13, 1945.
112. Norman M. Naimark, *The Russians in Germany: A History of the Soviet Zone of Occupation, 1945–1949* (Cambridge, MA: Belknap Press of Harvard University Press, 1995), 79.
113. Tatiana Metternich, *Tatiana: Full Circle in a Shifting Europe*, rev. ed. (London: Elliot & Thompson, 2004), 245–55.
114. John A. Armitage, "The View from Czechoslovakia," in *Witnesses to the Origins of the Cold War*, ed. Thomas T. Hammond (Seattle: University of Washington Press, 1982), 216–17.
115. LOC, Steinhardt Papers, box 83, Ambassador Steinhardt, 30 Pine Street, New York City, to the Hon. Rudolf Schoenfeld, the American Embassy near the Czechoslovakia Government, London, May 21, 1945.
116. Interview with Spencer L. Taggart, April 23, 1999, Logan, UT.
117. OSA 300-30-22, box 8.
118. "It Ends Where It Began," *New York Times*, May 10, 1945.
119. Bruins, *Life of a Family*, 218.
120. Drtina, *Československo můj osud*, 46.
121. Ivan Savický, *Osudová setkání : Češi v Rusku a Rusové v Čechách, 1914–1938* (Prague: Academia, 1999), 260, Vladimír Bystrov, *Osud generála* (Prague: Academia, 2007), 477–531; see also Sergei Davydov, "Al'fred Liudvigovich Bem (1886–1945)," *Pushkin Review* 1 (1998): 35–38.
122. "Presidentova cesta Prahou," *Rudé Právo*, May 17, 1945.
123. "Dnes přijíždí president," *Rudé Právo*, May 16, 1945.
124. NARA, Chargé d'Affaires ad interim Rudolf E. Schoenfeld, U.S. Embassy near the Czechoslovak Government, London, to the Secretary of State, Washington, May 22, 1945, 860f.001/5-2245.
125. "President Dr. E. Beneš v Praze," *Rudé Právo*, May 17, 1945.
126. NARA, Counselor of the U.S. Embassy, Alfred W. Klieforth, Prague, to the Secretary of State, Washington, June 8, 1945, 860f.01/6-845.
127. "Sovětský svaz nás nikdy nezradil," *Rudé Právo*, October 5, 1945.
128. NARA, General John Magruder, OSS Intelligence Service, to General Julius Holmes, Assistant Secretary of State, Washington, May 18, 1945, 860f.00/5-1845.
129. The myth persisted for decades to come; see Jan Galandauer and Miroslav Honzík, *1945: Nikdy nekvetly šeříky tak krásně* (Prague: Svoboda, 1985).
130. C. L. Sulzberger, "'Zones of Interest' Shifting in Europe," *New York Times*, May 20, 1945.

## Chapter 3

1. John Thompson, "Konrad Henlein Kills Himself," *Chicago Daily Tribune*, May 11, 1945;"Free Life Begins Once More," *Los Angeles Times*, May 11, 1945.
2. "K. H. Frank na Pankráci," *Rudé Právo*, August 8, 1945.
3. OSA, 300-30-22/box 3, Radio Prague, August 5, 1951. On jazz after the war, see Josef Škvorecký, *Talkin' Moscow Blues* (New York: Ecco, 1990), 91.
4. According to *Národní Politika*, Prague had seventy-nine movie theaters in early 1945. The films offered included *Come Back to Me!*, *The Singing Girl*, *The Eighteen-Year-Old*, and *La Paloma*.
5. Jan Slavík, "Kus sovětského Ruska u nás," *Svobodné Slovo*, July 4, 1945.
6. LOC, Steinhardt Papers, Francis T. Williams, State Department, Washington, to Laurence Steinhardt, U.S. Embassy, Prague, n.d., possibly July 1945; NARA, Department of State, Washington, to the United States Embassy, London, for Rudolph E. Schoenfeld, Chargé d'Affaires ad interim, April 4, 1945, 860f.01/3-2845.
7. Interview with Kurt Taub, March 5, 2000, Salzburg, Austria; Pavel Žáček, "O.S.S. a české povstání," *Národní Osvobození*, May 10, 2001, 8.

8. Interview with Kurt Taub, March 5, 2000.

9. SFA, Bundesarchiv Bern, E 2200. 190,-/3, Bd. 1, 1928–1945, Jahresbericht 1941 des Schwizerischen Generalkonsulates in Prag; Swiss Federal Archives, E 2200.56-/3, Der Schwizerische Generalkonsul und Frank Novotny, Der Verwalter des Regierungsbesitzes der Vereinigten Staaten in Prague, December 22, 1941.

10. SFA, Bundesarchiv Bern, B. 24. USA (2) o-1, U.S.A. en Allemagne et en Pays Occupés, Remise des Archives et des Intérets, July 5, 1945, Albert Huber, Prague, to Abteilung für Fremde Interessen des Eidgenössischen Politischen Departements, Bern.

11. Interview with Kurt Taub, Salzburg, Austria, March 6, 2000.

12. Interview with Janet Edwards, Katek's daughter, Potomac, MD, July 19, 2000.

13. Information on Mr. Bruins is from Dorothy Bruins, *Life of a Family*, unpublished manuscript, and from my interview with his son, William, Wellesley, MA, April 29, 2004. I am grateful to Mr. Bruins for a copy of his mother's memoirs.

14. *Register of the Department of State* (Washington: Office of Public Affairs, 1950), 66.

15. Bruins, *Life of a Family*, 202–8.

16. LOC, Steinhardt Papers, "U.S. Embassy in Prague," William Walton Cable no. 22, sent from Austria, June 30, 1945.

17. AMFA, Diplomatic Protocol, USA, 1945–1955, box 55, A. W. Klieforth, Chargé d'Affaires a.i., to Vladimír Clementis, Acting Minister for Foreign Affairs, June 7, 1945. See also "U.S. Envoys in Prague," *New York Times*, June 2, 1945.

18. "Americans Fly to Pilsen," *New York Times*, May 30, 1945.

19. Chargé Alfred W. Klieforth, U.S. Embassy, Prague, to the Secretary of State, Washington, via Ambassador Jefferson Caffery, U.S. Embassy, Paris, June 5, 1945, in *Foreign Relations of the United States, 1945*, vol. 4 (Washington, DC: U.S. Government Printing Office, 1968), 455–56.

20. AMFA, Diplomatický protokol, cizí ZU v Praze, USA, 1945–55, box 55, Alfred W. Klieforth, Chargé d'Affaires a.i. to Vlado Clementis, Prague, June 7, 1945. See "Velvyslanectví USA v Praze oznamuje," *Svobodné Slovo*, June 15, 1945.

21. LOC, Steinhardt Papers, box 47, State Department, Washington, to Ambassador Laurence Steinhardt, 30 Pine Street, New York, June 14, 1945; NARA, Chargé A. W. Klieforth, Prague, to the Secretary of State, Washington, June 8, 1945, 860F.01/6-845.

22. LOC, Steinhardt Papers, box 47, Chargé d'Affaires A. W. Klieforth, U.S. Embassy, Prague, to James W. Riddleberger, Central European Division, Department of State, Washington, June 4, 1945.

23. LOC, Steinhardt Papers, box 47, State Department, Washington, to Ambassador Laurence Steinhardt, 30 Pine Street, New York, June 14, 1945; NARA, Chargé A. W. Klieforth, Prague, to the Secretary of State, Washington, June 8, 1945, 860F.01/6-845.

24. NARA, Chargé A. W. Klieforth, U.S. Embassy, Prague, to the Secretary of State, Washington, June 13, 1945, 860F.515/6-1345.

25. Walter Birge, "Prague, Czechoslovakia," 11, unpublished manuscript.

26. LOC, Steinhardt Papers, box 47, U.S. Embassy, Prague, William Walton Cable no. 22, Sans Origine (Austria) to David Hulburd, sent June 30, 1945.

27. LOC, Steinhardt Papers, box 47, Chargé d'Affaires A. W. Klieforth, U.S. Embassy, Prague, to James W. Riddleberger, Central European Division, Department of State, Washington, June 4, 1945. See also NARA, U.S. HQ, European Theater, Paris, France, to War Department, June 1, 1945, 860F.01/6-245.

28. Robert B. Pynsent, ed., *The Phoney Peace: Power and Culture in Central Europe 1945–49* (London: School of Slavonic and East European Studies, London, 2000), 9.

29. LOC, Steinhardt Papers, box 47, Chargé d'Affaires A. W. Klieforth, U.S. Embassy, Prague, to James W. Riddleberger, Central European Division, Department of State, Washington, June 4, 1945.

30. Jan Stransky, *East Wind over Prague* (New York: Random House, 1951), 56–57.

31. NARA, HQ, European Theater, Paris, France, to the Department of War, June 1, 1945, 860f.01/6-245.

32. Zdeněk Roučka, *Američané a západní Čechy 1945* (Pilsen: ZR & T, 2000).

33. NARA, A. W. Klieforth, U.S. Embassy, Prague, to the Secretary of State, Washington, "Beneš's Visit to Pilsen," June 16, 1945, 860F.001/6-1645.

34. NARA, General E. N. Harmon, HQ XXII Corps, to Chargé A. W. Klieforth, U.S. Embassy, Prague, July 6, 1945, enclosure to 860F. 01/7-745.

35. NARA, Vladimír Clementis, Ministry of Foreign Affairs, Prague, to A. W. Klieforth, U.S. Embassy, Prague, June 30, 1945, Enclosure no. 1 to A. W. Klieforth to the Secretary of State, Washington, July 7, 1945, 860F.01/7-345.

36. NARA, A. W. Klieforth, U.S. Embassy, Prague, to Vladimír Clementis, Ministry of Foreign Affairs, Prague, July 3, 1945, Enclosure no. 2 to A. W. Klieforth to the Secretary of State, Washington, July 7, 1945, 860F.01/7-345.

37. NA, General Secretariat, CC CPC, 1945–1951, fond 100/1, file 64, archival unit 524.

38. E. N. Harmon, *Combat Commander: Autobiography of a Soldier* (Englewood Cliffs, NJ: Prentice-Hall, 1970), 272.

39. Harmon, *Combat Commander*, 274.

40. NARA, General E. N. Harmon, HQ 22 Corps, to Chargé A. W. Klieforth, U.S. Embassy, Prague, July 7, 1945, enclosure to 860F.01/7-1145.

41. NARA, Ambassador W. Averell Harriman, U.S. Embassy, Moscow, to the Secretary of State, Washington, June 26, 1945, 860F.00/6-2645.

42. NARA, Chargé A. W. Klieforth, U.S. Embassy, Prague, to the Secretary of State, Washington, July 5, 1945, 860F.01/7-545; NA, ACC CPC, fond 100/24, archival unit 1157, June 8, 1945.

43. NARA, Chargé A. W. Klieforth, U.S. Embassy, Prague, to the Secretary of State, Washington, July 6, 1945, 860F.01/7-645.

44. NARA, Joseph C. Grew, Acting Secretary of State, Washington, Department of State Telegram to the U.S. Embassy, Prague, Urgent and Secret, July 6, 1945, 860F.01/7-645. The reference number is identical with that of the document cited in the note above, although it denotes a different document.

45. NARA, Chargé A. W. Klieforth, U.S. Embassy, Prague, to the Secretary of State, Washington, July 9, 1945, 860F.01/7-945; Department of State Telegram to the U.S. Embassy, Prague, by Secretary of State James F. Byrnes, 860F.01/7-445.

46. John MacCormack, "Prague is Crucible of Allied Tensions, *New York Times*, July 8, 1945. See also Alfred W. Klieforth, U.S. Embassy, Prague, to the Secretary of State, Washington, June 21, 1945 in *Foreign Relations of the United States 1945*, vol. 4, *Europe* (Washington, DC: Government Printing Office, 1968), 459–60, 476–77 (henceforth *FRUS 1945*).

47. AMFA, Generální sekretariát, 1945–1954, box 191, Ambassador Nichols to the Ministry of Foreign Affairs, regarding the incident of June 20, 1945.

48. AMFA, Diplomatic Protocol, USA, 1945–1955, box 54, the United States Embassy, October 18, 1945.

49. NARA, Chargé A. W. Klieforth, U.S. Embassy, Prague, to the Secretary of State, Washington, June 29, 1945, 860F.01/6-2945.

50. Ambassador Averell Harriman, U.S. Embassy, Moscow, to the Secretary of State, Washington, July 9, 1945; Chargé Alfred W. Klieforth, U.S. Embassy, Prague, to the Secretary of State, Washington, July 14, 1945, in *FRUS 1945*, 475–77.

51. Acting Secretary of State Joseph Grew, Washington, to Ambassador Laurence Steinhardt, U.S. Embassy, Prague, August 7, 1945, in *FRUS 1945*, 482; Ambassador Laurence Steinhardt, U.S. Embassy, Prague, to the Secretary of State, Washington, July 23, 1945, *FRUS 1945* 478–79.

52. LOC, Steinhardt Papers, box 47, Chargé Klieforth, United States Embassy, Prague, to Ambassador Steinhardt, August 23, 1945.

53. AMFA, Diplomatic Protocol, USA, 1945–1955, box 54, U.S. Embassy, October 18, 1945.

54. Interview with George and Virginia Bogardus and Louise Schaffner, January 30 1999, Washington, DC, and Bethesda, MD, and Walter Birge, November 2, 1998, Kingston, MA.

55. LOC, Steinhardt Papers, box 47, Chargé d'Affaires A. W. Klieforth, U.S. Embassy, Prague, to Ambassador Laurence Steinhardt, c/o Department of State, Washington, June 4, 1945.

## Chapter 4

1. NARA, Office of Strategic Services, Research and Analysis Branch, "Report on Czechoslo-vakia: Pivot Point of Europe," July 4, 1945.
2. Interview with Louise Schaffner, January 29, 1999, Washington, DC.
3. Interview with Dulcie-Ann Steinhardt Sherlock, June 18, 1998, Washington, DC.
4. LOC, Steinhardt Papers, box 68, "The Current Situation in Czechoslovakia," lecture presented at the National War College, Washington, DC, December 15, 1947.
5. Unless otherwise indicated, information on Steinhardt is from my interviews with Dulcie-Ann Steinhardt Sherlock, Steinhardt's daughter; Laurene A. Sherlock, Steinhardt's grand-daughter; and Peter R. and Naomi Rosenblatt; Mr. Rosenblatt is Steinhardt's nephew. I am most grateful to Ms. Sherlock and Mr. and Mrs. Rosenblatt for their kindness and for sharing with me Mrs. Steinhardt Sherlock's unpublished manuscript "R.S.V.P." Some details are from John A. Garraty and Mark C. Carnes, eds., *American National Biography* (New York: Oxford University Press, 1999).
6. Bill Santin, Columbia University, Registrar's Office, February 9, 2006.
7. Jocelyn K. Wilk, Columbia University Archives, February 8, 2006.
8. G. E. R. Gedye, "Ambassador to the USSR," *New York Times*, April 21, 1940.
9. LOC, Steinhardt Papers, box 57, November 11, 1948.
10. Steinhardt Sherlock, "R.S.V.P.," 25.
11. LOC, Steinhardt Papers; see Steinhardt's letter from Stockholm to his wife at the Ritz Hotel, Paris, September 29, 1933 (box 90); interview with George Bogardus, June 3, 1998, Bethesda, MD.
12. Steinhardt Sherlock, "R.S.V.P.," 146.
13. Walter Birge, "Istanbul," 11, unpublished manuscript,
14. Steinhardt Sherlock, "R.S.V.P.,"22.
15. "Bonaparte Jewels Found, Seller Gone," *New York Times*, March 2, 1930; "Napoleon Necklace Returned by Buyer," *New York Times*, March 22, 1930.
16. Interview with Peter and Naomi Rosenblatt, October 27, 2007, Bethesda, MD; Dennis J. Dunn, *Caught Between Roosevelt and Stalin: America's Ambassadors to Moscow* (Lexing-ton: University of Kentucky Press, 1998), 93.
17. LOC, Steinhardt Papers, box 68; "Plan to Reorganize Swedish Match Co.," *New York Times*, November 30, 1932.
18. "Democratic Funds Reach $1,427,118," *New York Times*, November 5, 1932.
19. LOC, Steinhardt Papers, box 57. In May 1948, Steinhardt contributed $15,000.
20. "Robbins and Steinhardt Confirmed," *New York Times*, May 5, 1933.
21. Jan Lowenbach, "Nový americký velvyslanec," *Týdeník Čechoslovák*, January 12, 1945.
22. Steinhardt Sherlock, "R.S.V.P.," 34.
23. See David Mayers, *The Ambassadors and America's Soviet Policy* (New York: Oxford University Press, 1995); and Dunn, *Caught Between Roosevelt and Stalin*.
24. "Nazis Assail U.S. Envoys," *New York Times*, April 24, 1939.
25. LOC, Steinhardt Papers, box 68.
26. Lowenbach, "Nový americký velvyslanec."
27. Charles E. Bohlen, *Witness to History, 1929–1969* (New York: Norton, 1973), 19.
28. Dunn, *Caught Between Roosevelt and Stalin*, 101–3.
29. Dunn, *Caught Between Roosevelt and Stalin*, 107.
30. Steinhardt Sherlock, "R.S.V.P.," 47–73.
31. Steinhardt Sherlock, "R.S.V.P.," 67.
32. Bohlen, *Witness to History*, 88–89, 95, 108.
33. Ibid., 69–83, 86–87; Hans Heinrich Herwarth, *Zwischen Hitler und Stalin: Erlebte Zeitge-schichte 1931 bis 1945* (Frankfurt: Propyläen, 1982).
34. "Envoys Cheer Poles Leaving Soviet Post," *New York Times*, October 10, 1939.
35. "Final Report Presented by Former Ambassador Grzybowski," in *Documents on Polish-Soviet Relations, 1939–1945*, vol. 1, *1939–1945* (London: Heinemann, 1961), 89–90.
36. Gary Kern, "How 'Uncle Joe' Bugged FDR," *Studies in Intelligence* 47, no. 1 (2003): 20. See also Elizabeth Kimball MacLean, *Joseph E. Davies: Envoy to the Soviets* (Westport, CT: Prae-ger, 1992), 40; George F. Kennan, *Memoirs 1925–1950* (Boston: Little, Brown, 1967), 189.

37. Bohlen, *Witness to History*, 46.
38. LOC, Steinhardt papers, box 78, Laurence Steinhardt, Moscow, to Frank Walker, Washington, February 1, 1940.
39. LOC, Steinhardt papers, box 78, Laurence Steinhardt, Moscow, to Sumner Wells, Washington, January 11, 1940.
40. Dunn, *Caught Between Roosevelt and Stalin*, 106.
41. Marcia Davenport, *Too Strong for Fantasy* (New York: Scribner's, 1967), 364.
42. "Envoy Saves US Girl Doomed by Soviet," *New York Times*, May 10, 1941.
43. Lowenbach, "Nový americký velvyslanec."
44. Steinhardt Sherlock, "R.S.V.P.," 55–56.
45. Laurence Steinhardt, Moscow, to the Secretary of State, Washington, December 23, 1940, in *Foreign Relations of the United States 1940*, vol. 3 (Washington, DC: Government Printing Office, 1958), 436–37.
46. Regarding the fate of U.S. citizens in Stalin's Russia, see Tim Tzouliadis, *The Forsaken: From the Great Depression to the Gulags : Hope and Betrayal in Stalin's Russia* (London: Little, Brown, 2008).
47. Laurence Steinhardt, Moscow, to the Secretary of State, Washington, October 30, 1940, in *Foreign Relations of the United States 1940*, vol. 3, 400–403.
48. Léopold L. S. Braun, *In Lubianka's Shadow: The Memoirs of an American Priest in Stalin's Moscow, 1934–1945* (Notre Dame, IN: University of Notre Dame Press, 2006).
49. "Church Desecration Protested by U.S.," *New York Times*, March 5, 1941.
50. Interview with Laurene Sherlock and Peter Rosenblatt, October 27, 2007.
51. The NKVD penetrations of the U.S. Embassy are described in V. K. Vinogradov et al., eds., *Sekrety Gitlera na stole u Stalina: Razvedka i kontrarazvedka o podgotovke germanskoi agressii protiv SSSR* (Moscow: Izdatel'stvo "Mosgorarkhiv," 1995); and Ovidy Gorchakov, "Nakanune, ili tragedia Kassandry," *Gorizont* 6 (1988): 30–42, continued in *Gorizont* 7 (1988): 51–63.
52. Peter R. Rosenblatt, personal correspondence, January 25, 2008.
53. Steinhardt Sherlock, "R.S.V.P.," 66.
54. Gorchakov, "Nakanune, ili tragedia Kassandry."
55. Anthony Read and David Fisher, *Deadly Embrace: Hitler, Stalin, and the Nazi-Soviet Pact* (New York: Norton, 1988), 606.
56. Record of Conversation of S. A. Lozovsky with U.S. Ambassador Steinhardt, April 15, 1941, in L. E. Reshin and V. P. Naumov, *1941 god: v 2-kh knigakh* (Moscow: Mezhdunar. fond Demokratii, 1998), 2:80–81.
57. Record of Conversation of S. A. Lozovsky with U.S. Ambassador Steinhardt, June 5, 1941, in Reshin, *1941 god*, 2:315–21.
58. Steinhardt Sherlock, "R.S.V.P.," 65; interview with Laurene Sherlock and Peter Rosenblatt, October 27, 2007.
59. David E. Murphy, *What Stalin Knew: The Enigma of Barbarossa* (New Haven, CT: Yale University Press, 2005).
60. Mayers, *The Ambassadors*, 132–33.
61. Steinhardt's successor, William C. Standley, also "criticized the policy of unconditional aid." See Dunn, *Caught Between Roosevelt and Stalin*, 207.
62. The same fate awaited Ambassador Standley. Dunn, *Caught Between Roosevelt and Stalin*, 185.
63. "Roosevelt-Stalin Letters," *New York Times*, November 7, 1941.
64. Mayers, *The Ambassadors*, 132.
65. Steinhardt Sherlock, "R.S.V.P.," 69.
66. LOC, Steinhardt papers, box 57.
67. Ibid.
68. "Litvinoff's Airplane Lands Safely at Baku," *New York Times*, November 15, 1941; "Steinhardt Resumes Trip," *New York Times*, November 19, 1941.
69. "Reticent on Steinhardt's Status," *New York Times*, December 6, 1941.
70. LOC, Steinhardt papers, box 57. See also Joachim Petzold, *Franz von Papen: Ein deutsches Verhängnis* (Munich: Union, 1995) and Steinhardt Sherlock, "R.S.V.P.," 87.

71. "Moscow to Ankara," *New York Times*, January 8, 1942.
72. Birge, "Istanbul," 14, unpublished manuscript.
73. Ibid., 38A.
74. Steinhardt Sherlock, "R.S.V.P.," 91.
75. David J. Alvarez, "The Embassy of Laurence A. Steinhardt: Aspects of Allied-Turkish Relations, 1942–1945," *East European Quarterly* 9, no 1 (1975): 39–52.
76. Ibid., 46.
77. Ibid.
78. Ibid., 48–49.
79. "Turkey Declares War on Axis to Get San Francisco Parley Seat," *New York Times*, February 24, 1945.
80. Interview with Dulcie-Ann Steinhardt Sherlock, June 18, 1998. All direct quotations are from Ms. Steinhardt Sherlock.
81. Steinhardt Sherlock, "R.S.V.P.," 96.
82. Steinhardt had failed to learn that the heavy cruiser USS *Quincy* took Roosevelt from the United States only to Malta, where the president rested and then transferred to a large airplane with a wheelchair lift (the *Sacred Cow*) that brought him near the site of the Yalta Conference, arriving there on February 3, 1945. USS *Catoctin*, an auxiliary ship served as a communications platform and headquarters for the advance party planning the Yalta conference. She had arrived in Sevastopol harbor earlier, on January 26, 1945.
83. LOC, Steinhardt Papers, box 68, "The Current Situation in Czechoslovakia," lecture presented at the National War College, Washington, December 15, 1947.
84. Birge, "Istanbul," 27–28, unpublished manuscript.
85. The original Guggenheimer, Untermyer & Marshall became Guggenheimer and Untermyer after Mr. Marshall left in the thirties. Communication with Peter R. Rosenblatt, February 15, 2008.
86. NARA, Office of Strategic Services, Research and Analysis Branch, "Report on Czechoslovakia: Pivot Point of Europe," July 4, 1945.
87. LOC, Steinhardt Papers, box 83, Ambassador Steinhardt, Pine Street, New York City, to Rudolf Schoenfeld, the American Embassy near the Czechoslovak Government, London, May 21, 1945.
88. "Velvyslanec Steinhardt do Prahy," *Svobodné Slovo*, June 8, 1945.

## Chapter 5

1. LOC, Steinhardt Papers, box 83, Laurence Steinhardt, New York, to A. W. Klieforth, Chargé d'Affaires ad interim, U.S. Embassy, Prague, June 22, 1945.
2. The description of the flight from Turkey to Czechoslovakia, see Dulcie-Ann Steinhardt Sherlock, "R.S.V.P.," unpublished manuscript, 102–4.
3. LOC, Steinhardt Papers, box 47.
4. *Rudé Právo*, July 17, 1945.
5. Interview with Louise Schaffner, January 29–30, 1999, Washington, DC.
6. NARA, Ambassador Laurence Steinhardt, U.S. Embassy, Prague, to the Secretary of State, Washington, July 26, 1945, 860F.00/7-2645.
7. R. H. Bruce Lockhart, *Jan Masaryk: A Personal Memoir* (New York: Philosophical Library, 1951), 46–47.
8. Interview with Spencer L. Taggart, April 24, 1999, Logan, Utah.
9. Interview with Kurt Taub, March 5, 2000, Salzburg, Austria; interview with George Bogardus and Louise Schaffner, January 29, 1999, Bethesda, Maryland.
10. Cecilia Sternberg, *The Journey* (London: Collins, 1977), 28–30.
11. "Velvyslanec Spojených států amerických nastoupil v úřad," *Rudé Právo*, July 22, 1945.
12. Archives of Thomas G. Masaryk, Beneš Archive, ATGM/BA, Speeches and Letters, box 6.
13. Steinhardt Sherlock, "R.S.V.P.," unpublished manuscript, 105–6.
14. Tatiana Metternich, *Tatiana: Full Circle in a Shifting Europe*, rev. ed. (London: Elliott & Thompson, 2004), 305–6.
15. Walter Birge, "Czechoslovakia," unpublished manuscript, 3.

16. Stanley B. Winters, "Conflicted Partners," paper presented at the 38th American Association for the Advancement of Slavic Studies National Convention, Washington, DC, April 18, 2006.

17. E. N. Harmon, *Combat Commander: Autobiography of a Soldier* (Englewood Cliffs, NJ: Prentice-Hall, 1970), 265–66.

18. LOC, Steinhardt Papers, box 68, Laurence Steinhardt, U.S. Embassy, Prague, to Francis Williamson, Division of Central European Affairs, Department of State, Washington, July 28, 1945.

19. LOC, Steinhardt Papers, box 47, Francis T. Williamson, Department of State, Washington, to Ambassador Laurence Steinhardt, U.S. Embassy, Prague, no date.

20. LOC, Steinhardt Papers, box 68, Laurence Steinhardt, Prague, to Julius Cecil Holmes, Department of State, Washington, July 23, 1945.

21. AMFA, foreign embassies in Prague, USA, 1945–55, box 55.

22. LOC, Steinhardt Papers, 83, Laurence Steinhardt, Prague, to G. Lewis Jones, Department of State, Washington, August 3, 1945.

23. LOC, Steinhardt Papers, box 83, Laurence Steinhardt, Prague, to James W. Riddleberger, Department of State, Washington, September 1, 1945.

24. LOC, Steinhardt Papers, box 83, Laurence Steinhardt, Prague, to James W. Riddleberger, Department of State, Washington, September 25, 1945.

25. LOC, Steinhardt Papers, box 83, Laurence Steinhardt, Prague, to Francis Williamson, Department of State, Washington, July 28, 1945.

26. LOC, Steinhardt Papers, box 83, Laurence Steinhardt, Prague, to Frederick Larkin, Rome, Italy, July 26, 1945.

27. LOC, Steinhardt Papers, box 83, Laurence Steinhardt, Prague, to James W. Riddleberger, Department of State, Washington, September 1, 1945.

28. LOC, Steinhardt Papers, box 83, Laurence Steinhardt, Prague, to Edwin C. Wilson, U.S. Embassy, Ankara, July 19, 1945.

29. LOC, Steinhardt Papers, box 47, Francis Williamson, Department of State, to Laurence Steinhardt, Prague, August 29, 1945.

30. LOC, Steinhardt Papers, box 83, Laurence Steinhardt, Prague, to Madam Romola Nijinsky, Hotel Sacher, Vienna, August 25, 1945.

31. LOC, Steinhardt Papers, box 83, Kabelogram, Laurence Steinhardt, Prague, to Dulcie Steinhardt, Rafael Hotel, Paris, September 11, 1945.

32. NARA, New York Passenger Lists, 1820–1957, Arrival: New York, Microfilm serial: T715, Microfilm roll: T715–6225.

33. LOC, Steinhardt Papers, box 83, Laurence Steinhardt, Prague, to Francis Williamson, Department of State, Washington, July 29, 1945.

34. LOC, Steinhardt Papers, 47, Francis Williamson, Department of State, to Laurence Steinhardt, Prague, August 29, 1945.

35. LOC, Steinhardt Papers, box 47, Viktor Petschek, New York City, to Edgard J. Goodrich at Guggenheimer, Untermyer & Goodrich, Washington, October 25, 1945.

36. LOC, Steinhardt Papers, box 83, Laurence Steinhardt, U.S. Embassy, Prague, to Francis Williamson, Department of State, Washington, July 28, 1945.

37. LOC, Steinhardt Papers, box 47, Viktor Petschek, New York City, to Edgard J. Goodrich at Guggenheimer, Untermyer & Goodrich, Washington, October 25, 1945.

38. Archives of the Presidential Office, APO, T 987/35, Edvard Beneš to Zdeněk Fierlinger, August 9, 1945.

39. AMFA, Diplomatic Protocol, foreign embassies in Prague, USA, 1945–55, box 55; Ministry of Foreign Affairs, Prague, to Ambassador Steinhardt, August 14, 1945 and Ministry of Defense, August 28, 1945. See also ATGM, Beneš Archive, correspondence, box 76, Zdeněk Fierlinger to Edvard Beneš, August 16, 1945.

40. "Ambassador's Residence," website of the United States Embassy in Prague, Czech Republic, http://prague.usembassy.gov/ambassadors_residence.html.

41. Steinhardt Sherlock, "R.S.V.P.," unpublished manuscript, 107.

42. Marie Vassiltchikov, *Berlin Diaries, 1940–1945* (New York: Knopf, 1987), 297–98.

43. Ibid., 299–302.

44. Letter from Dr. Miloš Říha, Kynžvart, December 7, 2007.
45. Interview with George Bogardus, June 3, 1998, Bethesda, MD.
46. Interview with Louise Schaffner, January 29, 1999, Washington, DC.
47. LOC, Steinhardt Papers, box 47, U.S. Embassy, Prague, William Walton Cable no. 22, Sans Origine (Austria) to David Hulburd, sent June 30, 1945.
48. LOC, Steinhardt Papers, box 68, Laurence Steinhardt: "Czechoslovakia," no date.
49. LOC, Steinhardt Papers, box 83, Laurence Steinhardt, U.S. Embassy, Prague, to James W. Riddleberger, Department of State, Washington, September 1, 1945.
50. Dulcie-Ann Steinhardt Sherlock, "R.S.V.P.," unpublished manuscript, 109.
51. AMI, Steinhardt, 36/5, September 18, 1945.
52. LOC, Steinhardt Papers, box 47, Laurence Steinhardt, U.S. Embassy, Prague, record of General Eisenhower's visit of October 11, 1945.
53. NARA, Secretary of War to the Secretary of State, Washington, October 15, 1945, 860F.01/10-1545.
54. Dorothy Bruins, "Opal of Many Hues," unpublished manuscript, 232.
55. Zdeněk Roučka, *Američané a západní Čechy 1945* (Pilsen: ZR & T, 2000), no page numbers.
56. NARA, Laurence Steinhardt, U.S. Embassy, Prague, to the Secretary of State, Washington, August 23, 1945, 860F.00/8-2545.
57. AMFA, fond Politické zprávy, Washington, J. Hanč, Czechoslovak Embassy, Washington, to the Ministry of Foreign Affairs, December 23, 1947. See also LOC, "Nationalization Laws and American Investments in Czechoslovakia," Division of Research for Europe, Office of Intelligence Research, OIR Report no. 3715.2, May 5, 1947, OSS/State Department: Intelligence and Research Reports, Part V, 861.2091.
58. NA, Archives of the Central Committee of the Communist Party of Czechoslovakia, František Kolář, the Commission on National Economy of the Central Committee, to Rudolf Slánský, General Secretary, May 28, 1947, fond 100/1, file 82, unit 612. See also LOC, Jan Krč, "Czechoslovak Gold: U.S. Claims Controversy," Congressional Research Service, December 8, 1981. The author lists the following claims by corporations: Mobil ($5 million), ITT ($3 million), IBM ($3 million), and Singer ($1.6); among the principal private claimants were Betty Papanek ($3 million) and Victor Petschek ($2.9 million).
59. NARA, Ambassador Laurence Steinhardt, U.S. Embassy, Prague, to the Secretary of State, Washington, August 14, 1945, 860F.00/8-1445.
60. NARA, Ambassador Laurence Steinhardt, U.S. Embassy, Prague, to the Secretary of State, Washington, August 23, 1945, 860F.00/8-2545.
61. NARA, "Report on Czechoslovakia: Pivot Point of Europe," Office of Strategic Services, Research and Analysis Branch, July 4, 1945.
62. Bulletin of the Ministry of Information, no. 4, Prague, August 13, 1945.
63. LOC, Steinhardt Papers, box 68, Laurence Steinhardt, U.S. Embassy, Prague, to Harold L. Smith, Hotel Claridge, Paris, August 28, 1945.
64. "Czechs Attempt to End Film Row," *New York Times*, September 1, 1945.
65. NARA, Ambassador Laurence Steinhardt, Prague, to the Secretary of State, Washington, August 23, 1945, 860f.00/8-2545.
66. NARA, "Report on Czechoslovakia: Pivot Point of Europe," The Office of Strategic Services, Research and Analysis Branch, July 4, 1945.
67. LOC, Steinhardt Papers, box 68, Laurence Steinhardt, Prague, to John Foster Dulles, Cromwell and Sullivan, New York, December 26, 1945.

## Chapter 6

1. Interview with George Bogardus, June 3, 1998, Bethesda, MD.
2. LOC, Steinhardt Papers, box 47.
3. LOC, Steinhardt Papers, box 83, Laurence Steinhardt, Prague, to Countess Cecilia Sternberg, Velkopřevorské Sq., Prague, August 16, 1945.
4. Cecilia Sternberg, *The Journey* (New York: Collins, 1977), 31–39.

5. Sternberg, *The Journey*, 28–29.

6. AMI, Lawrence Steinhardt, file 36/5.

7. NARA, "Report on Czechoslovakia: Pivot Point of Europe," Office of Strategic Services, Research and Analysis Branch, July 4, 1945.

8. Libuše Otáhalová and Milada Červinková, eds., *Dokumenty z historie československé politiky 1939–1943* (Prague: Academia, 1966), 91.

9. R. H. Bruce Lockhart, *Jan Masaryk: A Personal Memoir* (London: Putnam, 1956), 19, 38.

10. NARA, "Report on Czechoslovakia: Pivot Point of Europe," The Office of Strategic Services, Research and Analysis Branch, July 4, 1945.

11. NARA, Ambassador Laurence Steinhardt, U.S. Embassy, Prague, to the Secretary of State, Washington, December 7, 1945, 860F.00/12-745.

12. NARA, "Report on Czechoslovakia: Pivot Point of Europe," Office of Strategic Services, Research and Analysis Branch, July 4, 1945.

13. NARA, William J. Donovan, Director, Office of Strategic Services, to James C. Dunn, Assistant Secretary of State, Washington, June 16, 1945, 860F.01/6-1645.

14. NARA, Lester C. Houck, Reporting Board, OSS, Washington, to Julius Holmes, Assistant Secretary of State, Washington, August 1, 1945, 860F.00/8-145.

15. LOC, Steinhardt Papers, box 83, Ambassador Laurence Steinhardt, U.S. Embassy, Prague, to G. Lewis Jones, Chief, Near Eastern Division, Department of State, Washington, August 3, 1945.

16. LOC, Steinhardt Papers, box 83, Laurence Steinhardt, U.S. Embassy, Prague, to Walton C. Ferris, Department of State, Washington, August 7, 1945.

17. NARA, Ambassador Laurence Steinhardt, U.S. Embassy, Prague, to the Secretary of State, Washington, July 24, 1945, 860F.01/7-2445.

18. "KSČ nejsilnější stranou v republice," *Rudé Právo*, July 17, 1945.

19. NARA, Ambassador Laurence Steinhardt, U.S. Embassy, Prague, to the Secretary of State, Washington, July 26, 1945, 860F.00/7-2645.

20. ABS, 10999. The Czech security services kept a detailed record of Steinhardt's card-playing and hunting aristocratic friends. In addition to Count and Countess Sternberg, they included Countess Lobkowitz, who often entertained Steinhardt at the castle in Mělník (ABS 10946), Prince Liechtenstein, Count Pálffy, Count Czernin, Count Szembek, Count Nádherný, and Baroness Hrubá.

21. NARA, Ambassador Laurence Steinhardt, U.S. Embassy, Prague, to the Secretary of State, Washington, August 14, 1945, 860F.00/8-1445.

22. NARA, Ambassador Laurence Steinhardt, U.S. Embassy, Prague, to the Secretary of State, Washington, August 18, 1945, 860F.5034/8-1845.

23. LOC, Steinhardt Papers, box 83, Ambassador Laurence Steinhardt, U.S. Embassy, Prague, to James W. Riddleberger, Chief, Central European Division, Department of State, Washington, September 1, 1945.

24. John MacCormack, "Prague a Paradox," *New York Times*, July 9, 1945.

25. Interview with Vladimír Kabeš, January 30, 1999, Washington, DC.

26. NARA, "Report on Czechoslovakia: Pivot Point of Europe," Office of Strategic Services, Research and Analysis Branch, July 4, 1945.

27. LOC, Steinhardt Papers, box 83, Laurence Steinhardt, U.S. Embassy, Prague, to James W. Riddleberger, Department of State, Washington, September 1, 1945.

28. LOC, "Nationalization Laws and American Investments in Czechoslovakia," Department of State, Office of Intelligence Research, Division of Research for Europe, OIR Report no. 3715.2, May 5, 1947, OSS/State Department Intelligence and Research Reports, Part V, Postwar Europe, no. 86/2091.

29. LOC, "Czechoslovakia: Intelligence Research Report," Department of State, Office of Intelligence Coordination and Liaison (OCL 3793.4), September 4, 1946, OSS/State Department Intelligence and Research Reports, Part V, Postwar Europe, no. 86/2091.

30. LOC, "Czechoslovak Decrees on Nationalization," OSS/State Department Intelligence and Research Reports, Part V, no. 3439, January 25, 1946, Washington, 861.2091.

31. NARA, Ambassador Laurence Steinhardt, U.S. Embassy, Prague, to the Secretary of State, Washington, October 28, 1945, 860F.5034/10-2845.

32. LOC, "Czechoslovak Decrees on Nationalization: An Analysis," OSS/State Department Intelligence and Research Reports, Part V, Postwar Europe, no. 3439, January 25, 1946, Washington, 861.2091.

33. LOC, "American Investments in Czechoslovakia," OSS/State Department Intelligence and Research Reports, Part V, OIR Report no. 3715.2, May 5, 1947, 861.2091.

34. NARA, Ambassador Laurence Steinhardt, U.S. Embassy, Prague, to the Secretary of State, Incoming Telegram via War Department, October 23, 1945.

35. NARA, Secretary of State James F. Byrnes, Washington, to U.S. Embassy, Prague, Outgoing Telegram, October 31, 1945.

36. NARA, Ambassador Laurence Steinhardt, U.S. Embassy, Prague, to the Secretary of State, Washington, November 30, 1945, 860F.51/11-3045.

37. NARA, Ambassador Laurence Steinhardt, U.S. Embassy, Prague, to the Secretary of State, Washington, November 21, 1945, 860F.50/11-2145.

38. "Komuniké z konference tří mocností," *Rudé Právo*, August 4, 1945.

39. See especially Norman M. Naimark, *Fires of Hatred: Ethnic Cleansing in Twentieth-Century Europe* (Cambridge, MA: Harvard University Press, 2001), 108–38; and Benjamin Frommer, *National Cleansing: Retribution Against Nazi Collaborators in Postwar Czechoslovakia* (Cambridge: Cambridge University Press, 2005), passim.

40. Prokop Drtina, *Československo můj osud: Kniha života českého demokrata 20. století*, vol. 2, part 1, *Emigrací k vítězství* (Toronto: Sixty-Eight Publishers, 1982), 60–65.

41. "Odsun Němců začne 15. října," *Rudé Právo*, October 10, 1945.

42. "Bílá hora odčiněna," *Rudé Právo*, July 3, 1945.

43. " Věrní pravdě Husově," *Rudé Právo*, July 8, 1945.

44. LOC, Steinhardt Papers, box 83, Laurence Steinhardt, Prague, to Francis Williamson, Department of State, Washington, October 20, 1945.

45. LOC, Steinhardt Papers, box 47, A record of the briefing by Steinhardt, no date.

46. LOC, Steinhardt Papers, box 83, Laurence Steinhardt, Prague, to Francis Williamson, Department of State, Washington, October 20, 1945.

47. NARA, Ambassador Robert Murphy, Berlin, to the Secretary of State, Washington, October 19, 1945, 860F.00/10-2545; NARA, Ambassador Laurence Steinhardt, U.S. Embassy, Prague, to the Secretary of State, Washington, December 7, 1945, 860F.00/12-745.

48. LOC, Steinhardt Papers, box 83, Laurence Steinhardt, Prague, to Francis Williamson, Department of State, Washington, October 20, 1945.

49. NARA, Ambassador Laurence Steinhardt, U.S. Embassy, Prague, to the Secretary of State, Washington, August 25, 1945, 860F.01/8-2545.

50. NARA, Ambassador Robert D. Murphy, Berlin, to the Secretary of State, Washington, August 31, 1945, 860F.01/8-3145.

51. NARA, Ambassador Laurence Steinhardt, U.S. Embassy, Prague, to the Secretary of State, Washington, August 31, 1945, 860F.01/8-3145.

52. NARA, Ambassador Laurence Steinhardt, U.S. Embassy, Prague, to the Secretary of State, Washington, September 4, 1945, 860F.01/9-445.

53. Ibid.

54. NARA, Acting Secretary of State Dean Acheson, Washington, to Ambassador Laurence Steinhardt, U.S. Embassy, Prague, September 11, 1945, 860F.01/9-445.

55. NARA, Ambassador Laurence Steinhardt, U.S. Embassy, Prague, to Acting Secretary of State Dean Acheson, Washington, September 14, 1945, 860F.01/9-1445.

56. NARA, Acting Secretary of State Dean Acheson, to Secretary of State James F. Byrnes, Washington, September 28, 1945, 740.00119.

57. NARA, Secretary of State, James F. Byrnes, Washington, to Ambassador Laurence Steinhardt, U.S. Embassy, Prague, November 2, 1945, 860F.01/11-245.

58. NARA, Ambassador Laurence Steinhardt, U.S. Embassy, Prague, to the Secretary of State, Washington, November 8, 1945.

59. NARA, George Kennan, U.S. Embassy, Moscow, to the Secretary of State, Washington, September 23, 1945, 860F.01/9-2345.

60. NARA, Ambassador Laurence Steinhardt, U.S. Embassy, Prague, to the Secretary of State, Washington, October 31, 1945, 860F.00/10-3145.
61. NARA, Secretary of State James F. Byrnes, Washington, to Ambassador Laurence Steinhardt, U.S. Embassy, Prague, November 9, 1945.
62. NARA, Ambassador Laurence Steinhardt, U.S. Embassy, Prague, to the Secretary of State, Washington, November 8, 1945, 860F.01/11-845.
63. NARA, Ambassador Robert Murphy, U.S. Political Advisor for Germany, Berlin, to the Secretary of State, Washington, December 27, 1945, 861.23/12-2745.
64. "US Czechoslovakia Force to be Withdrawn by December 1," *New York Times*, November 10, 1945.
65. "Slavnostní přehlídka na Václavském náměstí," *Rudé Právo*, November 15, 1945.
66. "Praha nadšeně uvítala maršála Koněva," *Rudé Právo*, October 13, 1945.
67. NARA, Ambassador Laurence Steinhardt, U.S. Embassy, Prague, to the Secretary of State, Washington, December 6, 1945, 860F.00/12-645.
68. NARA, Ambassador Laurence Steinhardt, U.S. Embassy, Prague, to the Secretary of State, Washington, November 16, 1945, 860F.01/11-1645.
69. "Prague Honors Americans," *New York Times*, November 4, 1945.
70. "Masaryk Lauds US," *New York Times*, November 21, 1945.
71. NARA, Ambassador John G. Winant, U.S. Embassy, London, to the Secretary of State, Washington, December 5, 1945, 860F.51/12-545.
72. Zdeněk Roučka, *Američané a západní Čechy 1945* (Pilsen: ZR & T, 2000).
73. "American Troops Leave Pilsen," *New York Times*, December 2, 1945.
74. NARA, Ambassador Laurence Steinhardt, U.S. Embassy, Prague, to the Secretary of State, Washington, December 6, 1945, 860F.01/12-645.

## Chapter 7

1. The CPC infiltrated the democratic parties with secret agents who kept the party bosses informed about their opponents, while the latter knew nothing about the Communists. This is described in great detail in numerous books by Karel Kaplan. See also František Hanzlík, *Únor 1948: Výsledek nerovného zápasu* (Prague: Prewon, 1997); and Hanzlík, *Bez milosti a slitování: B. Reicin—fanatik rudého teroru* (Prague: Ostrov, 2011). Especially revealing is a chapter in Prokop Tomek, *Život a doba ministra Rudolfa Baráka* (Prague: Vyšehrad, 2009), 101–8.
2. Robert B. Pynsent, ed., *The Phoney Peace: Power and Culture in Central Europe 1945–49* (London: School of Slavonic and East European Studies, University College London, 2000); Bradley F. Abrams, *The Struggle for the Soul of the Nation: Czech Culture and the Rise of Communism* (Lanham, MD: Rowman & Littlefield, 2004).
3. Milan Kundera, *Žert* (Prague: Československý spisovatel, 1969), 70.
4. Inspired by Soviet propaganda, the CPC intermittently hinted at the possibility that Hitler was alive. "Hitler mluvil do rádia?" *Rudé Právo*, August 4, 1945. See also Gustav Bares, "Aby se již nikdy neopakoval Mnichov," *Rudé Právo*, September 30, 1945.
5. Růžena Kříženecká, Zdeněk Šel, and Jiří Zeman, *Československo 1945–1948: Kronika* (Prague: Kabinet Ústavu Dějin KSČ, 1968), 26.
6. See František Hanzlík, *Vojenské obranné zpravodajství v zápasu o politickou moc* (Prague: Úřad Dokumentace a Vyšetřování Zločinů Komunismu, 2003); František Hanzlík and Václav Vondrášek, *Armáda v zápase o politickou moc v letech* (Prague: Ministerstvo Obrany ČR, 2006); František Hanzlík and Jaroslav Pospíšil, *Soumrak demokracie: Reicinovo obranné zpravodajství na cestě KSČ k moci* (Vizovice, Czech Republic: Lípa, 2000).
7. NARA, Record Group 84, Confidential file, 1949, box 7, Chargé d'Affaires John H. Bruins, U.S. Embassy, London, to the Secretary of State, Washington, November 8, 1949. ABS, Archives of the Special Services, Statement by General Heliodor Píka (ret.) for President Klement Gottwald, no date.
8. Zdeňka Psůtková and Zdeněk Vahala, *I nám vládli nemocní? Naši první prezidenti očima medicíny* (Liberec, Czech Republic: King, 1993).

9. Karel Kaplan, *Poslední rok prezidenta: Edvard Beneš v roce 1948* (Prague: Ústav pro Soudobé Dějiny AV ČR, 1993), 84–85.

10. NARA, Ambassador Laurence Steinhardt, U.S. Embassy, Prague, to the Secretary of State, Washington, December 18, 1945, 860F.00/12-1845.

11. NARA, Ambassador Laurence Steinhardt, U.S. Embassy, Prague, to the Secretary of State, Washington, December 18, 1945, 860F.00/12-1845; Laurence Steinhardt, U.S. Embassy, Prague, to the Secretary of State, Washington, January 30, 1946, 861.00/1-3046.

12. NARA, Ambassador Laurence Steinhardt, U.S. Embassy, Prague, to the Secretary of State, Washington, November 26, 1945, 860F.00/11-2645. Ducháček was responding to an article by Ladislav Štoll, "Východ a západ," *Rudé Právo*, August 19, 1945.

13. NARA, Ambassador Laurence Steinhardt, U.S. Embassy, Prague, to the Secretary of State, Washington, November 17, 1945, 860F.00/11-1745.

14. The information on Walter Birge is from my interviews with him and his wife, Virginia, at Kingston, MA, and from his unpublished manuscript "Mémoirs," 5–103.

15. Birge, "Mémoirs," 105–17.

16. Ibid., 119–24.

17. Ibid., 125–55.

18. Ibid., 156–73.

19. Ibid., 175–98.

20. Ibid., 199.

21. Ibid., 200.

22. Ibid., 203–4.

23. AMI, 305-141-7, February 14, 1947.

24. NA, Ministry of the Interior, box 11981, Directorate of National Security, Prague, to the Ministry of the Interior, Prague, July 4, 1946.

25. NARA, Ambassador Laurence Steinhardt, U.S. Embassy, Prague, to the Secretary of State, January 18, 1946, 860F.00/1-1846.

26. NARA, Ambassador Laurence Steinhardt, U.S. Embassy, Prague, to the Secretary of State, January 21, 1946, 860F.00/1-2146.

27. Ibid.

28. NARA, Ambassador Laurence Steinhardt, U.S. Embassy, Prague, to the Secretary of State, February 1, 1946, 860F.00/2-146.

29. AMI, S-451-9, Prague, October 25, 1953, "Štěchovický archiv."

30. ABS, Ambassade de France a Prague, to Ministére des Affaires Etrangéres, Prague, 13. Octobre 1945.

31. ABS, Brigadier General J. Flipo, French Military Attaché, Prague, to the Fifth Department, Ministry of Defense, Prague, January 18, 1946.

32. AMI, S-451-9, October 25, 1953.

33. AMI, S-451-9, Statement by Captain Stephen M. Richards, February 14, 1946.

34. NARA, War Department, Classified Message Center, Lt. Colonel Taylor, US Embassy, Prague, to General Hoyt Vandenberg, War Department, February 16, 1946, nos. 13–16.

35. NARA, War Department, Classified Message Center, Lt. Colonel Taylor, US Embassy, Prague, to General Hoyt Vandenberg, War Department, February 15, 1946, nos. 12–15.

36. NA, State Central Archives, Office of the Prime Minister, UPV-T, archival unit 2407, sign 301/3/1, Ministry of National Defense, OBZ, Main Directorate, Prague, to the Prime Minister Zdenko Fierlinger, February 18, 1946.

37. NARA, War Department, Classified Message Center, Incoming, Lt. Colonel Taylor, US Embassy, Prague, to War Department, February 15, 1946, nos. 12–15.

38. František Hanzlík, Jan Pospíšil, and Jaroslav Pospíšil, *Sluha dvou pánu* (Vizovice, Czech Republic: Lípa, 1999), 178–218.

39. NARA, War Department, Classified Message Center, Incoming, Lt. Colonel Taylor, US Embassy, Prague, to War Department, February 15, 1946, nos. 12–15.

40. NA, State Central Archives, Archives of UML, fond 83, archival unit 258, Report on the Secret Meeting of the Czechoslovak Government, February 15, 1946. See also NA, State Central Archives, Archives of UML, fond 83, archival unit 259, Report on the Secret Meeting of the Czechoslovak Government, February 19, 1946.

41. AMI, S-451-6, Report by Rotmistr Vocílka Urban.
42. NARA, War Department, Classified Message Center, Incoming, Ambassador Steinhardt, Prague, to the Secretary of State, Washington, February 18, 1946.
43. AMI, S-451-9, Steinhardt's conversation with Captain Vítek, February 18, 1946.
44. AMI, Katek, H-686, "Opis materiálu na Charles Katek."
45. NARA, War Department, Classified Message Center, Incoming, Lt. Colonel Taylor, US Embassy, Prague, to War Department, February 16, 1946, nos. 13–16.
46. NA, State Central Archives, Office of the Prime Minister, UPV-T, Archives of the Prime Minister's Office, inventory no. 2407, signature 301/3/1.
47. AMI, S-451-6, Report by Lt. Colonel Karel Staller, March 2, 1946.
48. AMI, S-451-6, Captain Hašek, March 3, 1946.
49. "Czechs to Regain Papers Army Took," *New York Times*, February 24, 1946.
50. L. S. B. Shapiro, "Bohemia Raiders Gambled," *New York Times*, February 25, 1946.
51. T. Dennis Reece, "Mission to Stechovice, " *Prologue* 39, no. 4 (2007): 18–27.
52. *Rudé Právo*, February 23, 1946, "What do the Stolen Boxes Contain?"
53. Rudé Právo, February 24, 1946, "American Ambassador Has Apologized."
54. NA, State Central Archives, Office of the Prime Minister, UPV-T, inventory no. 2407, signature 301/3/1, MZV to the Office of the Prime Minister, March 25, 1946.
55. LOC, Steinhardt Papers, Francis T. Williamson, Department of State, April 1, 1946. Williamson quotes from a memorandum from Prague, February 2, 1946, box 68.
56. NARA, Ambassador Laurence Steinhardt, U.S. Embassy, Prague, to the Secretary of State, March 15, 1946, 860F.00/3-1546.
57. NARA, Dean Acheson, Acting Secretary of State, Washington, to the Hon. Vito Marcantonio, New York, NY, November 6, 1946, 860F.51/10-2046.
58. LOC, Steinhardt Papers, Francis T. Williamson, Department of State, to Ambassador Laurence Steinhardt, Prague, April 1, 1946, box 68.
59. NARA, Ambassador Laurence Steinhardt, U.S. Embassy, Prague, to the Secretary of State, January 25, 1946, 760F.61/1-2546.
60. NARA, Ambassador Laurence Steinhardt, U.S. Embassy, Prague, to the Secretary of State, February 26, 1946, 860F.51/2-2646.
61. NARA, Ambassador Laurence Steinhardt, U.S. Embassy, Prague, to the Secretary of State, September 17, 1946.
62. LOC, Jan Krč, "Czechoslovak Gold: U.S. Claims Controversy," Congressional Research Service, December 8, 1981.
63. LOC, Steinhardt Papers, box 68, Francis T. Williamson, Department of State, to Ambassador Laurence Steinhardt, Prague, April 1, 1946.
64. NARA, Ambassador Laurence Steinhardt, U.S. Embassy, Prague, to the Secretary of State, July 30, 1946, 860F.51/7-3046.
65. NARA, Ambassador Laurence Steinhardt, U.S. Embassy, Prague, to the Secretary of State, August 14, 1946, 860F.24/8.
66. NARA, Ambassador Laurence Steinhardt, U.S. Embassy, Prague, to the Secretary of State, August 26, 1946, 860F.24/8.
67. NARA, Secretary of State, James F. Byrnes, Paris, to Acting Secretary of State, Washington, August 30, 1946, 740.00119.
68. NARA, Ambassador Laurence Steinhardt, U.S. Embassy, Prague, to the Secretary of State, November 5, 1946, 860F.00/11-546; Statement by Vladimír Clementis before the National Assembly, October 31, 1946.
69. NARA, Secretary of State, James F. Byrnes, Paris, to Ambassador Laurence A. Steinhardt, Prague, October 14, 1946, 711.60F/10-1446.
70. NARA, Department of State to the Czechoslovak Embassy, September 28, 1946.
71. NARA, Ambassador Laurence Steinhardt, U.S. Embassy, Prague, to the Secretary of State, November 5, 1946, 860F.00/11-546.
72. H. F. Margh, "Decision on Czech Loan," *New York Times*, November 1, 1946; NARA, James W. Riddleberger, Department of State, December 3, 1946, 860F5034/12-346.
73. NARA, Ambassador Laurence Steinhardt, U.S. Embassy, Prague, to the Secretary of State, December 23, 1946, 860F.00/12.

74. Albion Ross, "Czechs Disturbed," *New York Times*, October 28, 1946.
75. NARA, Richard Salvatierra, the Department of State, to the Secretary of State, October 31, 1946, 860F.50/0-1846.
76. R. H. Bruce Lockhart, *My Europe* (London: Putnam, 1952), 97.
77. NARA, Ambassador Laurence Steinhardt, U.S. Embassy, Prague, to the Secretary of State, October 25, 1946, 711.60F/10-2546.
78. NARA, Ambassador Laurence Steinhardt, U.S. Embassy, Prague, to the Secretary of State, October 7, 1946, 711.60F/10-746.
79. NARA, Ambassador Laurence Steinhardt, U.S. Embassy, Prague, to the Secretary of State, October 11, 1946, 711.60F/10-1146.
80. NARA, Ambassador Laurence Steinhardt, U.S. Embassy, Prague, to the Secretary of State, February 20, 1946, 860F.00/2-2046.
81. NA, State Central Archive, fond 60, Václav Nosek, 60/6/3, box 2.
82. NARA, Ambassador Laurence Steinhardt, U.S. Embassy, Prague, to the Secretary of State, February 25, 1946, 860F.00/2-2546.
83. Mark Kramer, "Stalin, Soviet Policy, and the Consolidation of a Communist Bloc in Eastern Europe, 1944–1953," unpublished manuscript.
84. John MacCormack, "Beneš Sees No War But Notes Spheres," *New York Times*, March 10, 1946.
85. *Rudé Právo*, March 30, 1946.
86. "Slavný VIII. Sjezd KSČ," *Rudé Právo*, March 29, 1946.
87. NARA, Ambassador Laurence Steinhardt, U.S. Embassy, Prague, to the Secretary of State, April 4, 1946, 860F.00/4-446.
88. NA, Archives of the CC CPC, fond 100/36, vol. 401–0, 1786, May 10, 1946.
89. NARA, Ambassador Laurence Steinhardt, U.S. Embassy, Prague, to the Secretary of State, May 15, 1946, 860F.00/5-1546.
90. NARA, Ambassador Laurence Steinhardt, U.S. Embassy, Prague, to the Secretary of State, May 21, 1946, 861.2360F/5-2146.
91. NARA, Ambassador Laurence Steinhardt, U.S. Embassy, Prague, to the Secretary of State, May 21, 1946, 861.2360F/5-2146.
92. NARA, Ambassador Laurence Steinhardt, U.S. Embassy, Prague, to the Secretary of State, May 23, 1946, 860F.00/5-2346.
93. "Frank Hanged for Lidice Crime," *New York Times*, May 23, 1946.
94. "26. května 1946 všichni s komunisty!" *Rudé Právo*, May 12, 1946.
95. *Rudé Právo*, May 14, 1946; Petr Hruby, *Osudné iluze: čeští spisovatelé a komunismus 1917–1987* (Rychnov nad Kněžnou, Czech Republic: Ježek, 2000), 237.
96. NARA, Ambassador Laurence Steinhardt, U.S. Embassy, Prague, to the Secretary of State, May 15, 1946, 860F.00/5-1546.
97. John MacCormack, "Czechs Will Vote on Regime Today," *New York Times*, May 26, 1946.
98. NA, Fond 2, 2-105/4. Intelligence Section, no. 21, May 28, 1946.
99. "U.S. Envoy's Letter Tells of Right-Wing Victory Hopes," *Daily Worker*, June 1, 1946; "U.S. Envoy's Secret Letter Bares Wall Street Pressure on Czechs," *New York City Sunday Worker*, June 2, 1946.
100. LOC, Steinhardt Papers, Harold F. Sheets, New York City, to Laurence Steinhardt, U.S. Embassy, Prague, June 3, 1946, and Harold Sheets to Laurence Steinhardt, June 6, 1946, box 51.
101. "KSČ největší stranou v republice," *Rudé Právo*, May 28, 1946. The district where the CPC came in second was Zlín.
102. Prokop Drtina, *Československo můj osud: Kniha života českého demokrata 20. století*, vol. 2, part 1, *Emigrací k vítězství* (Toronto: Sixty-Eight Publishers, 1982), 285.
103. *Práce*, May 29, 1946.
104. Interview with George F. Bogardus, June 3, 1998, Bethesda, MD.
105. LOC, OSS/State Department Intelligence and Research Reports, part V, reel 2 of 10, 86/2091, Office of Strategic Services, Research and Analysis Branch, The Czechoslovak Party System, September 1, 1945, R&A 3140.
106. Drtina, *Československo můj osud*, 172.

107. AMFA, fond "Politické zprávy," Washington; Czechoslovak Embassy, Washington, to Prague, May 29, 1946. The report singles out a *New York Times* article of May 27, 1946 and a *New York Herald Tribune* analysis of May 28, 1946.
108. NARA, Ambassador Laurence Steinhardt, U.S. Embassy, Prague, to the Secretary of State, June 3, 1946, 860F.00/6-346.
109. NARA, Chargé d'Affaires John H. Bruins, U.S. Embassy, Prague, to the Secretary of State, June 4, 1946, 860F.00/6-446.
110. "Edvard Beneš opět presidentem," *Svobodné Slovo*, June 20, 1946.
111. NARA, Ambassador Laurence Steinhardt, U.S. Embassy, Prague, to the Secretary of State, July 3, 1946, 860F.00/7-650 (some digits are hard to read).
112. Steinhardt's daughter believed that her father "respected" Gottwald but "hated" Slánský. Interview with Dulcie-Ann Steinhardt Sherlock, January 18, 1998, Chevy Chase, MD.
113. Pavel Tigrid, "Věčná otázka našich dějin," *Lidová Demokracie*, July 14, 1946.
114. NARA, Ambassador Laurence Steinhardt, U.S. Embassy, Prague, to the Secretary of State, August 12, 1946, 860F.00/8-1246.
115. NARA, Colonel E. F. Koenig, Prague, to the Department of Intelligence, War Department, Washington, August 21, 1946, dispatch no. A-121-46, 200.2, Czechoslovakia.
116. NARA, War Department, Strategic Services Unit, Washington, reference DB-633, August 23, 1946.
117. NARA, Colonel E. F. Koenig, Prague, to the Department of Intelligence, War Department, Washington, August 28, 1946.
118. NARA, Ambassador Laurence Steinhardt, U.S. Embassy, Prague, to the Secretary of State, September 20, 1946, 860F.607/9-2046.
119. NARA, Ambassador Laurence Steinhardt, U.S. Embassy, Prague, to the Secretary of State, October 2, 1946, 860F.00/10-246.
120. OPR, inventory no. 1586/A. Record of December 16, 1946.
121. NA, CC CPC, fond 100/24, archival unit 1157.
122. Drtina, *Československo můj osud*, 237–40.
123. NARA, Ambassador Laurence Steinhardt, U.S. Embassy, Prague, to the Secretary of State, Washington, December 23, 1946, 860F.00/12-2346.
124. NARA, Ambassador Laurence Steinhardt, U.S. Embassy, Prague, to the Secretary of State, Washington, November 20, 1946, 860F.00/11-2046.
125. Hubert Ripka, *Únorová tragédie: Svědectví přímého účastníka* (Brno, Czech Republic: Atlantis, 1995), 150–52; Prokop Drtina, *Československo můj osud*, 134–46.
126. Lord Vansittart, November 23, 1949, in *Parliamentary Debates*, Lords, 5th ser., vol. 165 (1949); Mohan K. Wali, "Vladimir Krajina (1905–1993): A Tribute," *Bulletin of the Ecological Society of America* 75, no. 4 (December 1994): 194–95.
127. C. Adamec, "Psychosa strachu jako překážka výzkumu veřejného mínění," *Veřejné mínění* 2 (September 1946): 4–6. See NARA, Chargé d'Affaires John H. Bruins, Prague, to the Secretary of State, Washington, February 7, 1947, 860F.00/2-747.
128. ABS, H-105, Top Secret Memorandum no. 157, unit 701-A, officer 0623/Tk, October 18, 1950.
129. NARA, Secretary of State, James F. Byrnes, Washington, to the U.S. Embassy, Prague, January 9, 1947, 860F.00/12-2346.

## Chapter 8

1. Interview with Kurt Taub, March 5, 2000, Salzburg, Austria.
2. All information in this section is from my interview with Janet Edwards, Colonel Katek's daughter, July 19, 2000, Washington, DC and from AMI, H-686.
3. Janet Edwards recalled that "When Katek entered a room, people stepped back and made space as if he owned the place." Interview with Janet Edwards on July 19, 2000. Taub noted that "when Katek entered, a personality entered." Interview with Kurt Taub, March 5, 2000. Louise Schaffner remembered that Katek had "cornball charisma." Interview with Louise Schaffner, January 30, 1999.
4. Interview with Janet Edwards on July 19, 2000.

5. Archives of Northwestern University, Evanston, IL. The defense took place in July 1942, and Katek's major professor was Franklin D. Scott. I am grateful to Professor Benjamin Frommer, who helped me acquire this information.
6. Interview with Janet Edwards, July 19, 2000.
7. Kurt Taub, letter to author, November 2, 1999.
8. State Central Archives (SCA), Prague, 61-19-5.
9. Archives of Úřad pro Zahraniční Styky a Informace (AUZSI), 11549/320.
10. NA, SCA, Arnošt Heidrich, Secretary General, Ministry of Foreign Affairs, to the Prime Minister's Office, May 23, 1946, to the Prime Minister's Office, Secret, A of Úřad Předsednictva Vlády, Tajné (UPV-T), no. 2760, signature 378/4/2.
11. AMI, Z-651, file 13, LT COL Bedřich Reicin and CPT Karel Vaš, OBZ, Ministry of Defense, 302-592-1, no. l 50.457/secret report—2c-/1946, January 24, 1946.
12. Archiv Bezpečnostních Složek (ABS), 302-200-5, "Mise Katek," no date.
13. ABS, II Directorate, report of informer no. 7040, April 16, 1954.
14. AMI, H-686; Louise Schaffner, interview, January 29, 1999, Washington, DC.
15. AMI, H-686, Tracy E. Strevey, Chicago, to Charles Katek, Prague, November 20, 1945, Ministry of National Defense, Main Directorate of the OBZ.
16. Interview with Mr. and Mrs. George Bogardus, Otilia and Vladimír Kabeš, and Mrs. Louis Schaffner, Bethesda, MD, January 30, 1999.
17. Joseph Wechsberg, "Why Girls Leave Home," *This Week Magazine*, March 14, 1948.
18. AMI, H-686, "A Review of Evidence on Charles Katek," February 1947.
19. AMI, H-686, "Katek."
20. Archives of the Ministry of National Defense (AMND), Main Directorate of the OBZ, 302-592-1.
21. AMI, H-686, unsigned report of an informer, Ministry of National Defense, Main Directorate of the OBZ, January 31, 1946.
22. AMI, H-686, a typed paragraph, signed R/Ch, June 19, 1946, see also H-686, March 29, 1946, Ministry of Foreign Affairs to the Ministry of National Defense.
23. All information on the case of Kurt Taub comes from my correspondence and interviews with Taub (Kurt L. Taylor), in Salzburg, Austria, March 5–6, 2000. After the interview had taken place, I was also able to consult documents from the AUZSI, 11-850/300 I and II called "Central Intelligence Service." Finally, I gained access to documents from ABS. These include the complete file ABS 11-850/300–I and ABS 11-850–II. Most illuminating are documents in ABS 44 808 011, ABS 44 808 020, ABS 44 808 021, ABS 44 808 022, ABS 44 808 023, and ABS 44 808, file 12176, archival no. 570512.
24. AUZSI, 11-850/300. Vojna was second secretary of the Soviet embassy in Stockholm. See the KGB assessment of the Taub-DABL case for the Czechs of June 12, 1957.
25. One of the draftees at Camp Croft was Henry Kissinger.
26. Interview with Kurt Taub, March 5, 2000, Salzburg, Austria.
27. AUZSI, 11-850/300; the Soviet analysis is dated June 12, 1957.
28. "Two Czechs Sentenced to Die as Spies," *The Milwaukee Journal* (September 29, 1948). The Prague supreme military court sentenced Sgt. Čepelka and Sgt. Soloviev to death by hanging because they had provided a western embassy with economic, political, and military secrets. The case of Sergei Soloviev is described in *Some of Us . . .* (Prague: Office of the Government of the Czech Republic, 2008).
29. ABS 44 808, file 12176, archival no. 570512. Statement by Josef Madar, June 5, 1948.
30. Interview with Kurt Taub, March 5, 2000, Salzburg, Austria.
31. AMI, H-686, "Record," no date; deals with a dinner party at the Mission on November 10, 1947.
32. ABS, 302-200-5, "Excerpt from an informer's report," February 16, 1947.
33. AMI, H-686, Interrogation of Marie Tumová, July 11, 1950.
34. AMI, H-686, Section 29, "Record," March 19, 1948, signed 29d.
35. ABS 302-200-5, a handwritten note. "Excerpt from an informer's report," no date.
36. ABS 302-200-5, a typed note, no signature, May 8, 1947.
37. AMI, H-686, "A Review of Evidence on Charles Katek," February 1947.
38. AMI, H-686, "Excerpts from the Record," November 1946.

39. Interview with Warren Frank, December 1, 2006, Falls Church, VA.

40. Correspondence with Pete Bagley, April 21, 2009. Mr. Bagley quoted the opinion of a colleague who knew Katek.

41. Interview with Spencer Taggart, April 23, 1999.

42. The following information is based on my interviews with Spencer Taggart in April 1999, various telephone conversations with him and his family, our correspondence, and his two unpublished manuscripts.

43. Spencer Taggart, "Becoming a Mormon Missionary," unpublished manuscript, 1.

44. Interview with Spencer Taggart, April 23, 1999.

45. Visitors to Mr. Taggart's home in Utah in 1999 could read his poem "Gifts of Self":

> A friendly greeting
> A kind word
> An understanding ear
> A sharing heart
> A forgiving soul.

46. ABS, Z-10-66. This whole file deals with Taggart and his acquaintances.

47. Interview with Spencer Taggart, April 24, 1999.

48. ABS, 302-200-5, Section 29, October 26, 1947, signed "29."

49. AMI, H-686, Section 29, "Record," December 8, 1947.

50. ABS, 302-200-5, Section 29, October 26, 1947, signed "29."

51. ABS, 302-200-5, Section 29, October 26, 1947, signed "29."

52. ABS, Z-10-66.

53. Interview with Marga Meryn, Samuel's wife, July 5, 1999.

54. AMI, V 5443, Nechanský and company, appendix. Meryn's arrival in Prague is from V 5443, Vyšetřovací spis, KV StB, Prague, October 25, 1949.

55. Personal interviews with Reinhold Pick, April 10–11, 1999. All information on Mr. Pick is from my interviews and documents that he kindly provided.

56. I am grateful to Reinhold Pick for a copy of this letter.

57. Interview with Frank Warren, December 1, 2006, Falls Church, VA.

## Chapter 9

1. G. Wightman and A. H. Brown, "Changes in the Levels of Membership and Social Composition of the Communist Party of Czechoslovakia, 1945–73", *Soviet Studies*, 27, no. 3 (July 1975): 396–417.

2. John Shute, "Czechoslovakia's Territorial and Population Changes," *Economic Geography* 24, no. 1 (January 1948): 35–44.

3. Drew Middleton, "Moscow Predicts 'Victories' in 1947," *New York Times*, January 2, 1947. Middleton quotes *Pravda*, January 1, 1947.

4. "Poland: Free Election," *Time*, January 13, 1947; Arthur Bliss Lane, *I Saw Poland Betrayed: An American Ambassador Reports to the American People* (New York: Bobbs-Merrill, 1948), 1, 199–204.

5. László Borhi, *Hungary in the Cold War, 1945–1956: Between the United States and the Soviet Union* (Budapest: Central European University Press, 2004); *Parliamentary Debates*, Lords, 5th ser., vol. 151 (1947), cols. 993–1010; AMFA, Fond Politické zprávy, Washington, Ambassador Slávik, Washington, to the Foreign Ministry, Prague, March 7, March 27, March 28, 1947.

6. "The Truman Doctrine, 1947," United States Department of State, Office of the historian, http://history.state.gov/milestones/1945-1952/TrumanDoctrine.

7. NARA, Office of Intelligence Research, OIR Report no. 4181, "Domestic and Foreign Politics of Czechoslovakia since the Liberation," April 22, 1947.

8. NA, ACC CPC, fond 100/36, vol. 401–0, 7325.

9. NARA, Ambassador Laurence Steinhardt, U.S. Embassy, Prague, to the Secretary of State, Washington, January 7, 1947, 860F.00/1-747.

10. Truman awarded Steinhardt the Medal of Merit for his service in Turkey. See "Steinhardt on Way Here," *New York Times*, January 21, 1947; "Steinhardt Calls on Truman," *New York Times*, February 6, 1947; and "Steinhardt is Honored," *New York Times*, February 15, 1947.

11. AMFA, Fond Politické zprávy, Washington, Ambassador Slávik, Washington, to the Foreign Ministry, Prague, February 7, 1947.

12. NARA, Chargé d'Affaires John H. Bruins, U.S. Embassy, Prague, to the Secretary of State, Washington, March 14, 1947, 860F.00/3-1447.

13. NARA, Chargé d'Affaires John H. Bruins, U.S. Embassy, Prague, to the Secretary of State, Washington, March 5, 1947, 860F.00/3-547. See also NARA, Chargé d'Affaires John H. Bruins, U.S. Embassy, Prague, to the Secretary of State, Washington, March 13, 1947, 860F.00/3-1347.

14. "Czech Recovery Indicated," *New York Times*, December 29, 1946.

15. Albion Ross, "Czechoslovakia Tests Policies," *New York Times*, March 3, 1947.

16. Albion Ross, "'Let Them Eat Cake," *New York Times*, March 7, 1947.

17. John MacCormack, "Czech Expansion," *New York Times*, April 28, 1947.

18. "Czech Premier Likes Art," *New York Times*, January 14, 1947.

19. NARA, Ambassador Laurence Steinhardt, U.S. Embassy, Prague, to the Secretary of State, Washington, March 31, 1947, 860F.00/3-3147.

20. NARA, Ambassador Laurence Steinhardt, U.S. Embassy, Prague, to the Secretary of State, Washington, April 18, 1947, 860F.5043/4-1447.

21. Albion Ross, "Well-to-do Czechs," *New York Times*, February 2, 1947.

22. R. H. Bruce Lockhart, *My Europe* (London: Putnam, 1952), 95–96, 113.

23. C. L. Sulzberger, "West's Coolness Handicaps Czechs," *New York Times*, May 9, 1947.

24. *Le Saint Siège et les victimes de la guerre, janvier–décembre 1943* (Vatican City: Libreria Editrice Vaticana, 1975), 177n5.

25. NARA, F. T. Williamson, Division of Central European Affairs, Department of State, Washington, March 24, 1947, 860F.00/3-2447.

26. Anton Raška, *Proces s dr. J. Tisom* (Bratislava, Czechoslovakia: Tatrapress, 1990).

27. NARA, F. T. Williamson, Division of Central European Affairs, Department of State, Washington, March 24, 1947, 860F.00/3-2447; NARA, Acting Secretary Dean Acheson, Department of State, Washington, to Ray J. Madden, House of Representatives, April 25, 1947, 860F.004-1647. See also NARA, Durward Sandifer, Department of State, to Michael A. Feighan, House of Representatives, May 7, 1947, 860F.00/4-1647.

28. NARA, Ambassador Laurence Steinhardt, U.S. Embassy, Prague, to the Secretary of State, Washington, May 6, 1947, 860F.415/5-647.

29. NARA, Ambassador Laurence Steinhardt, U.S. Embassy, Prague, to the Secretary of State, Washington, May 16, 1947, 860F.00/5-1647.

30. NARA, Colonel E. F. Koenig, former U.S. Military Attaché, War Department, Washington, to Director of Intelligence, War Department, Washington, July 23, 1947, MID 380.01 MIA Czechoslovakia.

31. ABS, Prague, Z-10-175, includes an analysis of the Captain Novak case, no date, no signature.

32. NARA, Colonel E. F. Koenig, former U.S. Military Attaché, War Department, Washington, to Director of Intelligence, War Department, Washington, July 23, 1947, MID 380.01 MIA Czechoslovakia.

33. Ibid.

34. ABS, Prague, 302-197-4.

35. ABS, Prague, Z-10-175.

36. AMI, Z-621; ZV 119, folder 13/5, "Means and methods of American imperialism in Czechoslovakia," November 14, 1949, no. 246/032-1949, AMI 1-3-4; AMI, A 2/1-1527, Deputy Prime Minister Viliam Široký to Karol Bacilek, Minister of National Security, November 5, 1952.

37. Telephone interview with Colonel Jack Novak (ret.), December 12, 1998.

38. NARA, Ambassador Laurence Steinhardt, U.S. Embassy, Prague, to the Secretary of State, Washington, May 22, 1947, 860F.00/5-2247.

39. NARA, Ambassador Laurence Steinhardt, U.S. Embassy, Prague, to the Secretary of State, Washington, May 23, 1947, 860F.00/5-2347.

40. Ladislav Feierabend, *Politické vzpomínky*, vol. 3 (Brno, Czech Republic: Atlantis, 1996), 336–41.

41. NARA, Ambassador Laurence Steinhardt, U.S. Embassy, Prague, to the Secretary of State, Washington, May 27, 1947, 860F.00/5-2747.

42. NARA, Ambassador Laurence Steinhardt, U.S. Embassy, Prague, to the Secretary of State, Washington, June 2, 1947, 860F.00/6-247.

43. NARA, Ambassador Laurence Steinhardt, U.S. Embassy, Prague, to the Secretary of State, Washington, July 1, 1947.

44. NARA, Ambassador Laurence Steinhardt, U.S. Embassy, Prague, to the Secretary of State, Washington, June 2, 1947, 860F.00/6-247.

45. NARA, Ambassador Laurence Steinhardt, U.S. Embassy, Prague, to the Secretary of State, Washington, June 4, 1947, 860F.00/6-447.

46. The following account of the Marshall Plan is based on Prokop Drtina, *Československo můj osud: Kniha života českého demokrata 20. století*, vol. 2, part 1, *Emigrací k vítězství* (Toronto: 68 Publishers, 1982), 323–54; Hubert Ripka, *Únorová tragédie: Svědectví přímého účastníka* (Brno, Czech Republic: Atlantic, 1995), 65–80; Feierabend, *Politické vzpomínky*, 349–57. Czech documents are in Karel Kaplan and Alexandra Špiritová, eds., *ČSR a SSSR, 1945–1948: Dokumenty mezivládních jednání* (Brno, Czech Republic: Doplněk, 1997).

47. See Michael Cox and Caroline Kennedy-Pipe, "The Tragedy of American Diplomacy? Rethinking the Marshall Plan," *Journal of the Cold War Studies* 7, no. 1 (Winter 2005): 97–134.

48. "Czechs for Marshall Plan," *New York Times*, July 2, 1947.

49. AMI. This secret—and illegal—communication link connecting Stalin with Gottwald was opened in July 1945 when two Soviet NKVD officers installed a radio transmitter on the top floor of the residence of CPC general secretary Rudolf Slánský. It is described in an unsigned document from the Czech Ministry of the Interior, AMI, no date, no title, that deals with the history of Czechoslovak intelligence.

50. Jiří Kocián, Jiří Pernes, and Oldřich Tůma, *České průšvihy: aneb prohry, krize, skandály a aféry českých dějin let 1848–1989* (Brno, Czech Republic: Barrister & Principal, 2004), 197.

51. "Zápis o návštěvě u generalissima J. V. Stalina 9. července 1947," in Drtina, *Československo můj osud*, 684, and Kaplan and Špiritová, *ČSR a SSSR*, doc. no. 160, 369.

52. Feierabend, *Politické vzpomínky*, 350.

53. NA, International Department, ACC CPC, 1945–1962, fond 100/24, 18, 545. See also *Rudé Právo*, July 13, 1947.

54. Drtina, *Československo můj osud*, 340–41; Feierabend, *Politické vzpomínky*, 353–54.

55. Interview with George Bogardus, June 3, 1998; interview with Kurt Taub, March 5, 2000.

56. NA, ACC CPC, Fond 100/36, file 401–4, October 26, 1947.

57. James Reston, "Czechs Bow East," *New York Times*, August 5, 1947.

58. NARA, John H. Bruins, Counselor of Embassy, Prague, to the Secretary of State, Washington, June 6, 1947, 860F.00B/6-647.

59. LOC, box 68, Steinhardt Papers, record of a conference at the Embassy, with Ambassador and Staff, September 24, 1947.

60. NARA, Ambassador Laurence Steinhardt, U.S. Embassy, Prague, to the Secretary of State, Washington, July 19, 1947, 860F.00/7-1847.

61. NARA, Ambassador Laurence Steinhardt, U.S. Embassy, Prague, to the Secretary of State, Washington, July 30, 1947, 860F.00/7-3047.

62. Dulcie-Ann Steinhardt Sherlock, "R.S.V.P.," unpublished manuscript, 115–17.

63. NARA, Records of the Office of East European Affairs, Record Group 59, LOT 54D426, CSR, box 1, From: CE—Coburn Kidd, To: Mr. Scull, Subject: Embassy at Prague, July 9, 1947.

64. Rudolf Slánský, *Rudé Právo*, May 20, 1947.

65. NARA, Message Unsigned, U.S. Embassy, Prague, to the Secretary of State, Washington, August 20, 1947, 860F.00/8-1947.

66. NARA, Ambassador Laurence Steinhardt, U.S. Embassy, Prague, to the Secretary of State, Washington, August 19, 1947, 860F.00/8-1947.
67. NARA, Charles W. Yost, U.S. Embassy, Prague, to the Secretary of State, Washington, August 27, 1947, 860F.00/8-2647.
68. Václav Veber notes that the data (published in *Rudé Právo*, September 4, 1947) regarding the alleged millionaires and their wealth were grossly exaggerated. Veber, *Osudové únorové dny 1948* (Prague: Lidové Noviny, 2008), 133–38.
69. NARA, Charles W. Yost, U.S. Embassy, Prague, to the Secretary of State, Washington, September 8, 1947, 860F.00/9-547.
70. Drtina, *Československo můj osud*, 369–76; Veber, *Osudové únorové dny*, 138–42.
71. NARA, Charles W. Yost, U.S. Embassy, Prague, to the Secretary of State, Washington, September 11, 1947, 860F.00/9-1147.
72. NARA, Charles W. Yost, U.S. Embassy, Prague, to the Secretary of State, Washington, September 13, 1947, 860F.00/9-1247.
73. Veber, *Osudové únorové dny*, 138–42.
74. Drtina, *Československo můj osud*, 376, 396.
75. Čepička was the Communist Party's postwar star. Yet when he became a minister of internal trade (December 1947), the U.S. embassy called him a "hitherto obscure Moravian lawyer." NARA, John H. Bruins, U.S. Embassy, Prague, to the Secretary of State, Washington, December 4, 1947, 860F.002/12-447.
76. Drtina, *Československo můj osud*, 407.
77. NARA, Charles W. Yost, U.S. Embassy, Prague, to the Secretary of State, Washington, September 11, 1947, 860F.00/9-1147.
78. NARA, Ambassador Laurence Steinhardt, U.S. Embassy, Prague, to the Secretary of State, Washington, November 28, 1947, 860F.00/11-2447.
79. NARA, Chargé John H. Bruins, U.S. Embassy, Prague, to the Secretary of State, Washington, January 23, 1948, 860F.00/1-2348.
80. NARA, Chargé John H. Bruins, U.S. Embassy, Prague, to the Secretary of State, Washington, January 27, 1948, 860F.00/1-2348.
81. See Mark Kramer, "Stalin, Soviet Policy, and the Consolidation of a Communist Bloc in Eastern Europe, 1944–1953," unpublished manuscript, 27; L. Ya. Gibianskii, "Forsirovanie sovetskoi blokovoi politiki," in *Kholodnaya voina, 1945–1963 gg.: Istoricheskaya retrospektiva, Sbornik statei*, ed. N. I. Egorova and A. O. Chubar'yan (Moscow: OLMA-PRESS, 2003), 105–36.
82. NARA, George Kennan, Department of State, to Robert Lovett, Department of State, October 6, 1947, 861.00/10-647.
83. NARA, Ambassador Laurence Steinhardt, U.S. Embassy, Prague, to the Secretary of State, Washington, October 8, 1947, 860F.00/10-847; Charles W. Yost, U.S. Embassy, Prague, to the Secretary of State, Washington, October 21, 1947, 860F.00/9-1647;Veber, *Osudové únorové dny*, 158.
84. NARA, Ambassador Laurence Steinhardt, U.S. Embassy, Prague, to the Secretary of State, Washington, October 1, 1947, 860F.00/9-3047.
85. NARA, MID 200.3, MIA Czechoslovakia, R. F. Ennis, Colonel, GSC, Chief, Intelligence Group, September 7, 1947.
86. NARA, Ambassador Laurence Steinhardt, U.S. Embassy, Prague, to the Secretary of State, Washington, October 7, 1947, 860F.00/10-647.
87. *Rudé Právo*, October 24, 1947, and October 28, 1947.
88. NARA, Ambassador Laurence Steinhardt, U.S. Embassy, Prague, to the Secretary of State, Washington, November 1, 1947, 860F.00/10-3147.
89. NARA, Ambassador Laurence Steinhardt, U.S. Embassy, Prague, to the Secretary of State, Washington, October 23, 1947, 860F.00/10-2347. NARA, Ambassador Laurence Steinhardt, U.S. Embassy, Prague, to the Secretary of State, Washington, November 8, 1947, 860F.00/11-847.
90. NARA, Ambassador Laurence Steinhardt, U.S. Embassy, Prague, to the Secretary of State, Washington, November 12, 1947, 860F.00/11-1247.
91. NARA, Ambassador Laurence Steinhardt, U.S. Embassy, Prague, to the Secretary of State, Washington, November 21, 1947, 860F.00/11-1947.

92. Albion Ross, "Czech Socialists," *New York Times*, November 17, 1947.
93. NARA, Ambassador Laurence Steinhardt, U.S. Embassy, Prague, to the Secretary of State, Washington, November 18, 1947, 860F.00/11-1747.
94. NARA, Ambassador Laurence Steinhardt, U.S. Embassy, Prague, to the Secretary of State, Washington, November 21, 1947, 860F.00B/11-2047.
95. NARA, Second Secretary Walter Birge, U.S. Embassy, Prague, to the Secretary of State, Washington, December 23, 1947, 860F.00/12-2347.
96. Klement Gottwald's speech, *Rudé Právo*, November 29, 1947.
97. NARA, Ambassador Laurence Steinhardt, U.S. Embassy, Prague, to the Secretary of State, Washington, November 24, 1947, 860F.00/11-2447.
98. C. L. Sulzberger, "Mikolajczyk's Departure Marks Failure of a Policy," *New York Times*, October 29, 1947.
99. Albion Ross, "Benes Says Czechs Must Find Middle Way," *New York Times*, November 12, 1947.
100. "Steinhardt to the U.S.," *New York Times*, November 24, 1947.
101. AMFA, Fond Politické zprávy, Washington, 1947, Ambassador Slávik, Washington, to the Ministry of Foreign Affairs, Prague, December 19, 1947.
102. Albion Ross, "Stalin Doubles Grain to Czechs," *New York Times*, December 2, 1947.
103. "Czech Film Market Closing Against US," *New York Times*, December 21, 1947.
104. "German Poll Prefers Nazism to Communism," *New York Times*, December 23, 1947
105. C. L. Sulzberger, "Soviet Pressure," *New York Times*, December 28, 1947.
106. Harry S. Truman Library, Papers of Harry S. Truman, Files of the White House Naval Aide, G. C. M., Secretary of State, Memorandum for the President, November 7, 1947.
107. Woodrow J. Kuhns, ed., *Assessing the Soviet Threat: The Early Cold War Years* (Washington, DC: Center for the Study of Intelligence, CIA, 1997), 162–63.

## Chapter 10

1. Prokop Drtina, *Československo můj osud: Kniha života českého demokrata 20. století*, vol. 2, part 1, *Emigrací k vítězství* (Toronto: 68 Publishers, 1982), 440.
2. C. L. Sulzberger, "Benes in Failing Health," *New York Times*, January 18, 1948.
3. NARA, Laurence Steinhardt, U.S. Embassy, Prague, to the Secretary of State, Washington, October 22, 1947, 860F.001/10-2247.
4. NARA, John H. Bruins, U.S. Embassy, Prague, to the Secretary of State, Washington, January 22, 1948, 860F.001/1-2248.
5. NARA, John H. Bruins, U.S. Embassy, Prague, to the Secretary of State, Washington, January 28, 1948, 860F.001/1-2848.
6. LOC, Steinhardt Papers, box 57, Chargé John Bruins, Prague, to Laurence Steinhardt, New York City, January 23, 1948.
7. LOC, Steinhardt Papers, box 57, Chargé John Bruins, Prague, to Laurence Steinhardt, New York City, January 6, 1948.
8. LOC, Steinhardt Papers, box 57, Chargé John Bruins, Prague, to Laurence Steinhardt, New York City, January 30, 1948 and February 13, 1948.
9. "Czech Parties Look For Election in May," *New York Times*, January 23, 1948.
10. "Atentát byl připravován v Krčmáni," *Svobodné Slovo*, January 22, 1948.
11. Albion Ross, "Czechs Say Radio is Pro-Communist," *New York Times*, January 24, 1948.
12. Drtina, *Československo můj osud*, 458.
13. LOC, Steinhardt Papers, box 57, Chargé John Bruins, Prague, to Laurence Steinhardt, New York City, January 20, 1948.
14. NARA, Chargé John Bruins, Prague, to the Secretary of State, Washington, January 28, 1948, 860F.00B/1-2848.
15. NARA, Secretary of State George Marshall, Washington, to the Embassy in Czechoslovakia, February 4, 1948, 860F.00B/1-2848.
16. "Figure Skating Champions Receive Awards," *New York Times*, January 27, 1948.
17. Interview with Nathaniel Davis, March 2, 2003.
18. Interview with Ralph Saul, Philadelphia, April 16, 2004.

19. Ibid.
20. Unless indicated otherwise, all information in this section comes from my interviews with Louise Schaffner, Arlington, VA, June 11, 1998, January 29–30, 1999.
21. Interview with Louise Schaffner, January 29, 1999.
22. ABS, List A, no. 11, April 2, 1949.
23. JSCU, "Přednáška Profesora Dr. Vladimíra Krajiny," BBC, February 20, 1949.
24. NARA, C. Offie, Political Officer, Frankfurt, to the Secretary of State, Washington, March 2, 1948, 860F.00/4-248.
25. JSCU, "Mss: Jaromír Smutný, Beneš (notes & manuscripts)."
26. Walter Birge, "Mémoirs," unpublished manuscript, 219; interview with Nathaniel Davis, March 2, 2003.
27. NARA, Secretary of State George C. Marshall, Washington, to Certain American Missions, March 12, 1948, 860F.00/3-1248.
28. Vladimír Krajina, Vysoká hra: Vzpomínky (Prague: Eva, 1994), 191–93.
29. Drtina, Československo můj osud, 485.
30. Krajina, Vysoká hra, 195.
31. JSCU, "Mss: Smutný, J. Beneš (notes & mss.)."
32. Drtina, Československo můj osud, 470; Jindřich Veselý, Kronika únorových dnů 1948 (Prague: Státní Nakl. Politické Literatury, 1958).
33. Drtina, Československo můj osud, 470–72.
34. AMFA, Prague, Section A, the Cabinet of State Secretary and Minister, 1945–1950, Jiří Wehle, Ministry of Interior, to State Secretary Vladimír Clementis, March 5, 1948.
35. AMFA, Section A, the Cabinet of State Secretary and Minister, 1945–1950, Jiří Wehle, Ministry of Interior, to State Secretary Vladimír Clementis, March 5, 1948.
36. NARA, John H. Bruins, U.S. Embassy, Prague, to the Secretary of State, Washington, February 5, 1948, 860F.00/2-548.
37. NARA, John H. Bruins, U.S. Embassy, Prague, to the Secretary of State, Washington, February 12, 1948, 860F.00/2-1148.
38. NARA, John H. Bruins, U.S. Embassy, Prague, to the Secretary of State, Washington, February 18, 1948, 860F.00/2-1848.
39. LOC, Steinhardt Papers, box 57, Laurence Steinhardt, Prague, to Marquis W. Childs, New York City, March 30, 1948.
40. AMFA, Section A, the Cabinet of State Secretary and Minister, 1945–1950. From Jiří Wehle, Ministry of Interior, to State Secretary Vladimír Clementis, March 5, 1948. Compare with "The Current Situation in Czechoslovakia," by Laurence A. Steinhardt, Presented at the National War College, Washington, December 18, 1947, LOC, Steinhardt Papers, box 68.
41. Interview with George Bogardus, January 30, 1999. Mr. Bogardus recalled the name of the Pan Am manager as Peter Wenzel.
42. Galina Murashko, "Fevralskii krizis 1948 g. v Chekhoslovakii i sovetskoe rukovodstvo: Po novym materialam rossiiskikh arkhivov," Novaya i Novieshaya Istoria 3 (1998): 50–63.
43. Karel Kaplan, Pět kapitol o únoru (Brno, Czech Republic: Doplněk, 1997), 352.
44. NARA, Laurence Steinhardt, U.S. Embassy, Prague, to the Secretary of State, Washington, February 20, 1948, 860F.00/2-2048.
45. Drtina, Československo můj osud, 495.
46. JSCU, "Dr. J. Jína's record of the February crisis."
47. JSCU, "Mss: Smutný, J. Beneš (notes & mss.), 7."
48. NARA, Laurence Steinhardt, U.S. Embassy, Prague, to the Secretary of State, Washington, February 27, 1948, 860F.00/2-2748.
49. NARA, Laurence Steinhardt, U.S. Embassy, Prague, to the Secretary of State, Washington, March 12, 1948, 860F.00/3-1248.
50. Interview with Vladimír and Otilia Kabeš, January 30, 1999, Washington, DC.
51. I am grateful to Dr. Kabeš for providing a copy of the Jan Masaryk letter.
52. NARA, Laurence Steinhardt, U.S. Embassy, Prague, to the Secretary of State, Washington, February 21, 1948, 860F.00/2-2148.

53. NARA, Laurence Steinhardt, U.S. Embassy, Prague, to the Secretary of State, Washington, March 12, 1948, 860F.00/3-1248.
54. Interview with Vladimír and Otilia Kabeš, January 30, 1999, Washington, DC.
55. Kaplan, *Pět kapitol*, 360.
56. NA, Prague, Archives of the Central Committee of the Communist Party of Czechoslovakia [ACC CPC], fond 100/36, vol. 131/6. See also Jan Kalous, "Československý bezpečnostní aparát 1945–1948," paper delivered at a seminar in Jinonice on February 21, 2003.
57. NA, ACC CPC, f. 100/36, vol. 401/04.
58. NARA, Ambassador Jefferson Caffery, U.S. Embassy, Paris, to the Secretary of State, Washington, February 22, 1948, 860F.00/2-2248.
59. NARA, Laurence Steinhardt, U.S. Embassy, Prague, to the Secretary of State, Washington, February 23, 1948, 860F.00/2-2348.
60. Drtina, *Československo můj osud*, 543–48.
61. NARA, Laurence Steinhardt, U.S. Embassy, Prague, to the Secretary of State, Washington, March 12, 1948, 860F.00/3-1248.
62. Harry S. Truman Library, Papers of Harry S. Truman, Files of the White House Naval Aide, G. C. M., Secretary of State, Memorandum for the President, November 7, 1948.
63. NARA, Secretary of State, George Marshall, Washington, to Jefferson Caffery, U.S. Embassy, Paris, February 24, 1948, 860F.00/2-2448.
64. NARA, Memorandum of Conversation, "The Current Situation in Czechoslovakia," February 24, 1948, 860F.00/2-2448.
65. Klement Gottwald, *Sebrané spisy, 1925–1929* (Prague: Svoboda, 1951), 314–16, 323.
66. NARA, Laurence Steinhardt, U.S. Embassy, Prague, to the Secretary of State, Washington, February 26, 1948, 860F.00/2-2648.
67. NARA, Laurence Steinhardt, U.S. Embassy, Prague, to the Secretary of State, Washington, February 25, 1948, 860F.00/2-2548.
68. Drtina, *Československo můj osud*, 558.
69. "Soviet Sees Reaction Set Back in Prague," *New York Times*, February 26, 1948.
70. NARA, Ambassador Lewis W. Douglas, U.S. Embassy, London, to the Secretary of State, Washington, February 25, 1948, 860F.00/2-2548.
71. NARA, Laurence Steinhardt, U.S. Embassy, Prague, to the Secretary of State, Washington, March 1, 1948, 860F.00/3-1248.
72. Harold B. Hinton, "Dictatorship Seen: Joint Protest Charges Crisis was Instigated to End Free Rule, Calls Result a Disaster," *New York Times*, February 27, 1948.
73. NARA, Laurence Steinhardt, U.S. Embassy, Prague, to the Secretary of State, Washington, March 1, 1948, 860F.00/3-148.
74. NARA, Bonbright, U.S. Embassy, Paris, to the Secretary of State, Washington, February 29, 1948, 860F.00/2-2848.
75. Bertram D. Hulen, "Reign of Terror," *New York Times*, March 11, 1948, and AMFA, Generální sekretariát, box 194, Czechoslovak Embassy, Washington, to the Ministry, Prague, March 11, 1948.
76. Arnold A. Offner, *Another Such Victory: President Truman and the Cold War, 1945-1953* (Stanford, CA: Stanford University Press, 2002), 237–38.
77. NARA, Laurence Steinhardt, U.S. Embassy, Prague, to the Secretary of State, Washington, February 26, 1948, 860F.00/2-2648.
78. NARA, Laurence Steinhardt, U.S. Embassy, Prague, to the Secretary of State, Washington, February 27, 1948, 860F.00/2-2748.
79. "Gottwald Threat to Benes is Cited," *New York Times*, February 26, 1948.
80. NARA, Laurence Steinhardt, U.S. Embassy, Prague, to the Secretary of State, Washington, February 27, 1948, 860F.00/2-748.
81. Václav Černý, *Paměti*, vol. 3 (Brno, Czechoslovakia: Atlantis, 1992), 184–90.
82. Josef Korbel, *The Communist Subversion of Czechoslovakia, 1938–1948: The Failure of Coexistence* (Princeton, NJ: Princeton University Press, 1959), 233.
83. The prevalent opinion today—based on scientific tests and analyses—leans toward the view that Masaryk was murdered. There is still no incontrovertible proof.

84. AMFA, Fond Political Reports, Washington, 1948, Chargé d'Affaires Josef Hanč, Czecho-slovak Embassy, Washington, to the Ministry of Foreign Affairs, March 31, 1948.

85. AMFA, Prague, Fond Political Reports, Washington, 1948. Ambassador Vladimír Procházka, Czechoslovak Embassy, Washington, to the Ministry of Foreign Affairs, August 29, 1951.

86. NARA, Ambassador Jefferson Caffery, U.S. Embassy, Paris, to the Secretary of State, March 12, 1948, 860F.002/3-1148.

87. NARA, Ambassador Laurence Steinhardt, U.S. Embassy, Prague, to the Secretary of State, March 10, 1948, 860F.00/3-1048.

88. Interview with Louise Schaffner, Washington, January 29, 1999. In March 1948, a young Czech woman came to her apartment and was received by her mother. The visitor said that her father was a doctor who had examined Masaryk's body. He told her that Masaryk had been murdered—he was hit with a wet sandbag, then the body was pushed out the window.

89. NARA, Laurence Steinhardt, U.S. Embassy, Prague, to the Secretary of State, Washington, April 7, 1948, 860F.00/4-748.

90. NARA, Laurence Steinhardt, U.S. Embassy, Prague, to the Secretary of State, Washington, April 9, 1948, 860F.002/4-848.

91. Spencer L. Taggart, "Witnessing Freedom's Loss," unpublished manuscript, 4.

92. NARA, Laurence Steinhardt, U.S. Embassy, Prague, to the Secretary of State, Washington, March 12, 1948, 860F.002/3-1248.

93. NARA, Ambassador Laurence Steinhardt, U.S. Embassy, Prague, to the Secretary of State, March 10, 1948, 860F.00/3-1048.

94. Drew Middleton, "London and Paris Shocked by Coup in Czechoslovakia," New York Times, February 26, 1948.

95. Interview with Kurt Taub, March 5, 2000, Salzburg, Austria.

96. ABS, H-686.

97. Taggart, "Witnessing Freedom's Loss."

98. Interview with Spencer L. Taggart, April 23, 1999, Logan, UT.

99. NARA, Laurence Steinhardt, U.S. Embassy, Prague, to the Secretary of State, Washington, March 17, 1948, 860F.00/3-1748.

100. NARA, C. Offie, Political Officer, U.S. Political Adviser for Germany, to the Secretary of State, March 22, 1948, 860F.00/3-2248.

101. AMFA, Papers of Minister Vladimír Clementis, ZS report of March 5, 1948, no. 0511/1948, signed Dr. J. Wehle (for the minister).

102. NARA, Laurence Steinhardt, U.S. Embassy, Prague, to the Secretary of State, Washington, April 30, 1948, 860F.00/4-3048.

## Chapter 11

1. Delbert Clark, "Red Push Must End," The New York Times, March 5, 1948.

2. NARA, Counselor of the Embassy Gerald Keith, U. S. Embassy, London, to the Secretary of State, Washington, April 20, 1948, 761.00/4-3048.

3. "Byrnes Advocates 'Action' on Russia," The New York Times, March 14, 1948.

4. Edwin James, "Soviets Accusing Scandinavian Nations," The New York Times, April 4, 1948.

5. George Axelson, "Finns Warn Communists," The New York Times, March 28, 1948.

6. "Visit to Norway," The New York Times, April 7, 1948.

7. NARA, Ambassador Laurence Steinhardt, U.S. Embassy, Prague, to the Secretary of State, Washington, April 5, 1948, 860F.4212/4-348.

8. AMI, 310-35-5/1-6, Jindřich Veselý, circular note, April 23, 1948, Group III-A.

9. Archives of the Ministry of Foreign Affairs (AMFA), General secretariat, box 192, United States Embassy to the Ministry of Foreign Affairs, August 1, 1948.

10. AMFA, General secretariat, box 192, United States Embassy to the Ministry of Foreign Affairs, no. 4699, June 18, 1948.

11. AMFA, General secretariat, box 192, United States Embassy to the Ministry of Foreign Affairs, Aide Memoire, June 30, 1948.

12. NARA, Ambassador Laurence Steinhardt, U. S. Embassy, Prague, to Harold Vedeler, Department of State, Washington, April 15, 1948, 860F.001/4–1548.

13. AMFA, General secretariat, 1945-1954, box 4, United States Embassy, Prague, to the Ministry of Foreign Affairs, no. 4819, July 19, 1948.

14. ABS, ZS-GS (Military Intelligence), 8041, Birge.

15. Walter W. Birge, "Mémoirs," unpublished manuscript, 221–27, and my interviews with Mr. Birge.

16. LOC, Steinhardt Papers, box 58. Steinhardt had arranged for U.S. visas for Count Leopold and Countess Cecilia Sternberg.

17. Feierabend sought to hide with Steinhardt's deputy, John Bruins, who refused to shelter him on the grounds that he would be risking his career. See Ladislav Feierabend, *Politické vzpomínky*, vol. 3 (Brno, Czech Republic: Atlantis, 1996), 390.

18. Birge drove Ryšavý into the U.S. zone in the fall of 1948. He became a White House chef during the Eisenhower administration.

19. Birge had had no idea who his partner in BLACKWOOD was. The mystery was solved in 1974 when he received a letter from Josef Hybler, a Czech fighter pilot who fought in the ranks of the Royal Air Force. Flight Lieutenant Hybler was arrested in March 1949 and released from Communist prisons after eleven years of extra harsh treatment. He escaped from Czechoslovakia during the Prague Spring of 1968, moved to England, and—after years of searching—met with Birge.

20. NA (previously State Central Archives), fond 02/1 sign. P 66/88, item P4570. The Secretariat of the Central Committee of the CPC concluded that 170,938 citizens had escaped from the country between 1948 and 1987.

21. NARA, Robert Murphy, Berlin, to the Secretary of State, Washington, April 16, 1948, 860F.00/4-1648.

22. The following account is based on my interviews with Reinhold Pick (April 10, 1999; August 3, 2000) and Jerry Horak (August 3, 2000), and on Birge, "Mémoirs," 227–31.

23. Birge, "Mémoirs, 227.

24. I am grateful to Mr. Pick for a copy of the card.

25. Interview with Reinhold Pick, April 10, 1999; Birge, "Mémoirs," 234–41; interview with Jerome V. Horak, August 3, 2000; I also have a letter from Mr. Horak, February 2, 1999.

26. Birge, "Mémoirs," 235.

27. Ibid., 237.

28. NA (State Central Archives), fond 100/24, 102, 1156.

29. AMFA, United States Embassy, Prague, to the Ministry, September 20, 1948, Diplomatic Protocol, foreign missions in Prague, United States, 1945–1955, box 55.

30. AMFA, James K. Penfield, U.S. Embassy, Prague, December 10, 1948, Diplomatic Protocol, United States, 1945–1955, box 55.

31. LOC, Steinhardt Papers, box 58.

32. Interview with Spencer Taggart, April 23, 1999.

33. Birge, "Mémoirs," 240–41.

34. NA, A CC CPC, fond 100/36, vol. 322.7.

35. Birge, "Mémoirs," 241–45.

36. Ibid., 245.

37. Ibid., 253–54.

38. Ibid., 253.

39. Ibid., 234.

40. Criminals did murder would be refugees in the border area for private gain. See AMI, 310-98-1.

41. Tennent H. Bagley, *Spy Wars: Moles, Mysteries, and Deadly Games* (New Haven, CT: Yale University Press, 2007), 110, 130–31.

42. Prokop Tomek, "Amon Tomašoff," *Securitas Imperii* 12 (2005): 5–28.

43. AMI, 319-38-6, AMI 13065, and AMI 4219. I have learned much from my interview with Eva Pokorná, Mr. Prošvic's daughter, and Ivonne Pokorny, Mr. Prošvic's granddaughter, August 6, 2011, Vonoklasy, Czech Republic.

44. AMI, 13065, "Statement by Josef Janoušek," July 7, 1948.

45. AMI, 13065. "Statement by Jan Prošvic," July 3, 1948, StB, Prague.
46. AMI, 4219.
47. Interview with Eva Pokorná, August 6, 2011, Vonoklasy, Czech Republic.
48. AMI, 319-38-6. "Jan and Jiřina Prošvic. For comrade Minister," January 7, 1957.
49. Ibid.
50. AMI, 319-22-6.
51. AMI, file 13065, "Statement by Oldřich Maláč," July 12, 1948, StB, Prague.
52. AMI A-8-354-379. "The former Air Force Major Josef Hnátek," October 25, 1956.
53. AMFA, General secretariat, 1945–1954, box 192, U.S. Embassy note no. 4680, June 15, 1948.
54. AMFA, General secretariat, 1945–1954, box 192, U.S. Embassy note, July 2, 1948.
55. AMI, sector II Ab to sector III Aa, June 24, 1948, Jiří Wehle, chief of III/Ab; AMI, sector III Aa to sector III Ab, "Reply to the American Protest Note."
56. AMI, 44516, AMI, 319-38-6, AMI, 596973, "Causa Zoltan Joseph Havas"; AMI, H 796, Stanislav Liška, "False Border," Ludwigsburg. Liška was recruited to work for the United States by his chief, Lt. Col. František Havlíček, who worked for Lt. Col. Zoltan J. Havas, U.S. Army intelligence (MIS), stationed in Regensburg and Straubing. Like other networks of this kind, this one was wrapped up by the StB: the two leaders were sentenced to death and executed, and others were sent to prison for many years.
57. AMI, A8-1355.
58. Interview with Spencer L. Taggart, April 23, 1999.
59. AMI, V-5443, file no. 1, Interrogation of Nechanský, September 5, 1949; interview with Spencer L. Taggart, April 23, 1999.
60. Interview with Louise Schaffner, January 29, 1999.
61. AMI, V 5443, "Nechanský and comp.," "Interrogation of Jarmila Dudešková."
62. The following is based on AMI, V 5443 and on my correspondence (July 26, 2001) with Táňa Wahl's second husband, Mr. Herman.
63. Táňa Wahl, "Život a prokletí Slávka Wahla," and "Veleslav Wahl," in *Zpravodajská brigáda: Pravdou ke svobodě; Vydáno k 60. výročí vzniku Zpravodajské brigády*, ed. Josef Daněk (Prague: Ministerstvo Obrany České Republiky, 1999), 50–54 and 112–14.
64. Veleslav Wahl, *Pražské ptactvo: Ptáci velkoměsta a jeho okolí* (Prague: Česká Grafická Unie, 1944).
65. See Daněk, *Zpravodajská brigáda*, 186.
66. I am grateful to Jaromír Klika, MD, for information and printed materials about the Intelligence Brigade he sent me with his letter of September 24, 2001.
67. AMI, V 5443. "Nechanský and comp.," subfile 3; Interrogation of J. Dudešková.
68. Birge, "Mémoirs," 218.
69. AMI, V 5443, "Nechanský and comp."
70. AMI, Z-651, file 13. OBZ (Main Directorate), Ministry of Defense, Reports 302-592-1.
71. AMI, V-5443, Nechanský's interrogation on September 5, 1949.
72. Birge, "Mémoirs," 254–55.
73. Interview with Louise Schaffner, January 29, 1999, and a typed text by Táňa Wahl.
74. AMI, V-5443, file no. 2.
75. AMI, V-5443.
76. "Another U.S. Aide Ousted by Czechs," *New York Times*, October 26, 1949.
77. "Prague Imprisons U.S. Aide," *New York Times*, October 22, 1949.
78. "New Big Spy Ring Foiled, Czechs Say," *New York Times*, October 23, 1949.
79. Telephone interview with Colonel Jack Novak, December 12, 1988.
80. For instance, "Zrádci ve službách imperialismu," *Práce*, April 21, 1950.
81. AMS, fond Klos.
82. State Prosecutor to the Ministry of Justice, November 3, 1950. I am grateful to Mr. Herman for a copy of this document.
83. Birge, "Mémoirs," 256–57.
84. Interview with Louise Schaffner, June 11, 1998.
85. "Prague Imprisons U.S. Aide," *New York Times*, October 22, 1949.
86. Personal interviews, as listed above.

87. AMFA, Teritoriální odbor, tajné, 1960–64, USA, box 2, MZV Internal Memorandum on Czechoslovak-American Relations, July 24, 1961.

88. Spencer L. Taggart, "Witnessing Freedom's Loss," unpublished manuscript, 15.

89. "Memorandum from the Assistant Secretary of State for European Affairs to the Under Secretary of State," January 4, 1955, in *Foreign Relations of the United States, 1955–1957*, vol. 25 (Washington, DC: Government Printing Office, 1990), 7.

90. R. H. Bruce Lockhart, *My Europe* (London: Putnam, 1952), 105, 128–29.

91. Prokop Tomek, "Počty obětí komunistického režimu v Československu v letech 1948–1989," unpublished manuscript. I am grateful to Dr. Tomek for a copy of this document.

# SOURCES

Research for this book was conducted primarily in the United States National Archives and Records Administration in College Park, Maryland.

Additional archives consulted in this project included the following archives in Prague, Czech Republic:

- Archives of the Ministry of Foreign Affairs (AMFA)
  - Fond Political Reports, Czechoslovak Embassy, Washington, DC
  - Fond Political Reports, Czechoslovak Embassy, Washington, DC, Secret
  - Fond Territorial Section, Secret (TO-T)
  - Fond U.S. Embassy, Prague, 6th Section
  - General Secretariat (all diplomatic correspondence between Czechoslovakia and the U.S. embassy in Prague)
  - Diplomatic Protocol, Foreign Embassies in Czechoslovakia
  - Nezařazené (*Varia*)

- Archives of the Ministry of Interior (AMI)
  - U.S. embassy
  - Western embassies
  - Security Collegium
  - Jaromír Nechanský
  - Veleslav Wahl
  - Operation TRUST FUND
  - Operation KÁMEN
  - Emil Sztwiertnia
  - "Anglo-American Offensive against Czechoslovakia"
  - Operation GENERAL

- State Central Archives, Loreta (now part of the Czech National Archives, NA)
  - Archives of the Ministry of Interior
    Passport Section
    Fond 2, Ministry of Interior, London
    Fond 42, Presidium, Police Directorate
    Fond 61, Czechoslovak Intelligence in London
    Fond 200, Intelligence Central, Police Directorate
    Fond 207, Presidium of the Land Bureau in Prague

- State Central Archives, Karmelitska Street (now part of the Czech National Archives [NA])
  — Archives of the Central Committee of the Communist Party of Czechoslovakia
     Fond 100/3, International Department
     Fond 100/24, Klement Gottwald
     Fond 100/45, Václav Kopecký
     Fond 100/50, Rudolf Slánský
     Fond 60, Václav Nosek
     Fond 110
     Fond 02/5, Political Secretariat
     Fond 02/1, Politburo
     Fond 02/2
     Fond 02/4, Secretariat

- Swiss Federal Archives, Bundesarchiv Bern
- Harry S. Truman Presidential Library
- Bakhmeteff Archive, Columbia University, New York (JSCU):
  Jaromír Smutný Papers

- Unpublished manuscripts:
  Walter Birge, "Mémoires"
  Dorothy Bruins, "Life of a Family"
  Frank Munk, "My Century and My Many Lives"
  Dulcie-Ann Steinhardt Sherlock, "R.S.V.P."

- Interviews:
  Walter Birge
  George F. Bogardus
  Robert and Dagmar Bronec
  Nathaniel Davis
  Hana Disher
  Jane Edwards
  Foss Foote
  Warren Frank
  Tanja Gard
  Jerome Horak
  Vladimír and Otilia Kabeš
  Miloš Knorr
  Marga Meryn
  James E. Mrazek
  Herbert Němec
  Jack C. Novak
  Reinhold Pick
  Eva Pokorná
  Arthur P. Price
  Peter R. and Naomi Rosenblatt
  Ralph S. Saul
  Louise Schaffner
  Alois Šeda
  Laurene A. Sherlock
  Dulcie-Ann Steinhardt Sherlock
  Spencer L. Taggart
  Kurt Taub

# INDEX